BANFF, JASPER & GLACIER
NATIONAL PARKS

KORINA MILLER

SUSAN DERBY

DAVID LUKAS

LONELY PLANET PUBLICATIONS
Melbourne · Oakland · London · Paris

Banff, Jasper & Glacier National Parks
1st edition – March 2004

Published by
Lonely Planet Publications Pty Ltd ABN 36 005 607 983
90 Maribyrnong St, Footscray, Victoria 3011, Australia

Lonely Planet Offices
Australia Locked Bag 1, Footscray, Victoria 3011
USA 150 Linden St, Oakland, CA 94607
UK 7282 Rosebery Ave, Clerkenwell, London EC1R 4RW
France 1 rue du Dahomey, 75011 Paris

Photographs
Many of the images in this guide are available for licensing from
Lonely Planet Images.
W www.lonelyplanetimages.com

Front cover photograph
Paddling on Moraine Lake,
Banff National Park (Andrew Brown/Lonely Planet Images)
Back cover photograph
Canada's Bighorn sheep,
Jasper National Park (Mark Newman/Lonely Planet Images)

ISBN 1 74059 562 9

text & maps © Lonely Planet Publications Pty Ltd 2004
photos © photographers as indicated 2004

Printed through Colorcraft Ltd, Hong Kong
Printed in China

BANFF, JASPER & GLACIER
CONTENTS

THE AUTHORS

Korina Miller

Born on Vancouver Island, Korina first visited Banff at the age of three. She began roaming the world at age 18, but returns to Banff and Jasper whenever she has the chance. Her travels, studies and work have taken her to many corners of the world, from Alaska to Sicily and Columbia to Scotland. She studied in Japan and Denmark; worked with remote tribal peoples in India and Southwest China; ran a hotel in Ecuador and arts organisations in London and Vancouver. En route, she picked up a degree in Communications and an MA in Migration Studies, focusing on Canada's Native peoples. Korina is co-author of Lonely Planet's *China*, *South-West China*, *Fiji*, *South Pacific* and the author of *Beijing Condensed*.

Susan Derby

Susan spent a summer working in Glacier National Park at the age of 19 and fell in love with the region during wanders in the backcountry. She has road-tripped extensively through Montana and the Rockies region, and along the way, has become acquainted with extreme weather, wild wildlife, intriguing humans and more mountains than malls. When not on the road, Susan spends a lot of time moving-house in California, where she gets by as a freelance writer. She spent two years working as an in-house editor and scribe for lonelyplanet.com and CitySync products, and has contributed to Lonely Planet's *Out to Eat: San Francisco*, *USA* and *India*.

David Lukas

David has been an avid student of the natural world since he started memorizing field guides at age five. This same love took him around the world for 10 years to study animals and ecosystems in Borneo, the Amazon Basin, and much of Central America. Now working as a professional naturalist, David leads natural history tours, conducts biological surveys, and writes about natural history. His articles have appeared in *Audubon*, the *Los Angeles Times*, *Orion*, *Sunset*, and elsewhere. His most recent book is *Wild Birds of California*, and he just completed revising *Sierra Nevada Natural History*. David also contributed to Lonely Planet's *Yosemite National Park*, *Yellowstone & Grand Teton National Parks* and *Grand Canyon National Park*.

From the Authors

Korina Miller Thanks and love to Paul for braving the bears alone on some of the hikes, for endless amounts of help and for unwavering support. Thanks to Mum and Dad for the camping equipment and tips for RVers, to Bob and Heather for the temporary home and garden, to Kathleen at Lonely Planet for her patience and guidance and to my co-authors, Susan and David. A big thank-you to the staff at Parks Canada for doling out information and to all of the campers, hikers, tour operators, business proprietors and local residents who were full of friendly advice and good cheer.

Susan Derby To the amazing Kathleen Munnelly at LP, huge thanks and grizzly-bear hugs for allowing me to re-explore one of my favorite places in the world. The incredible rangers and volunteers of Glacier and Waterton parks helped me every step of the way. Special thanks to Clare Landry and Clay Rubano at the Many Glacier Ranger Station, Ellen Blickhan at the Goat Haunt Ranger Station and Pat Hagan. I'm very grateful to my hiking buddies, especially Claire and Chris from Calgary and Nick from Oakland. Thanks also to Kris K from Melbourne for his amusing tales. Endless gratitude goes to my incredible partner, Johnny, for unwavering support, whether I'm home frantically writing or on the road. And to my communities at home, I am ever grateful for your love, friendship and silliness.

David Lukas Special thanks to Burnett and Mimi Miller for their generous hospitality and friendly company while I was researching and writing these chapters. Thanks also to Brett Hall Jones of the Squaw Valley Community of Writers for her unstinting support, and to Angie Bartlett of The Friends of Banff National Parks for her tireless assistance securing research materials.

THIS BOOK

The first edition of *Banff, Jasper & Glacier National Parks* was researched and written by Korina Miller, Susan Derby and David Lukas. Coordinating author Korina Miller researched and wrote the Banff, Jasper and Icefields Parkway chapters, as well as the Introduction and the majority of Itineraries, Activities, Planning, History and the Appendix. Susan Derby researched and wrote the Glacier-Waterton chapter, and contributed to the Itineraries, Activities, Planning and History chapters. David Lukas wrote the Geology and Ecosystem chapters.

Credits

Banff, Jasper & Glacier National Parks was produced in Lonely Planet's Oakland office under the leadership of US Regional Publishing Manager Maria Donohoe. The title was commissioned, developed and project managed by Kathleen Munnelly. Design manager Candice Jacobus designed the cover, color pages and the template for the series and the title. She oversaw the layout done by Emily Douglas and Shelley Firth, and chipped in on layout as well. Wade Fox edited the book, and Wendy Taylor proofed, with the help of Alex Hershey. Cartographer Bart Wright created the maps, assisted by Tim Lohnes, Kat Smith and John Spelman. Hayden Foell drew the illustrations, and Alex Hershey researched the historic photographs. Ken DellaPenta compiled the index.

ACKNOWLEDGEMENTS

Grateful acknowledgement is made to the Glenbow Archives for the use of the photographs on pages 66 and 162 and to the National Park Service for the other historic photographs throughout the book.

THE LONELY PLANET STORY

The story begins with a classic travel adventure: Tony and Maureen Wheeler's 1972 journey across Europe and Asia to Australia. There was no useful information about the overland trail then, so Tony and Maureen published the first Lonely Planet guidebook to meet a growing need.

From a kitchen table, Lonely Planet has grown to become the largest independent travel publisher in the world, with offices in Melbourne (Australia), Oakland (USA), London (UK) and Paris (France).

Today Lonely Planet guidebooks cover the globe. There is an ever-growing list of books and information in a variety of media. Some things haven't changed. The main aim is still to make it possible for adventurous travelers to get out there – to explore and better understand the world.

At Lonely Planet we believe travelers can make a positive contribution to the countries they visit – if they respect their host communities and spend their money wisely. Since 1986 a percentage of the income from each book has been donated to aid projects and human rights campaigns, and, more recently, to help wildlife conservation.

SEND US YOUR FEEDBACK

We love to hear from travelers – your comments keep us on our toes and help make our books better. Our well-traveled team reads every word on what you loved or loathed about this book. Although we cannot reply individually to postal submissions, we always guarantee that your feedback goes straight to the appropriate authors, in time for the next edition. Each person who sends us information is thanked in the next edition – and the most useful submissions are rewarded with a free book.

To send us your updates – and find out about LP events, newsletters and travel news – visit our award-winning website: **www.lonelyplanet.com**.

Note: We may edit, reproduce and incorporate your comments in Lonely Planet products such as guidebooks, websites and digital products, so let us know if you don't want your comments reproduced or your name acknowledged. For a copy of our privacy policy, email privacy@lonelyplanet.com.au.

INTRODUCTION

The national parks of the Canadian Rocky Mountains are filled with dramatic, untamed wilderness. Rugged mountaintops scrape the skyline while enormous glaciers cling to their precipices. Glassy lakes flash emerald, turquoise and sapphire, and are filled by waterfalls tumbling down cliff faces and thundering through bottomless canyons. Lush forests blanket wide valleys, and lofty alpine meadows explode with vibrant wildflowers. It's the scenery that you only expect to see on postcards, right there at your fingertips. And through it wander a cast of elusive characters, like bears, elk, moose, marmots, wolves and bighorn sheep.

Banff, Jasper, Kootenay, Yoho, Glacier and Waterton Lakes National Parks, along with surrounding provincial and state parks, create one of the largest areas of protected wilderness in the world. Straddling the Canadian–US border and declared a UNESCO world heritage site, a visit to any one of these parks will leave you spellbound. Despite the throngs who come for a glimpse of the parks' more infamous spectacles, like Lake Louise, or elbow for a dip in the Miette Hot Springs, it's by no means difficult to escape to a more tranquil experience of this sublime wonderland.

No matter how you choose to explore the parks, you'll uncover the unique personality of each, from the remoteness of Jasper to the much heralded splendor of Banff and the diversity of Glacier and Waterton Lakes. Camp in the backcountry, pamper yourself at an alpine resort, cross crisp powder on snowshoes, raft down turbulent rivers, haul yourself up a cliff face, dogsled, ride horseback, canoe, ski, enjoy the view from a train window or simply head down a trail on foot. Whether you're an adrenaline-seeker or a spectator, there's a unique experience waiting for you.

USING THIS GUIDEBOOK

With a few tips, you'll be on the way to seeing the sights, finding a great place to stay and choosing activities that will keep the kids, the dog and the folks happy. We'll show you how to see the best of the parks in a day or how to fill a month. No matter how many times you've visited the Rockies, there's always something new to discover.

A quick flip through our photo highlights will give you an overview of top sightseeing options throughout the parks. If you're looking for ideas on where to go, check out the Itineraries chapter for suggested routes to suit both the flyby traveler and the hiker with two weeks to spare. Want to know just what you can do in the parks? The Activities chapter will leave you spoiled for choice.

For pointers on when to go and what to bring, and for tips on how to find last-minute accommodations, look in the Planning chapter. The destination chapters provide in-depth coverage of specific parks and areas, including sights, places to stay, where to eat, detailed trail descriptions, driving tours and nearby excursions. And if you're curious about who originally roamed these parts, just how old those mountains are or how a bear spends its winters, the History, Geology and Ecology chapters will satisfy your curiosity.

Some Notes on Terminology

Glacier National Park in the United States and Waterton Lakes National Park in Canada are known collectively as Waterton-Glacier International Peace Park, an abiding symbol of the friendship between the two countries. When these parks are covered or referenced individually, they bear their individual names; at other times, they are referenced by their collective name.

You'll also see references to the Canadian Rocky Mountains throughout. This term does not exclude Glacier National Park in the United States; geologically and ecologically, Glacier is a part of the Canadian Rocky Mountains, although it is not a part of Canada. (The geology and ecosystem of the US Rocky Mountains are quite different).

The Icefields Parkway runs through both Banff and Jasper National Parks. With many sights and an independent reputation, the Parkway is a destination in its own right, which is why it is covered in its own chapter.

Because this book covers parks in two countries that use the same name for their currencies, we've established a code for prices. If prices are in Canadian dollars, they're marked as CAD$50; prices in United States dollars are written as USD$50.

ITINERARIES

Perhaps, like many visitors, you've only got a few hours in a park and want to make the most of it. Or maybe you have a month to tour the Rockies at large and want to see the best of each park. Ultimately, how you decide to spend your time will be dictated by what activities you're interested in pursuing. Below are suggested itineraries to get you started, ranging from half a day in one park to four weeks of delving into each of them.

Banff National Park

HALF A DAY

- Head out down the **Bow Valley Parkway** (p77), following the driving tour and keeping your eyes peeled for wildlife.
- Stop at **Johnston Canyon** (p86) for a dramatic walk to the **Upper Falls**.
- Continue along the parkway to **Lake Louise** (p75), stopping for lunch at **Deer Lodge** (p114).
- Wander along the flat **Lakeshore Trail** (p88) to enjoy the gorgeous scenery and leave the crowds behind.

ONE DAY

- Follow the half-day tour above to **Lake Louise** (p75), where you can rent a boat or kayak and paddle out through the turquoise water. In winter, go **ice-skating** on the lake instead.
- Return to **Banff Town** (p72) along the Trans-Canada Hwy, following the **driving tour**.
- Once in town, ride the **Banff Gondola** (p74) for panoramic views of the Rockies.
- Have dinner at the **Maple Leaf Grillé & Spirits** (p113) for contemporary Canadian cuisine and, if you've still got some energy, head to the **Rundle**

Lounge (p115) at **Banff Springs Hotel** (p74) for a drink with glamour, or try out your two-step at **Wild Bill's Legendary Saloon** (p115).

TWO DAYS

Take in the sights and activities listed under One Day for your first day.

Day Two
- Rent a bike and head out from Banff Town on the **Sundance Trail** (p101) along the Bow River. Take a packed lunch to have along the way. In winter, spend the morning exploring trails near **Banff Town** (p72) on snowshoes.
- After lunch, spend the afternoon in Banff Town, taking in **Canada Place** (p73) or the **Whyte Museum of the Canadian Rockies** (p72).
- Finish off the day with a soak in the **Upper Hot Springs** (p74).

FOUR DAYS

Fill your first two days with the previous itineraries.

Day Three
- Head out for a full day's walk to suit your ability – either **Garden Path Trail & Twin Cairn Meadows** (p94), **Lake Agnes & the Big Beehive** (p89) or **Aylmer Lookout** (p84).

Day Four
- If you're beat on the fourth day, drive up the **Icefields Parkway** (p134) as far as **Peyto Lake** (p136) for some majestic scenery, or take a **white-water rafting trip** (p102) for an adrenaline rush.
- For meals, taste your way through Banff's fantastic restaurant scene.
- Spend an evening at the theater of **Banff Centre** (p116).

ONE WEEK

Spend your first four days following the previous itineraries.
- If you didn't take in the **Icefields Parkway** (p134) yet, do so now.
- Consider camping for a few of days at the basic but peaceful **Mosquito Creek** (p146), where you can head out on some excellent nearby day hikes.
- For a true adventure in the wild, head out on an overnight, backcountry trip. **Egypt Lake** (p98) and **Lake Minnewanka** (p98) trails are great options.
- If you're keen to try out a new activity or pursue one that's already a favorite, Banff is the perfect place to do so. Test out rock climbing, horseback riding, cross-country skiing or snowboarding.
- Consider spending a day in one Banff's neighboring parks, like **Yoho National Park** (p124) or **Kananaskis Country** (p121).

Jasper National Park

- To beat the crowds, head out early along the **Icefields Parkway** (p134) to **Mt Edith Cavell** (p143) for a short walk highlighted with the soaring **Angel Glacier** (p141) and an iceberg-speckled lake.
- Stop at **Athabasca Falls** (p138), then head into Jasper Town for lunch at the **Soft Rock Café** (p188). From the patio, look for the **Old Man** sleeping atop **Roche Bonhomme**.

ONE DAY

Follow the half-a-day itinerary, and then:

- Head to **Maligne Lake** (p167), following the **driving tour** (p168) and watching for wildlife.
- Escape the crowds by renting a boat and paddling out into the lake, where you'll be rewarded with fantastic views.
- Dine at the atmospheric **Tekarra Restaurant** (p189), south of Jasper Town.

TWO DAYS

Fill the first day with activities and sights previously listed.

Day Two

- Pack a picnic lunch with lots of goodies from the **Bear's Paw Bakery** (p188) and delve into the woods along the **Valley of the Five Lakes** (p144) trail. In winter, spend the morning **snowshoeing** (p184).
- After lunch, head to **Columbia Icefield** (p137) for a walk on the **Athabasca Glacier**.
- Take a trip at dusk on the **Jasper Tramway** (p166) and later dine on fancy fish & chips at **Fiddle River** (p189), in Jasper Town.

FOUR DAYS

For the first two days, take in the sights and activities previously listed.

Day Three

- Head out on a full-day hike; both **Bald Hills** (p173) and **Sulphur Skyline** (p176) are fantastic options. In winter, spend the day cross-country skiing.
- Afterward, take a well-earned soak in **Miette Hot Springs** (p166).

Day Four

- Spend the morning swimming at **Lake Annette** (p167), skating on **Pyramid Lake** (p167) or nosing around the **Jasper-Yellowhead Museum** (p165).
- Take a hair-raising driving tour along **Celestine Rd** (p169).
- Spend your evenings sampling Jasper Town's multiethnic cuisine.

Combine some of the activities and sights listed previously.

- Rent a bike and test it out on the popular **Overlander Trail** (p182), drive a dogsled team or join a tour in search of wildlife.
- Learn a new sport, like rock climbing, white-water rafting or fly-fishing.
- Before the week is out, be sure to head down the **Icefields Parkway** (p134) for spectacular views.
- Consider taking a side trip to **Mt Robson Provincial Park** (p191) to see the highest peak in the Canadian Rockies.
- Spend a few days really experiencing the park with a backcountry hike or horse trip. Both the **Skyline Trail** (p180) and **Tonquin Valley** (p181) offer amazing views, opportunities to see wildlife and camping or lodging en route.

Wateron-Glacier International Peace Park

HALF A DAY

- Load up on picnic supplies in West Glacier. Get an early start on **Going-to-the-Sun Rd** (p200).
- Visit the Continental Divide at **Logan Pass** (p200).
- If you have a couple hours to spare, walk to the gorgeous **Hidden Lake Overlook** (p204). If you have less time, test out a portion of the **Highline Trail** (p205).
- If you'd rather hike in the Lake McDonald area, try out the lush **Trail of the Cedars** (p203); it's paved and will take just a half hour. If time warrants, continue up to **Avalanche Lake** (p204; 2.5 hours).
- Stop at Sun Point for lunch, off Going-to-the-Sun Rd just 14.5km/9 miles west of **St Mary** (p201). From there, see St Mary Lake and its surrounding peaks.
- If you have time to stretch your legs, take the easy 2.6km/1.6-mile roundtrip trail along the lake.

ONE DAY

- Spend the morning taking in **Going-to-the-Sun Rd** (p200).
- Do one of the hikes listed earlier, or carry on to **Many Glacier** (p208).
- Fill your tummy at a restaurant in **St Mary Village** (p196), outside of the park. Enter the park again at the superbly scenic Many Glacier.
- In the afternoon, the **Highline Trail** (p205) boasts truly awesome scenery. How about a memorable glacial lake? The **Iceberg Lake Trail** (p208) is a journey that visitors rave about. Either hike will take six hours or less. Travelers looking for a gentler, less time-consuming hike might enjoy the **Redrock Falls Trail** (p209), which takes about two hours.
- After your day's accomplishments, treat yourself to a feast at Many Glacier Hotel's **Ptarmigan Dining Room** (p225).
- If you still have some evening to fill, check out the *Glacier Explorer* schedule for **campfire programs**.

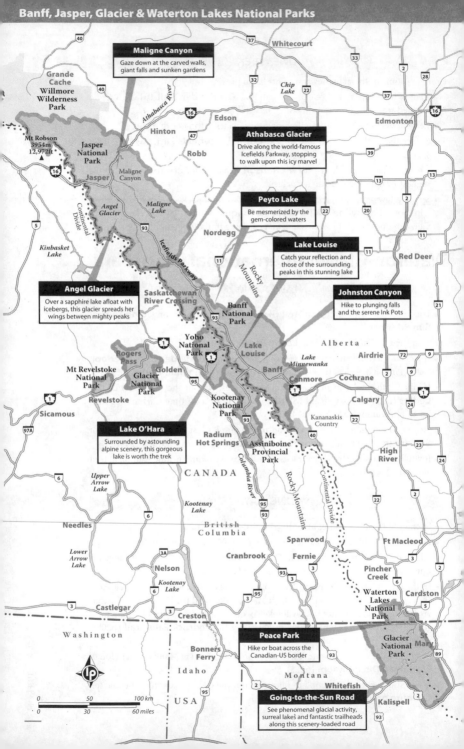

Banff, Jasper, Glacier & Waterton Lakes National Parks

Maligne Canyon
Gaze down at the carved walls, giant falls and sunken gardens

Athabasca Glacier
Drive along the world-famous Icefields Parkway, stopping to walk upon this icy marvel

Peyto Lake
Be mesmerized by the gem-colored waters

Lake Louise
Catch your reflection and those of the surrounding peaks in this stunning lake

Johnston Canyon
Hike to plunging falls and the serene Ink Pots

Angel Glacier
Over a sapphire lake afloat with icebergs, this glacier spreads her wings between mighty peaks

Lake O'Hara
Surrounded by astounding alpine scenery, this gorgeous lake is worth the trek

Peace Park
Hike or boat across the Canadian-US border

Going-to-the-Sun Road
See phenomenal glacial activity, surreal lakes and fantastic trailheads along this scenery-loaded road

Serene and utterly majestic, the National Parks of the Rockies inspire awe and wonder with their dramatic beauty, like this dusk view of Mt Rundle and Vermillion Lakes in Banff.

BANFF, JASPER & GLACIER
HIGHLIGHTS

From paddling across a gem-colored glacial lake to scaling remote and rugged peaks, Banff, Jasper, Glacier and Waterton Lakes National Parks offer thousands of ways to experience their wild splendor. No matter how you choose to explore the parks, be it through driving tours or backcountry skiing, you're sure to find your own highlights. Encounters with wildlife, hidden valleys, unexpected fields of wildflowers and some of the starriest night skies you'll ever set eyes on lend a constant element of surprise to your visit. The more you see, the more you'll come to appreciate the parks' magic – and the more you'll want to discover.

PEYTO LAKE The mesmerizing blue of this glacial lake is brilliant in the sunlight.

ELK Boasting gigantic antlers, elk are some of the Rockies' most prominent residents.

RICK RUDNICKI

MARK LIGHTBODY

CHATEAU LAKE LOUISE Surrounded by glaciated peaks, this posh hotel enjoys stellar views of glassy Lake Louise.

MARK NEWMAN

BOW RIVER Paddle down this serene river or stroll along its banks for a peaceful respite from the hustle of downtown Banff.

BANFF **HIGHLIGHTS**

SNOWBOARDING With some of the continent's best slopes, Banff is a winter-sports paradise.

RICK RUDNICKI

BANFF SPRINGS HOTEL The glamour of this gothic castle is rivaled only by its dramatic setting.

ICEFIELDS PARKWAY Cycle past breathtaking peaks, enormous glaciers and iridescent lakes on North America's highest road.

WHITE-WATER RAFTING Hang on tight for a heart-stopping ride over wild rapids.

GARETH MCCORMACK

MARK LIGHTBODY

JASPER **HIGHLIGHTS**

THE CANADIAN ROCKIES Hop on a gondola, don your hiking boots or take a helicopter tour to get a view across this sea of magnificent peaks.

RICK RUE

MALIGNE LAKE Hugged by sky-scraping peaks, Maligne Lake offers a tranquil retreat for kayakers and canoers.

JASPER TOWN The Canadian flag flies proudly outside a quaint church in this pleasant town.

ICE CLIMBING Crawling your way up a glacier is an exhilarating alpine pursuit.

KRAIG LIEB

St Mary Lake One of the windiest spots in Glacier, dazzling St Mary Lake stands still to pose.

CAROL POLICH

JOHN ELK III

Horse Riding Give your feet a break and hitch a ride on a sturdy pack horse.

Mt Reynolds Wildflowers blanket a meadow in front of majestic Mt Reynolds, a glacial horn.

SUNRIFT GORGE Views of this stunning gorge are easily accessed and well worth your while.

CAROL POLICH

BIGHORN SHEEP A young member of this generally shy species gets up close.

MARK LIGHTBODY

GLACIER HIGHLIGHTS

MT SINOPAH Glacier's many mountains include this sturdy gem.

CAROL POLICH

WATERTON-GLACIER INTERNATIONAL PEACE PARK From the plains to the mountains, Canada and the US join hands under the big sky.

RICK RUD

WATERTON LAKES NATIONAL PARK The moon rises over a rocky mountain ridge.

GARETH MCCORMACK

PRINCE OF WALES HOTEL This grand hotel holds its own amid Waterton's breathtaking beauty.

GARETH MCCORMACK

TWO DAYS

Day One

On the first day, spend the morning on activities and sights listed previously. Alternatively, stop at one of the boat-rental docks at **Apgar** (p196) or **Lake McDonald** (p200) and go kayaking or canoeing for an hour or two.

- At lunchtime, find a place along the lakeshore to dive into your picnic lunch, or tuck into Italian fare at **Jammer Joe's Grill & Pizzaria** (p225), near Lake McDonald Lodge.
- A few hours of **horseback riding** (p219) might be just the thing to while away the afternoon hours; there's a corral at Lake McDonald.
- Late afternoon to early evening is a great time to continue eastward on Going-to-the-Sun Rd if you haven't explored the entire route yet. Stop at overlooks en route, or do one of the short hikes mentioned earlier.
- The **Trail of the Cedars** (p203) loop can make for a serene end to the day.
- Rising Sun Campground and St Mary Visitors Center usually have **evening programs**; see the *Glacier Explorer*.

Day Two

- Delve into one area of the park on a day hike. See the One Day section for hiking in the **Many Glacier** (p208) area.
- **Two Medicine Valley** (p210) is less crowded but is filled with incredible natural beauty. Past its entrance station, stop by the Running Eagle Falls Trail for a quick and scenic half-hour.
- Head onward to a longer hike, like the easy **Upper Two Medicine Lake Trail** (p210), which takes about five hours.
- Plan time to take in a **boat cruise** (p199) before you leave. The last departure from the Many Glacier boat dock is 4pm, while the last boat leaves Two Medicine at 5pm.
- If you fancy a drive, take in a **driving tour** (p201) on the forested US 2, where you can watch goats lick salt.

FOUR DAYS

Take in the sights and activities previously mentioned for the first two days.

Day Three

- Head north to **Waterton Lakes National Park** on the Canadian side, and hightail it for the trails. If you are there early enough in the morning to catch a boat departure (9am and 10am) from the townsite's marina to its trailhead, the **Crypt Lake Trail** (p239) is a relatively strenuous but certainly fun hike that is sure to please. It's an all-day venture. The five-hour **Rowe Lakes Trail** (p240) is a little easier and very scenic.
- In the evening, relax in the charming **Waterton Townsite** (p235), where you can dine, stroll along the lake or have a cocktail.

Day Four

- Top off your trip with the 6.5-hour **Carthew-Alderson Trail** (p238); it's a 19km/11.8-mile one-way hike, requiring a shuttle to the starting point, at Cameron Lake.

ITINERARIES

- If daylight hours remain after the hike, drive down **Red Rock Parkway** (p237). It culminates at the colorful Red Rock Canyon, which is circuited by a short self-guided loop trail. Wildlife-watching is often successful along both Red Rock Parkway and **Akamina Parkway** (p236).
- Alternatives to hiking include boat tours on **Upper Waterton Lake** (p235), and **horseback riding** (p243).

ONE WEEK

Fill the first four days with the sights and activities listed previously.

Day Five

- Spend one more day in Waterton, or head back down to **Many Glacier** (p208) for another day of hiking.
- Alternately, spend all day on a scenic or white-water **rafting** (p217) trip on the North or Middle Fork of the Flathead River, along Glacier park's boundary.

Day Six

- Head to the remote **North Fork Valley** (p211) for a couple days of peace. The primitive campgrounds along the dusty **Inside North Fork Rd** (p221) are truly places to get away from it all. On the way, stop at the one-of-a-kind village of **Polebridge** (p224) and load up on delicious pastries from its one store. Kintla Lake, at the top of the road, is a stellar destination for a picnic, a float or simply quiet time.
- If you want to hike, start the **Boulder Pass Trail** (p214).
- Dinner and drinks at the **Northern Lights Saloon** (p227), in Polebridge, is the ideal way to wind down.
- Finally, say 'so long' to Glacier National Park and spend your day exploring the surrounding area. The **Blackfeet Indian Reservation** (p229) has a fascinating museum, as well as hiking and fishing opportunities.
- If you're heading south for your departure, the massive Flathead Lake is a stunner worth checking out. Kayak or take a boat tour (looking out for Flathead Nessie, the lake's monster). Eat mahogany cherries picked from lakeside orchards, and dine in the charming village of Polson.

Canadian Parks Sampler

ONE WEEK

- Spend three days in **Banff National Park** (p67), taking in the world-renowned **Lake Louise**, (p75), hiking up to **Lake Agnes & the Big Beehive** (p89) and exploring the sights in **Banff Town** (p72).
- On the fourth day, head up the **Icefields Parkway** (p134), the highest road on the continent. Spend the night at one of the remote hostels or campgrounds en route, and take in **Peyto Lake** (p136), the **Columbia Icefields** (p137) and the **Athabasca Falls** (p138).
- Spend the last two days in **Jasper National Park** (p162), boating on **Maligne Lake** (p167), hiking up **Bald Hills** (p173) or soaking in **Miette Hot Springs** (p166).

Fill the first week with the sights and activities from the One Week section.

- Take a side trip from Banff to **Yoho National Park** (p124), either doing an overnight backcountry hike to **Lake O'Hara** (p124) or taking in **Emerald Lake** (p125) and **Takakkaw Falls** (p124) and staying at the quaint town of **Field** (p126).
- Dip down into **Kootenay National Park** (p128) to see Marble Canyon and the Paint Pots, maybe splashing out on a night at the cozy and romantic **Storm Mountain** (p130).
- From Jasper, take in **Mt Robson Provincial Park** (p191) to set your eyes on the highest peak in Canada.

Follow the two-week itinerary.

- Take a trip to **Waterton Lakes National Park** (p232), where you can hike the stunning **Carthew-Alderson** (p238) or **Crypt Lake** (p239) **Trails**. Or take to the backcountry with the **Tamarack Trail** (p242) for magnificent views.
- En route between Waterton Lake and Banff, explore **Kananaskis Country** (p121) and stay in the peaceful campgrounds, watching for moose.

Rocky Mountain Parks Explorer

If you're determined to see all of the national parks, you'll need four weeks. Here's the best of each.

Begin with just under a week in the southern **Waterton-Glacier International Peace Park** (p194).

- Follow the driving tour along the stunningly scenic **Going-to-the-Sun Rd** (p200) for lots of viewpoints and a good introduction to the park.
- Head out on a day hike along **Iceberg Lake Trail** (p208) or **Carthew-Alderson Trail** (p238), the area's top trails.
- Hop on a **boat tour** (p235) of Upper Waterton Lake to Goat Haunt; stay on for a roundtrip boat or walk back via the pleasant **Waterton Lakeshore Trail** (p235).
- If you'd like to experience the backcountry, spend two spectacular days on the **Tamarack Trail** (p242).
- For wining and dining, head to **Waterton Townsite** (p235) and the unique **Polebridge Village** (p224).
- Head north through **Kananaskis Country** (p121) to **Canmore** (p118) and on to **Banff National Park** (p67).

Spend a week in **Banff National Park** (p67).

- Take in the major sights, like **Lake Louise** (p75), the **Banff Gondola** (p74), the **Upper Hot Springs** (p74) and the **Whyte Museum of the Canadian Rockies** (p72).
- Follow the driving tour along the **Bow Valley Parkway** (p77) for a good chance of spotting wildlife.
- Head out along some of the park's best trails, like **Lake Agnes & the Big Beehive** (p89), **Plain of Six Glaciers** (p88) or **Johnston Canyon** (p86).
- Paddle a canoe up the **Bow River** (p102), rent a bike and cycle along the endless trail system or go white-water rafting along the raging rivers.

WEEK THREE

From Banff, spend two days in **Kootenay National Park** (p128).
- Cross the **Continental Divide** (p128).
- Stop to see **Marble Canyon** (p128).
- Dine or even spend the night at **Storm Mountain** (p130).
- Take in **Stanley Glacier** on one of the area's most popular day hikes (p129).
- Soak in **Radium Hot Springs** (p129).
- Head west to **Yoho National Park** (p124).
- Spend three days hiking to and around **Lake O'Hara** (p124) or visit it on a day trip, basing yourself in quaint **Field** (p124). Take in some of the park's other sights like **Takakkaw Falls** (p124) and ride horses around **Emerald Lake** (p125).
- Return to Banff via Yoho and spend two days following the **Icefields Parkway** (p134), arguably the most gorgeous drive in the Rockies.
- Stay in a remote campground, hostel or lodge.
- Take in the blue-blue **Peyto Lake** (p136), the **Athabasca Falls** (p138), or the **Columbia Icefields** (p137).
- Head out on a day hike for spectacular views of the surrounding peaks. Try **Bow Glacier Falls** (p138) or **Wilcox Pass** (p143).
- Visit **Mt Edith Cavell** (p143).

WEEK FOUR

Spend your final week in **Jasper National Park** (p162).
- Paddle on **Maligne Lake** (p167).
- Rest in **Miette Hot Springs** (p166).
- Take a plunge into **Lake Annette** (p167).
- Hike along the park's superb trails, like the **Maligne Canyon** (p177), **Bald Hills** (p173) or **Jacques Lake** (p176).
- If you want to spend a few days in the backcountry, head for the **Skyline Trail** (p180) or **Tonquin Valley** (p181).

The Canadian Rocky Mountains are an outdoor enthusiast's paradise. Whether you're eager to scale a cliff, drive a dogsled team, hike, bike, ski or play a round of golf, the parks have plenty to offer, all set amid stunning mountain scenery.

ACTIVITIES

Most activities are offered at every level, from beginner to expert; if you're tempted to try something new, the Rockies are the place to do it.

Hiking & Backpacking

Going for a hike is one of the best and easiest ways to experience the wilderness of the Rockies. No matter which of the parks you choose to visit, opportunities for hiking are fantastic and, all totaled, the number of trails is staggering. From one-hour strolls to multiday hikes, there are trails suitable for everyone. For short ventures, you need next to no equipment and can easily escape the bustling crowds as you delve into deep forests and lofty meadows. Perhaps it's the surrounding peacefulness or simply a sense of accomplishment, but views achieved through hiking always appear more striking, encounters with wildlife feel like even more of a privilege, and mountains look even grander than those seen through the car window. If you only do one activity while you're visiting the parks, make it a hike.

Excellent hikes are spread throughout each of the parks, and which trail you set out on will largely depend on your interests (alpine lakes, glaciers, wildlife, solitude, easy walks or tough slogs). In **Banff**, some of the best day hikes are found around Lake Louise, where you can leave the tour groups behind and find alpine lakes in hidden, hanging valleys. In **Jasper**, trails are even more remote; head out to **Maligne Lake** for walks with lots of wildlife, and head south along the **Icefields Parkway** for magnificent glaciers and stunning lakes. In **Glacier**, trails around Many Glacier lead through lush forests to gorgeous glacial lakes. Trails through the tiny **Waterton Lakes** lead almost immediately into the backcountry, where you'll find sweeping, majestic views. For more details on specific areas and hikes, see the destination chapters.

Opportunities for hiking don't end at the park borders, since there are many neighboring recreational areas. **Yoho** is famous for its walks around Lake O'Hara, and **Kootenay** is known for the day hikes near its northern border. **Kananaskis Country**, east of Banff, has a multitude of beautiful trails that see few hikers. **Mt Assiniboine Provincial Park** is accessible only by foot and is many hikers' favorite haunt. Each year, backpackers return to the Valley of a Thousand Falls, in **Mt Robson Provincial Park**. South of Glacier National Park in the USA, the **Bob Marshall Wilderness Complex** has lots of trails humming with geology, plants and wildlife.

All of the national parks have information centers which dole out trail maps, current conditions and lots of helpful advice. Each Canadian national park has a 'Friends Of' society that sells specialists guidebooks and topographical maps and operates guided hikes. See each destination chapter for contact details, tour companies and ranger-guided hikes.

WHEN TO HIKE

The majority of hiking takes place from mid-May to late September. Hikes that are lower in elevation are accessible earliest in the season (sometimes as early as April). Hikes leading up to lofty heights can still have snow coverage in mid-July or later. If you're planning to head into the backcountry, July and August are the best months to go, although they're also the busiest months on the trails. The weather might not be as nice in June, as there are regular showers, but you're more likely to have the path to yourself. September can bring clear, blue skies, as well as a sudden drop in temperature.

In winter, a number of short trails remain open around Banff Town and Jasper Town. Visit the information centers for winter trail maps and further details.

DIFFICULTY LEVEL

In order to help you find an appropriate trail, hikes listed within this guide are graded as follows:

Easy: Generally flat and easy to navigate, these trails are often accessible to wheelchairs and suitable for young children.

Moderate: Trails have some elevation gain and may be narrow or not as well defined but can be done by anyone of average fitness.

Difficult: Steep climbs, tricky route finding and an overall strenuous endeavor make these trails the grounds of the fit.

DAY HIKES

The majority of hikes detailed within this guide are day hikes, taking 45 minutes to eight hours (not including breaks). If a particular hike catches your fancy but is longer than you have the time or energy for, consider doing the first hour or two and turning back. This is true for backcountry hikes as well; a mere two hours of a three-day hike can often be very worthwhile. Trail descriptions in the destination chapters detail sights and viewpoints en route.

Always set out with a full bottle of water, rain gear (weather is very unpredictable in the mountains), a hat, sunscreen, bug repellent and a friend. If you're going to be gone for any length of time, carry snacks and a basic first-aid kit. See Safety (p32) for more details.

BACKCOUNTRY HIKES

For a wilderness experience that's more vivid and encompassing than is achievable from a car or even on a day hike, try an overnight backcountry trail. Hikes vary in length (from two days to the better part of a month) and in difficulty. As long as you're reasonably fit, well equipped and realistic about your ability, you should have no problem finding an appropriate backcountry trail. **Egypt Lake** in Banff, **Tonquin Valley** in Jasper and **Lake O'Hara** in Yoho can all be reached within eight hours of moderate hiking and offer accommodations other than camping. Other popular

HIKING IN BANFF

NAME	TYPE	LOCATION START	DISTANCE R/T	DURATION	CHALLENGE	ELEVATION CHANGE	FEATURES	FACILITIES	DESCRIPTION	PAGE
Aylmer Lookout	Day Hike	Minnewanka Area	23.3km/ 14.4mi	8 hrs	difficult	560m/ 1706ft			After a tough slog, rewards hikers with brilliant lake and mountain views.	84
Bow River Falls	Day Hike	Banff Town	4.4km/ 1.4mi	1.5 hrs	easy	negligible			An easy stroll along the river, with views of Bow Falls.	52
Consolation Lakes	Day Hike	Lake Louise Area	5.8km/ 3.6mi	1 hr 40 min	easy-moderate	65m/ 213ft			Delves into the heart of the park and provides spectacular views with little effort.	92
Egypt Lake	Overnight	Sunshine Meadows	26.4km/ 16.4mi	9 hrs	moderate-difficult	655m/ 2148ft			Sparkling alpine lakes, meadows blanketed with wildflowers and lots of side-trip options.	98
Fenland Trail	Day Hike	Banff Town	2.1km/ 1.3mi	0.5 hr	easy	none			A picturesque trail through marshland.	82
Garden Path Trail & Twin Cairns Meadow	Day Hike	Sunshine Meadows	8.3km/ 5.1mi	3.5 hrs	easy-moderate	185m/ 607ft			Passes through an enchanted area of alpine meadows, glassy lakes and other magnificent views.	94
Healy Pass	Day Hike	Sunshine Meadows	18.4km/ 11.4mi	6 hrs	moderate-difficult	655m/ 2148ft			A hike to lush alpine meadows and uninterrupted views across the Great Divide.	95
Johnston Canyon	Day Hike	Bow Valley	5.4km/ 3.4mi	2.5 hrs	easy	120m/ 394ft			One of Banff's most popular walks; goes along a spectacular gorge to raging falls.	86
Lake Agnes & The Big Beehive	Day Hike	Lake Louise Area	10.2km/ 6.4mi	3 hrs	difficult	520m/ 1706ft			Pretty lakes in hidden valleys and astounding vistas; one of the area's best day hikes.	89
Lake Louise Lakeshore Trail	Day Hike	Lake Louise Area	3.8km/ 2.4mi	1 hr	easy	none			Continuous views across a milky-green lake to surrounding peaks and glaciers.	88
Lake Minnewanka	Overnight	Minnewanka Area	59km/ 36.6mi	17 hrs	moderate	45m/ 148ft			A relatively easy backcountry hike along the lakeshore to Devil's Gap.	98
C-Level Cirque	Day Hike	Minnewanka Area	7.8km/ 4.8mi	3 hrs	moderate-difficult	445m/ 1493ft			A steady ascent to an impressive amphitheater with views en route and pika to greet you.	83
Moraine Lake Shoreline Trail	Day Hike	Lake Louise Area	2.4km/ 1.4mi	40 min	easy	none			Ambles along a peaceful lakeshore, with views of glaciers on the Wenkchemna Peaks.	91
Mt Assiniboine & Magog Lake	Overnight	Mt Assiniboine	57.6km/ 35.8mi	4 days	moderate-difficult	44m/ 1310ft			Gorgeous views en route to brightly colored lakes and the Matterhorn of the Rockies.	99
Plain of Six Glaciers	Day Hike	Lake Louise Area	13.5km/ 8.4mi	4 hrs	moderate	340m/ 1115ft			Climbs high into the mountains to a remote lookout surrounded by enormous rivers of ice.	88
ICEFIELDS PARKWAY										
Bow Glacier Falls	Day Hike	Icefields Parkway	7.2km/ 4.4mi	2 hrs	easy-moderate	95m/ 310ft			A well-worn trail taking in Bow Lake, a deep gorge and a waterfall.	133
Helen Lake	Day Hike	Icefields Parkway	12km/ 7.4mi	4 hrs	moderate-difficult	550m/ 1804ft			Cuts through an alpine valley with heavy marmots; offers beautiful views and solitude.	140
Peyto Lake & Bow Summit Lookout	Day Hike	Icefields Parkway	6.2km/ 3.8mi	2 hrs	moderate-difficult	235m/ 768ft			From the Peyto Lake lookout, the trail heads up to a grassy knoll with panoramic views.	139

routes include the trail to **Mt Assiniboine** from Banff, the **Skyline Trail** in Jasper and, in Glacier, the **North Circle** (or Highland Trail). For all of these routes, reserve your permits early.

The majority of backcountry trails are open from mid-June until mid-September; however, continuously changing weather patterns and late thaws can leave snow hanging around well into the summer. Always check with the appropriate information center before you go. Backcountry hikes covered in this guide are the more popular and, generally, easier options. For information on difficult or more remote hikes, visit the parks' information centers.

Responsible Backcountry Camping

If there are no tent pads, pitch your tent at least 50m/164ft from the trail and 70m/230ft from any water source. To discourage unwanted visitors, such as bears or wolves, hang all food, toiletries and garbage from food-storage cables. If no cables are provided, hang your food between two strong trees, at least 4m/13ft above the ground and 2m/7ft from either tree trunk. (You'll need two 20m/66ft lengths of rope to accomplish this.)

Fires are not permitted at many campgrounds, and bans are often imposed if forest-fire hazards are high. While campfires evoke nostalgia for many campers, they also cause environmental degradation; try to cook on a lightweight stove whenever possible. While it may look as if you are surrounded by an endless sea of trees, there is not an inexhaustible supply; only use deadfall, and never cut branches or trees down. Keep the fire small, and ensure that it is completely out before you go to sleep or leave the site.

At designated sites you'll find pit toilets; however, if you need to relieve yourself along the trail, there are a number of guidelines to follow.

- Always move well away from the path and at least 70m/230ft from any water source.
- Dig a hole, do the deed, and then cover it with dirt.
- Pack out toilet paper in a sealed plastic bag.

Housekeeping in the wilderness also requires some special considerations. Pour dishwater far from water and campsites. In high alpine areas, even biodegradable soap may not degrade. Try using sand or a kitchen scourer to clean your dishes. Finally, pack out all garbage. Not only is it the law, it also helps to preserve the park. A small piece of glass or foil is enough to magnify the sun's rays and start a forest fire, and animals quickly lose their wildness if accustomed to scavenging.

HIKING SAFETY

Avalanches, rockslides and agitated wild animals are a few of the dangers that you're unlikely to encounter but should be prepared for nonetheless. Always be prepared for a sudden change in weather, and be well versed in how to deal with wildlife encountered on the trail (p59). It is never wise to travel alone, and if you're on going on a backcountry hike, it's always advisable to register with the park staff or let someone at home know when to expect you back. If you do opt to go on your own, see Going Solo (p34) for hints.

It's also important to know your limits; sprained ankles and falls are much more likely to happen to weary hikers. When planning your route, allow plenty of time for rests en route and to ensure that you reach your destination before dark.

River crossings can also pose risks; check with information centers for river levels before you go. Use a stick or interlock arms with others when crossing rivers and

NAME	TYPE	LOCATION START	DISTANCE R/T	DURATION	CHALLENGE	ELEVATION CHANGE	FEATURES	FACILITIES	DESCRIPTION	PAGE
Annette Lake Loop	Day-hike	Jasper Town	2.4km/1.5mi	40 min	easy	none			Surrounded by views of well-known peaks; can be finished with a plunge in the lake.	173
Bald Hills	Day-hike	Maligne Lake	10.4km/6.4mi	3.5 hrs	moderate-difficult	480m/1574ft			Leads to lofty meadows, spectacular views and endless opportunities for exploring.	173
Celestine Lake & Devona Lookout	Day Hike	Celestine Lake Rd	18.4km/11.4mi	5 hrs	moderate	325m/1066ft			Takes in tranquil lakes and a view, stretching along the Athabasca Valley.	178
Jaques Lake	Day Hike	Maligne Lake	24km/14.9mi	8 hrs	moderate	90m/295ft			Ends up in a remote valley surrounded by massive mountains and bejeweled with a turquoise lake.	176
Lorraine & Mona Lakes	Day Hike	Maligne Lake Rd	5km/3.1mi	1.5 hrs	easy	negligible			A peaceful walk beneath the canopy of the forest to picturesque lakes.	175
Maligne Canyon	Day Hike	Maligne Lake	4.2km/2.6mi	1.5 hrs	moderate	100m/328ft			One of the Rockies' deepest canyons; provides dramatic views of waterfalls and sunken gardens.	177
Mary Schaffer Loop	Day Hike	Maligne Lake	3.2km/2.2mi	45 min	easy	negligible			Holds the famous view first seen by Mary Schaffer (see p253).	175
Mina & Riley Lakes Loop	Day Hike	Jasper Town	9km/5.6mi	3 hrs	easy-moderate	160m/525ft			Takes you deep into the woods to remote lakes.	171
Moose Lake Loop	Day Hike	Maligne Lake	2.6km/1.6mi	45 min	easy	negligible			Offers a peaceful, verdant forest and a chance to spot a moose.	174
Old Fort Point Loop	Day Hike	Jasper Town	3.2km/2.2mi	1.5 hrs	moderate	135m/443ft			Panoramic views of the mountaintops around Jasper Town.	172
Skyline Trail	Overnight	Miette Hot Springs	45.8km/28.7mi	2-3 days (one way)	moderate-difficult	1380m/4526ft			Mostly downhill; offers infinite views across the mountains.	180
Sulphur Skyline	Day Hike	Maligne Lake Rd	9.6km/6mi	3.5 hrs	difficult	700m/2296ft			Provides a staggering view and the opportunity to soak in hot springs after the hike.	176
Tonquin Valley	Overnight	Marmot Basin Rd	53.2km/33mi	2 days	difficult	700m/2296ft			Features wildlife, lush meadows and sparkling lakes, all beneath the shadow of The Ramparts.	181
ICEFIELDS PARKWAY										
Path of the Glacier & Cavell Meadows	Day Hike	Icefields Parkway	9.1km/5.6mi	3 hrs	difficult	400m/1300ft			Angel Glacier rests over a sapphire lake afloat with icebergs; the meadows trek offers amazing views.	141
Valley of the Five Lakes	Day Hike	Icefields Parkway	4.2km/2.6mi	1 hr 45 min	easy	negligible			Winds through the woods, taking in five serene lakes, each a different shade of blue and green.	144
Wilcox Pass	Day Hike	Icefields Parkway	11.2km/6.9mi	3.5 hrs	moderate	335m/1100ft			Allows hikers to look out to the Columbia Icefields and to some of the Rockies' highest peaks.	143

Legend: Swimming · Restroom · Ranger Station · Drinking Water · Picnic Sites · Backcountry Campsite · Restaurant · Wheelchair Access · Canoeing · Backcountry · Views · Wildlife Watching · Fishing · Great for Families · Waterfalls · Bicycles streams, and for deeper crossings, move through the water sideways. Always undo chest and waist straps on your backpack, just in case you fall.

There is never a guarantee that you'll be able to find a ranger or warden in an emergency, so you need to be as well prepared as possible to deal with difficult situations. Reception for cellular phones is also hit-and-miss in the wilderness and cannot be relied upon for emergency contact.

HIKING RULES & PERMITS

No matter where you're hiking, stay on the trails – even if it means treading through snow or mud. Crushing alpine plants or forging new paths damages the fragile ecosystem of the parks. Obey trail closures; they're due to fire or wildlife hazards, or occasional maintenance.

GOING SOLO

One of the most important things to take with you on a hike is a companion. Falls, sprains and getting lost are much easier to cope with if you're not alone; wildlife are more intimidated and likely to go their own way if encountering a group; and, in a serious emergency, there's somebody to run for help.

If you're traveling on your own but don't want to head off down the trail alone, **Friends of Banff** (☎ 403-762-8911) keeps a list of solo travelers looking for hiking partners. Also consider staying in hostels, where there's a good chance you'll find a friendly hiking partner or two. Inquire at information centers for ranger-led hikes; they're often interesting, if a little slow paced.

If you do decide to throw caution to the wind, be sure to let someone know where you're going and when to expect you back. If it's a longer or risky trip, register with Parks Canada or a ranger in Glacier. Sing your lungs out, clap loudly and chatter away to yourself to warn animals of your approach, particularly in dense forest, near streams or on windy days. Pack a first-aid kit and bear spray, and carry a map, trail description and compass. And don't forget your nerve.

Canadian National Parks

For all stops within Canada's national parks, you are required to purchase a **park pass**. Day passes for most parks cost adult/senior/child CAD$7/6/3.50. If you're planning to spend more than a week in the parks, it's worth buying a year pass, giving you unlimited access to all of Canada's national parks (adult/groups of up to five people CAD$38/75). Passes are available from park gates and from Parks Canada information desks. Day passes for Waterton cost adult/senior/child CAD$5/4.25/2.50.

For overnight stays in the backcountry, you must have a **wilderness pass** (CAD$8 per night per adult over 16 years in all parks), available up to 24 hours in advance from all Canada Parks information desks. You will be required to show your pass to any wardens you encounter on the trail. Reservations are recommended, as Parks Canada limits the number of hikers on each trail; contact **Parks Canada** (☎ 800-748-7275). The reservation fee is CAD$12.

Glacier National Park

A pass into Waterton does not include entry into Glacier National Park. Entering Glacier costs USD$10 per car or RV; those arriving on foot, bicycle or motorcycle pay

NAME	TYPE	LOCATION START	DISTANCE	DURATION	CHALLENGE	ELEVATION CHANGE	FEATURES	FACILITIES	DESCRIPTION	PAGE
GLACIER										
Avalanche Lake Trail	Day Hike	Lake McDonald Valley	6.4km/2.5mi	2.5 hr	easy	764m/475ft			Very popular forested walk to a stunning lake.	234
Boulder Pass Trail	Overnight	North Fork Valley	50.5km/31.4mi	4 days	moderate-difficult	1273m/4175ft			Climbs passes till you're just below the Canada border.	214
Cracker Lake Trail	Day Hike	Many Glacier Area	19.6km/12.2mi	7 hrs	moderate	378m/1228ft			Less crowded than other Many Glacier hikes; offers a spectacular lake destination.	209
Gunsight Pass Trail	Overnight	St Mary Valley	31.9km/19.8mi	2 days	moderate-difficult	1158m/3800ft			See snowfields, glaciers, lakes and more over two riveting days.	213
Hidden Lake Overlook Trail	Day Hike	Logan Pass	5km/3mi	2 hrs	moderate	150m/494ft			Quick scamper to spectacular lookout.	204
Highline Trail	Day Hike	Logan Pass	18.7km/11.6mi	5.5-7.5 hrs	easy	920m/3020ft			Phenomenal scenery for miles; heads to Granite Park Chalet.	205
Highline Trail/Ptarmigan Tunnel	Overnight	Many Glacier	80.8km/50.2mi	6 days	moderate-difficult	853m/2800ft			Backcountry hike offers the most diverse scenery of any park journey.	216
Iceberg Lake Trail	Day Hike	Many Glacier	14.5km/9mi	5.5 hrs	easy-moderate	363m/1190ft			Leads to one of the most impressive glacial lakes in the Rockies.	208
Medicine Grizzly Lake Trail	Day Hike	Two Med Valley	19.8km/12.4mi	6.5 hrs	easy-moderate	165m/540ft			Easy ascents and descents through bear country; the tranquil destination lake is lovely.	211
Red Eagle Lake Trail	Day Hike	St Mary Valley	24.5km/15.2mi	8 hr	easy	91m/300ft			Long but gentle hike to a lake favored for its serenity.	206
Redrock Falls	Day Hike	Many Glacier	5.8km/3.6mi	2 hrs	easy	64m/212ft			An easy stroll, with wildflower meadows on the way to waterfalls.	209
Siyeh Pass Trail	Day Hike	St Mary Valley	16.6km/10.3mi	7 hrs	moderate-difficult	1050m/3345ft			Diverse views on the way to a dramatic, windy pass.	207
Trail of the Cedars	Day Hike	Lake McDonald Valley	1.3km/0.8mi	30 min	easy	16m/52ft			A short, wheelchair-accessible loop trail through mature forest.	208
Upper Two Medicine Lake Trail	Day Hike	Two Medicine Valley	15.1km/9.4mi	5 hrs	easy	101m/330ft			Pleasant daytrip via forest and meadows to a lake, with side trip to waterfalls.	211
WATERTON										
Carthew-Alderson Trail	Day Hike	Cameron Lake	19km/11.8mi (OW)	6.5 hrs	moderate	600m/1968ft			Memorable hike offers beautiful scenery and sweeping views.	238
Crypt Lake Trail	Day Hike	Upper Waterton Lake	17.2km/10.3mi	6.5 hrs	moderate-difficult	700m/2296ft			Involves tunnel-crawling and a cable-assisted walk over sheer cliffs.	239
Rowe Lakes	Day Hike	Akamina Parkway	12.6km/7.8mi	5 hrs	moderate	548.6m/1800ft			A beautiful scenic hike, with an option to ascend a ridge.	240
Crandell Lake Trail	Day Hike	Red Rock Parkway	4km/2.4mi	1.5 hrs	easy-moderate	100m/328ft			Clear Crandell Lake makes a great place to hang out for a while.	241
Avion Ridge Loop	Day Hike	Red Rock Canyon	22.5km/14mi	8.5 hrs	moderate-difficult	981m/3218ft			Unusual route traverses a high, scree-covered ridge with spectacular views.	241

See Legend on page 32, used for Hiking in 3 zones. All distances and duration information is for round-trip unless otherwise specified. *OW (One Way)

USD$5 per person. Passes are valid for seven days. An annual Glacier National Park Pass goes for USD$20.

You do not need a permit for day hikes within the park. For overnight trips, you must purchase a **wilderness permit** *(adult/child USD$4/2, season pass USD$50, under 9yrs free)*. These can be arranged at the ranger stations at Many Glacier, Two Medicine or Polebridge. For reservations, contact the **Apgar Backcountry Office** *(☎ 406-888-7857, fax 406-888-5819).*

White-Water Rafting & Float Trips

Raging rivers, giant rapids and an adrenaline-pumping ride – with some of the best **white-water rafting** in the country, you can definitely find all of this in the Rockies. Take a beginner's course or have a go at heli-rafting. If you prefer to stay dry or are just after something a little more peaceful, almost all rafting companies in the parks offer **float trips** as well. These are ideal for families and are a good opportunity for spotting wildlife. The season for rafting is May through September, with highest river levels (and therefore the most rapids) in spring.

Rafting along the powerful Kicking Horse and Kananaskis Rivers is world-class; arrange trips through outfitters in Banff Town, Golden, Canmore or Radium Hot Springs. From Jasper Town, trips run along the beautiful Athabasca River. For details on rafting in each of the parks, see Activities in the destination chapters.

Rafting can look precarious and feel chaotic, and there are inherent risks involved. Nevertheless, serious accidents are incredibly rare, and getting wet is the most that's likely to happen to you if you fall out of the raft. The smaller the boat, the wilder the trip; larger boats are sturdier. A guide trained in life-saving is mandatory on all trips, and all participants are provided with lifejackets.

Cycling

With lots of hiking trails open to cyclists, **mountain biking** is a popular way to explore many of the parks between May and October. In Banff there are a number of rides around Banff Town, as well as some popular routes near Lake Louise. Scores of trails in Jasper, where you can enjoy superb views or skirt gorgeous lakes, are well geared for cyclists. Along the Icefields Parkway, linking Banff and Jasper, many of the backcountry trails are open to mountain bikes. Trails in both parks range from family-friendly, flat routes to difficult, steep, root-riddled rides.

You'll also find biking trails in Waterton National Park, Kananaskis Country and Canmore. Kicking Horse Resort, in Golden, allows cyclists to take their bikes up the gondola in summer, followed by an extreme ride down the mountainside. In Banff Town you'll find tour companies offering guided bike rides. See the destination chapters for recommended routes.

Biking in the parks is allowed on designated trails only; ask at information centers for trail maps. All off-trail riding is strictly forbidden, as it damages vegetation and displaces wildlife. Avoid riding when it's extremely wet, muddy or dry; it damages trails, as does skidding and sliding. Cyclists must give way to hikers and horseback riders on the trails.

Road riding is popular along the Bow Valley Parkway and Minnewanka Loop Rd in Banff, and on the Icefields Parkway. Be wary of drivers, whose minds are on wildlife-watching and rarely on looking for cyclists. In Glacier, biking is not permitted on any trails, though you can cycle down some of the scenic roads in and around the park.

Bikes and equipment can be rented in Banff Town, Jasper Town, Waterton Village, Kananaskis Village, Canmore and Golden. Full and front suspension bikes, car racks, kids' bikes and tot trailers are all available. You can have your bike repaired at most rental companies.

Hills that don't seem so steep on foot can be much more difficult when you're on a bike. If you're a novice at mountain biking, start with an easy trail. Helmets are mandatory, and if you're heading anywhere remote, take basic repair gear and a first-aid kit. On remote trails, because bikes are quiet and fast, cyclists are more vulnerable to dangerous bear encounters. To warn bears of your presence, ride slowly, stay aware and make lots of noise, particularly in deep forests, near streams and on windy days. Bear bells are not enough.

Canoeing, Kayaking & Boating

Skimming along the top of brilliantly colored glacial lakes and down rivers winding beneath mountaintops can be a serene way to experience the parks and offers a good chance for watching wildlife. The season runs from mid-May to early October, depending on spring thaws, autumn weather conditions and the elevation of the body of water. Nonmotorized boats are permitted on almost all waters. Motorized boats can be launched on very few of Canada's national park waters (with Banff's Minnewanka Lake being a major exception), but motorized boats are permitted on many lakes in Glacier. Visit an information center for current regulations.

In Banff, Vermillion Lakes is a popular hangout for wildlife and hence is a popular place to **canoe**; rentals are available from nearby Banff Town. Bow River and lakes in the Minnewanka area are also good places to set adrift. At Lake Louise and Moraine Lake, you can rent a variety of boats to paddle through the icy water. Maligne Lake, in Jasper, also has boat rentals, and paddling out into the middle of the water is one of the best ways of appreciating its beautiful setting. You can also rent boats on Pyramid Lake.

In Glacier Village, rent kayaks, canoes and **rowboats** for a trip on the stunning lakes of Glacier National Park; sailors can try out the enthusiastic winds on St Mary Lake. In Waterton Lakes, hire a boat to explore the exquisite Cameron Lake. Just outside Glacier, Flathead Lake has picturesque

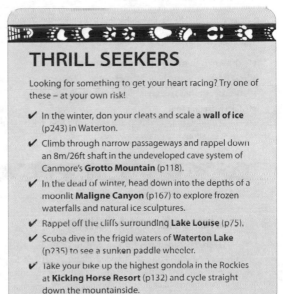

THRILL SEEKERS

Looking for something to get your heart racing? Try one of these – at your own risk!

✔ In the winter, don your cleats and scale a **wall of ice** (p243) in Waterton.

✔ Climb through narrow passageways and rappel down an 8m/26ft shaft in the undeveloped cave system of Canmore's **Grotto Mountain** (p118).

✔ In the dead of winter, head down into the depths of a moonlit **Maligne Canyon** (p167) to explore frozen waterfalls and natural ice sculptures.

✔ Rappel off the cliffs surrounding **Lake Louise** (p75).

✔ Scuba dive in the frigid waters of **Waterton Lake** (p235) to see a sunken paddle wheeler.

✔ Take your bike up the highest gondola in the Rockies at **Kicking Horse Resort** (p132) and cycle straight down the mountainside.

bays ideal for **kayaking**, canoeing and marine campgrounds. See each destination chapter for more details.

Depending on the popularity of the lake, boat and kayak rentals range anywhere from CAD$10 to CAD$20 per hour in the Canadian national parks and USD$10 to USD$15 in Glacier National Park. Life jackets are included in all rentals. If you're heading off down a river, be sure to know what's ahead of you; slow-running water can suddenly pick up its pace and rush into deep canyons or over giant falls.

If you'd prefer to sit back and relax as you cruise across the waters, regular boat tours are available down the length of Minnewanka Lake in Banff and Maligne Lake in Jasper. Trips on Maligne Lake are extremely popular and fill up fast. In Glacier, boat trips set out from hotels for a whole slew of lakes – McDonald, St Mary, Swiftcurrent and Josephine.

Rock & Ice Climbing

Giant ranges and countless cliff faces make Banff a mecca for **rock climbers**, but tough approaches and ever-changing weather patterns make those peaks all the more challenging. In Banff Town, first-timers can take lessons, and experienced climbers can join tours. Jasper is also popular for climbing, and lessons are available from Jasper Town. Half-day trips cost around CAD$60 to $70, and two-day beginner courses are around CAD$150. Gear is available in both Banff Town and Jasper Town. **CMH Mountaineering** (☎ 800-661-0252; **W** *www.cmhmountaineering.com*) organizes incredible multiday climbing trips throughout the region, with first ascents, spires and glaciers.

Mountains in areas like Mt Assiniboine, Waterton Lakes and Glacier are made of decaying limestone, making rockslides common and climbing treacherous. Even experts should seek local advice before setting out.

In winter, Waterton Lakes becomes a popular haunt for **ice climbing**. Tours also head out for icy cliffs from Banff Town. Don't even think about wandering onto a glacier; snow drifts often hide deep, deadly crevasses.

RAINY DAY FUN

The weather doesn't have to put a damper on your vacation. When Mother Nature decides to give the scenery a good watering, try one of these activities:

✔ Visit a **museum** in Banff Town or Jasper Town

✔ Go **rafting** – you're bound to get wet anyway

✔ Head for the **hot springs** in Banff, Jasper or Kootenay

✔ Take a **driving tour**

✔ Ask at information centers about **sheltered hikes** that aren't all about mountain views (try Johnston Canyon in Banff

---

Horseback Riding

From lakeside rides for tiny tots to overnight backcountry trips, horseback riding is well established in the parks. In both Banff and Jasper you can take your horse down many of the hiking trails; ask for a map at the information centers. If you're galloping off into the backcountry, you need to purchase a grazing permit (CAD$1 per horse per night) in addition to your own wilderness pass. **Tonquin Valley** is popular with horseback riders, as is the approach to Mt Assiniboine Park from Kananaskis Country. Always check with park information about the level of any rivers you might have to ford.

If you didn't bring your own horse, you can hop on one with a tour from Jasper Town, Banff Town, Waterton Lakes, Glacier, Kananaskis Country and the Bob Marshall Wilderness Area. Many outfitters run multiday trips into the wilds. Lakeside ambles are also available at Emerald Lake in Yoho. Prices vary, depending on accommodations, equipment, skill level etc.

Alberta Outfitters Association (☎ 800-742-5548, **W** *www.albertaoutfitters.com*) is worth contacting for a membership directory of outfitters throughout the province, as is **Montana Outfitters & Guides Association** (☎ 406-449-3578; **W** *www.moga-montana.org*). See Activities in the destination chapters for more details.

Wildlife Watching

In the stomping grounds of bears, wolves, elk, bighorn sheep, caribou, moose and cougars, you're bound to cross tracks with wildlife. Of course, your chances are higher in some places than others. Jasper is relatively remote, with elk often meandering down the main streets of town, and offers excellent opportunities to set your eyes on mountain creatures. For an almost guaranteed sighting, join one of the many **wildlife tours** from Jasper Town. Even in Banff, the busiest of the parks, slower roads (like the Bow Valley Parkway) offer a good chance to see elk and bears. Kananaskis Country, with its many roadside marshes, is the best place for spotting those elusive moose. The best time to see animals is in early morning and at dusk. Boat tours are also a great, safe way to get a look at wilderness and its occupants.

ELK ETIQUETTE & MOOSE MANNERS

Seeing a bear foraging alongside the road or happening upon a moose swimming in a remote lake are the highlights of many visitors' trips to the parks. Keep in mind, however, that you're a guest in their home. A number of guidelines and laws exist to protect both you and the animals.

✔ Keep your distance – at least 10 bus lengths from bears, cougars and wolves and three bus lengths from elk, deer, sheep, goats and moose. If a bedded animal gets up or a feeding animal stops chewing, you're too close. Animals don't like the spotlight, and those that feel threatened can (and do!) charge.

✔ Wildlife watching is a spectator sport only; do not approach, entice or in any way disturb wildlife. Many people move closer and closer in an attempt to get a close-up photo, frightening the animal and putting the photographer in a dangerous situation.

✔ Never feed wildlife. Parks rangers are almost always forced to put down animals that become accustomed to people, as the animals generally turn aggressive over time.

✔ If you see an animal from your car, slow down – it could dart in front of you at any moment. If you decide to stop, do so carefully and stay inside your car.

✔ Be particularly wary of animals that appear indifferent to your presence; they may appear cute, cuddly and even docile, but they're not afraid of you.

For tips on specific hikes, drives or areas to see wildlife, see Where the Wild Things Are (p174) in the Jasper chapter and Spotting Animals (p220) in the Glacier chapter. Also check out Wildlife Watching under Activities in the destination chapters.

Many people spend many of their hiking hours fretting over a bear encounter. Your chances of spotting a bear on the trail are not great, especially if you take precautions like hiking in a group and singing or talking loudly as you walk. Tying bear bells onto your pack certainly won't do any harm, but they're not a substitute for making noise. Consider investing in bear spray if you're going to be hiking in remote areas or on trails where bears are commonly sighted. Make sure you know how to use the spray before you hit the trail, and reserve it for emergency situations only; a bear with no plans to attack may do so if shot at with bear spray. Watch for signs that a bear is near at hand, namely clawed logs, large dead animals or bear poop (which looks more like dog or human stools than those left by horses or deer). Bears are not true hibernators as is commonly believed; they do wake up occasionally during the winter, so don't let your guard down.

PHOTOGRAPHY TIPS

With all that gorgeous scenery, there's never a shortage of subjects to photograph in the parks, but you may be wondering just what camera equipment to bring, and when and how to get the best shots.

Unless you're a professional, the lighter and more compact your equipment, the better; even if you are a professional, you might want to reassess what is essential to bring along. What feels light from the hotel room to the car can become onerous a mile or two up the trail. Tripods can be particularly burdensome; improvise with boulders and backpacks instead. If you're climbing, over-the-shoulder camera bags can pull you off balance. Instead, try a small backpack or photographer's belt.

Panoramic shots are not only some of the most stunning, they're also some of the easiest shots to make. Water is very photogenic, especially at some of the more reflective lakes; develop a panoramic photo of Lake Louise taken on a still day, and it's difficult to tell top from bottom.

Dusk and dawn are fantastic times to capture the wilderness on film. Focus on objects that the light is reflected on, like mountains, water or clouds, rather than directly photographing the sinking or rising sun. If the sun goes behind a cloud, don't take that as a signal to put away your camera. Some of the best pictures are taken in soft light; you'll get clean, even colors rather than bleached or drab shots. Shooting directly into the sunlight can turn your plant, friend or marmot into a silhouette. Try to find places where the sun is reflected off some aspect of the landscape, like snow or granite.

Wildlife is perhaps the greatest challenge to photographers. Those wide-angle lenses that are great for mountain scenery make distant animals seem even smaller; try to carry something with a zoom lens. Animals often move quickly, suddenly or constantly – particularly bobbing, twitching birds; try fast-speed film. One of your best opportunities for taking snapshots of wildlife is from the car window, as animals are generally much less disturbed than if you approach on foot, and therefore less likely to bolt.

Film can be bought at most tourist shops, camp stores and gas stations within the parks. Equipment and repairs can be found in Banff Town and Jasper Town, and you'll find one-hour processing there and in Whitefish, Kalispell, Pincher Creek and Cardston.

For further tips, pick up a copy of Lonely Planet's *Travel Photography*. Pointers in Galen Rowell's *Mountain Light* may be too technical, but the pictures are sure to inspire.

Park wardens and rangers post warnings of sightings at trailheads and in information centers; if there is considered to be a great risk, trails will be closed, or you'll be required to hike with at least five companions. For more details on how to prepare yourself for bear encounters and how to distinguish a black bear from the more aggressive grizzly, see p267 in the Ecosystem chapter.

Fishing

With so many lakes and waterways flowing through the landscape, fishing has unsurprisingly become popular in many of the parks. Arctic grayling, rainbow trout, brown trout, brook trout, lake trout, northern pike, mountain whitefish and lake whitefish are plentiful; many other species, like bull trout and kokanee salmon, are found in Canadian park waters but are protected.

Fly-fishing is particularly popular in Banff and Jasper, with the season running from June to September and peaking near the end of July. Waters open as early as May and close as late as October. In winter you can try **ice-fishing** in a few of the parks' waters; however, regulations are strict. Lots of outfitters offer spring and summer fishing trips and lessons from Banff Town and Jasper Town; if you want to set out on your own, try the Bow River, the Vermillion Lakes and waters in the Minnewanka area. In Jasper, locals head for Celestine Lake and Princess Lakes, Maligne Lake and Pyramid Lake. Along the Icefields Parkway, the Valley of the Five Lakes and the Athabasca and Sunwapta Rivers are good bets.

The waters in Waterton are also hopping with fish, and have similar opening dates to those in Banff and Jasper. Head for Bertha Lake, Upper and Middle Waterton Lakes, Akamina Lake and Cameron Lake.

Montana is mad about fly-fishing, and some of that fever carries over into Glacier National Park. Lake fishing here is year-round and popular in Lake McDonald, St Mary Lake and some more remote locations, like Oldman and Red Eagle Lakes. The season for stream and river fishing runs from May to late November; test out Red Eagle Creek, in St Mary, or Cut Bank Creek.

Outside the parks, cast your line in Kananaskis Country in Sibbald Meadows Pond or Lower Kananaskis Lake. East of Glacier, the Blackfeet Indian reservation boasts some good fishing.

In all parks and areas, seasons vary from year to year and from one lake or river to another; always check with park information centers for which waters are currently open. Many areas are closed to fishing at all times, and bans can be put in place if a species of fish is threatened.

FISHING LICENSES

In Canadian national parks, provincial fishing licenses are not valid; you must purchase a national park fishing permit (annual/seven-day permit CAD$13/6). Children under 16 years can fish without a permit if accompanied by a permit-holder over the age of 16.

The maximum daily catch and possession limit is two fish; if someone under 16 years is fishing with you, you have a maximum of two fish between you. Once you have caught your limit, it is unlawful to continue fishing until the next day. If you are unsure of what you've caught, throw it back; fines for catching protected species are high. You will be given a list of catch and possession limits when you purchase your fishing permit.

It is illegal to fish with natural bait, chemical attractants or lead tackle; stick to the likes of tinsel, silk and feathers. You cannot have more than one line in at a time and may not fish from two hours after sunset to an hour before sunrise. Fishing outside of Canada's national parks is subject to provincial laws.

Across the border in Glacier National Park, a state fishing license is not required. Five fish is the general possession limit, although this depends on what you've caught. A number of waters are catch-and-release zones only. Casting on the park's boundaries may require a Montana state fishing license, and waters on Blackfoot reservation land (such as part of Lower Two Medicine Lake) require proper permits from the reservation.

Golf

Golfing in the Rockies is like nowhere else – jagged peaks, unrivaled views and elk wandering across the course make it tricky to keep your eye on the ball.

Banff Springs Golf Course and **Jasper Lodge Golf Course** are both world-class. Designed by Stanley Thompson in the 1920s, both courses are as challenging as they are stunning. The price for a round in summer is about CAD$150. You'll also find courses in East and West Glacier, Waterton Lakes, Radium Hot Springs and Kananaskis Country.

Downhill Skiing & Snowboarding

Big mountains and lots of snow equal a skiing paradise in the Rockies. Banff boasts some of the continent's best ski slopes, attracting flocks of downhill skiers and snowboarders each winter. Mt Norquay, Lake Louise and Sunshine Village are all popular ski resorts that are easily accessible from Banff Town, offering full facilities like lessons, snowboarding terrain parks, groomed and powder slopes for all levels and sensational views.

New on the scene, Golden's **Kicking Horse Resort** (☎ 250-439-5400; W www .kickinghorseresort.com) is taking the ski world by storm; limited grooming makes it a haven for intermediate to expert skiers. In Jasper, head for **Marmot Basin** (☎ 780-852-3816; W www.skimarmot.com), on the Icefields Parkway, for lessons and novice to expert runs. You can also slide down the slopes of **Nakiska** (☎ 403-591-7777; W www.skinakiska.com), in Kananaskis Country, the site of the 1988 Winter Olympics. Down the road, **Fortress Mountain** (☎ 403-591-7108; W www.ski fortress.com) is popular with snowboarders.

Just south of Glacier, **Big Mountain Resort** (☎ 406-862-2900, 800-858-4157; W www.bigmtn.com) is a popular winter destination with lots of prime terrain and a 762m/2500ft vertical drop. The slopes are 11.2km/7 miles from downtown Whitefish.

Skis, poles, boots and snowboards can all be rented at all ski resorts, as well as in Banff Town and Jasper Town. Depending on the whims of Mother Nature, the season runs from about November to May.

Cross-Country Skiing

While most visitors wait for spring thaw to visit the parks, others find that snow-laced trees and mountainsides and the pervading stillness create the most beautiful time of year. Cross-country skiing is one of the best ways to experience the serenity of the wilderness in winter, and many trails in the parks remain open for this pursuit from December through March.

A number of popular trails are track set and easily accessible from both Jasper Town and Banff Town; pick up a trail map from the information centers and see the destination chapters for more details. Hiking trails are also open to skiers in Kananaskis Country, Glacier and Waterton Lakes, where information centers dole out trail maps. Trails are often not marked, so it is essential to carry a topographical map with you and wise to register with the warden before you go.

You can also slide on into the backcountry; popular long-distance cross-country trails lead to Lake Magog in Mt Assiniboine (via Assiniboine Pass from Kananaskis Country), Lake O'Hara in Yoho and Tonquin Valley in Jasper. At the end of each of these trails you can warm-up at alpine lodges. These trips should only be attempted by experienced skiers. Avalanches are frequent in the Rockies, and so skiers must be equipped for self-rescue. Always check with park information centers for current warnings and conditions before setting out.

HOT TIPS FOR COLD DAYS

Wondering what you can do in the snow-covered parks?

✔ Ice skate on Banff's magnificent Lake Louise
✔ Head through Jasper's deep forests on **snowshoes**
✔ Enjoy the views as you **downhill ski** at Banff's top ski resorts
✔ Drive a **dogsledding team** through the valleys of Banff or Jasper
✔ Explore Glacier's Going-to-the-Sun Rd on **cross-country skis**
✔ Put your sleeping bag to the test with **winter camping** at Waterton Lakes' Pass Creek

Snowshoeing

Walking in deep snow may seem more like work than fun; but strap on some snowshoes and venture through crisp snow and sleepy forests, and you'll soon change your mind. One of the easiest winter sports to master, snowshoeing is a superb means of exploring the parks in winter.

All of the parks have trails open to snowshoeing in winter, with Jasper, Banff and Glacier offering the most opportunities. The area around Jasper Town is an ideal location for snowshoeing, with groomed trails and trail maps available from the information center. See destination chapters for details, and in all parks, visit the information center for current trail conditions. You can rent snowshoes in Jasper Town, Banff Town and Poleridge.

Other Winter Activities

Ice-skating atop a glacial lake, with snowy forests and rugged mountaintops surrounding you, is magical. Areas of Lake Louise in Banff, Lac Beauvert and Pyramid Lakes in Jasper, and Emerald Lake in Yoho are maintained from around November to January. Drive your own **dogsledding** team across icy meadows from Jasper Town or Banff Town, or follow a tour through Maligne Canyon to see frozen waterfalls and ice formations.

Ranger Programs

Each summer, Parks Canada runs interpretive programs in Banff, Jasper, Waterton and Kootenay. These are generally based in the larger campgrounds but can be attended by anyone for a small donation. Programs include nature walks, campfire talks, slideshows and films, as well as activities for kids. The nonprofit Friends of Banff, Jasper, Yoho and Kootenay runs similar programs, with great activities for children like butterfly counting and 'bug-ology.' They also often host free nature walks. For details, see Activities in the destination chapters and visit the information centers in the parks.

In Glacier, rangers run summer programs that include heaps of activities, like morning strolls and day hikes, as well as evening talks and slideshows. Programs take place at visitors centers and campgrounds; look for the more than 40 listings every other week in the *Waterton/Glacier Guide* newspaper.

Classes

The **Banff Arts Centre** (☎ 800-565-9989; W *www.banffcentre.ca*) holds a huge variety of spring and summer courses, summits and professional development workshops lasting from a weekend to six weeks. Classes include aboriginal arts, dance, theater, opera and music. Retreat-style independent residencies are also available for established artists.

The Banff Centre's **Mountain Culture Programs** (☎ 800-298-1229) runs a weeklong spring Heritage Interpreter's course, focusing on the history, ecology and geology of the area, as well as interpreter skills. You can also do this course at a professional level with the **Mountain Park Heritage Interpreter's Association** (W *www.mphia.org*) in May of each year. **Friends of Yoho** (W *www.friendsofyoho.ca*) also run a summer institute, with opportunities to study within the park with leading researches and informed guides.

Each November, the **Banff Mountain Summit** (☎ 403-762-6100; W *www.banff mountainfestivals.ca/festivals/summit; single event/day pass/event CAD$10-20/100/299*) is four days of celebrating and scrutinizing a particular aspect of mountain environment. Seminars and discussion panels are led by scientists, researchers and writers.

The **Glacier Institute** (☎ 406-756-1211; W *www.glacierinstitute.org*) runs a field camp located within the park, 0.8km/0.5 mile from West Glacier. Afternoon to weeklong field classes cover topics such as birding, mushroom hunting, river ecology, geology, photography and more. Some classes offer credit through the University of Montana and Flathead Valley Community College.

Routes to Learning (☎ 613-530-2222, 866-745-1690) runs a range of scheduled multiday educational tours in Waterton Lakes and other areas in the Canadian Rockies.

Volunteering

Both **Friends of Banff** (☎ 403-762-8918; W *www.friendsofbanff.com*) and **Friends of Jasper** (☎ 780-852-4767; W *www.friendsofjasper.com*) have opportunities for volunteers to get involved in everything from trail maintenance to community educational programs. Check their websites for details.

Parks Canada occasionally accepts volunteers to help within the park. Canadian citizens should contact the parks' information centers directly, and foreign applicants should request an application from Parks Canada **National Volunteer Program** (*25 Eddy St, 4th floor, Hull, Quebec, Canada K1A 0M5*). The deadline for summer and autumn placement is December 1 of the previous year; for winter and spring placement, the deadline is June 30.

If you love camping and campers, volunteer with Parks Canada's **Campground Host Program** (☎ 250-343-6100; e *yoho.reception@pc.gc.ca*). Give out information and greetings at self-registration campgrounds in exchange for a free site and a park pass, valid for the whole year. These positions disappear fast.

In Glacier, the National Park Service runs a volunteer program (**W** *www.nps.gov/volunteer*). Job possibilities include campground hosting, staffing a visitors center or maintaining park trails. Apply online. Many more volunteer opportunities are available through the **US Forest Service** (**W** *www.fs.fed.us/r4/volunteer*).

Kids' Activities

You shouldn't have any difficulty keeping your kids entertained in the park. The chance to see wildlife, row a boat on the lake, touch a glacier, peer down into a canyon and wander through the woods is usually enough. Children of all ages seem to adapt remarkably well to hiking; start off with short, easy walks, and progress from there.

The parks are very family-oriented. Most activities, like white-water rafting, biking, skiing, boating and snowshoeing, are easily accessible to kids with appropriately sized gear for hire, and there are outfitters who tailor trips and tours for tots.

Friends of Banff and Friends of Jasper run hands-on **Junior Naturalist** programs in summer for kids aged six to 10. One-hour programs explore the environment and wildlife. Classes are run by donation, and space fills up quickly; register at information centers.

For young naturalists (ages six to 12) eager to learn about the park, Glacier runs the **Junior Ranger Program**. Request the *Junior Ranger Newspaper* at a visitors center or ranger station. It provides activities (from drawing to hiking) to be completed, after which a badge is earned. The **Glacier Institute** (☎ *406-756-1211*; **W** *www.glacierinstitute.org*) runs day and overnight theme camps for children, focusing on topics from fly-fishing to ecology. Parents and children can learn together in one of the institute's summer Family Day programs. For a schedule, contact the institute.

IN SEARCH OF SOLITUDE?

If you came to the parks for a little peace and quiet, check out these spectacular yet less-visited sights.

- ✔ **Moraine Lake**, Banff. Most visitors head straight for neighboring Lake Louise.
- ✔ **Canada Place**, Banff. Lots of interactive exhibits to keep the whole family entertained.
- ✔ **Mistaya Canyon**, Icefields Parkway. Water plunges dramatically through carved limestone walls.
- ✔ **Horseshoe Lake**, Icefields Parkway. Incredibly blue, these lakes are often unnoticed by tourists speeding by.
- ✔ **Pyramid Lake**, Jasper. From tiny Pyramid Island, look across the lake for great mountain views.
- ✔ **Jasper-Yellowhead Museum**, Jasper. Packed with interesting exhibits.
- ✔ **Kintla Lake**, Glacier. Incredibly beautiful and amazingly quiet.
- ✔ **Avion Ridge**, Waterton. Way-up-high spot for adventurous hikers.

For some people, planning a vacation amounts to little more than packing a toothbrush and filling the car with gas. Others need a detailed strategy and long itineraries. Whether you fit into either of these groups or are somewhere in the middle, you should consider a few things when planning your trip to the national parks.

PLANNING THE TRIP

Firstly, the parks cover an enormous amount of land. Unless you have a lot of time (at least a month), it's wiser to concentrate on one park or area rather than trying to see everything. If your visit is going to be very brief, careful planning can be a huge asset; knowing beforehand what you want to do and see, how you're going to get around and where you're going to stay can save a lot of precious time. And many activities require planning; particularly backcountry hikes, where reservations are often imperative. And if you're interested in a particular tour, a fishing trip or a climb, reservations can't hurt. The same goes for accommodations and transportation; if you're on a tight budget or a tight schedule, or if you have your heart set on a certain hotel, book ahead. Reservations are especially advisable in July and August, when the parks receive the majority of their visitors.

Try, nevertheless, not to overplan your trip. A spare hour here or an extra day there gives you the flexibility to enjoy the unexpected – wildlife crossing your path, a sparkling lake to laze by or a white-water rafting trip that you suddenly feel inspired to join.

When to Go

While all of the parks are open throughout the year, the seasons play a huge part in what you can and can't do, as well as how busy the parks are likely to be. Many of the more remote facilities and services are closed throughout the winter months (from November to May), particularly in Glacier and along the Icefields Parkway. Each season brings a distinct look and feel to the parks. Summer is vibrant and busy; autumn sprinkles the trees with color and calms the crowds; winter is a hushed and brilliant white wonderland; and spring is lush and filled with wildlife and birdsong.

SEASONAL HIGHS & LOWS
Spring
Join the wildlife in welcoming warmer temperatures and green grass. Spring brings a special atmosphere to the parks, as the snow begins to melt, flowers begin to blossom and the forests wake up. Facilities and services begin to reopen, but prices remain lower than in summer.

Frequent rains put many travelers off visiting at this time of year, and sights and gateway towns remain relatively quiet. Many trails do not open until summer, and those that do are often muddy. Other activities, like white-water rafting, can be particularly wild, as the water levels rise considerably. Most summer activities become accessible around mid-May; however, a late or early thaw can alter the date considerably.

Summer

Summer is the busiest time of year in all of the parks. The land thaws, the majority of outdoor activities – like hiking, rafting, fishing, biking, camping, boating and horseback riding – are all possible, and the sun stays up until around 10pm, meaning you can pack a huge amount into a day. A further summertime advantage is that every amenity is open; a disadvantage is that you'll be paying peak-season rates.

The only guarantee you'll have weather wise in summer is unpredictability. In one day, you may well see all four seasons, with the sun beaming brightly one minute and clouds from nowhere bursting into a torrential downpour the next. Snow often falls on the mountaintops well into July, so if you're backcountry hiking or camping, come prepared.

Summer can be a good time for seeing wildlife, as those animals not scared off by the crowds spend copious amounts of time fattening themselves up for the next winter. Wildflowers explode with color atop alpine meadows in August. Dry, hot summers can bring the threat of forest fires, which often equates to campfire restrictions and, if fire does break out, area closures.

Autumn

Autumn brings a whole new beauty to the parks, with leaves turning to vibrant reds and oranges. September is an ideal time to visit if you don't mind chillier evenings. While temperatures begin to drop and can reach freezing, they don't usually plummet until mid-October and November. September offers fewer crowds, yet most facilities and activities are still available. Gateway towns remain open and prices begin to drop. Some campgrounds do shut down and, as snow begins to fall in the higher ranges, hikes can become infeasible. All totaled, early September is wiser than later in the month.

Winter

Winter is a magical time to visit the parks but requires a certain hardiness. While the buzz around Banff Town – and, to a lesser extent, Jasper Town – isn't quite as great as in summer, it keeps pace, with the droves of skiers and snowboarders. Other parks take on a hushed, tranquil quality, with many services closing. While gateway towns have some facilities that are open year round, other areas, like Glacier and the Icefields Parkway, offer no accommodations other than a primitive campground or two. Prices drop in all the parks, except over Christmas and New Year. January is the coldest month, when the average maximum temperature is a bitter -9°C/16°F.

If you can handle the climate, you'll be treated to what is arguably the most beautiful time of year in the parks. Cross-country skiing, snowshoeing, and short hikes take you into a gorgeous winter wonderland. Early in the season, you'll also have the opportunity to participate in unique activities, like skating on glacial lakes or driving a dogsled. Wildlife that is often far from view in the high ranges come down to lower plains in search of food and relative warmth.

COPING WITH CROWDS

Most people visit the parks to escape the hustle and bustle of the city. Unfortunately, more than half of the city seems to come along via tour buses, motorhomes and streams of cars. In summer, all of the parks have busy areas; crowds tend to concentrate around major sights, along stretches of the most popular scenic routes and in gateway towns. While the prospect of crowds may influence how you plan your trip, don't let it discourage you from visiting.

Visit the most popular sights early in the morning or later in the afternoon, when the throngs have moved on. If you're heading off down a trail, choose one long route rather than a couple short ones; your chances of losing the masses after the first hour or so are great. Take scenic drives early in the morning, when you're most likely to see wildlife; you'll also avoid the tourist convoys. If you do choose a scenic drive, remember that the aim is to enjoy the views. Don't bother if you're in a hurry. Making advance reservations for activities and accommodations is always wise. Even if you're booking that morning, you'll have a much greater chance of getting a room or securing a place on the tour if you call ahead.

Banff

Banff Town, Lake Louise and the highways in between are definitely the busiest areas of the park – in fact, they are the busiest of the entire region. The Bow Valley Parkway sees less traffic than the Trans-Canada Hwy, but the traffic's much slower, with wildlife spotters inching their way along. Surprisingly, many of the trails around Lake Louise and Banff Town are relatively quiet; for even more peace, head to the Minnewanka area or Moraine Lake. While reasonably priced accommodations can fill up in Banff, there are enough restaurants and (in most cases) activity outfitters to go around.

Icefields Parkway

As a tourist route, this road sees lots of RVs and slow-moving vehicles. It's far from congested, but be prepared to go slowly. Not that you'll mind – the scenery is fantastic. Major sights like the Columbia Icefields, Athabasca Falls, Peyto Lake and Angel Glacier get mobbed in summer, but many of the trails are extremely quiet, and campgrounds are far less busy than in the rest of Banff and Jasper.

Jasper

In recent years, Jasper Town has gained a more cosmopolitan air, with services and facilities booming. With a much smaller town and fewer sights, Jasper can still feel busy in summer. Nevertheless, it remains a quieter, slower alternative to Banff. Trails never get too busy, and those away from major sights are always quieter. Campgrounds north of town are much quieter than those just south, and the ever-burgeoning restaurant scene means you shouldn't have to wait for a table.

Glacier

In Glacier National Park, Going-to-the-Sun Rd is where you will see the largest concentration of car bumpers and Harleys, although there isn't a more beautiful place to be stuck in a traffic jam. Day hikes that get their start off Going-to-the-Sun Rd or from

Many Glacier Valley tend to be some of the busier trails in the park. Less-populated trails line the North Fork, Cut Bank and Two Medicine areas. On the busiest days, cars scope out campsites like vultures. Get there early to get the best spot.

Waterton Lakes

Waterton is much smaller than Glacier and has far fewer stretches of road, so the more popular trails can get really crowded in July and August. The charming town-site is also bustling in these months, but you will always find a place to park, will rarely have to wait for a table at the restaurants and won't see the tour-bus traffic that can crowd Banff.

SPECIAL EVENTS

Events and festivals can mean more crowds, but they can also bring a wealth of activities to enjoy. Consider planning your trip around one of the following. For further information and contact details, see Festivals & Events in the destination chapters.

Banff

Banff's biggest event is the **Summer Arts Festival**, from mid-July to mid-August in Banff Town. Well worth attending, the festival is packed with daily performances by resident and visiting artists. Banff also goes all out for **Canada Day** on July 1, with fireworks, concerts and the RCMP Musical Ride, which features Mounties performing cavalry drills to music.

In autumn, movie buffs will enjoy the **Banff Mountain Film Festival**, and the **book festival**, around late October, draws book lovers en masse.

Ice Magic will thrill you and your kids, as ice carvers from around the globe create elaborate sculptures along Lake Louise's shoreline from January to March. The **Banff/Lake Louise Winter Festival** is 10 days of merrymaking throughout Banff, when sports events, barn dances and art exhibitions draw locals and visitors out of hibernation in late January.

Take your kids to Canmore's **Children's Festival**, in May, for juggling, storytelling, dancing, puppets, games and workshops. In June, on **Banff Day**, enter Banff Town's Whyte Museum for free, and antique cars cruise the streets for the **Touring Tin's Annual Show & Shine**.

Jasper

On July 1, **Canada Day** is celebrated in true Canadian style, with a patriotic pancake breakfast, parade and fireworks. **Parks Day**, the third weekend in July, brings free guided hikes, exhibits and kids' activities. Every few years, **Jasper Heritage Folk Festival** brings musicians to Jasper Town in early August, and the **Jasper Heritage Rodeo** in mid-August features bull riding, steer wrestling, calf roping and barrel racing.

Family events wash away the winter blues with **Jasper Welcomes Winter**, in early December. **Jasper in January** is held over the last two weeks of the month and includes snow-sculpture contests, performances and parades. Each year Jasper also hosts a number of one-off events.

Glacier

The weekend of **July 4th** is the busiest in the park, when the gateway village of Polebridge erupts in funky festivities. Over four days in July, **North American Indian**

Days takes place on the Tribal Fairgrounds in Browning, on the Blackfeet Indian reservation outside of Glacier. The program includes a parade, dancing, games and ceremonies and is one of the largest gatherings of US and Canadian tribes.

Polebridge celebrates once more in winter, with the **Root Beer Classic Sled Dog Races** in January. In April, you may just find yourself putting skis on your old sofa for Big Mountain's zany **Annual Furniture Race** in Whitefish.

Waterton Lakes

The **Waterton International French Film Festival** (W *www.watertoninternational frenchfilmfest.com)* screens in early June. Enter the park free in celebration of **Canada Day** (July 1) and **Parks Day** (third Saturday in July). In mid-September, the **Heritage Ball** is your chance to dance.

PETS IN THE PARK

A few days out in the wilderness may seem like a big treat for your pooch, but before you pack bones and a blanket, consider the following. Dogs resemble prey for bears and cougars, putting both you and your pet at increased risk. To other animals, like caribou and elk, dogs look like wolves and coyotes, causing wildlife increased stress and displacing them farther off the trail than you alone would. Being continuously leashed for days on end may also upset your dog.

If you do bring you pet to the park, be extra cautious in spring and summer, when wildlife are mating and rearing young and are more prone to aggression. Parks Canada allows dogs on trails and in campgrounds, so long as they're on a leash at all times. In Glacier, leashed pets can stay in campgrounds and parking areas but are not allowed on any trails. Few hotels in any of the parks will accept pets.

Please take care not to leave anything behind; cleaning up after your pet is required by law.

Gathering Information

Parks Canada (W *www.parkscanada.gc.ca)* manages the country's national parks. For information, call the following numbers:

Banff   (☎ 403-762-1550)
Jasper   (☎ 780-852-6176)
Waterton (☎ 403-859-5133)

In Banff and Jasper, you can get limited information on accommodations from the following sources:

Banff–Lake Louise Tourism Bureau (☎ 403-762-8421; W *www.banfflakelouise.com)*
Jasper Tourism & Commerce   (☎ 780-852-3858; W *www.jaspercanadianrockies.com)*
National Park Hotel Guide   (☎ 866-656-7127; W *www.nationalparkhotelguide.com)*

Contact the appropriate Parks Canada desk for information on campgrounds.

Across the border, Glacier National Park is administered by the USA's **National Park Service** (NPS; ☎ 406-888-7800; W *www.nps.gov).*

Glacier Park, Inc (☎ 406-892-2525; W *www.glacierparkinc.com)* can provide information on the accommodations and restaurants that they run in Glacier and Waterton, as well as make reservations.

SUGGESTED READING

Ben Gadd's *Handbook of the Canadian Rockies* is a comprehensive look at the geology, ecology and history of the area, with tips on safety and emergency. Although a little heavy to lug around, it provides some good pre- and post-trip reading. Gadd also wrote *Raven's End*, a recent work of fiction looking at mountain life and adventures from the perspective of these big birds. It's unusual but highly praised.

The award-winning *Switchbacks: True Stories from the Canadian Rockies*, by Sid Marty, is a readable portrait of creatures, people and life in the mountains, dabbling in climbing, tourism and politics.

For books that are handy for traveling with youngsters, see Bringing the Kids (p57). Also check out the Amazing Indian Children series, which includes *Om-kas-toe: Blackfeet Twin Captures and Elkdog*, by Kenneth Thomasma, and is geared toward children ages nine to 13.

The Group of Seven in Western Canada, edited by Catherine Mastin, is a recent look at the influence that the western regions had on some of Canada's most famous artists. The mountains play a big part in this story, and the essays are broken up with bold, colorful, modernist paintings. Douglas Leighton's *Canadian Rockies* is a beautiful book of photographs sure to inspire you to pack your bags.

History

A Hunter of Peace: Old Indian Trails of the Canadian Rockies is Mary Schaffer's account of exploring the Bow Valley, surrounding mountains and her 1907 discovery of Maligne Lake. Originally printed in 1911, this more recent edition is illustrated with her drawings and colored lantern slides. *No Ordinary Woman: The Story of Mary Schaffer*, by Janice Sanford Beck, is a detailed look at Mary's life as a woman in the mainly male world of mountaineering and independent travel.

For a lighthearted look at the history of the area, pick up *Mountain Madness: An Historical Miscellany*, by Edward Cavell and Jon Whyte. Through campfire tales, newspaper accounts, reminiscences, photographs and letters, you'll get a unique – if sometimes bizarre – view of life in the parks.

The Glacier Natural History Association, in West Glacier, publishes many useful books and natural-history guides, including *Man in Glacier*, by CW Buchholtz, an interesting account of Glacier from the 1700s to the 1970s.

There are lots of books relaying the stories of the Blackfeet Nation of the Glacier region. A particularly engaging one is *The Old North Trail: Life, Legends and Religion of the Blackfeet Indians*, by Walter McClintock, a white man who was adopted into the tribe. *Blackfeet Tales of Glacier National Park*, by James Willard Schultz, is another good read, though Schultz is often accused of peppering his nonfiction with fiction.

For a comprehensive look at the history of Waterton, pick up Graham A MacDonald's *When the Mountains Meet the Prairies: A History of Waterton Country*.

Ecology

In *Bears*, Kevin Van Tighem doles out advice and information from his firsthand experience with bears. *The Bear's Embrace* is Patricia Van Tighem's true story of surviving a grizzly bear attack; while both moving and inspiring, you may want to pass this one up until you return home, and instead read James Gary Shelton's *Bear Encounter Survival Guide*. In it, he demystifies cultural myths and common fears about bears.

Animal Tracks of Western Canada, by Joanne Barwise, will help you tell the prints of a housecat from a cougar and a moose from a mountain goat. Pocket-sized and easy to use, it has brief descriptions and pictures of the tracks and the animals that leave them.

Plants of the Rocky Mountains, by Kershaw, MacKinnon and Pojar, is a comprehensive, colorful guide to over 1360 wildflowers, trees, shrubs, berries and mosses found from New Mexico to British Columbia. A botanist's bible, *A Guide to Rocky Mountain Plants* has recently been revised by Roger Williams and will help you to identify more than 350 species of plant in the Rockies, with lots of drawings and photos. *Leave No Trace*, by Annette McGivney, is an excellent guide on how to minimize your impact on the environment when camping, hiking, kayaking, canoeing or rafting in the wilderness.

Activities

Lonely Planet's *Hiking in the Rocky Mountains* details day hikes and backcountry trips in Glacier, Waterton and other areas in the US Rockies.

For detailed trail descriptions of day and overnight hikes in all of the parks, see *The Canadian Rockies Trail Guide*, by Patton and Robinson. Also pick up the pocket-sized hiking guide produced by Friends of Banff, which gives a good rundown of day hikes in the park.

Hiking Glacier & Waterton Lakes National Parks, by Erik Molvar, is a very good resource, with detailed descriptions. The slimmer *Hiker's Guide to Glacier National Park*, published by the Glacier Natural History Association, is another smart choice.

For pointers on everything from nutrition to navigation to how to tie knots, check out *Backpacker's Field Manual*, by Rick Curtis. Tired of freeze-dried food in a bag? *The Well-Fed Backpacker*, by June Fleming, is a collection of recipes and suggestions on how to liven up the palate on the trail.

Canadian Mountaineering Anthology: Stories from 100 Years on the Edge, edited by Bruce Fairley, is an inspirational ode to the art of mountain climbing.

INTERNET RESOURCES

For up-to-the-minute information, the Internet offers a wealth of resources. A good place to begin is at **Lonely Planet** (**W** www.lonelyplanet.com), where you'll find current summaries on the ins and outs of traveling in the area. Also on the site, the **Thorn Tree** bulletin board gives you the chance to post questions to other travelers (and dispense advice when you get back). You can also scroll through previous questions and answers, bringing up lots of recent tips and ideas.

Next, visit the general websites of Parks Canada (www.parkscanada.gc.ca) and the National Parks System (www.nps.gov) for an overall look at the way the parks operate, fees, regulations and any current issues.

Banff & Japer National Parks

Atlas (**W** *www.atlas.gc.ca*) Maps of Canada, including downloadable reference maps, covering everything from historical facts to aboriginal statistics to forests.

Banff Tourism Bureau (**W** *www.bannflakelouise.com*) Information on services, accommodations, activities and events in and around Banff Town.

Canada World Web (**W** *www.canada.worldweb.com*) Hotel reservations, health, travel articles and vehicle rental links, with spotlights on family and outdoor travel.

Jasper Tourism & Commerce (**W** *www.jaspercanadianrockies.com*) Information on services, accommodations, activities and events in Jasper Town.

Parks Canada *(w www.parkscanada.gc.ca)* Information on parks and road and trail conditions, bulletins, avalanche reports, sights, maps, services, safety and links to other sites.

Peakfinder *(w www.peakfinder.com)* Descriptions and photos of mountains in the Canadian Rockies.

Travel Alberta *(w www.travelalberta.com)* General traveling information, photos, accommodation links, activities and sights across the province.

Glacier & Waterton Lakes National Parks

American Park Network *(w www.americanparknetwork.com/parkinfo/gl/index.html)* General information on Glacier and other US parks.

Blackfeet Nation *(w www.blackfeetnation.com)* History, culture and news of the Blackfeet Indians.

Discover Waterton *(w www.discoverwaterton.com)* A convenient stop, offering links to accommodations, activities and more.

Glacier National Park *(w www.glacier.national-park.com)* Personal site with a lot of information on activities and more.

Glacier Natural History Association *(w www.glacierassociation.org)* Purchase books from its website before your trip.

NPS Glacier National Park *(w www.nps.gov/glac)* Comprehensive downloadable park information, including maps and backcountry-campground availability.

Parks Canada's Waterton *(w www.parkscanada.gc.ca/waterton)* Straight from the horse's mouth – information on the park.

Waterton Visitors Association *(w www.watertonchamber.com)* A comprehensive resource on park offerings and facilities.

Waterton Park Information Services *(w www.watertonpark.com)* Informational site on townsite amenities and the park as a whole.

MAPS

Gem Trek Publishing *(☎ 403-932-4208; w www.gemtrek.com)* produces excellent topographical maps of Banff, Jasper, Yoho and Kootenay National Parks (scale 1:100,000). These maps include major trails and are water- and tearproof. Check the website for the nearest dealer.

If you're driving to the parks, **Map Art Publishing** *(☎ 403-278-6674; w www.mapart.com)* have regularly updated road maps covering the Canadian Rockies. They also produce *Fast Track – Alberta*, a waterproof card map that's not extremely detailed but will get you where you're going.

National Geographic's *Trails Illustrated* offers topographical, waterproof, tearproof maps of Glacier and Waterton Lakes Parks, with 24m/80ft contour intervals. The United States Geological Survey (USGS) publishes a 1:1000 topographical map for Glacier National Park and its immediate surrounds (though nothing on the Canadian side). Canada's **Geographical Services** has put out an easy-to-use 1:50,000 map of Waterton Lakes National Park, which includes northern Glacier.

USEFUL ORGANIZATIONS

Friends of Banff *(☎ 403-762-8918; w www.friendsofbanff.com)* and **Friends of Jasper** *(☎ 780-852-4767; w www.friendsofjasper.com)* are nonprofit groups that work with Parks Canada in maintaining the parks and providing educational and research opportunities. Both are responsible for many of the summer ranger programs, like kids' activities and guided walks, and run book and gift shops at the information centers. **Friends of Kootenay** *(☎ 250-347-6525; w www.livingwithwildlife.ca)* and **Friends of Yoho** *(☎ 250-343-6393; w www.friendsofyoho.ca)* offer similar, though somewhat pared down, services.

In addition to running programs for climbers and backcountry skiers, the **Alpine Club of Canada** (☎ *403-678-3200;* W *www.alpineclubofcanada.ca*) doles out lots of information on activities in the Canadian Rockies and can answer most questions you have on the backcountry.

In the USA, **Glacier Natural History Association** (☎ *406-888-5756;* W *www .glacierassociation.org*) works with the NPS to offer similar services to Canada's Friends Of societies and is responsible for many free park publications and the Native American programs scheduled in the summer. **Glacier Institute** (☎ *406-756-1211;* W *www.glacierinstitute.org*) offers opportunities to learn about Glacier through its field classes, and the volunteer-run **Montana Wilderness Association** (☎ *406-443-7350;* W *www.wildmontana.org*) champions causes that protect and preserve the state's wilderness areas.

The nonprofit **Waterton Natural History Association** (☎ *403-859-2624*) encourages education and appropriate land use in Waterton Lakes National Park. It offers courses and operates a small museum in the townsite.

What's It Going to Cost?

How much you spend can vary dramatically, depending on whether you opt for camping, or indoor accommodations. In Canadian parks, campgrounds near park towns have showers and flush toilets and cost around CAD$25 per site. With hookups, a site is about CAD$30, and if you head to more remote grounds and rough it a little, sites are around CAD$15. In Glacier, campgrounds inside the gateway towns are cheaper – as low as USD$10 – and those inside the park are USD$12 to $17.

B&Bs are the most affordable accommodations in Banff Town and Jasper Town. You can get a double for as little as CAD$50. Except for a few atmospheric lodges, most mid- to top-end hotels are overpriced. You'll save a little money staying in gateway towns like Canmore or Field. Hotel rooms in Glacier's gateway towns cost around USD$60.

Budget travelers can opt for hostels in all parks, although those near or within park towns aren't cheap (around CAD$30 for a dorm), and the private rooms are often pricier and not as pleasant as B&Bs. Remote, basic hostels have dorms for around CAD$15.

You can eat well for fairly little in the parks. Jasper Town and Banff Town both have average-priced grocery stores; even if you're not camping, picnicking is a great way to save a little on lunch and spend more time outdoors. If you're visiting Glacier, stock up on groceries before you enter the park for cheaper prices. Budget restaurants can be found in all park towns, where you can fill up for around CAD$12. There are also lots of restaurants worth splurging on.

While you can hike, bike, cross-country ski, attend ranger programs and see the majority of sights for the price of the park permit, activities like rafting, downhill skiing and rock climbing can quickly bite into your budget. Renting a car or RV can also be pricey, although it will give you flexibility. Tour buses, coaches and shuttles can be more expensive than a rented car if you're planning on doing a lot of moving around. Bringing your own vehicle is by far the best and cheapest option.

All totaled, if you stay in the cheapest accommodation, cook your own food, rely on public transportation as much as possible and restrict your main activity to hiking, you might just squeeze in at around CAD$50/USD$40 per day. If you've rented a car, camp and cook some of your meals, you're more likely to spend CAD$80 to $100 (USD$60 to $75). If you stay in B&Bs or hotels, add at least another CAD$50 to $150 (USD$40 to $115).

Accommodations

Every park has pleasant, forested campgrounds, but be aware that, except for Glacier, all of the national parks dole out sites on a first-come, first-served basis. Finding a vacancy can be tricky in the height of summer. The majority of campgrounds outside the parks accept reservations.

For those after a few more home comforts, like a roof and a bed, your options range from basic dorms in Banff and Jasper's remote hostels to top-end hotels and posh resorts in all of the parks. If you can fit them into your budget, historical lodges are a fantastic option. Lodges, which are some of the oldest buildings in the park, are generally atmospheric and have amenities ranging from basic to luxurious.

If you're not camping or staying in a hostel, budget accommodations can be tricky to find. Banff Town is notorious for its pricey hotels, and Jasper Town isn't far behind; your best bet is to look for a B&B. Waterton Lakes has only one hostel as a budget option; the rest of the lodging is mid to top end.

LAST-MINUTE ACCOMMODATIONS

You've heard the horror stories about needing to book accommodations in the parks 12 months in advance, yet there you are, on the outskirts of the park, reservationless and beginning to contemplate just how uncomfy snoozing in the car is going to be. Don't despair. While campgrounds, lodges and hotels do fill up quickly, finding somewhere to stay doesn't have to be traumatic.

Even if you're only a few hours from your destination, it's worth stopping at the nearest telephone and calling a hotel to make a reservation, especially if it's the height of summer or later in the day.

Banff – There is no central reservation desk in Banff. Your best bet is to head for the information center, where you'll find a list of accommodations with prices and vacancies. Once you've pinpointed a few places, call from the pay phones outside; in the time it takes you to find the hotel, the final room could be snatched up. Also pick up a list of B&Bs; there are oodles of them in Banff Town for every price range. For mid to top-end hotels, try calling **National Park Hotel Guide** (☎ 866-656-7127). If you're camping, ask at the parks desk for vacancies. If all else fails, head for Canmore or Field.

Jasper – Jasper doesn't have a central reservation desk either, but the information center keeps a list of accommodations and has courtesy phones inside where you can call around for vacancies. Jasper also has lots of accommodations in private homes; ask for a list from the tourist desk. Campgrounds north of town are much quieter than those to the south. Again, try the **National Park Hotel Guide** for pricier hotels.

Glacier & Waterton Lakes – Make same-day reservations with Glacier Park Inc Lodges for accommodations in both parks or at two of the National Park Service campgrounds in Glacier. There are no waiting lists for accommodations when the park is full; your best bet is to keep calling the reservations desk for last-minute cancellations. You'll often find rooms in the gateway towns of East Glacier, St Mary, Babb, Polebridge and West Glacier, or in Cardston, Mountain View or Pincher Creek, near Waterton. If campgrounds are full, head to Whitefish and Kalispell from Glacier, or to just outside the park entrance in Waterton.

WHAT TO PACK

Pack light. You won't regret it, whether carrying your gear up a mountain, hauling it into the hotel or trying to fit it into the trunk of the car. If you forget something, you can usually purchase it in the outdoor equipment stores of Banff Town and Jasper Town. Most essentials are also available in many of the gateway towns. Consider the following when packing:

✔ **Clothing** – Bring layers; mountain weather is notorious for fitting four seasons into one day. A fleece sweater is necessary at every time of year.

✔ **Rain gear** – This is essential for everyone, no matter when you're visiting. Light and breathable is best.

✔ **Footwear** – For day hiking, light boots are ideal. For backcountry hiking, sturdy boots are essential, particularly if you're carrying a heavy pack. Thick socks will protect tender feet on those first few days on the trail. For kayaking, rafting or wandering around camp, waterproof sandals (like Tevas) are a good option.

✔ **Hat** – Fleece is good for cold weather and dries quickly too. Light-colored cotton hats with brims are great for summer.

✔ **Bandana** – This is an all-purpose item that's handy for everything from wiping the kid's nose to using as sling.

✔ **First-aid kit** – Include a tensor bandage for sprains, bandages, disinfectant, tweezers, antibiotic cream, Deep Heat and painkillers.

✔ **Camera** – Extra film and a spare battery will come in handy. Even if you're taking a fancy camera, a light, disposable camera can come in handy on longer hikes.

✔ **Towel** – Anyone who has lugged around a wet towel appreciates having a small towel rather than a bath-sized one.

✔ **Water purifier** – Essential if you're heading into the backcountry. Tablets are lighter than a filter. Also bring a refillable water bottle.

✔ **Camping gear** – In addition to the obvious, take extra tent stakes, a tarp for shelter and waterproof matches or a lighter. A sleeping pad (like Therm-a-Rest) makes a huge difference in staying warm and comfy. Choose a sleeping bag that can withstand the damp (ie not goose down), especially if you're off into the backcountry.

✔ **Flashlight or headlamp** and **small binoculars**

✔ **Other handy items** – Moisturizer (it gets dry in the mountains), insect repellent, sunscreen (the mountain sun can burn even in winter), resealable bags, garbage bags and a whistle.

Worth remembering are the gateway towns outside the parks. Canmore and Field (outside of Banff), East Glacier, St Mary, Babb, Polebridge and West Glacier (outside Glacier) and Cardston and Pincher Creek (outside Waterton Lakes) all offer more humbly priced options and, in the cases of Canmore, St Mary and West Glacier, top-end hotels more worthy of the price than many of the those inside the parks.

For more information on accommodations, see Places to Stay in the destination chapters. No matter where you're staying, reservations can eliminate the challenge of finding somewhere once you arrive.

Bringing the Kids

The national parks are some of the most family-friendly destinations you'll find. Camping in the woods, the chance to spot wildlife, and activities like rafting, canoeing and horseback riding put smiles on most kids' faces. Ranger programs are often geared for younger audiences, encouraging kids to interact with the environment through activities like hiking and drawing. You'll also meet lots of other families on the trails and in the campgrounds, giving your kids some peers to play with and giving you the chance to swap tips with other parents.

Let your kids in on planning your trip; this can get them excited and interested in activities before they even arrive. Pick up a copy of *Sleeping in a Sack: Camping Activities for Kids*, by Linda White, a colorful guide with ideas of what they can expect and suggestions of what they might like to do.

Consider staying close to amenities; the comfort of a dip in the hot springs or an ice-cream break can recharge tired youngsters and oldsters after a day on the trail. Most restaurants in and around the parks offer kids' menus; many also have kids' corners, where your youngsters can color up a storm while awaiting their meal. Banff Town in particular has lots to keep young minds interested, from the exhibits at Canada Place to the ice-cream shops along Banff Ave.

Most kids will amaze you on the trail, mustering more energy than their folks. Trails that wind through the woods and offer a mix of sights – waterfalls, lakes and canyons – seem to keep kids most interested. Johnston Canyon in Banff, Valley of the Five Lakes along Jasper's Icefields Parkway, and Crypt Lake Trail in Waterton are great options. Be particularly cautious with children when crossing streams. Rocks are often deceptively slippery. Also hang on to them near canyons, where trails often grow slippery from the spray of waterfalls; some canyon trails have sheer drops and not all have handrails.

For more ideas on what to do as a family, see Kids Activities (p45, and for some insider tips on traveling with kids, check out Lonely Planet's *Travel with Children*.

Health & Safety

If you have any emergencies while staying in the national parks, dial ☎ 911. Major centers like Banff Town, Jasper Town and Waterton Town have medical facilities; for contact details, see Essentials in the destination chapters. If you're out in the backcountry, you may encounter a warden or ranger, but this is far from guaranteed. Be prepared to cope with emergencies until you can reach help. If you're traveling out of your home country, be sure to purchase medical insurance before you leave. Medical services in Canada and the US are not reciprocal.

WATER PURIFICATION

While water running through the mountains may look crystal clear, much of it carries *Giardia lamblia*, a microscopic parasite that causes intestinal disorders. To avoid getting sick, boil all water for at least 10 minutes, treat it with water tablets or filter at 0.5 microns or smaller. Iodine doesn't destroy *Giardia*. Symptoms that you've ingested the bug include diarrhea, bloating and horrifying gas; treatment is by antibiotics. While many campgrounds have clean, safe water, treat all water with suspicion.

WEST NILE VIRUS

Little is known about this virus, but it's believed to be carried by mosquitoes that have fed on the blood of an infected bird. Many people who become infected with West Nile virus have no symptoms and do not get sick; others develop flu-like symptoms within two to 15 days, including headache, fever and body aches and occasionally mild rashes and swollen lymph glands. People with weaker immune systems, such as the elderly, are at greater risk of developing serious neurological effects; symptoms in these cases include the rapid onset of severe headache, high fever, stiff neck, vomiting, drowsiness, confusion, loss of consciousness, muscle weakness and paralysis. Severe cases can be fatal, and immediate medical attention should be sought. There is no vaccine for West Nile virus and no specific treatment. Watch for any warnings that the virus has been detected in the area, and do your best to avoid mosquito bites.

LYME DISEASE

While rare in Canada, Lyme disease can be acquired anywhere where ticks hang out – namely alpine meadows and forested areas. The disease is most commonly spread from May through August, when ticks feed on animals infected with microscopic *Borrelia burgdorferi* bacterium and then latch onto you. The first symptom is generally a red, slowly expanding bull's-eye rash that shows up within a few days to a month. This is often accompanied by general fatigue, fever, headache, stiff neck, muscle aches and joint pain. Treatment is by a long dose of antibiotics. If untreated, the disease can develop into arthritis, neurological abnormalities and, rarely, cardiac problems.

There is no vaccine for Lyme disease; the best prevention is to wear bug repellent and to tuck your trouser legs into your socks if you suspect ticks are in the area. Check yourself at the end of each day; ticks are most likely to transmit the disease after feeding off you for two or more days. For more details on ticks, see Tick Fever (p275).

HYPOTHERMIA

In winter, take precautions against hypothermia and frostbite. If you're camping or hiking at high altitudes, hypothermia is a risk throughout the year. Hypothermia occurs when your body temperature drops below normal, causing rapid physical and mental breakdown. Symptoms include shivering, loss of coordination, slurred speech and disorientation or confusion. These symptoms can be accompanied by exhaustion, numbness, irrational or violent behavior, lethargy, dizzy spells, muscle cramps and even bursts of energy.

To treat hypothermia in its early stages, get the victim out of the wind or rain, replace wet clothing with dry clothing and give them hot liquids (not alcohol) and high-calorie, easily digestible food, like granola bars or chocolate. Put the victim in a warm sleeping bag and get in with them. If possible, position the victim near a fire or in a warm (not hot) bath. Do not rub a victim's skin.

SUNBURN

As you gain elevation, your risk of sunburn increases greatly, even on cloudy or snowy days. Use sunscreen of SPF30 or greater, wear a hat and sunglasses, and try to avoid hiking at midday.

ALTITUDE SICKNESS

Altitude sickness can strike anyone heading up into the mountains, whether it's your first visit or your 100th. Thinner air means less oxygen is reaching your muscles and brain, requiring the heart and lungs to work harder. Many trailheads begin at high elevations (particularly along the Icefields Parkway), meaning that you don't have to go very far before feeling the effects. Symptoms include headache, lethargy, dizziness, difficulty sleeping and loss of appetite. To avoid altitude sickness, acclimatize yourself to high elevations before setting out on a hike. If you do begin to feel unwell, head down to somewhere lower and rest.

Dangers & Annoyances

Crime is not bad in any of the parks, but use your common sense; lock valuables in the trunk of your vehicle, try to avoid leaving anything in your car if you're parking it at a trailhead overnight, and never leave anything worth stealing in your tent.

AVALANCHES

Avalanches are a threat during and following storms, in high winds and during temperature changes, particularly when it warms in spring. Educate yourself about the dangers of avalanches before setting out into the backcountry. Signs of avalanche activity include felled trees and slides. Bears love avalanche shoots because of the fresh-frozen food they produce (casualties such as goats and sheep) – another good reason to steer clear. For up-to-date information on avalanche hazards, contact ☎ 403-762-1460 in Banff, Kootenay and Yoho, ☎ 780-852-6176 in Jasper and ☎ 250-837-6867 at Roger's Pass. For other areas, contact the **Canadian Avalanche Association** (☎ 800-667-1105) or local park information centers.

Before adventuring in Waterton, check with the **park warden** (☎ 403-859-5140) for avalanche updates, as winter trails are not maintained. In Glacier, call ☎ 406-257-8402 or ☎ 800-526-5329 for information. Local radio stations broadcast reports on area avalanche conditions studied by the Northwest Montana Avalanche Warning System.

If you are caught in an avalanche, your chance of survival depends on your ability to keep yourself above the flowing snow and your companions' ability to rescue you. The probability of survival decreases rapidly after half an hour, so the party must be self-equipped, with each member carrying an avalanche beacon, a sectional probe and a collapsible shovel.

MOSQUITOES

Mosquitoes can be rampant in all parks, particularly on summer evenings. In Banff and Jasper, you'll notice them around lakes and on wooded hikes, although many areas along the Icefields Parkway are mosquito-free due to the high elevation. In Glacier and Waterton Lakes, mosquitoes tend to be more annoying on the west side of the park than in the windier east. Use repellent, wear light-colored clothing, cover yourself in the evening, and hike with someone who tastes better to mosquitoes than you.

WILDLIFE

While spotting wildlife is exciting, don't let your senses run away with you – take precautions to protect both you and the animals. Your chances of seeing wildlife are very high; know how to behave in order to remain safe. See Watching Wildlife and Elk Etiquette & Moose Manners (p39) in the Activities section, and Bear Issues (p268) in the Ecosystem chapter.

ACCESS FOR ALL

The national parks have been created for the enjoyment of all, with opportunities for those in wheelchairs or with hearing, visual or other disabilities to experience the wilderness. Unfortunately, Parks Canada does not produce information or guides on accessibility within the parks. As recent planning and management changes are continuously increasing access, your best bet for gaining reliable and current information is to contact the parks' information centers directly. In the USA, the National Parks Service produces the *Accessibility Guide*, with lots of helpful information and details for Glacier.

BANFF

Major sights in Banff, including Lake Louise, Banff Town's museums, Upper Hot Springs and Peyto Lake along the Icefields Parkway are all accessible to those in wheelchairs, as is the information center. Johnston Canyon, Lake Louise Shoreline and the initial stretch of the Bow River Falls are all popular, paved trails. Johnston Canyon, Lake Louise, Moraine Lake and the Bow Valley Parkway have interpretive signs for those with hearing impediments, and Parks Canada has some audiotapes for those with visual difficulties.

Most campgrounds within Banff have designated sites close to wheelchair-accessible facilities. The hostels in both Banff Town and Lake Louise Village have wheelchair-accessible rooms and facilities, and almost all hotels have elevators, though few have fully accessible rooms. Most restaurants have ground-floor seating and accessible toilets.

In Kananaskis Country, William Watson Lodge has been designed specifically to give people with disabilities access to the area. See Around Banff in the Banff chapter for more details; make reservations, as this place books up fast.

JASPER

Jasper Town's museum, Miette Hot Springs, Maligne Lake, Medicine Lake, Jasper Tramway and the information center are all wheelchair-accessible, as is Athabasca Falls and the Icefields Centre, along the Icefields Parkway. The initial stretch of the Mary Schaffer Loop is an interpretive paved path accessible to wheelchairs and people with hearing difficulties. Annette Lake Loop and Pyramid Isle in Pyramid Lake are also paved interpretive routes and are lovely spots for a picnic.

Only four of Jasper's campgrounds have accessible facilities: Pocahontas, Whistlers, Wapiti and Wabasso, along the Icefields Parkway. Accommodations in Jasper are not always accessible, and you should call ahead to reserve a room on the ground floor if you require wheelchair access. For those not on a tight budget, Park Place is Jasper Town's top hotel and has one wheelchair-accessible room. Many of Jasper Town's restaurants are on ground floors and have accessible toilets.

GLACIER

Two short and scenic trails in the park are paved for wheelchair use: Trail of the Cedars, off of Going-to-the-Sun Rd, and the Running Eagle Falls Trail in Two Medicine. Hearing-impaired visitors can get information at TDD ☎ 406-888-7806. Some of the short nature trails have explanatory signposts along the trail and brochures at the trailhead explaining area flora and fauna. Park visitors centers have audiotapes for visually impaired visitors.

At least one or two wheelchair-friendly rooms are available at all in-park lodges – reserve well in advance; none of the lodges have elevators, so the rooms are on the ground floor. Several campgrounds have wheelchair-accessible bathrooms.

WATERTON LAKES

Waterton Townsite campground has wheelchair-accessible bathroom facilities. The hostel can accommodate travelers using a wheelchair, as can a few of the lodges in the townsite.

Getting There

BANFF & JASPER NATIONAL PARKS

Most visitors fly into Calgary or Edmonton, and some into Vancouver, all of which are serviced by most major US, European and Asian airlines. Calgary is closer to Banff (128km/79 miles), and Edmonton is closer to Jasper (366km/227 miles), but it's worth checking flight prices to both for deals. Vancouver is 847km/525 miles from Banff (a good 10-hour drive) and 794km/492 miles from Jasper. **Air Canada** (**W** www.aircanada.ca) is Canada's only major airline. It's often cheaper to fly with a US airline, like **Continental** (**W** www.flycontinental.com), **Delta** (**W** www.delta-air.com) or Northwest (**W** www.nwa.com).

To reach Banff Town from Calgary airport, hop on a **Brewster Airporter** (☎ 800-760-6934; **W** www.brewster.ca; adult/child CAD$42/21; May–late Oct), departing at 12:30pm and 4:55pm daily. Both buses stop at Canmore and carry on to Lake Louise; the early bus heads up the Icefields Parkway to Jasper. **Jasper Express** (☎ 800-661-4946; CAD$55) runs a daily shuttle between Edmonton airport and most hotels in Jasper Town, departing at 4:30pm. From Vancouver, catch the Greyhound (see Bus, later).

Train

VIA Rail (☎ 888-842-7245; **W** www.viarail.com) has passenger trains chugging along to Jasper from Edmonton (CAD$150) and Vancouver (CAD$210) three times per week.

Rocky Mountaineer Rail Tours (☎ 800-665-7245; **W** www.rockymountaineer .com; d/s CAD$669/739; depart Sun, Tue & Thu Apr-Oct) have a number of tourist-geared train trips that will land you in Jasper and Banff, departing from Vancouver. Two-day journeys travel in daylight only (hotel in Kamloops not included in price) to give you the best views.

To tour the Rockies in a vintage train, join a Pacific Luxury Rail Tour with the **Canadian Pacific Railway** (☎ 800-942-3301; **W** www.escortedcanadatours.com). The eight-day tour from Calgary to Banff, Columbia Icefields, Jasper and on to Vancouver costs CAD$8000 (including accommodations and meals). There's also a bargain version for CAD$1250.

Bus

Greyhound (☎ 800-661-8747; **W** www.greyhound.ca) has four daily departures to Jasper from Edmonton (CAD$55) and Vancouver (CAD$109); these buses do not follow the Icefields Parkway. Buses leave for Banff from Calgary (CAD$23; 4 times daily) and Vancouver (CAD$117; 3 times daily). Purchase tickets from the airports, the train station in Jasper (607 Connaught Dr; open 6am-7:15pm Mon-Fri, 8am-2pm & 5-7:15pm Sat, 10am-2pm Sun) and the bus depot in Banff (Mt Norquay Rd; open 7:30am-9pm).

Organized Tours

For a sight-filled three days in Banff and Yoho, join a Rocky Mountain Express bus tour with **Brewster** (☎ 877-791-5500; **W** www.brewster.ca; per person s/d CAD$1057/668, including accommodations & some meals) from Calgary. You can also do this tour from Calgary to Jasper.

Hop on a Canadian Rockies Circle Tour with **Anderson Tours** (☎ 780-464-0815, 800-548-7262; **W** www.albertatours.com; per person s/d CAD$1540/1040, including accommodations & some meals) for a weeklong whirlwind look at Calgary, Banff, Jasper and Edmonton.

Cardinal Tours (☎ 800-661-6161; Ⓦ *www.cardinaltraveltours.com; per person s/d CAD$2840/2000, including accommodations & some meals*) runs a 10-day trip from Calgary to Vancouver, taking in Banff and Jasper en route and other locations in British Columbia, like Whistler and Victoria.

Car & Motorcycle

From Calgary, follow Trans-Canada Hwy 1 west to Banff via Canmore. To reach Jasper from Edmonton, take Hwy 16 west. Between Edmonton and Calgary, Hwy 11 heads west of Red Deer, entering Banff along the Icefields Parkway, just south of the border with Jasper.

Coming from Vancouver, head east to Hope and follow the Coquihalia Hwy (Hwy 5) north to Kamloops; there is a CAD$10 toll to use this road. From there, head north on Hwy 5 to Jasper via Mt Robson Provincial Park. To reach Banff from Kamloops, follow Trans-Canada Hwy 1 east through Mt Revelstoke, Glacier (in Canada) and Yoho National Parks and Golden.

Getting There **Banff, Jasper, Glacier & Waterton Lakes National Parks**

Car Rental

Renting a car is a popular way to get around the parks. Most agencies provide road-side assistance with Canada's Automobile Association. Ask about hidden fees (like mileage caps or insurance excess) before you sign up. You can reserve vehicles online. Airport offices for the following agencies are open most hours of the day (around 6am to midnight). Offices in town keep regular business hours (8am to 5pm).

Avis (☎ 800-879-2847; W www.avis.com) Calgary, Edmonton and Vancouver airports, Banff Town and Jasper Town

Budget (☎ 800-268-8900; W www.budget.com) Calgary, Edmonton and Vancouver airports, Banff Town and Jasper Town

Discount Cars & Truck Rentals (☎ 800-263-2355; W www.discountcar.com) Edmonton, Calgary and Vancouver airports

Hertz (☎ 800-263-0600; W www.hertz.com) Calgary and Edmonton airports, Banff Town and Canmore

National (☎ 800-227-7368; W www.nationalcar.com) Calgary and Edmonton airports, Banff Town and Jasper Town

Thrifty (☎ 800-847-4389; W www.thrifty.com) Calgary, Edmonton and Vancouver airports, Jasper Town

RV & Camper Rentals

Make sure you're given a thorough tour of your RV before you head out. A popular option, **CanaDream Camper** (☎ 800-461-7368; W www.bluedtravel.com/canadream) rents a variety of RVs from offices in Calgary, Edmonton and Vancouver. A week in a midsized motorhome for four adults and two kids costs CAD$220 per night, with 100km/62 miles per day. For a smaller camper, just big enough for you and a friend, it's CAD$174 per night. **Cruise Canada** (☎ 888-278-1736; W www.cruiseamerica.com/rv_rentals) rents RVs from Calgary and Vancouver. For three nights and oodles of kilometers, it costs CAD$715 for a midsized motorhome.

GLACIER & WATERTON LAKES NATIONAL PARKS

Air

Glacier's nearest airport is **Glacier Park International Airport** (☎ 406-257-5994; W www.glacierairport.com), halfway between Whitefish and Kalispell and serviced by Delta, Alaska, United and Northwest Airlines. Destinations include Missoula, Salt Lake City, Minneapolis and Seattle. Save a good chunk of change by flying instead to **Great Falls International Airport** (☎ 406-727-3404; W www.gtfairport.com), 249km/155 miles from Glacier, or **Missoula International Airport** (☎ 406-728-4381; W www.msoairport.org), 241km/150 miles from the park, although the savings may be offset by the price of a rental car.

Spokane International Airport (☎ 509-455-6455; W www.spokaneairports.net) is 447km/278 miles west of West Glacier, in Washington. Arriving there and renting a car is worth pondering, as flights to Spokane tend to be much cheaper than anything into Montana. Train and bus services are also available from Spokane.

The closest fly-in point to Waterton Lakes is **Lethbridge County Airport** (☎ 403-329-4166; W www.lethbridgecountyairport.com), 129km/80 miles northeast of the Waterton Lakes entrance in Lethbridge, Alberta; it's served by Air Canada and Integra Air. It is generally cheaper to fly into **Calgary International Airport** (☎ 403-735-1200; W www.calgaryairport.com), served by over 25 airlines. It's 266km/165 miles to the north.

Train

Amtrak's *Empire Builder* follows the southern border of Glacier National Park, with stops at East Glacier (Glacier Park Station) and West Glacier (Belton Station). Eastbound trains stop at both stations in the morning (around 8am to 10am), and westbound trains stop in the evening (around 7pm to 8pm), with the ride in between taking approximately 30 minutes. Tickets are available at the **East Glacier Station** (☎ *406-226-4452; open 8-10:30am & 5-7:30pm)*; if you're boarding in **West Glacier**, buy tickets onboard. A one-way ticket from West/East Glacier is USD$10/24 to Whitefish, USD$68/37 to Havre and USD$117 to Seattle. Buy tickets at the **Whitefish railroad depot** (☎ *406-862-2268; 500 Depot St; open 6am-2pm & 4pm-11pm Mon-Fri, closes 1pm Sat-Sun)*. There is no train service in or near Waterton.

Bus

To reach Glacier Park International Airport from Whitefish (adult/child six to 12 USD$18/9) or Kalispell (USD$7.50/3.80), hop on a **Airport Shuttle Service** (☎ *406-752-2842)*. Intermountain Transport connects the **Kalispell bus station** (☎ *406-755-4011; 1301 S Main St; open 9am-5pm Mon-Fri, 9am-noon Sat-Sun)* to the Whitefish railroad depot; its buses also run to Missoula, Helena, Bozeman and Seattle.

No public buses make it to Waterton. **Greyhound Canada** (☎ *403-627-2716, 800-661-8747; 840 Main St)* connects Pincher Creek, 53km/33 miles from the townsite, with other locations in Alberta and Canada. To reach Banff from Pincher Creek, head for Fort Macleod, on to Calgary and then on to Banff. There is no direct service from Pincher Creek to Jasper.

'Jammer' buses run by Glacier Park, Inc (see p198) and charter buses ply the route between Glacier and Waterton.

Car & Motorcycle

The west side of Glacier is most easily reached from Whitefish, Kalispell and Flathead Lake; the east side is closer than the west to Great Falls and Helena. West Glacier and East Glacier are connected by US 2, below the southern boundary of the park.

People visiting Waterton from Glacier must go through customs at the border; enter Canada from US 17 via the **Port of Chief Mountain** (*open 7am-10pm Jun 1–Labor Day, 9am-6pm Labor Day–Sept 30, 9am-6pm May 15–May 31)*. In the nonsummer months, enter via the **Port of Peigan** (*open 7am-11pm year-round)* toward Cardston. Be ready to flash two forms of identification: a passport or birth certificate and a federal- or state-issued ID card (like a driver's license). **Canada Customs** can be reached at ☎ 403-653-3535.

From Calgary and Pincher Creek to the north, Hwy 6 shoots south toward Hwy 5 into the park. From Banff National Park, visit via Calgary and Cardston or, in the summer, Kananaskis Country.

The **Better World Club** (☎ *866-238-1137; W www.betterworldclub.com)* is an ecologically minded automobile club that offers roadside assistance to its members in the USA.

Car Rentals Glacier Park International Airport houses the following car rental agencies:

Avis (☎ *406-257-2727; W www.avis.com; open 7am-midnight Mon-Sat, from 8:30am Sun)*
Budget (☎ *406-755-7500, 800-527-0700; W www.budget.com; open 8am-midnight)*

Hertz (☎ 406-758-2220, 800 654 3131; **W** www.hertz.com; open 8am-midnight)

National (☎ 406-257-7144; **W** www.nationalcar.com; open 8am-midnight)

A plethora of other agencies are based in Kalispell, including **Dollar Rent A Car** (☎ 406-892-0009; **W** www.dollar.com; 5506 US 2 W; open 8am-8pm) and **Thrifty** (☎ 406-257-7333; **W** www.thrity.com; 4785 US 2 W; open 8am-8pm Mon-Sat, 9am-5pm Sun).

Rental agencies around the park are open for the summer season. In West Glacier try the **Glacier Highland Resort** (☎ 406-888-5427, 800-766-0811; open 8am-10pm). In East Glacier the **Glacier Park Trading Co** (☎ 406-226-4433, 800-331-1212; open 8am-9pm) handles Avis car rentals. All car rental companies offer vans and 4WD vehicles.

For Waterton, rental agencies at Lethbridge County Airport include **Budget** (☎ 403-328-6555, 800-527-0700; **W** www.budget.com; open 8:30am-8pm) and **Hertz** (☎ 403-382-3472, 800-654 3131; **W** www.hertz.com; open 8:30am-8pm).

Other Rentals By contacting **Cruise America** (☎ 480-464-7300; **W** www.cruise america.com) you can rent a range of RVs through local dealers in various US cities, though none in Montana; check the website for a dealer nearest you. In Glacier, trailers may be parked temporarily at campgrounds or at Sun Point, on the east side of the park.

On the other extreme, rent a Harley at **Scenic Harley Rentals** (☎ 406-892-7368; **W** www.shrentals.com; 7312 US 2 E, Columbia Falls; from USD$119). In Waterton Townsite, all-purpose **Pat's** (☎ 403-859-2266; 224 Mount View Rd; per day CAD$65) rents out scooters.

Organized Tours

Montana Rockies Rail Tours (☎ 200-265-0610, 800 519 7245; **W** www.montana railtours.com) offers Glacier Canada Tour, an eight-day train venture from Bozeman to Spokane, taking in Glacier, Waterton and surrounding sites. **Senior Women's Travel** (☎ 212-838-4740; **W** www.poshnosh.com) offers a tour to Waterton and Glacier Parks, as well as to other US national parks.

True North Tours (☎ 403-934-5972; **W** www.backpacker-tour.com) explores Waterton Lakes National Park over four days; transportation is by passenger van.

GLENBOW ARCHIVES NC32-15

Laden with glaciers and sprinkled with gem-colored lakes, the Rocky Mountains create a landscape of continuous change and awe-inspiring beauty throughout Banff National Park.

EXPERIENCING BANFF

Towering like giant castles in the sky, the mountains and valleys of Banff provide endless opportunities for wildlife watching, hiking, boating, climbing, biking, skiing or simply convening with nature. Lush canyons compete for your attention with lofty fields of alpine wildflowers; tranquil waterways meander past, and dense, emerald forests bid you to delve inside.

With a couple of days, it's possible to get a taste of the park's wonders, but if you really want to experience the magic of the region, take time to explore its quieter areas; rent a boat, don your hiking boots or strap on some snowshoes and get out into the wilds. The oldest national park in Canada, Banff is also by far the most popular; you'll soon come to appreciate why.

Despite the crowds that are drawn to the park each year (particularly in summer), with a little effort you can escape them at even the most popular sites, like Lake Louise. If you do so, you may well be rewarded by bumping into some of the park's more reclusive residents, like moose, elk, bears, pikas and marmots.

When You Arrive

Banff National Park is open year-round. Unless you're driving through on Trans-Canada Hwy 1, you are required to purchase a valid park pass. If you are found without a pass anywhere in the park (including Banff Town), you can be fined. Day passes to the park cost adult/senior/child CAD$6/4.50/3; if you're planning to spend more than a week here, it's worth buying a year pass, giving you unlimited access to all of Canada's national parks (adults/groups of up to five people CAD$38/75). Visa, MasterCard, American Express, travelers checks and good old-fashioned cash are all accepted as payment.

Tollbooths are located along Trans-Canada Hwy 1 at the eastern boundary of the park, as well as along the Icefields Parkway to the north. If you are entering the park along another route and do not find a tollbooth (or if the booth is vacant), purchase your pass from a Parks Canada office as soon as possible. Random roadside checks are often done near popular sights or areas.

At tollbooths you will be given The Mountain Guide, a Parks Canada publication containing basic maps and a brief description of sights within the park. Staff also have a mountain of other information and brochures stashed away in these booths; ask if you're after something specific.

ORIENTATION

Stretching over 6641 sq km/2564 sq miles, Banff National Park lies along Alberta's western provincial border with British Columbia. The busiest area is by far the southern half of the park, concentrated around Banff Town and Lake Louise. Banff Town is the first service hub en route from Calgary and is packed with activity outfitters, shops, restaurants and hotels. Lake Louise Village, 58km/36 miles northwest of Banff Town, is the first service hub for those entering from Golden and Yoho National Park. More of a hamlet than a town, Lake Louise Village has basic services, like a grocery store, post office, hotels and a few restaurants. On the far side of the village lies the access road to both Lake Louise and Moraine Lake. A glacier loaded area, the icy lakes are surrounded by magnificent snowy peaks.

Between Banff Town and Lake Louise lies the lush Bow Valley with the popular Johnston Canyon along its northern side. To the south of Bow Valley is Sunshine Meadows, with many alpine day hikes and winter ski runs. Northeast of Banff Town, the Minnewanka area is dotted with small lakes and is a favorite spot with boaters and campers.

North of Lake Louise, the stunning and much acclaimed Icefields Parkway heads northeast, entering Jasper National Park at 122km/75.6 miles. See the Icefields Parkway chapter (p134) for details.

Entrances

There are five road entrances into Banff National Park. All are open year-round, weather permitting. Highway 1 enters Banff from the east just west of Canmore and from the west via Yoho National Park. You can also enter from the south on Hwy 93 from Kootenay National Park; this entrance has no tollbooth and meets up with Hwy 1 about halfway between Lake Louise and Banff Town. From north of the park, enter along the Icefields Parkway from Jasper National Park or via Hwy 11 from Rocky Mountain House.

A number of hiking trails lead into the park. The most popular begins from Kananaskis Country (via Mt Assiniboine Provincial Park), although it is also possible to enter on foot or skis from Kootenay and Yoho National Parks.

Major Roads

Trans-Canada Hwy 1 is the country's major thoroughfare, crossing the continent from east to west. The section passing through Banff National Park is often busy with commuters and is notorious for collisions; drive defensively and with care. Those wanting to take their time can follow the Bow Valley Parkway (Hwy 1A), which runs parallel to Hwy 1 along the Bow Valley. The eastern section of this road (from Johnston Canyon) is closed in spring from 6pm to 9am to give wildlife some peace and privacy.

INFORMATION

At the **Banff Information Centre** (☎ 403-762-1550; **W** www.parkscanada.gc.ca /pn-np/ab/banff; 224 Banff Ave, Banff Town; open 8am-6pm spring & autumn, 8am-8pm summer, 9am-noon & 1-5pm winter) you'll find knowledgeable Parks Canada staff with lots of resources at their fingertips. Pick up maps, brochures, permits and trail and road reports. There are also exhibits and, in summer, talks on wildlife and the environment.

To the right as you enter the center is the **Banff Tourism Bureau** (☎ 403-762-8421; **W** www.banfflakelouise.com; opening hours as above), which gives out information on services and activities in and around Banff Town.

Also run by Parks Canada, the **Lake Louise Visitor Centre** (☎ 403-522-3833; beside Samson Mall, Lake Louise Village; open 9am-5pm spring & autumn, 9am-7pm summer, 9am-4pm winter) doles out information on the park, and under the same roof, the **Lake Louise Tourism Bureau** (☎ 403-762-8421; open 9am-7pm summer only) has information about activities and services in the village.

Friends of Banff (☎ 403-762-8911; **W** www.friendsofbanff.com; The Bear & Butterfly, 214 Banff Ave) is a nonprofit group that runs educational programs and is actively involved in park maintenance. They provide advice and information and sell an excellent selection of topographical maps. Tune your radio to 101.1FM/103.3FM for their park news in English/French.

The following numbers provide recorded up-to-date information:

Avalanche Hazards	☎ 403-762-1460
Park Warden Office	☎ 403-762-1470
Road Conditions	☎ 403-762-1450
Trail Conditions	☎ 403-760-1305

Bookstores

Friends of Banff (see Information, previous) has lots of topographical maps and a good selection of books covering flora, fauna and activities in the park. All profits go back into the organization.

For books on local activities as well as coffee-table books of the surrounding scenery, try **The Viewpoint** (☎ 403-762-0405; 201 Caribou St). **Cascade Mountain Books** (☎ 403-762-8508; lower level, Cascade Plaza, cnr Bear St & Banff Ave) carries Canadian fiction, travel books, maps and specialist books on outdoor activities.

Policies & Regulations

It is illegal to take or pick anything from the park, from more obvious things like antlers and artifacts to rocks, flowers and leaves. Pets must be kept on a leash at all times and are not allowed in backcountry shelters. Hunting and firearms are not permitted anywhere in the park. Most permits and passes listed can be ordered in advance for a CAD$12 reservation fee by calling ☎ 800-748-7275.

WILDLIFE

Encountering wildlife can be a highlight of your trip; however, keep in mind a number of regulations enforced to protect you and the animals. It is illegal to touch, entice, disturb or in any way harass any wild animals. Do not feed animals (even those inquisitive little squirrels), and keep all food and coolers inside your vehicle. Dispose of garbage in bear-proof bins; littering is illegal.

CAMPING

Only camp in designated areas. Reservations are not accepted for frontcountry campgrounds; sites are given out on a first-come, first-served basis. Checkout is at 11am, and there is a maximum stay of 14 nights. You can have one tent and up to two vehicles at one campsite.

The Bare Campground Policy requires you to keep your site clear of everything but outdoor furniture, tents and bedding. If you leave cooking equipment, food, soap, coolers or anything else lying around while you're out, it may be confiscated. All food must be stored in your vehicle or in bear-proof storage lockers, or must be hung from bear poles.

If camping just isn't camping without toasted marshmallows, purchase a required fire permit (CAD$6, including wood) from the campground entrance. Bring your own axe for kindling. Parks staff also ask that you be thrifty with the amount of wood you use in your fire pit. Restrictions are often placed on fires during dry seasons.

For information on backcountry camping, see Backcountry Hikes (p96).

HORSES

Horses are permitted on designated backcountry trails within the park. For backcountry horse trekking, purchase a wilderness pass and a grazing permit (CAD$1 per horse, per night). At the height of summer, reservations are recommended.

Enquire at the information center about high rivers you may have to ford (especially in spring), and pick up a *Horse User's Guide to Banff National Park,* which details trailheads and staging areas.

FISHING

Fishing seasons vary from one lake or river to another and from year to year. Generally, Bow River is open year-round, and Johnson Lake, Lake Minnewanka, Two Jack Lake and Vermillion Lakes are open mid-May to early September. Many areas are closed to fishing at all times.

The maximum daily catch and possession limit is two fish. Strict regulations govern which fish you may catch. Many, like bull trout and kokanee salmon, are protected. If you are unsure what you've caught, throw it back. (Wardens do not accept 'but I thought it was a lake trout' excuse and will slap on heavy fines.) You will be given a list of catch and possession limits when you purchase your fishing permit.

For up-to-the-minute information, check with parks information before you cast your line. For details on fishing licenses, see p41.

BIKING

Biking is only permitted on designated trails; ask at the Banff Information Centre for trail maps. Yield to hikers and horses, and avoid skidding (it causes erosion). Off trail riding is unlawful, and bike helmets are mandatory in Alberta.

Getting Around

Most people enter the park in their own vehicles. If you are not from the area, consider renting a car for maximum flexibility. Public transportation and shuttles are limited and won't take you to out-of-the-way trailheads or sites. Tours run to most major sights.

CAR & MOTORCYCLE

Speed limits for major routes are 90kmh/56 mph, dropping to 60kmh/37 mph or 30kmh/18.6 mph on secondary roads. Wildlife, weather and maintenance can result in temporary speed-limit reductions. Gas is available from service stations in Banff Town, Lake Louise Village and Castle Mountain Junction. For repairs, you'll do best in Banff Town.

Driving in Canada is on the right, and seatbelts are mandatory for all passengers, even in motorhomes. Unless there is a marked turning lane, it is illegal to cross a double solid line to reach rest stops and viewpoints on the opposite side of the road. At all times, be particularly cautious of wildlife – it is not unusual for animals to dart across the road. If you are in a motorhome, pulling a trailer or driving anything with a large blind spot, be particularly cautious of bikers.

In winter, you are required by law to have your vehicle equipped with snow tires or must carry chains on all roads within the park except Hwy 1. All roads are subject to closure due to winter weather conditions.

In Banff Town, parking is metered or limited to one or two hours. Many parking lots do not allow RVs; you're better off parking at the trailer/RV parking lot on Banff Ave and catching the bus into town.

BUS

Banff Transit Service (☎ 403-760-8294; CAD$1/0.50 adults/6-12 yrs, under 5 yrs free; daily 7am-midnight May-Sep, noon-midnight winter) is geared for tourists and will help you reach most sights in town. The Banff Ave–Banff Springs route runs from the trailer/RV parking lot on Banff Ave to the Banff Springs Hotel. The Tunnel Mountain–Downtown route runs from Village One at Tunnel Mountain Campground on Tunnel Mountain Rd to the Luxton Museum. Both run every half hour.

Greyhound (☎ 800-661-8747; Gopher St) has four daily departures between Banff and Canmore (CAD$8.40) and three between Banff and Lake Louise (CAD$12.75). In summer book your return trip ahead.

SHUTTLE

The **Mountain Hostel Connector** (May-Oct daily) connects International Hostels in Banff Town, Lake Louise Village and Jasper Town, stopping at major sights and hostels along the Icefields Parkway. Heading north, the bus departs Banff Town at 6am and Lake Louise at 8:45am (CAD$8) and reaches Jasper Town at 12:15pm (from Banff/Lake Louise; CAD$51/45). Going south, the bus leaves Jasper Town at 1:30pm, reaching Lake Louise at 5pm and Banff Town at 5:45pm.

TRAIN

These days, standard passenger trains rush through town without stopping. Nevertheless, experiencing the parks by train is breathtaking and adds a historical element to your journey. **Rocky Mountaineer Rail Tours** (☎ 800-665-7245; W www.rocky mountaineer.com; d/s CAD$669/739; departs Sun, Tue & Thu Apr-Oct) have train trips for tourists that end up in Banff Town via Jasper. Two-day journeys from Vancouver travel in daylight only (hotel in Kamloops not included in price) to give you the best views.

ORGANIZED TOURS

If you prefer to sit back and let someone else do the planning, there are a number of popular tours to highlights in and around the park. Many upscale hotels run their own shuttles to sights. For a bird's eye-view of the park, check out the helicopter tours in Canmore (p118).

Brewster (☎ 403-762-6750, 877-791-5500; W www.brewster.ca; 100 Gopher St, Banff Town) is the largest and longest-running tour company in Banff, having carted early visitors to the hot springs more than a century ago. Today their big buses do tours of Banff Town (3 hours; adult/child CAD$43/21.50), Lake Minnewanka (including 1.5-hour boat ride; adult/child CAD$44/22) and the Icefields Parkway (adult/child one way CAD$95/47.50). You can also do a marathon tour of the Bow Valley, Lake Louise, Moraine Lake and Yoho National Park in one fell swoop (9.5 hours; adult/child CAD$65/32.50).

Discover Banff Tours (☎ 403-760-5007; W www.banfftours.com; Sundance Mall, 215 Banff Ave) has daily guided tours of Banff Town (CAD$45), Lake Louise & Moraine Lake (CAD$55) and Yoho National Park (CAD$60). They also run evening wildlife safaris (CAD$35), horse treks (CAD$30-75) and hiking tours (CAD$35–50). Tour groups are small (maximum 24 people), and children are generally half price.

UNDER NEW MANAGEMENT

It's a difficult balancing act, and one that Parks Canada has been trying to get right since Banff National Park's conception. On one side of the seesaw sits the tourism industry, with its highways, railway, businesses, pollution and more than five million annual visitors; on the other side rests the wilderness, with its fragile ecosystems and wildlife. By 1996, it had become apparent to many that the balancing act was about to collapse, that human encroachment had grown too hefty on the seesaw and threatened to send the wilderness soaring into a state of irreparable damage. Studies were done, recommendations were made, and the Banff National Park Management Plan was born, recognizing that wilderness stability is vital to sustaining the businesses and populations relying on the park for their livelihood.

As part of the management plan, caps have been put on the growth of both industry and populations in Banff Town and Lake Louise Village. New land is no longer released for commercial development, a few facilities outside the service hubs have been removed, and restrictions have been placed on driving and hiking. The main goal of the plan is to rehabilitate the Bow River Valley, a unique montane ecoregion and integral migration corridor for wildlife, as well as the most developed area of the park.

Not surprisingly, those sitting on the tourism end of the seesaw are not all smiles. Industry stakeholders argue that the park is as much for the benefit of people as wildlife and that the return to a mythical natural state is an environmental elitist dream.

While proposed actions and initial successes were applauded, the plan's implementation has not always left environmentalists whooping for joy either. The survival of species like the grizzly bear continue to remain seriously threatened; animals like moose, lynx and otter continue to be displaced from Bow Valley; and even the seemingly pervasive elk is considered in social turmoil. Vehicles and trains continue to run down wildlife, and development such as the Fairmont Chateau Lake Louise's conference center ensures a growing number of visitors and related problems.

Meanwhile, what some call an 'unholy marriage' between industry and the environment continues. The government spends giant sums on promoting tourism, which brings in more than CAD$750 million annually to Banff alone. At the same time, the government claims that restoring the ecological integrity of the park is a main priority and that the park must be left 'unimpaired for future generations.' The debate continues, the seesaw teeters, and the park's future rests in the precarious balance.

HIGHLIGHTS

If you only visit one ...

✔ museum, make it the **Whyte Museum of the Canadian Rockies** (p72), for excellent paintings, photographs and exhibits

✔ historic building, explore the Gothic glamour of the **Fairmont Banff Springs Hotel** (p74)

✔ neighboring park, check out the unusual scenery and watch for moose in **Kananaskis Country** (p121)

✔ tourist shop, save your pennies for the crafts, books and souvenirs in **The Bear & Butterfly** (p116), run by the Friends of Banff

✔ viewpoint, hike or take the **Banff Gondola** up Sulphur Mountain (p74) for a panoramic look at the Rockies

✔ cowboy hangout, don your Stetson and try out your two-step at **Wild Bill's Legendary Saloon** (p115)

✔ teahouse, huff and puff your way up to the **Six Glacier Teahouse** (p89), a 1927 relic from Lake Louise's original Swiss mountain guides

✔ lake, head for **Lake Louise** (p75) on a still day for the amazing reflections of its surrounding peaks and glaciers

In spring and summer, **Gray Line Sightseeing** (☎ 800-661-4919; W *www.gray line.ca*) runs daily tours to Lake Louise and surrounding highlights (CAD$52), Lake Minnewanka (CAD$44), Emerald Lake (CAD$51) and the Icefields Parkway (CAD$95 one way to Jasper). Buses depart from most hotels in Banff Town as well as from the bus depot. Reservations are required on most tours, and children ride for half-price.

Sights

You'll never be stumped for something to see or do in Banff National Park – the whole place is a sight. Breathtaking natural attractions like world-renowned Lake Louise, lofty Castle Mountain or the bizarre Hoodoos are set in a wonderland of scenery and wildlife. And when you've had enough of the outdoors, duck into one of Banff Town's unique museums, check out its historical buildings or relax in the bubbling water of Upper Hot Springs Pool.

BANFF TOWN
MAP 2

Unlike most national parks, this park's major hub is more than a general store, a warden's cabin and a hut or two. A major destination in its own right, Banff Town offers excellent facilities, chic restaurants, shopping, entertainment and some worthwhile museums and sights. Nobody will blame you if you're unable to drag yourself away from downtown for a few days. Judging from the number of tourists that crowd the sidewalks in summer, you're not alone.

Whyte Museum of the Canadian Rockies

With excellent, diverse displays on glaciers, resident artists, mountaineers and local life in the 1900s, the **Whyte Museum** (☎ 403-762-2291; W *www.whyte.org*; 111 Bear St;

adults/students & seniors/ family of 4 CAD$6/3.50/15; open 10am-5pm) is well worth a couple of hours. Special exhibitions get you better acquainted with particular personalities or aspects of the area. The museum also hosts films, lectures and concerts (check their website for details) and runs Historic Banff Walks (90 min; CAD$7; 3pm daily, June-Sept) as well as private tours of historical homes in town (call to reserve).

Canada Place

Loaded with interactive activities, the small **Canada Place** (☎ *403-760-1338;* ☒ *www.canadaplace.gc.ca/cprc/alta/index.html; Mountain Ave; free; open 10am-6pm daily spring & summer, noon-5pm daily autumn, 1pm-4pm Wed-Sun winter)* will entertain the entire family. Exhibits are packed with information on Canadian art, heritage and history. Sit in a birch-bark canoe, find out how successful you'd have been as an early explorer or travel across Canada through digitally displayed paintings. The museum is surrounded by beautifully manicured gardens built by relief workers during the 1930s depression.

Cave & Basin

Used therapeutically by natives for over 10,000 years, **Cave and Basin** *(Map 1;* ☎ *403-762-1566; adult/senior/youth CAD$4/3.50/3; open 9am-6pm daily in summer, 11am-4pm Mon-Fri & 9.30am-5pm Sat & Sun in winter)* has been drawing tourists with its eggy-smelling sulphur waters for more than 110 years. It was largely the springs' popularity that led to the establishment of the original natural reserve that later widened into Banff National Park. Today you can still see the bubbling waters and wander around the restored complex (1914), but dips are no longer allowed. Exhibits tell the history and geology of the sight, and tours

ELIXIR OF LIFE?

It wasn't just the beautiful mountain scenery that drew Europeans to Banff in the late 1800s. Nor was it simply the promise of a hot bath. It was the reputed powers of the hot springs that brought them flocking, powers that promised to heal, rejuvenate and make visitors the picture of health. By the early 1900s, the precious water was pumped to a sanatorium built on the present-day site of Canada Place; the aspiring resident doctor issued a pair of crutches to every patient walking in and then displayed those left behind as proof of the water's curative strength. Companies bottled and sold the water to train passengers as far away as Winnipeg, and bars opened up along Banff Ave selling glasses of gin or rum with a splash of mineral water. The water was claimed to cure everything from poor digestion to liver conditions to physical disabilities.

Is it simply an old wives' tale or is there really something magical in that water? The heat of the water alone increases circulation, and the minerals are believed to help with insomnia, aches and pains and detoxification. In particular, lithium is believed to calm nerves, raise spirits and perhaps even strengthen the immune system. So go on, immerse yourself in a bit of history.

are available (11am, daily in summer, weekends in winter) for a more in-depth account.

Banff Park Museum

The longest-standing Parks Canada facility, **Banff Park Museum** (☎ *403-762-1558; 93 Banff Ave; adult/child CAD$3/2; open 10am-6pm daily summer, 1-5pm daily winter),* is beginning to feel the burden of its years. Housed in what was once a Canadian Pacific Railway building (1903), the museum was closed indefinitely at the time of writing due to serious deterioration of its wooden structure. Once the museum is reopened, you will be able to step back in time to exhibits that have changed little since the museum's opening in 1895. Check out plants, birds, wood, mammals and mineral samples found in the park in the late 1800s.

Luxton Museum of the Plains Indians

Housed in what looks like a wooden fort, the small **Luxton Museum** (☎ 403-762-2388; 1 Birch Ave; adult/senior & student/child CAD$8/6/2.50; open 9am-6pm) celebrates the cultures of First Nations from the Northern Plains and Rockies. The traditional clothing, tepee, crafts and hunting equipment may be interesting for those unacquainted with First Nations' culture.

Banff Gondola

Board the **Sulphur Mountain Gondola** (☎ 403-762-5438; Mountain Ave; W www .banffgondola.com; adult/child CAD$21.50/10.75, under 6 yrs free; open daily, 7:30am-9pm summer, 10am-4pm winter, reduced hours spring & autumn, closed Jan 6-17) at the bottom of Sulphur Mountain, and eight minutes later you'll have an endless 360° view of mountaintops. The gondola carries you up to 2281m/7486ft above sea level, where you can grab a pricey coffee or lunch, visit the observation terrace and wander over to the historic **weather station**.

You can reach the gondola's lower terminal, 4km/2.5 miles south of downtown Banff, on a **Brewster shuttle bus** (adult/child CAD$5; hourly May-Oct; cnr Banff Ave & Caribou St). If you're up for a good workout, hike up the mountain (5.5km/3.4 miles; 2 hours; difficult) and ride the gondola back down for free.

Fairmont Banff Springs Hotel

Designed in the style of a Scottish castle, the **Banff Springs Hotel** (☎ 403-762-6860; Spray Ave) has a Gothic interior that winds into turrets and opens into grand ballrooms. Restorations have done nothing to diminish the hotel's original 1928 glory; even if you're not staying here (p109), it's well worth having a wander around. You can also soak up a bit of the glamour with a drink in the lounge or dinner at one of the hotel's restaurants (p114).

Upper Hot Springs Pool

If you're feeling weary from a long hike, a long drive or even a long winter, step into the **Upper Hot Springs Pool** (☎ 403-762-1515; end of Mountain Ave; adult/child & senior/family CAD$7.50/6.50/23; open 9am-11pm daily in summer, 10am-10pm Sun-Thur & 10am-11pm Fri & Sat in winter). The scalding mineral water (47°C/116°F) is cooled to around a mere 40°C/104°F before entering the pools and is believed to carry healing properties. You can also indulge in a massage (CAD$70 per hour), reiki (CAD$70 per hour) or a facial (CAD$65 per hour). Bathing suits, towels and lockers are for hire.

Lake Minnewanka Map 3

Surrounded by peaks and forests, **Lake Minnewanka** is a popular escape from downtown Banff. **Lake Minnewanka Boat Tours** (☎ 403-762-3473; W www .minnewankaboattours.com; adult/child CAD$30/13, under 5 yrs free; 4-5 departures daily, 10:30am-7pm mid-May–Sep, 10:30-5pm Sep–early Oct) give you a closer look at the park's largest reservoir and fill you in on the history and geology of the area. You can also fish here or hike the **Aylmer Lookout** trail (p84) for spectacular vistas across and beyond the lake. While only 11km/6.8 miles from Banff Town, there is no public transportation to the lake; see Organized Tours (p70).

Bow Falls

More tumbling rapids than plunging falls, **Bow Falls** offer a popular viewpoint near the confluence of the Bow and Spray Rivers. You can reach the falls by a pleasant forested walk along Bow River or by a short stroll from Banff Springs Hotel. There's also a parking lot along Glen Rd.

Hoodoos

Looking as if they've been transported directly from the desert, **Hoodoos** are peculiar pillars of sandstone that appear to have risen up from the ground. In fact, the ground fell away from them, eroded by the Bow River, which now snakes far below. To see the giant, natural sculptures, head up to the viewpoint on Tunnel Mountain Rd, where a short interpretive walk begins.

Castle Mountain

Marking the end of the Front Ranges and the official start of the Rockies' Main Ranges, the majestic **Castle Mountain** claims the northern horizon as you head west from Banff Town. Its crimson-hued slopes are stacked horizontally, sandwiching limestone layers between shale and quartz. The force of nature has weathered its top into buttresses and pinnacles, giving the mountain its fortresslike appearance. Located halfway between Banff Town and Lake Louise Village, there are lookout points on Hwys 1 and 1A.

LAKE LOUISE & AROUND
MAP 1

In 1882, a Stoney guide led Tom Wilson to the 'Lake of Little Fishes.' Tom preferred to call the gorgeous spectacle Emerald Lake but had little sway before the government, who eventually named it Lake Louise in honor of Queen Victoria's daughter. Since Tom's arrival at the lakeshore, many have followed in his footsteps; the umpteen glaciers, craggy peaks and bright-colored lakes make this area a don't-miss.

Parking lots at Lake Louise and Moraine Lake fill up quickly in summer. Try to visit on a weekday, early in the morning or later in the afternoon. The road to Moraine Lake is winding and narrow, open only from June to October and unsuitable for RVs.

Lake Louise

Despite the enormous hotel and busloads of tourists that crowd along the southern shoreline of **Lake Louise**, this magical place is well worth exploring. With stunning emerald-green water and tall, snowy peaks that hoist the hefty Victoria Glacier up for all to see, Lake Louise has captured the imaginations of mountaineers, artists and visitors for more than a century. Depending on the stillness of the water and the angle of the sun, the lake's color will appear slightly different from each viewpoint and with each visit. On calm days, you may witness extraordinary reflections of the surrounding scenery.

A number of walks begin at the lakeshore and offer spectacular views, peaceful settings and even an alpine teahouse or two. Rent a canoe from Lake Louise Boathouse (p101) and paddle yourself through the icy waters. Canoes can carry three adults or two adults and two kids. Life jackets are supplied.

Lake Louise Gondola

The **Lake Louise Gondola** (☎ *403-522-3555, 800-258-7669; off Hwy 1A;* **w** *www .skilouise.com; adult/senior & student/child CAD$20/18/10; open 9am-4pm May, 8:30am-6pm Jun-Sep)* lands you at a lofty 2088m/6850ft for a view of Lake Louise and the surrounding glaciers and peaks. At the top you'll also find the **Wildlife Interpretation Centre** *(admission free; open May-Sep)* and regular theater presentations and themed guided walks. Travel the 14-minute ascent in either an open ski lift or an enclosed gondola.

Moraine Lake

You'll be dazzled by the scenery before you even reach **Moraine Lake**, set in the Valley of the Ten Peaks. En route, the narrow, winding road gives off fabulous views of imposing Wenkchemna Peaks. Look familiar? For years this scene was carried on the back of the Canadian $20 bill. In 1894, explorer Samuel Allen named the peaks with numbers from one to ten in the Stoney Indian language *(wenkchemna* means 'ten'); all but two of the mountains have since been renamed. You'll quickly notice the **Tower of Babel**, ascending solidly toward the heavens at the northeastern edge of the range.

With little hustle or bustle and lots of beauty, many people prefer the more rugged and remote setting of Moraine Lake to Lake Louise. Smaller than its popular neighbor, the turquoise waters of Moraine Lake are surprisingly clear for a glacial reservoir. (Its source, meltwater from a dormant glacier far up the mountainside, carries little mud, snow or rock down with it.) Take a look at the surrounding mountains through telescopes secured to the southern shore (free!) or hire a boat and paddle to the middle for a 360° view (p101). There are also some great day hikes from here and, to rest your weary legs, a café, dining room and lodge. The road to Moraine Lake and its facilities are open June to early October.

SILENT LEGACY

If you wandered upon the site today, deep in the Bow Valley forest, you'd find nothing more than a rusted pot, some barbed wire fence and maybe a few whitewashed stones. Little is left to attest to more than 600 prisoners held there between 1915 and 1917. Nevertheless, the prisoners left their mark in other ways – in the expansion of Banff Spring's Golf Course, in the building of the Cave and Basin pool and in the construction of the Bow Valley Parkway.

Few visitors to the park know that the infrastructure they enjoy was largely built by internees of W W I, the majority of them Ukrainian immigrants loyal to the British Crown and all settlers originally from enemy countries. Held in a camp beneath Castle Mountain during the summer and near Cave and Basin during winter, prisoners suffered harsh conditions and brutal treatment. Separated from their families (women and children were imprisoned elsewhere), they were stripped of their possessions and property and forced to labor on public works. For most, their only crime was having left Ukraine in search of a better life in Canada. It was wartime, and fear and xenophobic spirits ran high in Canada.

In 1994, a small monument was finally erected along the Bow Valley Parkway, near the site of the camp. Take a moment to acknowledge the prisoners' unheralded contribution to the park.

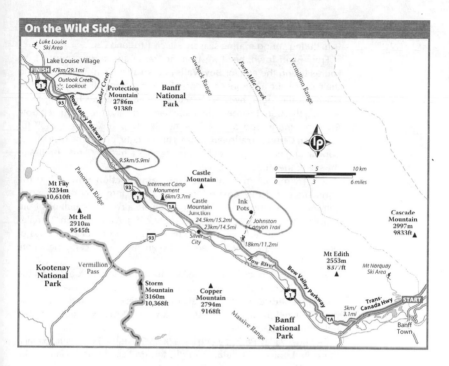

On the Wild Side

Lake Louise Ski Area

Lake Louise Village

FINISH 47km/29.1mi

Outlook Creek Lookout

Baker Creek

Sawback Range

Forty Mile Creek

Vermillion Range

Protection Mountain 2786m 9138ft

Banff National Park

93

Bow Valley Parkway

9.5km/5.9mi

Castle Mountain

Interment Camp Monument

6km/3.7mi

Mt Fay 3234m 10,610ft

Panorama Ridge

93 1

Castle Mountain Junction

Ink Pots

Cascade Mountain 2997m 9833ft

Mt Bell 2910m 9545ft

1A

24.5km/15.2mi

23km/14.5mi

Johnston Canyon Trail

93

Silver City

18km/11.2mi

Bow River

Bow Valley Parkway

Mt Edith 2553m 837/ft

Mt Norquay Ski Area

Kootenay National Park

Vermillion Pass

Storm Mountain 3160m 10,368ft

Copper Mountain 2794m 9168ft

Massive Range

1

Trans-Canada Hwy

START

5km/ 3.1mi

1A

Banff National Park

Banff Town

0   5   10 km
0   3   6 miles

Driving Tours

Banff's scenery will wow you before you ever even get out of your car. Below are some of the most scenic drives that the park has to offer, many of which are en route to popular sights and trailheads.

ON THE WILD SIDE
Route: Banff Town to Lake Louise Village, Bow Valley Parkway (Hwy 1A)
Distance: 52km/32.2 miles one way
Speed Limit: 60kmh/37 mph

The picturesque Bow Valley Parkway winds from Banff Town to Lake Louise Village along the bottom of the valley. Unfenced and less hectic than driving down Hwy 1, a trip along this road is one of your best chances for spotting wildlife from the car. Your prospects for an encounter are even greater if you start out early or late in the day. It's worth combining this tour with the Valley of the Giants driving tour for a fantastic loop.

Much narrower than many of the thoroughfares in the area, the Bow Valley Parkway should be savored rather than sped through; each year, wildlife is hit and killed along here. The eastern half of this route (from

Banff Town to Castle Mountain Junction) is closed to traffic from 6pm to 9am during spring mating season (March 1 to June 25).

From Banff Town, head west on the Trans-Canada Hwy toward Lake Louise, taking the exit for **Bow Valley Parkway** at 5km/3.1 miles. Along the parkway are a number of interesting and scenic pull-offs (marked 'e') where local geography is explained. The road continues heading west, winding through the trees, with mountain peaks and the very green **Bow River** coming in and out of view. At 18km/11.2 miles, the turnoff for **Johnston Canyon Trailhead** appears on the right, one of the park's most popular and worthwhile walks. From here it's a further 5km/3.1 miles to the site of the short-lived **Silver City**.

At 24.5km/15.2 miles, **Castle Mountain Junction** turns off to the right. The distinctive **Castle Mountain** looms into view on the right, crimson and enormous. Past the junction are a couple of pull-offs from which you can enjoy views of this majestic giant. A further 6km/3.7 miles up the road, you'll pass a **monument** depicting one of thousands of Ukrainian immigrants who were held in an internment camp near here from 1915 to 1917.

At 9.5km/5.9 miles from Castle Mountain Junction is a lookout on the left with incredible views across the river and southwest to the **Panorama Ridge**; watch for a few wooden steps heading down off the road. Just before the end of the parkway is **Outlook Creek**, another pull-off with superb views.

The Bow Valley Parkway ends at 47km/29.1 miles. Take a left to reach the **Lake Louise Gondola** or a right toward Lake Louise Village, **Lake Louise**, **Moraine Lake** or the Trans-Canada Hwy.

VALLEY OF THE GIANTS
Route: Banff Town to Lake Louise Village, Trans-Canada Hwy 1
Distance: 55km/34.1 miles one way
Speed Limit: 90kmh/56 mph; 70kmh/43 mph near Lake Louise

While the word *highway* may make you think of overpasses, industrial zones and congested traffic, the Trans-Canada Hwy between Banff Town and Lake Louise is one of the most scenic routes through the park. The highway runs through the Bow Valley, following the route of the Pacific Railway, with giant mountain ranges and craggy peaks sweeping up on either side of the road. The resulting perspective is much wider than on smaller roads with big, open vistas. Travel this route from east to west (as described here) to visit the pull-off viewpoints (only accessible to eastbound traffic). Consider linking this route with the **On the Wild Side** driving tour to make a complete loop.

Remember that you are traveling along one of Canada's main thoroughfares and need to balance scenery viewing with defensive driving. Regular commuters along this route often plow along at ridiculous speeds, and countless tourists slam on their brakes or wander across the highway to see elk. Resist the urge to follow suit; it puts you, other drivers and the animals at risk.

Head west out of Banff Town along Hwy 1. Almost immediately on your left are the **Vermillion Lakes**, a marshy area that's a popular hangout for wildfowl, elk and the occasional moose. To your right is the southern end of the Sawback Range and to your left lie the impressive Massive Range. The green Bow River passes under the highway just after Vermillion Lakes, where it winds and twists its way beside the highway for the remainder of the drive. The highway here is fenced on either side to protect wildlife; you'll see grassy overpasses where animals can cross safely to the other side.

Continuing between the ranges, the popular **Cascade Mountain Viewpoint** at 21km/13 miles is worth stopping for. **Castle Mountain** looms to the northwest and is difficult to miss in all its crimson glory. At **Castle Mountain Junction**, the four-lane highway is reduced to two lanes and the fencing disappears. Be extra cautious along this section of the road, both for madcap drivers and wildlife.

The **Panorama Ridge** rises up on the left, after which the enormous **Mount Temple** comes into view, towering at 3542m/11,620ft. Stop at the **Mt Temple Viewpoint** for a good look. The turnoff for **Lake Louise Village** is about 24km/14.9 miles from Castle Mountain Junction. For **Lake Louise** and **Moraine Lake**, turn left; take a right for **Lake Louise Gondola** or to hook up with the **Bow Valley Parkway**.

LOOPIN' THE LAKES
Route: return loop from Banff Town; Minnewanka Loop Drive
Distance: 16.5km/10.2 miles roundtrip to Hwy 1
Speed Limit: 50kmh/31mph

This short drive gives you a stunning and ever-changing view of the mountains and ranges east of Banff Town, bringing you close to three lakes in the area and numerous trailheads. This route is closed November 15 to April 15 due to winter conditions.

Head out of Banff Town on Banff Ave, crossing under Trans-Canada Hwy 1 to meet **Minnewanka Loop Drive**. Immediately on your left looms **Cascade Mountain**, with small waterfalls streaming down its walls and rugged shapes and pinnacles carved along its top. On the right is the turnoff to **Cascade Ponds**, a picnic area around small pools of water.

Pass by the turnoff on the right to Johnson Lake and continue north as the road winds up through the trees. At each bend you'll be given new perspectives of the mountains, with the **Palliser Range** directly ahead. At 3km/1.9 miles there is a turnoff on the right for **Lower Bankhead**, once the site of a coal plant that operated from 1904 to 1922. The mine supported around 1000 people; the buildings and machinery they left behind remain dilapidated. You can follow an **interpretive walk** around the site to learn more. The actual mine was located up the hill at **Upper Bankhead**, now the trailhead for **C-Level Cirque** (p83).

Lake Minnewanka comes into view at about 6km/3.7 miles. The largest lake in the park, it snakes west for 19.7km/12.2 miles, between Palliser

Range to the north and the **Fairholme Range** to the south. You'll also find the **Aylmer Lookout** and **Lake Minnewanka** trailheads here.

The road follows a bank along the lake's eastern side to **Two Jack Lake**, with gorgeous views south of **Mount Rundle**, particularly at dusk. You'll inevitably see mountain goats along this stretch of the loop, often wandering down the middle of the road.

On the right, about 11km/6.8 miles along the route, is the junction for **Johnson Lake**. Just under 3km/1.9 miles from the main road, this lake is popular for fishing, picnicking and even swimming on warm summer days. There's also a walk around the lake (3km/1.9 miles; 45 minutes; easy). Past the turnoff for the lake, the road loops around into a meadow where elk and deer often graze. The road twists back down to complete its loop; turn left to return to Banff Town.

Festivals & Events

WINTER

Ice Magic – International Ice Sculpture Competition & Exhibition

Teams of ice carvers from around the globe transform 150kg/300lb blocks of ice into giant, elaborate sculptures along Lake Louise's shoreline during **Ice Magic** (☎ 403-762-8421; admission free; competition Jan, exhibition Jan-Mar). Carvers practice their art in Lake Louise Village, where children (and parents too!) can have a go at whittling out a shape at the Little Chippers Ice Station, Samson Mall.

Banff/Lake Louise Winter Festival

A tradition in Banff since 1916, the **Winter Festival** (☎ 403-762 0270; Banff Town, Lake Louise Village & Sunshine Village; most events free; late Jan-early Feb) is ten days of merrymaking. Comic and serious sports events, barn dances, art exhibitions and the Banff Town Party draw locals and visitors out of hibernation. Contact the Banff Tourism Bureau for information on this year's events.

SPRING

Children's Festival

Juggling, storytelling, dancing, puppets, games and workshops in everything from drumming to story writing will keep kids (and parents!) entertained during the Children's Festival (☎ 403-678-1878; W www.canmorechildrens festival.com; Canmore; event tickets free-CAD$4; May long weekend).

Banff Day

In celebration of the history of Banff, the Whyte Museum swings its door ajar for an open house on Banff Day (☎ 403-762-2291; Banff Town; free; Jun).

Touring Tin's Annual Show & Shine

Antique cars head over the mountains to Banff each year to be shown in Touring Tin (☎ 403-678-9260, 780-453-2921; recreation center, Banff Town; free; mid-Jun). Even if you don't attend the show, you'll see the cars cruising around downtown Banff.

SUMMER

Canada Day

Banff goes all out in displaying its national pride on **Canada Day** (☎ 403-762-8421; *Banff Town; Jul 1*). Check out food booths, fireworks and concerts. The RCMP Musical Ride brings in the crowds, with Mounties in red coats performing cavalry drills on horseback, just like on the postcards.

Banff Summer Arts Festival

Each summer, the Banff Centre devotes four weeks to showcasing the best its resident and visiting artists have to offer. Originating in the 1930s as a summer drama program, the **Summer Arts Festival** (☎ 403-762-6301; W *www.banffcentre.ca/bsaf; Banff Town; tickets CAD$10-20 per show; mid-Jul–mid-Aug*) has gradually expanded to include a myriad of activities and performances, including music, dance, First Nations arts, opera, theater and guided art walks. For a full schedule or to book tickets, visit the website.

AUTUMN

Banff Mountain Film Festival

Since the mid-1970s, the three-day **Film Festival** (☎ 403-762-6301; W *www.banff mountainfestivals.ca/festivals/film; Banff Centre, Banff Town; tickets/pass CAD$15-40/140; early Nov*) has celebrated the spirit of mountain adventure through films, videos and lectures. You'll also find an adventure trade show and an arts and crafts sale. Reserve tickets online.

Banff Mountain Book Festival

On the go for over a decade, the **Book Festival** (☎ 403-762-6675; W *www .banffmountainfestivals.ca/festivals/book; Banff Centre, Banff Town; tickets/pass CAD$15-30/130; late Oct/early Nov*) draws book lovers en masse. Events include presentations, readings and seminars on mountain and adventure travel books from around the world, as well as a Mountain Book Fair and Adventure Trade Show (free).

Day Hikes

Whether you're up for climbing a mountain or just stretching your legs on a quiet stroll through the woods, hiking in Banff is one of the best ways to experience its sublime beauty. Even if you're only in the park for a day or two, be sure to include at least one hike on your itinerary. Trails range from flat, easy and short (1 hour roundtrip) to longer, more strenuous endeavors. Many are excellent for families, some are wheelchair accessible, and the majority of trailheads begin from major sights. No matter what your level, there's a hike out there for you. For those looking for a multiday hike, see Backcountry Hikes (p96) later in this chapter.

While you do not require a special permit for day hikes, you do need to have a park permit to be within the park boundaries. For more information on safety when hiking, see the Activities chapter (p29).

BANFF TOWN & AROUND

Only have an hour or two to spare? Take one of these short walks for a glimpse of the park's personality.

BOW RIVER FALLS
Distance: 4.4km/2.8 miles roundtrip
Duration: 1.5 hours roundtrip
Challenge: Easy
Elevation Change: Negligible

A pleasant wander from town, you'll be impressed at just how well this trail manages to delve into the wilderness despite being surrounded by downtown Banff. From the trailhead at the Bow River Boathouse (corner of Wolf St and Bow Ave), follow the paved path downstream toward town. Stroll along the edge of **Central Park**, filled on sunny days with picnicking families, before crossing the Bow River Bridge. Continue downstream along an increasingly wooded trail with views down the river and up to some of the nearby peaks. After about 30 minutes, the trail scales a couple of wooden staircases before descending to a viewing platform from which you can take in the burbling **Bow Falls**.

As this trail crosses directly through Banff Town, it can be joined at Central Park or Bow River Bridge. The path is wheelchair accessible and popular with cyclists as far as the staircases.

FENLAND TRAIL
Distance: 2.1km/1.3 miles roundtrip
Duration: 0.5 hour roundtrip
Challenge: Easy
Elevation Change: None

This picturesque trail follows the green **Echo** and **Forty Mile Creeks** through the fenlands. Wooden bridges pass over reed-filled marshes, birds chatter in the trees, and benches en route give you a chance to soak it all in. A popular route for locals, this is a well-maintained, flat loop with only one drawback – the notso-distant sound of Hwy 1 rushing past, not entirely muffled no matter how loud the stream flows or the birds sing. Nevertheless, this trail is a very worthwhile escape from downtown if you're short on time or energy.

You can extend the walk by crossing the large bridge about halfway round the loop and heading left down the road to the **Vermillion Lakes**, a wetland that's popular with wildlife (4km/2.5 miles roundtrip).

Begin the trail at the Forty Mile Picnic Area, just north of the 'Welcome to Banff' sign on Lynx St. If you're coming from downtown on foot, there's a

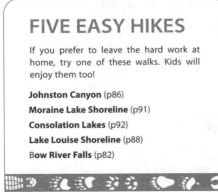

FIVE EASY HIKES

If you prefer to leave the hard work at home, try one of these walks. Kids will enjoy them too!

connecting trail on the left side of Lynx St, just over the railroad tracks. In late May and early June the trail is often closed due to aggressive female elk, who use the area for calving.

SULPHUR MOUNTAIN
Distance: 5.5km/3.41 miles to top
Duration: 2 hours up
Challenge: Difficult
Elevation Change: 655m/2150ft

A good leg (and lung) stretch, this trail zigzags back and forth across Sulphur Mountain on a steady ascent. Through the trees you catch glimpses and framed views of the surrounding peaks, and above you, the gondola pops in and out of view. About halfway up, you pass near a waterfall where the view opens up west to the snowy **Mt Rundle**. As you huff and puff your way up this mountain, remember that the endless 360° views of the Rockies from the summit are well worth the effort.

You'll find the trailhead at the end of Mountain Ave, at the northwest end of the gondola parking lot, closest to the Upper Hot Springs Pool. The tree-lined trail is well used (a daily workout for some of Banff Town's more fit residents). If you suffer vertigo, you may find the final ten minutes the most challenging; the trail grows narrow, with steep drop-offs. Once at the top, continue along a staircase to **Sanson Peak**, where you'll find a **weather station** left over from the 1900s and the most spectacular lookout. Between 1903 and 1933, meteorologist Norman Sanson hiked up this mountainside over 1000 times to check the weather.

You can hop on the gondola for a free trip back down the mountain (passengers are only charged for the trip up); if you plan to do this, double-check the time of the last lift down before you set out.

LAKE MINNEWANKA AREA
Popular with boaters, fishermen and those looking for a dose of fresh air, the Minnewanka area offers glittering lakes and majestic mountains.

C-LEVEL CIRQUE
Distance: 7.8km/4.8 miles roundtrip to cirque,
8.8km/5.4 miles roundtrip to lookout
Duration: 3 hours roundtrip to cirque, 4 hours roundtrip to lookout
Challenge: Moderate-Difficult to cirque, Difficult to lookout
Elevation Change: 455m/1493ft to cirque, 500m/1640ft to lookout

A steady ascent through peaceful, verdant forest, this hike will leave you breathless in more ways than one. After rewarding you with beautiful views south over the Bow Valley, the trail takes you directly beneath a looming peak of **Cascade Mountain**, into which is cut a natural amphitheater. If you're itching to see pika or to hear your own echo, pack your bug repellent and strap on your boots.

To reach the trailhead, follow Lake Minnewanka Rd north 3.5km/2.2 miles from Hwy 1 to the Upper Bankhead picnic area. From here the trail heads up into a forest sprinkled with wild violets in summer and teeming with mosquitoes. After 20 minutes (1km/0.6 miles) of climbing, you'll reach the shell of a concrete building. This is one of the few remnants left from the highest of the Bankhead coal mining sites (1904–22). Other telltale signs, including countless shafts and air vents, have been concealed by the forest. A number of rediscovered air vents are fenced off, but many more remain unmarked; be sure not to stray from the path lest you should land in one. The workers of the mine lived in the town of Bankhead, located back down at the bottom of the trail in the valley.

As the forest thins out nearer the top of the trail, watch for views through the trees of Banff Town, **Mt Rundle** and nearby lakes. The trail becomes narrower in places, with steep drop-offs. Eventually the path brings you through a pile of boulders where you can sit and take in the amphitheater, created by a glacier that has long since disappeared. At this near perspective, the top of the peak looks paper thin. Avalanche fall blankets the bottom of the cirque until midsummer, when a field of mountain lilies replaces it. Around you scurry ground squirrels, the occasional pika and, should you be so unlucky, wood ticks.

From here you can continue up a dirt path along the length of the theater. The trail rounds a bend and fades as it enters an area strewn with small boulders, home to countless hoary marmots. The final 20 minutes of this ascent is steep and difficult but rewards you with views back over the theater and across **Lake Minnewanka**.

AYLMER LOOKOUT
Distance: 23.2km/14.4 miles roundtrip
Duration: 7 hours roundtrip
Challenge: Difficult
Elevation Change: 560m/1837ft

This hike is a fairly tough slog with little scenery en route. Nevertheless, it's worth every bead of sweat for the incredible views at the top, stretching across Lake Minnewanka to the massive summits beyond. If you're well prepared for wood ticks, the grassy knoll of the lookout is an ideal spot to rest, picnic and enjoy the breathtaking vista.

The trailhead is located near the parking lot for Lake Minnewanka. Follow the paved road past the boat docks and picnic tables to the posted trail at the entrance to the woods. The wide, level path passes beneath the treetops and crosses the wide **Stewart Canyon Bridge** at 1.6km/1 mile. Beneath you, the green water of **Cascade River** flows through an impressive gorge.

The trail climbs up the opposite bank, branching right at the junction and bending into a few switchbacks. This area underwent a prescribed burn in 2003, leaving behind blackened trunks and encouraging lush new undergrowth. The trail soon turns rocky, with steep, precarious edges, and the forest thins and offers views of **Lake Minnewanka**; with its moody, green water and rocky shoreline, it possesses a sealike quality. A steep descent follows, and from here to the lookout, you'll catch only occasional views of the lake through the trees. The 5km/3.1 miles to Aylmer Pass Junction is fairly monotonous hiking; the trail is not difficult, though it is strewn with loose rock.

After about 1.5 hours, the forest opens up and turns to birch; cross a plank bridge over a small stream and continue for a further 15 minutes to the junction. As you head left from here, your true toil begins. Climbing north, the trail makes a steady ascent for the final 4km/2.5 miles to the lookout. A stream runs along the bottom of a gorge to your left, and over your shoulder, you'll get almost immediate but short-lived views across the lake. At 2.3km/1.4 miles, having climbed almost 600m/1968ft, you reach a junction; turn right along the narrowing path. Menacing drop-offs and some fantastic views skirt the edge of the ascending trail before it zigzags up a treeless hillside.

The trail winds behind the hill to the east and brings you up to its summit, a meadow strewn with wildflowers, the occasional sheep and the remains of old fire-lookout buildings. The captivating views before you have undoubtedly inspired many a hiker to burst into the chorus from *The Sound of Music*. The limestone cliffs of **Mt Inglismaldie** and **Mt Girourard** stand directly south, **Bow Valley** and **Mt Rundle** beckon from the southwest, and the enormous **Mt Aylmer** looms behind you. Be sure to tuck your trouser legs into your socks to deter the wood ticks that ply the meadow.

The return hike is almost entirely downhill. However, save some energy for a slippery, steep climb at around 7km/4.3 miles; it may well have escaped your notice on the way in, but it's a brutal assault on the return journey.

JOHNSON LAKE
Distance: 3km/1.86 miles roundtrip
Duration: 45 minute roundtrip
Challenge: Easy
Elevation Change: Negligible

This small, clear lake is skirted by an easy trail, providing ever-changing views of the surrounding mountain peaks. From the parking lot, follow the trail left (east). After passing a group of picnic tables, the paved trail turns to dirt; take the first branch right and the second left along the lakeside. From here, the path cuts alongside a grassy hill, which is sprinkled with bright wildflowers in summer.

As you continue following the trail around the lake, peer into its clear depths for a look at life below the water. Fish dart around tree stumps that line the lake's floor, telling of its past as a valley, before the construction of the dam on its eastern shore. The chilly waters are now a haven for rainbow trout and are also popular with boaters and the occasional brave swimmer. Also en route, watch for ancient Douglas fir trees, one of which is believed to be 700 years old and the oldest of its kind in Alberta.

To reach the lake, follow Lake Minnewanka Rd north of Hwy 1 and take the first right. The next junction is signposted right to Johnson Lake.

BOW VALLEY PARKWAY

Between Banff Town and Lake Louise, this flourishing area is home to oodles of wildlife. Popular as a driving tour (p77), it's worth getting out of your vehicle and having a wander.

JOHNSTON CANYON

Distance: 2.2km/1.4 miles to Lower Falls, 5.4km/3.5 miles to Upper Falls, 11.6km/7.2 miles to Ink Pots roundtrip
Duration: 1/2.5/5 hours roundtrip to Lower Falls/Upper Falls/Ink Pots
Challenge: Easy to Lower & Upper Falls, Moderate to Ink Pots
Elevation Change: 30m/98ft to Lower Falls, 120m/394ft to Upper Falls, 215m/705ft to Ink Pots

This popular trail takes you deep inside the lush Johnston Canyon. Below you, the clear waters of the **Johnston Creek** rush, plunge and pound against the cliffs, cutting ever deeper into the earth and carving irregular shapes into the limestone. Rising above you are the sheer canyon walls where, in even the smallest crevices, moss and ferns flourish. The path is alive with friendly ground squirrels, and you may spot the occasional water ouzel or black swift, which nest here from mid-June to late September. Trees line much of the trail, and, being both shaded and sheltered, it's a great walk to do in either the rain or the heat.

The trail takes in two sets of falls within the canyon. To the **Lower Falls**, the path is paved, relatively level and accessible to wheelchairs. Once you reach the Lower Falls, it's worth ducking through a small cave to get a closer (though wetter) look at the tumbling water.

Continuing on to the **Upper Falls**, the path becomes slightly steeper, with a few stairs. Just before the final staircase to the falls, take a detour to the right to see the unusually beautiful **Travertine Drape** – a wall of the canyon that's covered in algae and encrusted in minerals. The bridge here offers a peak at the bottom of the Upper Falls but definitely carry on to the top of the trail for a view of the falls as they dive over the edge.

From the Upper Falls the trail continues on to the **Ink Pots**. This is a backcountry trail that is far less traveled and will add a worthwhile hour and a half to your trek. The trail follows a

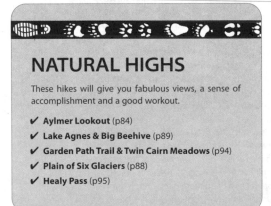

NATURAL HIGHS

These hikes will give you fabulous views, a sense of accomplishment and a good workout.

✔ **Aylmer Lookout** (p84)
✔ **Lake Agnes & Big Beehive** (p89)
✔ **Garden Path Trail & Twin Cairn Meadows** (p94)
✔ **Plain of Six Glaciers** (p88)
✔ **Healy Pass** (p95)

steady incline up through the forest and slightly inland from the creek. Eventually it opens into a vast clearing that's surrounded by remote snowy peaks and is home to the five Ink Pots, small springs of clear blue and green water. Johnston Creek runs alongside the Ink Pots, and bears have been known to drink from it; take precautions, and watch for warnings.

CASCADE AMPHITHEATRE
Distance: 6.6km/4.1miles one way
Duration: 2.5 hours one way
Challenge: Difficult
Elevation Change: 640m/2099ft

Lying beneath the limestone summit of **Cascade Mountain**, this hanging valley was cut into a natural amphitheater by long-ago glaciers. Carpeted by wildflowers in the height of summer, the peaceful valley is home to marmots and pika. While the hike up here is arduous, it promises satisfying views and a definite feeling of accomplishment.

To find the trailhead, start at the far end of parking lot number three of the Mt Norquay day lodge, at the end of Mt Norquay Rd out of Banff Town. Pass the ski lodge buildings to the north and continue along a service road. The trail passes a number of ski lifts; keep to the bottom of the valley. At the fourth and final ski run (0.8km/0.5 mile), the trail branches right (continuing north) from the Forty Mile Creek Trail, taking you behind the ski lift and entering the forest. Watch for trail markers.

Inside the forest, the trail broadens and quickly descends to **Forty Mile Creek**. Following the trail right and over the bridge, you'll soon have breathtaking views west to the sheer **Mt Louis**. To its left lie the jagged peaks of **Mt Edith**. From here the real climb begins as the trail continues up through the forest to a junction with the Elk Lake Summit Trail, at 4.3km/2.7 miles. Keep right and catch your breath for a series of brutal switchbacks that carry you 2.3km/1.4 miles up the pine-forested western slope of the mountain.

Just before arriving at the valley, the trail levels off and a number of faint paths head to the right. These lead to the ascent ridge – a dangerous climb that should only be attempted with proper equipment, topographical maps and up-to-date trail information. The main path enters an alpine meadow, sprinkled throughout the summer with a variety of wildflowers, from white anemone to yellow lilies. The trail becomes indistinct but continues for about 1km/0.6 mile to the upper end of the amphitheater, where the vegetation thins out and boulders litter the ground. Rest here for a while to see marmots and pikas scurrying between the rocks.

LAKE LOUISE & AROUND

The area surrounding Lake Louise is one of the most popular in the park for day hikes. Whether you hope to get up close to a glacier, seek panoramic vistas or want to experience a bit of Banff's remoteness, you can accomplish it here within a couple of hours.

Moraine Lake seems to be all the rage with grizzly bears; over the past few years, the bears have become rather complacent and even aggressive toward tourists. Warnings of sightings are well posted, and if danger is at all likely, restrictions are placed on hiking (such as requiring a minimum of six hikers in a party).

LAKE LOUISE LAKESHORE TRAIL
Distance: 3.8km/2.4 miles roundtrip
Duration: 1 hour roundtrip
Challenge: Easy
Elevation Change: None

The most popular walk at Lake Louise, this path offers continuous views across the lake to **Fairview Mountain**, along the southern shore, and **Victoria Glacier**, in the distant west. As you wander, you may notice the color of the lake change from pale turquoise to emerald, depending on the angle of the sun. The trail is wide, level and very well maintained, making it accessible to everyone. There are plenty of benches en route from which you can appreciate the grandeur that has made Lake Louise so famous.

At the end of the trail is a **quartz cliff wall** in all of its multicolored beauty. To reach the wall, you need to climb a flight of stairs, from which a trail continues to the marshy mouth of the river, which carries silty runoff from Victoria Glacier. While here, you may hear and then spot rock climbers training high above you on the quartz walls to your right. From the end of this trail, you can continue along the path to the **Plain of Six Glaciers**.

PLAIN OF SIX GLACIERS
Distance: 13.5km/8.4 miles roundtrip
Duration: 4 hours roundtrip
Challenge: Moderate
Elevation Change: 340m/1115ft

This hike takes you high into the mountains, affording almost constant views to snowy peaks and back down to the ever-diminishing Lake Louise. The destination? A remote lookout surrounded by giant rivers of ice. Follow the lakeshore walk 2.5km/1.6 miles, past the staircase and along the marshy river mouth.

From here, the trail takes a brief jaunt up through the forest before bringing you out into moraines with fantastic views of **Mt Lefroy** and **Mt Victoria**. This rocky terrain was shaped by Victoria Glacier as it marched down the valley. The glacier runoff flows below, sounding larger than life as it echoes against the mountainsides. You're also likely to hear the occasional rumble of rock and snowslides.

The trail continues climbing south through moraines, and although the scenery changes little, the glaciers grow ever nearer. At 3.3km/2 miles and again at 4km/2.5 miles, you'll meet trails branching off to the right.

Both lead to the **Big Beehive** and **Lake Agnes**; the second trail is the more gradual highland route. Beyond the second junction, the trail grows steeper, passing through boulder-strewn landscape and moraine ledges and eventually reaching a series of switchbacks.

After about two hours of climbing, you'll reach a tree-lined meadow and the **Plain of Six Glaciers Teahouse** (meals CAD$6; open 8am–6pm, Jun–mid-Oct) at 5.5km/3.4 miles. Built in 1927 as a halfway house for Swiss mountaineering guides, it has managed to retain much of its charm. Offering great views from the balcony, the teahouse serves up lunch, teas and hot chocolate to weary hikers. Watch out for the none-too-shy whisky jack birds, who'll fly off with your sandwich if given half a chance.

From here, it's a further 1.6km/1 mile uphill to the **Plain of Six Glaciers**. The trail is not particularly steep, but you'll have to scramble over rock and possibly snowslides amid howling winds. Although there is nothing to mark it, you'll know you've reached the **lookout** when you can see clearly back to Lake Louise, as well as the surrounding glaciers of Mt Lefroy and Mt Victoria. In the mid-1800s, Mt Victoria Glacier reigned over the terrain where you're standing. These days the lookout is covered in wildflowers in mid to late summer; in June there's still a thick layer of snow.

From the lookout, an indistinct, perilous path continues south along the top edge of a moraine; this leads to the rock face and is the territory of experienced climbers only. If you do venture out along this path for 1.3km/0.8 mile, you will have a view of Abbot Pass cutting between Mt Victoria and Mt Lefroy summits. If you look closely, you'll spot the stone **Abbot Pass Hut** at the top of Victoria Glacier. Built in 1922, it's now Canada's highest national historic site, run by the Alpine Club of Canada. The route up to this hut is about as tough as they come, passing the **Death Trap**, a steep, narrow, glacier-filled gorge. Avalanches are common here and only *very* experienced, well-equipped climbers should even consider it.

At any time of year, good shoes are a must on the Plain of Six Glaciers hike, particularly in spring and early summer, when you may have to traverse icy avalanche paths. Don't venture off the path; avalanche paths often have deep, hidden crevices nearby. It's a good idea to save this walk for a clear day when views are at their best. As it's often raining near the final lookout, be sure to take wind- and waterproof gear with you. The rocky and sometimes slippery terrain makes a walking stick a good companion.

LAKE AGNES & THE BIG BEEHIVE
Distance: 7km/4.4 miles to Lake Agnes,
10.2km/6.4 miles roundtrip to Big Beehive
Duration: 1.5 hours/3 hours roundtrip to Lake Agnes/Big Beehive
Challenge: Moderate/Difficult to Lake Agnes/Big Beehive
Elevation Change: 385m/1263ft to Lake Agnes,
520m/1706ft to Big Beehive

Sunlight filtering down through lofty treetops, gorgeous lakes hidden deep in valleys, and astonishing vistas make this one of the most beauti-

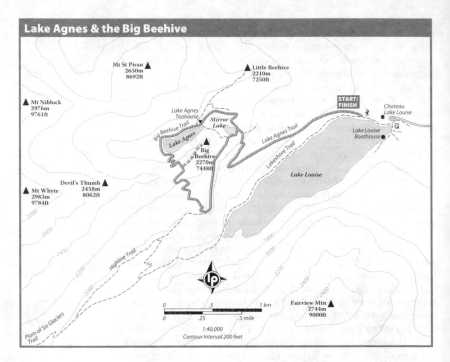

Lake Agnes & the Big Beehive

Mt St Piran
2650m
8692ft

Little Beehive
2210m
7250ft

Mt Niblock
2976m
9761ft

START/
FINISH

Chateau
Lake Louise

Lake Agnes
Teahouse

Mirror
Lake

Big Beehive Trail

Lake Agnes Trail

Lake Louise
Boathouse

Lake Agnes

Lakeshore Trail

Big
Beehive
2270m
7448ft

Lake Louise

Devil's Thumb
2458m
8062ft

Mt Whyte
2983m
9784ft

Highline Trail

Plain of Six Glaciers Trail

Fairview Mtn
2744m
9000ft

0   .5   1 km
0   .25   .5 mile

1:40,000
Contour Interval 200 feet

ful day hikes in the Rockies. If you can muster the energy, it's definitely worth continuing to the top of the Big Beehive for truly spectacular views.

From the northeast corner of the Lake Louise shoreline, the wide, even trail begins a steady (though not too steep) ascent through the forest. Watch for hares and ground squirrels bounding across the trail and for the occasional framed view back over Lake Louise. The path zigzags through the trees for about 45 minutes (2.5km/1.6 miles) before meeting up with a horse trail. Take a left and continue up the broad path for another five minutes to **Mirror Lake**. This small, round and very green body of water is crowned by the looming **Big Beehive**, which rests impressively on its far shoreline.

At Mirror Lake you are given a number of trail options. Turn left to hook up with the **Plain of Six Glaciers** walk. If you're headed for Lake Agnes or have plans to scale the Big Beehive, head right instead. While you can reach Lake Agnes via a shorter trail that runs beneath the Beehive to the left, it's arduous and takes much longer. You can also ascend Big Beehive by heading left, but it isn't as pleasant as the approach from Lake Agnes.

Heading right, the trail continues at a moderate climb for a further 15 minutes (0.8km/0.5 mile). The forest begins to thin out and reveals excellent 270° views of surrounding mountains and the striking Big Beehive. The path brings you alongside a thundering waterfall before a final staircase to Lake Agnes.

Set high in the mountains in a hanging valley and sheltered from the sun by towering stony peaks, **Lake Agnes** may still be covered in glassy ice and small icebergs if you visit in June. The Big and Small Beehives stand guard on either side while water from its clear blue depths rushes over the falls at the eastern end of the lake and into Mirror Lake, below. In 1890, Lady Susan Agnes Macdonald, the wife of then prime minister Sir John Macdonald, defied her many petticoats and made it to the shore of the lake, an event that left the lake with both a name and an enduring popularity.

You can take in the stunning scenery from the **Lake Agnes Teahouse** (*meals CAD$6; open Jun-Oct 8am-5pm*), an alpine cottage boiling up water straight from the lake to serve you teas and hot chocolate. Try the Lady Hannah tea, made from chunks of real fruit, and fill up on sandwiches or apple crumble.

From here, you can either return to Lake Louise by the same route or – for those after a challenge and better views – head for Big Beehive. Follow the trail from the teahouse along the northern shoreline of Lake Agnes. The path loops around the back of the lake, where you may have to cross over fairly flat avalanche slides or moraines. The trail then begins a short but very steep ascent of switchbacks, climbing up the southern side of the valley. This 40-minute (1.6km/1 mile) hike is difficult, but the rewards at the top are well worth the effort. Once at the summit, head left to the **Big Beehive Lookout**. This section of the trail is not clearly defined; haul yourself over the boulders to a small gazebo. From this sky-scraping vantage point you can take in the **Slate Range** to the northeast, the **Bow Valley** running southeast, and **Lake Louise** and its surrounding peaks far below you.

Returning from the lookout, pick up the trail again, turning left and descending through the forested southern side of the Beehive. This route does not give much in the way of views and may well turn your legs to jelly. Nevertheless, if you're still gung-ho once you reach the bottom, head right at the T-junction to hook up with the Plain of Six Glaciers hike. Otherwise, head left to return to Mirror Lake and descend north (right) to Lake Louise from there.

MORAINE LAKE SHORELINE TRAIL
Distance: 2.4km/1.4 miles roundtrip
Duration: 40 minute roundtrip
Challenge: Easy
Elevation Change: None

Follow this leisurely wooded trail for a peaceful walk around the western shore of Moraine Lake, with lots of opportunities to rest along the turquoise water and with clear views of the first five Wenkchemna Peaks. **Mt Fay** (Peak One) is the largest and most impressive of these and is topped with a hefty glacier.

This walk is far less crowded than the Lake Louise Shoreline Trail and exudes a bit of remoteness. While the dirt trail is fairly level and well defined, it's somewhat riddled with tree roots. A number of bridges take you over streams that trickle into the lake. Near the end of the walk, you'll reach a Y-junction in the trail; head left down to a short boardwalk that traverses the shallow water along the lake's edge. At the end of the boardwalk is the source of the lake, runoff from a dormant Wenkchemna Glacier, far up in the mountain range.

MORAINE ROCK PILE TRAIL
Distance: 0.7km/0.4 mile one way
Duration: 30 minute roundtrip
Challenge: Easy-Moderate
Elevation Change: 25m/82ft

Offering one of the most famous views in the Rockies, this short walk begins to the east of the parking lot, crossing a bridge and following the same initial route as the trail to **Consolation Lake**. At the top of the rocky hill, turn right and follow the steps as they wind their way up the rock pile. Signs along the way describe the area's past life as an ancient seabed, with **fossils** en route to prove it.

The views you behold from the top of the rock pile inspired early adventurer Walter Wilcox to write: "No scene had ever given me an equal impression of inspiring solitude and rugged grandeur" (1899). **Moraine Lake** lies below you, named on behalf of the very rock pile (or moraine) beneath your feet. The **Wenkchemna Peaks**, circling the lake, each rise to over 3000m/10,000ft, and from **Twenty Dollar View** you can gain a view that was carried on the back of the Canadian twenty-dollar bill from 1969 to 1986.

While this walk is not particularly difficult, it offers no shade and does require you to haul yourself up a flight of rock-slab steps. Don't forget your walking shoes and hat.

CONSOLATION LAKES
Distance: 5.8km/3.6 miles roundtrip
Duration: 1 hour 40 minute roundtrip
Challenge: Easy-Moderate
Elevation Change: 65m/213ft

For little effort, this hike offers some of the area's most spectacular views. While well traveled, it nonetheless retains a feeling of remoteness, leaving you with the impression that you dove deep into the heart of Banff.

Heading east from the parking lot (on the Moraine Rock Pile Trail), the path crosses a small bridge and heads up over a small rocky hill. About 50 million years ago, this area was covered by sea; today you can still see the work of the sand and water, which left ripples carved into many of the stones alongside the trail. At the top of the hill, turn left and descend to the foot of a giant rockslide, which was left behind by a receding glacier. Only 10 minutes from the parking lot, you'll already find fabulous views up the side of **Mt Babel** and back over the shoreline peaks of Moraine Lake. The trail crosses over the moraine; hop from boulder to boulder, heading east in the direction of the trees.

At the edge of the forest, the trail becomes a clearly marked dirt path that continues up into the woods. Eventually the path runs alongside the lively **Babel Creek**; you'll hear it first, and then, with views down to the left, you'll see it, cloaked in foam and mist.

The end of the trail brings you out into a huge valley that was long ago carved by ice into a perfect 'U' shape. Boulders of every size fill both the shoreline and mouth of the retreating creek. Perch yourself on one, or clamor over them to the lakeside, to take in the surrounding ring of towering peaks. The **Panorama Ridge** and **Mt Bell** lie to the left, **Mt Quadra**, **Bident Mountain** and **Mt Fay** are the iced giants to the south and **Mt Babel** climbs up to the right. Looking downstream, you'll see **Mt Temple** draped across in the skyline. Huge, thick layers of snow rest on the upper reaches of the peaks, threatening to tumble down.

The area around Consolation Lake is a popular bear hangout; watch for warnings and take precautions (like five friends).

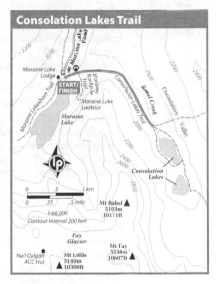

Consolation Lakes Trail

SUNSHINE MEADOWS

Following the Great Divide, Sunshine Meadows are 15km/9.3 miles of alpine and subalpine meadowland. A favorite haunt of flower spotters, this area blooms with an amazing variety of wildflowers each summer. Trails in the area have been widened and are well maintained in hopes that hikers won't wander off the path and damage the fragile terrain.

At the center of the area is Sunshine Village, a popular ski village and the trailhead for many of the area's hikes. The gondola from Bourgeau Parking Lot to the village no longer operates in summer. Instead, the **Sunshine Village Shuttle** (☎ 403-678-4099; **W** www.canadiannatureguides.com; CAD$18 roundtrip; depart 9:30am, 10:30am, 11:30am & 1:30pm, return hourly from 1-5pm, Jun-late Sep) climbs the dusty access road. It may seem pricey for a trip in a stuffy, yellow school bus, but it beats hiking up the road.

PEAK EXPERIENCE

By 1898, the Canadian Pacific Railway (CPR) knew it had to do something to keep mountaineering enthusiasts boarding its trains for the Rockies. One climber had already fallen to a tragic death, and it seemed inevitable that more would follow.

Enter Edward Feuz, Jr (1884–1981). Hailing from Switzerland, Edward and some of his fellow countrymen were hired by the CPR for their reputed ability to lead people skillfully and safely through the mountains. Edward was one of the first Swiss guides in the Rockies and was the first person to stand atop 70 Canadian peaks. During his 50-year career, he led over 100 new routes and never once lost a climber.

When visiting Lake Louise, take a look across the water to the towering Mt Victoria. Edward scaled this peak one last time in 1981 and then hung up his hiking boots for good. Not that anyone could blame him – he was 85, after all.

There is a trail from the parking lot to Wolverine ski lift (about halfway to the village), but you have to ford a stream numerous times and still end up hiking for one hour up the dust-clogged road. Tickets for the shuttle are available at the gondola station, or you can catch the first shuttle from Banff Town at 8:45am.

GARDEN PATH TRAIL & TWIN CAIRNS MEADOW
Distance: 4.2km/2.6 miles to Larix Lake;
**   8.3km/5.1 miles roundtrip via Twin Cairns Meadow loop**
Duration: 3.5 hours roundtrip via Twin Cairns Meadow loop
Challenge: Easy-Moderate
Elevation Change: 185m/607ft

From Sunshine Village, you don't have to hike far before the chairlifts and ski runs disappear into the background and you enter an enchanted area of alpine meadow, glassy lakes and magnificent views. While the landscape is wide open for the majority of the hike, it's far from barren, with bright wildflowers, peculiar tree islands and countless ground squirrels bouncing across the meadows.

To find the trailhead, turn right out of the lodge and head up the hill to a log cabin on your left; the trail begins immediately behind this cabin, from which it climbs a steady but moderately graded hill for 10 minutes. At the first fork, keep right. At the top of the hill, you enter the alpine meadows –

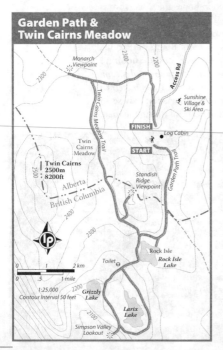

sprinkled with buttercups and white-flowered mountain avens. This area is home to a colony of **Columbian ground squirrels**; you'll see them darting underfoot as they head for their homes, which pock the landscape.

You soon reach the provincial divide and cross into British Columbia and Kootenay Park; keep right at this junction and follow the trail around a bend to **Rock Isle Lake**. As with each of the lakes you'll encounter along this trail, Rock Isle Lake seems to appear out of nowhere. Just above the lake, a short boardwalk to the left takes you to a **lookout** with views of **Standish Ridge** to the right, **Quartz Hill** to the left and, far in the distance, the peaks of **The Monarch** and **Mt Shanks**. In the center of the lake, the tiny **Rock Isle** is dotted with miniature trees and challenges your perspective as you follow the trail around the lakeshore.

Continue west along the trail, steering left at the next two junctions so that you continue along the western side of Rock Isle Lake. At the southwestern shore, the trail once again turns west and descends below the lake's water level. From here, the trail more or less flattens out as it winds into a picturesque, thin forest. Plank bridges cross crystal-clear streams bedded with brightly colored pebbles.

At the next junction, keep right and continue west to nearby **Grizzly Lake**, which is unusual for the gold and green streaks of color running through it. The trail follows the lake's eastern shore before reentering the forest. The next stop is **Simpson Valley Lookout**, just off the trail on the right, which is not to be missed for its breathtaking vista of the valley winding its way through snowcapped mountains and disappearing over the far horizon.

The trail then heads east, emerging from the forest and skirting deep green **Larix Lake** before climbing north to the junction. Keep right and return to Rock Isle Lake. While you can return to Sunshine Village the way you came, a far better option is to head back via **Twin Cairns Meadows**. This route involves only a slight climb, is but a few steps longer and is by far the more scenic choice. Follow Rock Isle Lake to its northern shore and take the first junction left.

The trail climbs for 0.5km/0.3 mile, with views back down to three lakes. If you're really gung-ho, take a right at the top of the hill and climb on for 0.5km/0.3 mile to **Standish Ridge Viewpoint**, where you can gaze down over Sunshine Valley, chairlifts and all. Back on the main trail, the grade levels off and you continue through a rolling, flower-strewn meadow hugged closely between **Standish Ridge** and **Twin Cairns**. After 2km/1.2 miles you reach a T-junction; take a short detour left to **Monarch Viewpoint** (100m) and views of **Mt Assiniboine**. The trail heading right from the junction returns back down to Sunshine Village (1.6km/1mile) via a pleasant, sparsely wooded trail.

HEALY PASS
Distance: 18.4km/11.4 miles roundtrip
Duration: 6 hours roundtrip
Challenge: Moderate-Difficult
Elevation Change: 655m/2148.4ft

Ideal for flower lovers, this hike unveils lush meadows and an uninterrupted vista of peaks and lakes. Beginning from Bourgeau parking lot, at the end of Sunshine Rd, you'll find the trailhead behind the base station, to the right. The initial, bulldozed service road is not particularly pleasant and climbs for 0.8km/0.5 mile before the Healy Pass Trail branches right into the forest. From here the trail ascends steadily (though not particularly steeply) along **Healy Creek Valley**, canopied by spruce and fir trees. At 3km/1.9 miles, the trail crosses **Healy Creek** and carries on to Healy Creek Campground at 5.5km/3.4 miles. Catch your breath; the 2km/1.2 mile climb from here to the meadows is somewhat steeper.

The forest opens up, and the trail levels off into a more gradual climb as it enters the open meadows, alive with wildflowers throughout July and August and dotted with alpine larch. The junction for Simpson Pass

Trail will appear on the left; continue ahead for a further 1.5km/0.9 mile to **Healy Pass**. At 2330m/7644ft, atop an escarpment called **Monarch Ramparts**, this pass offers truly magnificent views. Less than 1km/0.6 mile away from the Great Divide, mountains encircle you. To your left (southeast) is the distinct peak of **Mt Assiniboine**, soaring above the surrounding summits. Ahead of you, and not nearly so far away, stands **The Monarch**, identifiable by its pyramid shape. To your right (west) you'll see **Egypt Lake** and **Scarab Lake**, shining brightly beneath the **Pharaoh Peaks**, and behind you looms the aptly named **Massive Range**.

Backcountry Hikes

For true adventurers, nothing beats an overnight backcountry trip into the wilds of Banff. Hikes vary in length (from two days to the better part of a month) and in difficulty. As long as you're reasonably fit and realistic about your ability, you'll have no problem finding a hike. If you are traveling alone, Friends of Banff keeps a list of independent hikers looking for groups to head into the backcountry with. See Activities (p29) for more information on when to go, what to pack, backcountry camping and safety.

PERMITS

For overnight stays in the backcountry, you require a wilderness pass (CAD$8 per night per adult over 16 years) to camp. Reservations (☎ 800-748-7275) are recommended, as Parks Canada limits the number of hikers on each trail. You will be required to show your pass to any wardens you encounter on the trail.

Parks Canada also operates a voluntary safety registration program. If you do not return by your specified date, a search party will be initiated. While registration is voluntary, you must report back immediately upon your return or face legal action.

BACKCOUNTRY CAMPING

With 53 backcountry campgrounds, Banff is well suited for adventurers. Backcountry campgrounds are basic, with facilities limited to cleared sites, tent pads and pit toilets. Some of the most popular and better-developed campgrounds include **Fish Lake**, **Egypt Lake** and **Aylmer Pass Junction**. Random camping areas have no facilities.

You are only permitted to camp in campsites you've registered for when purchasing your wilderness pass and can only stay at each site for a maximum of three days. If you are registered at a random camping area, pitch your tent at least 50m/164ft from the trail and 70m/230ft from any water source.

BACKCOUNTRY LODGING

If you're eager to get out into the backcountry but don't fancy the idea of hauling your home around with you, there are other options in Banff.

Shelters

Parks Canada operates two backcountry trail shelters (CAD$5 per night), one at **Egypt Lake** and another at **Bryant Creek**. Both are extremely rustic and offer little more than a roof over your head. You'll still need to be completely self-sufficient, with your own bedding, food and cooking equipment. Book the shelters when you purchase your wilderness pass. Reservations can be made up to three months in advance, and there is a maximum stay of three nights.

Alpine Club of Canada's Huts

Ranging from portacabins to historic log and stone huts, the Alpine Club of Canada's backcountry huts offer a little more comfort in stunning surroundings. Although you must supply bedding and food, huts are equipped with Coleman stoves and lights (though not always propane), mattresses and cooking utensils. You must pack out all garbage and supply your own toilet paper, matches and dishcloth.

Reservations are required at all huts and can be made through the **Alpine Clubhouse** (☎ 403-678-3200; **w** www.alpineclubofcanada.ca; PO Box 8040, Indian Flats Rd, Canmore; CAD$9-24 per night, under 16 yrs half price). Visa and MasterCard are accepted. You are also required to have a Parks Canada wilderness pass. Nonmembers can reserve up to one month in advance. You are often given a lock combination for the hut when making your reservation.

The historic **Abbot Pass Hut** (Map 1; Mt Victoria; sleeps 24; summer access only) is perched atop an extremely difficult climb but rewards hikers with propane- and wood-burning stoves. **Castle Mountain Hut** (Map 1; Castle Mountain; sleeps 6; summer access only) is popular with rock climbers for the nearby limestone routes but can only be reached by a technical climb. Reaching both **Neil Colgan Hut** (Map 1; Valley of the Ten Peaks; summer/winter sleeps 18/16; open summer & winter) and **Scott Duncan Hut** (Map 8; Wapta Icefield; sleeps 12; open summer & winter) requires you to be adept and equipped for glacier travel.

The Alpine Club also operates huts along the Icefields Parkway (p134).

Lodges

There are two commercial lodges in Banff's backcountry, so you can reward yourself with the comforts of home after a long day's hike. You are still required to purchase a wilderness pass, and reservations are mandatory.

Skoki Lodge (Map 1; ☎ 403-522-3555; **w** www.skilouise.com/skoki; adult/child aged 5-12 CAD$120/60, including meals) is the highest guest lodge in the Canadian Rockies. At 2165m/7100ft, it commands a lofty view across the Skoki Valley, northeast of Lake Louise. Guests hike the 14.7km/9.1 miles to the lodge in summer and cross-country ski there in winter.

Shadow Lake Lodge (Map 1; ☎ 403-762-0116; **w** www.brewsteradventures.com; CAD$150 per person, including all meals; open late Jun–late Sep) has 12 snug cabins set amidst the trees near the large Shadow Lake. Hike or bike the 13.2km/8.2 miles to the lodge in summer or ski in winter. Once there you'll be plied with tasty meals and can explore on one of the many day hikes.

BACKCOUNTRY TRAILS

There are countless trails that will wind and carry you into Banff's backcountry. Below are three of the more popular and scenic routes to give you a taste of what's on offer. For more information on these and other hikes, visit Parks Canada or pick up a specialist guide in backcountry hiking. All of the backcountry campgrounds listed in the hikes below have basic cleared sites, tent pads, food-storage cables and pit toilets.

EGYPT LAKE
Distance: 26.4km/16.4 miles roundtrip
Duration: 2-4 days roundtrip, depending on side trips
Challenge: Moderate-Difficult
Elevation Change: 655m/2148.4ft

The hike to Egypt Lake via Healy Pass is one of the most scenic and most popular backcountry hike in Banff. Set in a high valley near the Continental Divide, the area has sparkling alpine lakes and is blanketed in wildflowers in the height of summer, and autumn is popular for its blaze of color. The hike is not particularly strenuous, and Egypt Lake is a great base for excellent half-day hikes. Unfortunately the campground can get crowded and generally reaches full capacity all summer long; be sure to reserve as far in advance as possible.

The trailhead begins from Bourgeau Gondola parking lot, at the end of Sunshine Rd, and follows the 9.2km/5.7 mile route to **Healy Pass** (p95). This three-hour trail takes you through forest and meadowland and opens up into a vast 360° view.

From Healy Pass, the trail continues northwest and heads down into the forest, where, at 3km/1.9 miles, you'll pass **Pharaoh Creek**. A little further on, you pass a trail on the right to **Egypt Lake Warden Cabin**, then cross a bridged creek into a meadow, where you'll find **Egypt Lake Campground** and shelter. **Egypt Lake** is a further 0.8km/0.5 mile southwest along the level Whistling Pass Trail, branching left after 0.5km/0.3 mile. With green, calm water, the lake is skirted with forest and is watched over by the **Pharaoh Peaks**.

Egypt Lake and the many peaks, meadows and smaller lakes surrounding it were pinpointed as the area's most "outstanding … for scenic charm and interest" in the Canadian Rockies by surveyor AO Wheeler, founder of the Alpine Club of Canada. Most people spend a couple days enjoying half-day hikes in the area. The most popular is the rather difficult trail to **Whistling Pass** (3.3km/2 miles one way), which zigzags for 1.9km/1.2 miles up through the forest, southwest from the campground. After crossing over a number of rockslides, the trail rolls out into a meadow from which you can hang a left for a side trip to **Scarab** and **Mummy Lakes** (2.8km/17.4 miles roundtrip). The trail continues to climb from the junction, reaching the rocky pass, with its breathtaking views across the eastern side of the Great Divide. On your right stands **Haiduk Peak** and on your left the **Pharaoh Peaks**. Ahead of you lies the glacier-roofed **Mt Ball** and **Haiduk Lake**. The pass is named for the whistling hoary marmots that you may hear echoing across the valley.

LAKE MINNEWANKA
Distance: 59km/36.6 miles roundtrip to Devil's Gap
Duration: 2-5 days roundtrip, depending on side trips
Challenge: Moderate
Elevation Change: 45m/148ft

You don't need to be a mountaineer to take on this hike and, because it's open earlier and later in the season than most hikes, it's a good choice for a relatively easy backcountry experience. With numerous campgrounds en route, you can adjust your route length to match your ability.

Follow the trail to **Aylmer Lookout** (p84) from the Lake Minnewanka parking lot to the Aylmer Lookout junction (two hours). Many people begin the hike late in the day and spend the first night in the wooded **Aylmer Pass Junction Campground**, near the shores of the lake. Another option is to begin early, set up camp at the junction and tackle the difficult side trip to Aylmer Lookout for some spectacular views.

From Aylmer Junction, the nearly level trail continues along the shoreline and opens into meadows that are scattered with colorful dryland wildflowers in summer. You'll pass a number of campgrounds along the way, including **Aylmer Canyon** (9.3km/5.8 miles), **Mt Inglismaldie Campground** (11.1km/6.9 miles) and **Mt Costigan Campground** (18.8km/11.7 miles). Each is set near the lake, with a rocky beach. Near the eastern end of Lake Minnewanka is **Narrows Campground**, where many hikers choose to spend their second night.

From the Narrows, continue east along the trail to the first **Ghost Lake**. The trail follows its northern shoreline to a small channel that connects it to the second **Ghost Lake**. Be prepared to get a little wet as you ford the channel to the south shore. Continue east into **Devil's Gap** and the boundary of Banff Park. Upon returning, you can either camp at **Ghost Lakes Campground**, on the south side of the channel, or continue back to Narrows or Mt Costigan Campground.

MT ASSINIBOINE & LAKE MAGOG FROM SUNSHINE VILLAGE
Distance: 57.6km/35.8 miles roundtrip
Duration: 4-5 days, depending on side trips
Challenge: Moderate-Difficult
Elevation Change: 44m/144ft

This backcountry hike will take you into Mt Assiniboine Park, where the 'Matterhorn of the Canadian Rockies' reigns over Lake Magog. The area is filled with alpine meadows and brightly colored glacial lakes, making it an excellent place to both explore on day trips and to rest up for the hike out.

While the shorter trail via Bryant's Creek is the traditional way to reach the Mt Assiniboine area, its poorer views, heavy commercial use and grizzly bear activity have hikers heading down the trail from Sunshine Village as an alternative. This route is far more scenic, offering excellent wide-open views along the Great Divide, and you'll hardly notice the extra 3km/1.9 miles among all the peace and quiet.

Day 1: Sunshine Village to Porcupine Campground *(4 hours, 13.7km/8.5 miles)* Begin the hike from Sunshine Village; it's definitely worth taking the shuttle up to the village to shave a dusty 5.7km/3.5 miles from the start of your day. Follow the **Garden Path Trail** (p94) up over the rocky hill and into the meadow, taking the junction left at 1.3km/0.8 mile toward Citadel Pass. The trail gives you a brief 1km/0.6

mile jaunt through British Columbia before reentering Alberta. Head downhill through a thin forest, cross a small meadow and begin a steep climb that takes you up to the summit of **Quartz Hill** (5.3km/3.3 miles). From here there is a long view of meadows and forest that lie between **Citadel Peak** to the right and **Fatigue Mountain** to the left. The trail descends to **Howard Douglas Lake**, on whose shore you'll find **Douglas Lake Campground**. The trail continues southeast to **Citadel Pass**, crossing between Citadel Peak and Fatigue Mountain before descending into **Golden Valley**. At 12.5km/7.8 miles the trail meets a junction; to reach **Porcupine Campground** (where most hikers spend their first night) head right, continuing down into the valley for a further 0.5km/0.3 mile. If you opt not to stop at this campground, head left at the junction into the Valley of the Rocks (see Day 2).

Day 2: Porcupine Village to Lake Magog *(6 hours, 15.1km/9.4 miles)* From Porcupine Campground, head southeast, keeping to the left at the first junction. This path will bring you back onto the main trail and into the aptly named **Valley of the Rocks**. The enormous boulders that crowd this lengthy valley are left over from a long-ago rockslide. The valley ends at **Og Lake** (22.2km/13.8 miles), where you'll find another campground. Continuing south, the trail gradually climbs through the open **Og Meadows**, scattered with wildflowers. You'll come to a junction with a trail heading left; keep to the right, where you'll be egged on by continuous views to **Mt Assiniboine**. A second four-way junction follows immediately after; again continue ahead. From here there are a number of signposted trails taking you east to **park headquarters** and southwest to **Lake Magog Campground** near the shores of the lake. There are a few accommodations options here; see **Mt Assiniboine Provincial Park** (p127).

Day 3-5: Day trips and return routes There are a number of day trips in Mt Assiniboine Park, including **Assiniboine Pass** (4.2km/2.6 miles roundtrip), **Ferro Pass** (21.4km/13.3 miles roundtrip) and **Wedgwood Lake** (14.8km/9.2 miles roundtrip). Ask at the park headquarters for details. You can return from the area via the same route over Citadel Pass to Sunshine Village, or you can head back by way of the Bryant Creek. For details on this route, contact Parks Canada.

Other Activities

Banff is a giant playground for outdoor enthusiasts. Many trails are geared for biking and horseback riding, most lakes are open to fishing and canoeing, and rock climbers are drawn to Banff like a magnet.

Many commercial businesses gear activities toward children and beginners, so if you've always wanted to trek on horseback, bounce over the rapids of a rushing river or find out what fly-fishing is all about, now's your chance.

CYCLING

Pick up a *Mountain Biking and Cycling Guide* from Parks Canada for details on bike-friendly trails in Banff Park. The majority of trails are open to bikes, particularly around Banff Town, but they're also shared with horse groups and hikers. The biking season is generally from mid-May to early October.

Popular routes around Banff Town include **Sundance** (7.4km/4.6 miles roundtrip) and **Spray River Loop** (12.5km/7.8 mile), both recommended for families. **Spray River & Goat Creek** (19km/11.8 miles one way) is a moderate ride, and **Rundle Riverside** (14km/8.7 miles one way) is a more challenging, rolling trail with rough root riding.

In the Lake Louise area, families can head for the gentle **Bow River Loop** (7.1km/4.4 miles). **Tramline** (9km/5.6 miles roundtrip) follows the historic tramway route (1912–1930) from Lake Louise train station to the lakeside. **Moraine Lake Highline** (20km/12.4 miles), the most demanding bike ride in the area, climbs the side of Mt Temple before descending to Moraine Lake. This route is closed from mid to late summer, when grizzly bears are given free rein to search for buffalo berries.

A number of commercial companies run mountain bike tours in Banff:

Snow Tips/Bactrax *(Map 2; ☎ 403-762-8177; w www.snowtips-bactrax.com; Bear St, Banff Town)* runs tours of Vermillion Lakes, Tunnel Mountain Rd, Bow Falls and the Lake Minnewanka Loop.

The Ski Stop *(Map 2; ☎ 403-762-5333; w www.theskistop.com; Bear St, Banff Town)* offers the same tours on a per hour basis, allowing you to travel at your own pace.

Giddy Goat Adventures *(☎ 403-609-9992; w www.giddygoatadventures.com)* will pick you and your bike up for trips to Goat Creek Trail or Kicking Horse Resort for a serious adrenaline rush.

If you're bikeless but up for adventuring out on your own, there are plenty of bike rental operations in Banff Town. For a full list of outfitters, ask at the Banff Information Center in town.

The Ski Stop *(see previous list)* rents town bikes (hr/day CAD$7/15), full suspension bikes (hr/day CAD$10/35), kids' bikes (hr/day CAD$4/14), child trailers and car bike racks.

Snow Tips/Bactrax *(see previous list)* rents town (hr/day CAD$8/30), trail (hr/day CAD$10/36) and front suspension bikes (hr/day CAD$12/42), as well as kids' bikes and carriers.

CANOEING & KAYAKING

Canoeing and kayaking are peaceful ways to experience the park and watch wildlife. The season runs from about mid-May to early October, depending on spring thaws and autumn weather conditions.

Vermillion Lakes is the most popular area to take to the water; this marshland has an abundance of wildfowl, muskrat, elk, beaver and sheep passing through it. The winding stretch of Bow River upstream from Banff Town is popular for kayaking, and Johnson Lake is a pleasant place for a float.

At both Lake Louise and Moraine Lake, where you can rent boats, private crafts are not permitted. **Lake Louise Boathouse** *(Map 1; CAD$32 per hr; open 10am-7pm Jun-mid Oct)* rents canoes big enough for three adults or two adults and two kids (total 22kg/55lbs), as does **Moraine Lake Boathouse** *(Map 1; CAD$27 per hr; open 9am-4pm Jun-Oct)*. Both boathouses include mandatory life jackets in their price.

Bow River Canoe Rental *(Map 2; cnr Bow Ave & Wolf St, Banff Town; hr/day CAD$16/40)* rents out canoes for paddles up the Bow River and through Vermillion Lakes.

Lake Minnewanka Boat Tours (p103) is a good option if you'd like to cruise the waters without the workout.

WHITE-WATER RAFTING & FLOAT TRIPS

Whether you're a novice, have the kids in tow or are after some serious rapids, you shouldn't have difficulty finding a river rafting trip in Banff. Companies listed below offer trips (CAD$60 to $100) for the mildly adventurous to the daring, as well as float (child/youth/adult from CAD$20/30/40) and family trips.

Canadian Rockies Rafting Company (☎ 403-678-6535; **w** www.rafting.ca) includes the chance to go cliff jump and bodysurfing on all tours.

Wild Water Adventures (☎ 403-522-2211; u www.wildwater.com) also runs two-day heli-rafting trips (CAD$149).

Inside Out Experience (☎ 403-949-3305; u www.insideoutexperience.com)

Hydra (☎ 403-762-4554; **w** www.raftbanff.com)

Rocky Mountain Raft Tours (☎ 403-762-3632; canoe docks, cnr Wolf & Bow, Banff Town)

CLIMBING

With all of those mountains and cliff faces, it's not surprising that climbing is a popular sport in Banff. The terrain is tough, made all the more difficult by ever-changing weather conditions. Novices should not venture out alone, and even experienced climbers should talk to locals before taking to the mountains.

Banff Adventure Centre *(Map 2; ☎ 403-762-8536; **w** www.mountainguide.com; 224 Bear St, 2nd floor of Mountain Magic Equipment; open daily 9am-9pm)* offers half-day trips (CAD$69) for those who've never given the sport a go and multiday climbs (CAD$240 to $530) for those with a little to a lot of experience. Instruction and all gear are included. In summer, an indoor evening class for absolute beginners (admission free; 7pm to 9pm Thursday) is held.

CMH Mountaineering (☎ 800-661-0252; **w** www.cmhmountaineering.com) puts together unbelievable climbing trips for beginning to advanced climbers. Think helicopters and first ascents up unnamed peaks, spires and glaciers.

Yamnuska (☎ 403-678-4164; **w** www.yamnuska.com) also offers half (CAD$225; 3 hours), full (CAD$340; 6 hours) and multiday climbs. If you bring along some friends (maximum four climbers), the rates decrease considerably. All equipment is included.

HORSEBACK RIDING

Horses are permitted on many of the backcountry trails in Banff; get a copy of *The Horse Users Guide* from Parks Canada for details.

If you didn't bring along your own horse, **Warner Guiding and Outfitting** *(Map 2; ☎ 800-661-8352; **w** www.horseback.com; 132 Banff Ave, Banff Town)* can help you out with a huge range of tours, including covered-wagon cookouts (CAD$63), explorer day rides (CAD$135) and two- to six-day backcountry lodge and tenting trips.

Timberline Tours (☎ 888-858-3388; **w** www.banff.net/timberline; Lake Louise Village) run 1½-hour (CAD$45) to full-day (CAD$120) rides and overnight trips (three to 10 days), and pony rides for tots. Tours take in trails around Lake Louise, including the Plain of Six Glaciers and Lake Agnes.

Also worth contacting is the **Alberta Outfitters Association** (☎ 800-742-5548; W *www.albertaoutfitters.com*), which produces a membership directory with details of outfitters in the Banff area.

GOLF

You can golf with the pros and the elk at **Banff Springs Golf Course** (Map 2; ☎ 403-762-6801; W *www.fairmont.com; 18-holes/tunnel 9 CAD$160/50; open May-Oct*). Established in 1928, this top course rests below the shadow of Mt Rundle and Sulphur Mountain. You'll need to dress up for the occasion; no denim, no sweats, dress shorts only and collared shirts for men. Shoe and club rentals are available.

RANGER PROGRAMS

Friends of Banff National Park (☎ 403-762-8911; W *www.friendsofbanff.com; The Bear & Butterfly, 214 Banff Ave, Banff Town*) runs a free summer program with guided walks and children's events and activities. Many of the evening events take place at Tunnel Mountain Campground, Two Jack Lakeside Campground and Johnston Canyon Campground. For full details of the program, contact Friends of Banff.

FISHING

There are a number of options for fishing in Banff Park, but be sure you're up on your fish-identification skills and know the current quotas (available from Parks Canada) before heading out. Fly-fishing is particularly popular in Banff; the season runs from around June to September, with the end of July being the top time.

Lake Minnewanka is the only lake within the park where motorized boats are permitted, and it is popular for lake fishing. **Lake Minnewanka Boat Tours** (☎ 403-762-3473; W *www.minnewankaboattours.com; 1st hr/additional hr CAD$32/12 including gear; mid May–early Sep*) will whiz you around the lake in a cushy cabin cruiser in search of trout.

Banff Fishing (☎ 403-762-4936; W *www.banff-fishing.com*) offers year-round fly-fishing, spin-casting and lake-trout fishing. They also do ice fishing and lessons for beginners. Prices depend on the group size and level of instruction needed.

Alpine Anglers (☎ 403-762-8223; W *alpineanglers.com; half day from CAD$375, full day CAD$440–500 including gear*) offers float trips on the Bow River in search of trout and Walk & Wade trips to small mountain streams. All fishing with this company is catch-and-release.

Other companies worth checking out are **Hawqwild Flyfishing Guides** (☎ 403-760-2446; W *www.flyfishingbanff.com; half/full day US$199/249*), **Adventures Unlimited** (Map 2; ☎ 403-762-4554; W *www.banffadventures.com; 211 Bear St, Banff Town; CAD$350–495*) and **Tightline Adventures** (☎ 403-762-4548; W *www.tightline adventures.com; CAD$350–495*). With all three companies, rates get cheaper with additional anglers. All offer instruction, gear and lunch.

Winter Activities

While the onset of cold temperatures brings hiking, biking and canoeing to a virtual halt, the arrival of snow draws a whole new crowd of adventurers to the park. With world-class slopes, Banff is a North American hotspot for skiers and snowboarders.

DOWNHILL SKIING & SNOWBOARDING

Banff is home to three well-known, well-loved ski and snowboarding resorts, and you may well find yourself unable to decide which one sounds best. Don't despair; the **Tri-Area Lift Pass** (☎ 403-762-4561; 3-day pass adult/child/senior CAD$186/64/164) gives you access to Mt Norquay, Lake Louise and Sunshine Village, as well as free shuttles to the mountains and a free night's skiing at Mt Norquay. Passes are available from three to 14 days, and some packages include lessons and accommodations.

If you don't fancy standing in line for skis at the resorts, head over to **Snow Tips** (Map 2; ☎ 403-762-8177; www.snowtips-bactrax.com; 225 Bear St, Banff Town; adult/shild ski package CAD$16–35/9, adult/child snowboard package CAD$25–28/20; open 7am-9pm daily) the night before. Discounts are available for multiday rentals.

Mt Norquay (Map 1; ☎ 403-762-4421; W www.banffnorquay.com; Mt Norquay Access Rd; full day adult/youth/child/senior CAD$49/38/16/38; open Nov–May) Its first ski runs were cut in 1926, and Norquay has had thrill seekers gliding down its slopes ever since. Located 6km/3.7 miles north of Banff Town, Norquay is smaller than its two rivaling ski resorts (30 runs), but it has lots of adrenaline-rushing black runs and snowboarding terrain park. Skiing and snowboarding lessons are available for all ages and levels. Special lift rates are available for hourly, afternoon, night skiing (Friday, January through March) and multiday skiing.

Lake Louise (Map 1; ☎ 403-522-3555; W www.skilouise.com; full day adult/student/child/senior CAD$61/50/15/50; open Nov–May) With four mountain faces and over 100 runs, you could ski Lake Louise for a week and still not see all of the runs. Blue and/or green runs can be found from every chairlift, as well as lots of powder, bowl skiing and super steeps for pros. And, of course, the views are fabulous. Day care, skiing and snowboarding classes, ski rentals and half-day rates are all available.

Sunshine Village (Map 1; ☎ 877-542-2633; W www.skibanff.com; adult/student/child/senior CAD$63/50/21/50) Favored by mother nature, Sunshine Village always seems to get a lot of snow. Ski through lots of powder on 90 runs across three mountains. You'll also find the Silver Bullet snowboard park, skiing and snowboarding classes, day care and rentals. Half-day rates are also available.

CROSS-COUNTRY SKIING

Cross-country skiing is a wonderful, peaceful way to get out and explore independently in winter. Slide along over 80km/50 miles of trails that Parks Canada maintains for the pursuit between December and March. There are lots of popular trails near Banff Town, including the **Spray River Loop, Cave & Basin Trail, Cascade Fire Rd** and the **Banff Springs Golf Loop**, great for beginners. From Lake Louise Village, head out along **Moraine Lake Rd** or the **Lake Louise Shoreline Trail**.

Always check with Parks Canada to see which trails are currently open; they'll also be able to recommend trails further afield. You can rent cross-country skis at all three ski resorts, as well as at **Snow Tips** (see Downhill Skiing).

OTHER WINTER ACTIVITIES

Strapping on a pair of **snowshoes** and heading out into the wilds can be an invigorating experience. Ask at Parks Canada for current trail information. Rent your snowshoes at **Snow Tips** (see Downhill Skiing) or join a tour with **Discover Banff Tours** (Map 2; ☎ 403-760-5007; W www.banfftours.com; Sundance Mall, 215 Banff Ave).

Early in the season, before the snow really heaps up, you can **ice-skate** on Lake Louise, where the Fairmont Lake Louise Chateau grooms a small area. You can also skate on Vermillion Lakes but should ask at Parks Canada first to ensure it's safe.

If you can't bear to put your climbing equipment away for the winter, **Yamnuska** (p102) runs **ice-climbing** courses in the winter. **Discover Banff Tours** offers guided **ice walks** and will take you out **dogsledding**.

Places to Stay

With over 3600 hotel rooms and 2254 campsites, you wouldn't think that finding a place to stay in Banff would be a problem. And it's not – if you've got an unlimited budget. Banff is notorious for its expensive hotels and lack of budget options, but if you plan ahead or know a few tricks, you can find a comfortable and affordable place to stay (see p55 for tips). Banff has some great campgrounds, a number of good quality hostels and countless well-priced bed and breakfasts. If you're looking for something splashy, you're in luck – Banff has some luxurious top-end hotels with plenty of atmosphere and stunning views.

CAMPING

Camping is unsurprisingly popular in Banff, and finding a site on a weekend in the height of the summer can prove challenging. Reservations are not accepted at any of the campgrounds, and sites are given out on a first-come, first-served basis.

CAMPING RULES

Keep the following laws in mind when you setting up home in the park.

✔ Camping is only permitted in designated areas. If you're caught camping in roadside pullouts, picnic areas or even in the middle of nowhere, you may be handed a whopping fine (up to CAD$2000).

✔ Find out when quiet hours are at the campground (usually after 10pm) and observe them.

✔ Dispose of dishwater down flush toilets or designated drains, not in natural water sources or around the campsite. Brush your teeth and wash in designated areas too, as even toothpaste can attract bears.

✔ Fires can only be lit if you have purchased a permit, and they must be kept in designated grates. Use the firewood provided (cutting trees or bushes will land you with a fine) and, with a mind to conservation, keep your fire small.

✔ Campsites in national parks practice the 'Bare Campground Programme.' This means nothing can be left unattended at your site except camping furniture, tents and bedding. All food, cooking equipment, coolers, dishes and toiletries must be stored in your vehicle or in lockers. If left unattended, these items may be confiscated.

✔ Pets must be kept on a leash at all times.

✔ Checkout is 11am. You can stay a maximum of 14 nights in any one campground.

So what are the tricks to finding a site? Get there early. Checkout is at 11am, and by that time, there can already be a line of waiting campers. If possible, plan to stay put on weekends; it's easier to find a site on Friday, and it's wise to hold onto it until at least Sunday. If you can rough it for a few days, you're in luck; campgrounds that don't have showers are also generally quieter, as are those away from Banff Town. If you still can't find a site in the park, try the campgrounds in Canmore, Kootenay Provincial Park and Yoho National Park and along the Icefields Parkway.

Other than Lake Louise Trailer Campground and Tunnel Mountain Village Two, Banff's campgrounds are closed in winter.

Banff Town Area Map 2

Tunnel Mountain *(Tunnel Mountain Rd, Banff Town; electricity/full hookups/tent/ tent with fire CAD$26/30/22/28)* Giant but well situated on the outskirts of Banff Town, this popular campground is divided into three. **Village One** (open May–late Sep) has 618 forested sites but no hookups. The trees grant some privacy but block most views; sites B31, 41 and 43 have a wonderful outlook to the peaks south. **Village Two** *(open year-round)* has electricity, picnic tables and somewhat forested sites but no views. **Tunnel Mountain Trailer Court** *(open May–late Sep)* offers full hookups in a field next to Village Two. While you'll find no shelter or privacy, the views of the surrounding mountains are superb. All sites have use of flush toilets and showers, and wheelchair-accessible sites are available in each village. An evening interpretive program is run regularly during July and August.

Lake Minnewanka Area Map 3

Two Jack Lakeside *(Minnewanka Loop Dr; no hookups/with fire CAD$17/23; open mid May–mid Sep)* This campground is deservedly popular, and its 74 sites fill up quickly. Set in the trees next to the lake, it's close to lots of day hikes in the Minnewanka area. Flush toilets, bear-proof lockers, showers, wheelchair-accessible sites and shelters are all here. Ask for a lakeside site.

Two Jack Main *(Minnewanka Loop Dr; no hookups/with fire CAD$13/18; open mid May-Sep)* Much larger than its lakeside extension across the road, the wooded Two Jack Main has 380 sites and caters mainly to RVs, although there are no hookups. You'll find flush toilets, shelters and bear-proof lockers.

Bow Valley & Lake Louise Area Map 1

Johnston Canyon *(Bow Valley Parkway; no hookups/with fire CAD$22/28; open early Jun–mid Sep)* One of Banff's finest campgrounds, this place is excellently located next to Johnston Creek, in the heart of Bow Valley. Its 132 wooded sites are clean and well maintained. Sites within the loops are more sheltered and private than those along the edges of the grounds. There are a number of wheelchair-accessible sites, as well as showers and flush toilets.

Protection Mountain *(Bow Valley Parkway; no hookups/with fire CAD$17/23; open Jun–Sep)* Wooded and generally quiet, this campground doesn't fill up as quickly as others. Facilities are basic but include flush toilets. Sites on the far north side are best. There are 89 sites, a few of which are wheelchair accessible.

Lake Louise Tent & Trailer *(off Lake Louise Dr, Lake Louise Village; tent/full hookups CAD$22/26; trailer park open year-round, tent sites open late Jun–late Sep)* Divided into two campgrounds with one access gate, this is the closest you can camp to Lake Louise. Tent sites are pleasant and private, but a large electric fence divides you from Bow River (and the bears!). Try to avoid sites along the perimeter of the grounds, which are less wooded and a bit dreary. Trailer sites are not as private but have beautiful mountain views. All sites have access to full facilities. Tent sites can have a fire (CAD$6), and a few sites are wheelchair accessible.

BANFF TOWN LODGING
MAP 2

Cruising the streets of Banff Town, you'll see hotel after hotel after hotel. Finding one that has a vacancy and that's within your budget can seem overwhelming. It's always wise to book ahead, particularly if you already know where you want to stay or are arriving in summer or late in the day. You can book through the **National Park Hotel Guide** (☎ 866-656-7124; **w** *www.nationalparkhotelguide.com*) or call hotels directly. Last-minute walk-in rates are sometimes available (particularly off-season), but if the hotel is busy, it's likely that only the more expensive rooms will still be available. If you arrive in town without a reservation, head to the Banff Information Centre. They keep a handy list of hotel and B&B availability and prices. The list is updated as frequently as the proprietors call the center.

Budget

'Budget accommodations' may sound like an oxymoron in Banff, but it is possible to find them. For those after a dorm bed, reservations are a very good idea, as hostels fill up quickly. If you're looking for a private room, consider a bed and breakfast.

D&Bs There are more than 40 in-town B&Bs, which are often housed in historical homes and full of atmosphere. B&Bs are generally far more comfortable and cheaper than the private rooms in hostels. The majority are well located, are open year-round, offer weekly rates and include a full breakfast in the price. Many accept children, though few allow pets. Doubles generally range $40 to $165. Contact Banff Information Centre for a full list.

Good B&Bs to try include the following:

Holiday Lodge (☎ 403-762-3648; **w** *www.banffholidaylodge.com*; *311 Marten St; doubles from CAD$65; open year-round*)

Beaver Street Suites & Cabins (☎ 403-762 5077; *220 Beaver St; doubles CAD$65 165, open year-round*)

McHardy Cabins (☎ 403 762-2176; *412 Marten St; doubles CAD$60-80; open Jun-Sep*)

Tan-Y-Bryn B&B (☎ 403-762-3696; *118 Otter St; doubles CAD$40-75*)

Global Village Backpackers (☎ 403-762-5521, 888-844-7875; **w** *www.global backpackers.com*; *449 Banff Ave; dorms/semiprivate double CAD$28/66*) The bright, homey and very relaxed Global Village is a popular stomping ground for young backpackers. Each room has four to six bunks with a full en suite and lockers. The central outdoor courtyard is a good place to chill out, and you can hop on the Internet or make reservations for activities from here.

HI Banff Alpine Centre (☎ 403-521-8421; **w** *www.hihostels.ca*; *801 Coyote Dr, off Tunnel Mountain Rd; members dorm/private from CAD$28/80, nonmembers dorm/private from CAD$32/87*) If you're after organized activities galore, this could be the place for you. Spacious buildings that are wheelchair accessible, fireplaces and big decks create an alpine – if not exactly homey – atmosphere. Facilities include a kitchen, sauna and family room. Located at the top of Tunnel Mountain, you can reach the hostel by taking a free shuttle from the bus depot or by hopping on the public bus from downtown.

Y Banff Mountain Lodge (☎ 403-762-3560, 800-813-4138; W www.ymountain lodge.com; 102 Spray Ave; dorm bed CAD$28, double with shared/private bath CAD$59/79-89) Long ago the town hospital, this hostel hasn't quite managed to shake off the building's institutional atmosphere. Dorms are fairly drab, private rooms are somewhat stuffy, and the kitchen is tiny. Nevertheless, the staff is extremely friendly. A minute's stroll from the town center, it's incredibly popular and fills up fast.

Arrow Motel (☎ 403-762-2207; W www.banffcaribouproperties.com; 337 Banff Ave; doubles CAD$129) These out-of-date, basic motel-style rooms are popular with those who just want a bed to crash in. There are no amenities to speak of, but it is one of the cheapest motel options in town.

Mid-range

The eastern end of Banff Ave is a string of mid-range hotels. The majority offer box-standard rooms with little atmosphere. Prices listed are high-season rates; expect considerable discounts in the winter. Also see B&Bs, earlier in this section, for some other great mid-range options.

Royal Canadian Lodge (☎ 403-762-3307; W www.charltonresorts.com; 459 Banff Ave; doubles CAD$200-345) While not quite luxurious, this hotel is definitely a good choice. Rooms are spacious and tastefully decorated with lots of dark wood, big windows and king-size beds. Amenities include a hot tub, sauna and restaurant. All rooms have fridges, and family and wheelchair-accessible rooms are available.

Banff Ptarmigan Inn (☎ 403-762-2207; W www.bestofbanff.com; 337 Banff Ave; doubles CAD$220-285) Recently renovated, rooms here are bright and fairly plush. Some have mountain views, and others face the central courtyard. The lobby has a cozy, alpine feel; amenities are numerous and staff is friendly.

Elkhorn Lodge (☎ 403-762-2299; W www.elkhornbanff.ca; 124 Spray Ave; doubles CAD$110-125, suites CAD$160-215) This small alpine lodge has a storybook look, with fairy lights outside and dark woods looming around its perimeter. Its eight rooms don't ooze atmosphere but are homey enough, and the owners are extremely friendly and helpful.

Banff Caribou Lodge (☎ 403-762-5887; W www.bestofbanff.com; 521 Banff Ave; CAD$220-350) This large wood lodge has all of the modern conveniences you'd expect of a 3½-star hotel. There isn't a lot of atmosphere, but rooms are comfortable and, relatively speaking, it's a good value.

Travellers' Inn (☎ 403-762-4401; W www.banfftravellersinn.com; 401 Banff Ave; doubles CAD$190) While lacking the glitz of many of its neighbors, Traveller's Inn is clean, pleasant and friendly. Standard rooms are bright and some of the cheapest in town – especially if you luck into one of their great walk-in rates.

Driftwood Inn (☎ 403-762-3577; W www.bestofbanff.com; 337 Banff Ave; doubles CAD$149-209) Basic and a little dated, this motel-style inn is geared for those on a budget. Rooms are clean, and you get full use of the amenities at the Ptarmigan Inn next door. Winter rates drop down to CAD$99. For reception, go to the Ptarmigan.

Top End

Fairmont Banff Springs *(☎ 103 762 2211, 000-441-1414, W www.fairmont.com; Spray Ave; doubles CAD$376-677 per person)* A virtual castle, the posh Banff Springs was built in 1928 and remains elegant and grand, with sweeping views across the mountains. Rooms are plush, and service will leave you feeling like royalty. Unfortunately you may need a king's treasure to foot the bill. Golfing, skiing, breakfast and visits to the spa are included in various room packages.

Rimrock Resort Hotel *(☎ 403-762-3356, 800-661-1587; W www.rimrockresort .com; 300 Mountain Ave; doubles CAD$350-410, extra adult CAD$20)* The Rimrock is classy, has spectacular mountain views and ranks as one of Banff's top hotels. Rooms are bright and spacious, with beds as comfy as clouds. There's also a great spa and pool. Some rooms have obstructed views or overlook the parking lot, so double-check when booking. It's also worth checking here for knockout walk-in rates.

Hidden Ridge Resort *(☎ 403-762-3544; W www.bestofbanff.com; 901 Coyote Dr; doubles CAD$195-400, children under 16 yrs free)* Great for families, these chalets have full kitchens, wood-burning stoves and barbecues, all set atop Tunnel Mountain. There's a giant hot tub nestled among the pine trees, and a number of rooms have lofts for the kiddies. Baby-sitting services are available.

Rundlestone Lodge *(☎ 403-762-2201; W www.rundlestone.com; 537 Banff Ave; standard rooms CAD$185-195, suites CAD$215-310)* Fairly pricey in the summer, the loft suites here become much more affordable in winter, when you'll most appreciate their Jacuzzis and wood-burning fireplaces. With a modern condo atmosphere and a touch of alpine, many suites also come complete with a mini-kitchen and mountain views. Standard rooms here are fairly run of the mill.

BOW VALLEY PARKWAY LODGING
MAP 1

Set midway between Banff Town and Lake Louise Village, the lush Bow Valley gives you a chance to experience the wilderness and is also convenient for day trips and hikes.

Castle Mountain Wilderness Hostel *(☎ 403-670-7580; W www.hihostels.ca/ hostels/Alberta; Castle Junction; dorms members/nonmembers CAD$19/23)* Banff's top hostel, this home-away-from-home has a bright, well-equipped kitchen and a cozy common area where you can hang out around a wood-burning stove. Big windows look out onto the surrounding peaceful wilderness. The atmosphere and amenities are the perfect combination of remoteness and comfort. Dorms are separated by gender, with 28 beds total.

Johnston Canyon Resort *(☎ 403-762-0868; W www.johnstoncanyon.com; Bow Valley Parkway; 2-person cottages CAD$129-179, 4-person cottages CAD$174-274; open May-Oct)* Set next to the busy Johnston Canyon, these cabins are often booked months in advance. Built in the 1920s, those at the lower end of the price scale have sadly lost much of their character to renovations. The pricier ones are tastefully decorated, particularly the two- and four-person bungalows There's both a restaurant and a coffee shop in the main lodge.

Baker Creek Chalets *(☎ 403-522-3761, W www.bakercreek.com; doubles CAD$170-285, quad CAD$250, additional adult CAD$15)* Deep in the Bow Valley, these wooden chalets have log furniture and can come with fireplaces, lofts and decks. Lodge suites are just as cozy. In winter you can snowshoe or cross-country ski from the door. There's a good restaurant (with a kids' menu), and you're ensured peace and quiet.

A WORKING PARTY

A German backpacker whipped up your cappuccino this morning, an Aussie sold you your ski pass, and a student from Quebec checked you into your hotel. The workforce in Banff Town is as international as the visiting tourists; in fact, many workers are simply long-term tourists who find jobs to support their addictions to skiing, climbing or biking. Rumors of how the work scene in Banff is really just one giant party may have already filtered back to your hometown; visit one of the local pubs, and you'll see just how true they are.

Employment isn't too hard to come by in Banff's hotels, bars, restaurants and ski areas, and a second language or training in a popular outdoor activity will boost your chances of landing a job. Finding work without a permit has become tricky for non-Canadians; most establishments ask for proper documentation. If you want to be absolutely sure of being able to earn some money, inquire about work visas at home before you start your trip.

It's worth contacting the **Job Resource Centre** (☎ 403-760-4447; **w** www.jobresourcecentre .com; 314 Marten St) before you arrive in Banff. Staff there offer sound advice and can sometimes arrange a job for you before you even get there. Also check out **w** www.banffjobs.com for employment opportunities. Both International Hostels, in Banff Town and Lake Louise, offer Working Holiday Survival Packages (CAD$260), including seven nights in a dorm, breakfast, 200 minutes of free Internet access, job hunting resources and assistance with setting up a bank account and acquiring a social insurance number.

The most challenging part of working in Banff (besides budgeting your beer allowance) is finding affordable accommodations. Some employers provide a place to live in exchange for rock-bottom wages; others may include a room at modest rates. In Lake Louise, all jobs come with accommodations (otherwise you'd be sleeping in the bushes).

If you're jobless and homeless upon arrival, hunt through the classified ads in the local *Crag & Canyon* newspaper, and keep an eye open for 'help wanted' signs in shop windows. You can always head to the pubs for advice from veteran workers and to get in a little practice with the social side of work.

Castle Mountain Chalets (☎ 403-762-3868; **w** www.decorehotels.com; Bow Valley Parkway, junction with Hwy 93; chalets CAD$185-330) With excellent views of Castle Mountain, you can almost forget that these log chalets are set next to the highway. Fireplaces and cozy quilts keep you snug, and there's a small grocery store so that you can whip up a meal in the kitchenette. Some come with Jacuzzis, and pets are allowed.

LAKE LOUISE LODGING
MAP 1

With the exception of one hostel, lodging in and around Lake Louise is pricey. The majority of hotels in Lake Louise Village are average but command top-end prices. Try the cabins and lodges closer to the lakes, where you'll find fabulous views and lots of character.

HI Lake Louise (☎ 403-670-7580; **w** www.hihostels.ca; Village Rd, Lake Louise Village; members dorm/private from CAD$24/75, nonmembers CAD$28/83) With a friendly, sociable atmosphere, this popular hostel has a lot going on. Join in with ski packages in winter or outdoor programs in summer. Four-bed dorm rooms are clean and bright; private rooms are very basic and seem overpriced. All rooms share bathrooms and showers. A popular restaurant is on-site.

Deer Lodge (☎ 403-522-3991, 800-661-1595; **w** www.crmr.com; 109 Lake Louise Dr; doubles CAD$165-260, additional adult CAD$25) Lake Louise's most atmospheric lodge was built in 1921 and is now a maze of corridors connecting the many rooms and towers of the shingled buildings. The hotel has managed to keep its genuine alpine feel intact, complete with a beautifully restored lounge and cozy sitting area. Lodge Rooms are fairly tiny but quaint, while spacious Heritage Rooms are in a newer wing. To promote tranquility, you won't find a TV in any of the rooms, and telephones are only in a few. Children are welcome.

Paradise Lodge & Bungalows (☎ 403-522-3595; w www.paradiselodge.com; 105 Lake Louise Dr; 2-4 person suites & bungalows CAD$195-270) Cozy and well restored, these 1940s bungalows are surrounded by woods and are only moments from Lake Louise's shore. Huge comfy beds, cast-iron stoves and tasteful alpine decor make them pleasantly plush. Try for cabin No 21, which has a very private deck overlooking endless forest.

Moraine Lake Lodge (☎ 403-533-3733; w www.morainelake.com; doubles CAD$395-490; open Jun-Oct) In the valley of the Ten Peaks, with lake and mountain views from every room, the cabins and lodge rooms here have a casual, relaxed air. Decor includes chunky log furniture, lots of cushions on the beds and, in most rooms, a wood burning fireplace. These rooms fill up very quickly – book ahead.

Post Hotel (☎ 403-522-3989, 800-661-1596; w www.posthotel.com; Village Rd, Lake Louise Village; doubles CAD$305-425, 3-4 person suites CAD$425-575, lodge suites & cabins CAD$360-650) The Post Hotel has comfortable rooms that verge on classy, despite the mismatched floral decor. Rooms along the front are slightly cheaper but look over the parking lot; those at the back have decks looking over the river. Suites and cabins have more character but fill up quickly. In summer, interpretive talks are presented in the cozy library.

Fairmont Chateau Lake Louise (☎ 403-522-3511; w www.fairmont.com; Lake Louise Dr, doubles CAD$831-1881 including breakfast) While something of an atrocity from the outside, the standard rooms in this giant lakeshore hotel are plush, with small windows commanding brilliant views across the famous lake. While it's claimed that the hotel's original structure is from the 1920s, they've hidden it well; much of its charm has been lost to renovations that leave it feeling rather stuffy. Lots of activities are available, including lakeview teas, interpretive walks and alpine hiking.

Places to Eat

Banff has more restaurants than you can shake a tent pole at. From lively downtown bistros and fine dining to log diners in the woods, and from Mexican to Swiss to Japanese cuisine, Banff is a food lover's haven and is home to many of Alberta's top dining options. If the mountains don't draw you back to Banff, the food will.

BANFF TOWN
MAP 2
Budget
Evelyn's Coffee Bar (☎ 403-762-0352; 201 Banff Ave; mains CAD$6; open 7am-11pm Mon-Sat, 7:30am-11pm Sun) Never mind the coffee, this place is just as popular for its freshly baked cookies and muffins. It's absolute mayhem come lunchtime because of its homemade sandwiches, wraps and soups. For a quieter version where you can lounge over your espresso, try **Evelyn's Too** (☎ 403-762-0330; Wolf & Bear St Mall; open 7am-10pm Mon-Sat, 9am-5pm Sun).

BARGAIN BITES

Trying to save your pennies for a trip up the gondola or a white-water voyage? Head to one of the following restaurants, where you can satisfy that grumbling belly for under CAD$10.

✔ **Aardvark Pizza** will fill you and a friend with their mouthwatering 12-inch pizzas.

✔ For gyros and served with a smile, try the Greek **Barpa Bill's** takeout.

✔ On Wednesday and Sunday nights, **Bruno's Bar & Grill** brings the spaghetti on (and on) until you say halt.

✔ Big bowls of steaming noodles from **East Express** will leave you bursting.

✔ **Bill Peyto's Café** serves up tasty lunches on their sunny patio.

✔ For the biggest bargain of all, head to the **Old Spaghetti Factory** for a four-course meal that's a steal.

Barpa Bill's (☎ 403-762-0377; 223 Bear St; mains CAD$8; open 11am-9pm) Barpa has it all going on, from gyros to souvlaki to the Barpa burger, topped with tzatziki and onions. Try the tasty dolmas or spanakopita, made fresh by the friendly Greek proprietors. If you can elbow a little counter space, eat in; otherwise you can get it to go. Barpa offers free delivery for orders of CAD$8 or more.

Aardvark Pizza & Sub (☎ 403-762-5500; 304a Caribou St; 12-inch/slice/sub CAD$14/3/6; open noon-4am) Come here after the bars close or if you can't be bothered to start the camping stove. Takeout pizzas and subs are loaded with fresh toppings and ooze with cheese. Call in your order early on the weekend, when the line of hungry people often snakes out the door.

Sushi House Banff (☎ 403-762-4353; 304 Caribou St; sushi CAD$1.80-4.60; open noon-10:30pm) This is an authentic Japanese sushi bar with a Canadian flair; instead of the filled plates simply spinning around on the conveyor belt, a huge assortment of freshly rolled sushi chugs around on the cars of a miniature Rocky Mountain train. The plates' colors denote the prices.

Old Spaghetti Factory (☎ 403-760-2779; 2nd floor, Cascade Plaza, Wolf St; mains CAD$12, kids' mains CAD$6; open 11:30am-9:30pm) It may be short of atmosphere but never of pasta. Penne, cannelloni, spaghetti, linguine, tortellini and lasagna are topped with staple sauces like spicy meatballs, mushroom, clam and pesto. All entrées include sourdough bread, soup or salad and dessert – a serious bargain. Geared for families, you'll find jovial servers, a kids' menu and highchairs.

East Express (☎ 403-760-3988; 202 Caribou St; mains CAD$8; open 11am-9pm) If you're looking for something quick and filling, East Express dishes up big plates of noodles and rice with beef, veggies, shrimp or pork. Have yours as soup, in wonton form or under a heap of curry sauce. It's busy and noisy, with plastic chairs and friendly counter service.

Mid-range

Sukiyaki House (☎ 403-762-2002; 2nd floor, 211 Banff Ave; mains CAD$15; open noon-10pm) Mouthwatering sauces, tender seafood and fresh noodles are all authentically prepared. Popular with Japanese tourists, Sukiyaki House has a wonderfully relaxed atmosphere and excellent, friendly service. This is the best place in town to meet your Nippon cravings.

Typhoon (☎ 403-762-2000; 211 Caribou St; lunch/dinner CAD$10/18; open 11am-3pm & 6-11pm) Fitting the bill as eclectic Asian cuisine, Typhoon manages to pick the best from the cuisines of Thailand, India and Indonesia. The interior is bright, colorful and intimate and it's the perfect place to sample curries and satays.

Cilantro Mountain Café (☎ 403-760-3008; Tunnel Mountain Rd; mains CAD$20; open 11am-11pm Dec-Oct, usually closed Mon & Tue) In a tiny wood cabin on top of Tunnel Mountain, a wood-burning oven churns out fresh pizzas, venison, duck and veggies to the delight of faithful patrons relaxing on the patio or at small tables in the cozy interior. Cilantro is quaint, popular and tasty.

Giorgio's Trattoria (☎ 403-762-5114; 219 Banff Ave; mains CAD$18; open 5-10pm) The candlelight and warm, authentic decor make this one of Banff's most romantic dining experiences. Gourmet Italian food is served with flair; try the garlic shrimp, the spinach gnocchi or the homemade sausage with polenta. Reservations are recommended.

Coyote's Deli & Grill (☎ 403-762-3963; 206 Caribou St; breakfast/lunch/dinner CAD$9/12/20; open 7:30-11am, 11:30am-4pm & 5pm-late) Popular for good reason, this lively bistro dishes up excellent Southwestern cuisine. The open kitchen gives you a bird's-eye view into the preparation behind black-bean chili, tasty polenta and blue-corn enchiladas. You'll also find a Mediterranean twist to the menu, with delicious pizzas and fresh pastas. Reservations are recommended.

Bruno's Bar & Grill (☎ 403-762-8115; 304 Caribou St; lunch/dinner CAD$9/15; open 9:30am-2pm) With excellent daily specials like all-you-can-eat spaghetti, Bruno's is a jumping place with friendly staff and great food. Giant omelettes and hash browns are served up for breakfast. For lunch and dinner, fill up on hearty burgers, scrumptious pastas and substantial salads. There are good veggie options, a pool table and a well-stocked bar.

Sunfood Café (☎ 403-760-3933; Sundance Mall, 215 Banff Ave; mains CAD$10; open 11am-9pm) This tiny restaurant serves creative vegetarian food in a casual, welcoming atmosphere. Try the creamy mushroom stroganoff or the grilled teriyaki tofu steak.

Magpie & Stump (☎ 403-762-4067; 203 Caribou St; lunch/dinner CAD$8/15; open noon-2am) Decorated with saddles, guns and sombreros, this Tex-Mex restaurant is one place you won't leave hungry; chimichangas, enchiladas and burritos are served in hearty portions. Order dishes mild or try them hot (there are lots of cocktails on the menu to cool the fires). This place is very kid-friendly, with highchairs and a children's menu.

Top End

Saltlik (☎ 403-762-2467; 221 Bear St; mains CAD$25; open 5-11pm) Not your typikal steakhouse, the funky Saltlik serves up ribs, sirloin, ribeye and seafood with inventive sauces like citrus-rosemary butter and blue-cheese cream. The timber-framed dining room is spacious and chic, with big blazing fireplaces and bright local artwork.

Maple Leaf Grillé & Spirits (☎ 403-760-7680; 137 Banff Ave; mains lunch/dinner CAD$15/25; open 11am-11pm) Stylish yet comfortable, this restaurant has a warm Canadian feel. Logs are stacked against the wall, fairy lights twinkle from branches, and a giant birchbark canoe hangs above the staircase. The menu is innovative, with wasabi-crusted salmon, arctic char and apple-crusted pork. Sounds good, eh?

Bow Valley Grill (☎ 403-762-6860; Banff Springs Hotel; lunch/dinner CAD$27/33; open 11:30am-2:30pm & 5:30-9:30pm) Big, semicircular booths and giant chandeliers give this place a 1930s feel. Not that you'll notice the decor or even the mountain views – you'll be too absorbed by the fantastic food, like duck, prime rib or chicken served with exotic and innovative sauces.

Grizzly House Restaurant (☎ 403-762-4055; 207 Banff Ave; mains lunch/dinner CAD$13/35; open 11:30am-midnight) One of Banff's more unique dining options, this is a true carnivore's paradise. Appropriately decorated with the stuffed heads of buffalos, elk and moose, this dimly lit restaurant dishes up game and seafood fondue-style. Feeling adventurous? Try the Exotic Fondue, with shark, alligator, rattlesnake, frog legs and buffalo. Lunch is a little more ordinary, with burgers, pastrami and soups.

Banffshire Club (☎ 403-762-6860; Banff Springs Hotel; 2/3/4 courses CAD$100/110/120; open 6-9:30pm Sun-Thu, 6-10pm Fri-Sat) With the flickering candlelight and harp music wafting through the room, the posh Banffshire exudes intimacy. Elaborate mains include cedar-roasted sablefish, pecan-crusted caribou and roasted partridge with truffles. The wine cellar is overflowing, with over 600 different labels. Denim is a no-go here; jackets are a must, and ties are optional.

BOW VALLEY PARKWAY
MAP 1

The Canyon Café (☎ 403-762-0868; Walter's Landing, Johnston Canyon, Bow Valley Parkway; breakfast/lunch & dinner CAD$5/8; open 8am-9pm May-Oct) With a true diner feel, this tiny place gets packed with hikers. Grab a booth or sit at the long counter and fill up on soups, fish 'n' chips or good old-fashioned pie. If you're looking for something a little more classy, try **Bridges** (mains breakfast/lunch/dinner CAD$6/9/23; open breakfast/lunch/dinner 8-11am/11am-3pm/6pm-9pm), in the same building, for steak, prawns and chicken.

Baker Creek Bistro (☎ 403-522-2182; Bow Valley Parkway; lunch/dinner CAD$15/30; open 8-10:30am & noon-6pm) This snug log cabin whips up gourmet fare like fillets of ruby red trout and sautéed venison in orange and gin sauce. For the lunch menu, think mushroom and sherry–filled crepes or salmon and pesto spaghetti.

LAKE LOUISE
MAP 1

Bill Peyto's Café (☎ 403-670-7580; HI Lake Louise, Village Rd; breakfast/lunch/dinner CAD$7/9/13, kids' menu CAD$4; open 7am-10pm summer, 7am-9pm winter) With live music and a good wine list, lively Peyto's is a popular hangout for guests and locals alike. The food is both filling and tasty; try the granola or the burrito huevo for breakfast and fill up on seafood, stir-fry or mac 'n' cheese at dinner. The staff is friendly, and there's a patio for when the sun (or moon) is shining.

Lake Louise Station Restaurant (☎ 403-522-2600; end of Sentinel Rd; lunch/dinner CAD$9/25; open 11:30am-midnight) Dine in the stationmaster's office surrounded by left luggage and an old oak desk, opt for the elegant dining cars, or lounge on the patio overlooking the rails. This is one of Banff's most atmospheric restaurants, a lovingly restored railway station constructed in 1909. Reasonably priced meals cover all the basics with flair. Families are welcome.

Deer Lodge Lounge & Dining Room (☎ 403-522-3991; 109 Lake Louise Dr; mains in lounge/dining room CAD$12/30; lounge open 11am-11pm, dining room open 6-10pm) Set in the atmospheric Deer Lodge, this restaurant makes dishes like burgers, buffalo pastrami and crab cakes, served in the casual log-framed lounge or on the patio with glacier views.

The more formal dining room caters to gourmet connoisseurs with seafood, game and excellent service. Reservations are a must for the dining room.

Moraine Lake Dining Room (☎ 403-533-3733; *lunch/dinner CAD$14/12/35; open 7-10:30am breakfast, 11am-3pm lunch & 5:30-9pm dinner Jun-Oct*) Head here for a peaceful meal in front of big picture windows looking out across the lake and to the peaks beyond. Specialties include partridge, seafood and game. For breakfast, try the buttermilk pancakes or bagels with smoked salmon.

For something a little more casual, try the more manic **Moraine Lake Café** (*mains CAD$5; open 9am-8pm July & Aug*) for sandwiches, soups and coffees. **Poppy Brasserie** (☎ 403-522-3511; *Fairmont Chateau Lake Louise; mains CAD$25; open 6:30am-2pm & 6-9pm*) It doesn't have a great deal of charm, but of the Chateau's restaurants, it offers the best value. The food is tasty, and the Poppy is casual enough to make you feel comfortable in your hiking boots and fleece. If you'd prefer to picnic, head upstairs to the **Chateau Deli** (*open 24 hrs; mains CAD$6*), where you can get take-out sandwiches, soups, cakes and a mug of coffee that you can refill all day.

Entertainment

Unlike many parks, there's more to do in the evening in Banff than roasting marshmallows around the campfire. Check 'Summit Up' in the local *Crag & Canyon* newspaper for listings. There are also evening events, often geared for kids, held in some of the most popular campgrounds.

Pubs & Bars

Wild Bill's Legendary Saloon (*Map 2;* ☎ 403-760-0333; *201 Banff Ave; 11am-late*) A true cowboy hangout, this is the place to chug pints of beer and two-step the night away. They even have calf-roping, and live bands take charge of the music. Don't be daunted by the big hats and boots – this is a friendly crowd. Hungry two-steppers can devour chicken wings, burgers, steaks and burritos.

Rundle Lounge (*Map 2;* ☎ 403-762-6860; *Banff Springs Hotel; Spray Ave; appetizers/ drinks CAD$14/8; open noon-1am*) If you'd like to soak up a little bit of glamour in Banff's ritziest hotel, the elegant Rundle Lounge is the place to be. Upstairs in the Banff Springs Hotel, the chandeliers sparkle, and the giant windows look out to the mountains. You can snack from the appetizer menu until midnight and sip cocktails, beer and wine.

Lic Lounge (*Map 2;* ☎ 403-762-2467; *downstairs at the Saltlik, 221 Bear St; open 11am-2am*) The hippest place to have a drink, the stylish Lic Lounge plays funky music and has big comfy couches and a heated patio. On Sunday evenings, DJs spin jazz, funk and downtempo.

Aurora Club (*Map 2;* ☎ 403-760-3343; *110 Banff Ave; 6pm-late*) A martini bar and cigar lounge, this place pumps out dance music, and the weekend crowds start to boogie around midnight.

Rose & Crown (*Map 2;* ☎ 403-762-2121; *202 Banff Ave; open 11am-late*) Going for that English pub feel, this smoky place has lots of beer on tap, a pool table, darts and pub food to soak up the beer. Sunday evening sees live bands, and there's a rooftop patio that's a pleasant place to be.

Also check out the **Barbary Coast** (*Map 2;* ☎ 403-762-7673; *119 Banff Ave*), which draws a young crowd, and **Saint James Gate** (*Map 2;* ☎ 403-762-9355; *205 Wolf St*), an Irish pub with over 30 tap beers, 10 whiskeys and 50 scotches to choose from.

Cinema & Performing Arts

Lux Cinema *(Map 2; ☎ 403-762-8595; Bear St; adult CAD$9.50)* Come here for popcorn and first-run movies straight from Hollywood. Tickets are cheap on Tuesdays, and occasionally there are midnight showings.

Banff Centre *(Map 2; ☎ 403-762-6301; W www.banffcentre.ca/bsaf; Banff Town; tickets CAD$10-20 per show)* For theatrical, dance and musical performances, check out the Banff Centre. Events and exhibits are programmed throughout the year; see the website for current listings.

Shopping
EQUIPMENT & SUPPLIES

Mountain Magic Equipment *(Map 2; ☎ 403-762-2591; 224 Bear St)* Just off the main shopping drag, Mountain Magic sells virtually everything you'll need to get out and about. Their prices for climbing, hiking, skiing, snowboarding and camping equipment are some of the best in town.

Abominable Sports *(Map 2; ☎ 403-762-2905; 229 Banff Ave)* This place carries lots of camping gear, backpacks, Gore-Tex and even the essential Albertan cowboy boots. Head downstairs to the hiking department for bear spray and climbing gear.

Rude Girls *(Map 2; ☎ 403-760-4412; 207 Caribou St)* Looking for a new snowboard or maybe something stylish to wear on your skateboard? Rude Girls has all the namebrand gear and clothing that you could ever desire. Guys can head to **Rude Boys** *(☎ 403-762-8480; Sundance Mall, 215 Banff Ave)*.

Mondo Sports *(Map 2; ☎ 403-762-4571; 129 Banff Ave)* One of Banff's oldest equipment shops, Mondo has two floors of high-quality camping and climbing gear. This is also the place meet all of your fly-fishing needs, with anglers on hand for any questions.

BOOKS

Cascade Mountain Books *(Map 2; ☎ 403-762-8508; basement, Cascade Plaza, 317 Banff Ave)* If you're hoping to bone up on your Canadian history, take in a little Margaret Lawrence or study local wildflowers, this shop will probably have the answer. Shelves are well stocked with Canadian fiction, nonfiction and specialist travel guides, as well as local maps and calendars with scenes of the Rockies.

The Viewpoint *(Map 2; ☎ 403-762-0405; cnr Caribou St & Banff Ave; open 10am-10pm)* You'll find lots of beautiful books of local scenery, as well as local activity, geology and wildlife books. This is also a great place for postcards.

Banff Book & Art Den *(Map 2; ☎ 403-762-3919; 94 Banff Ave; open 9am-9pm)* Stock up on specialty activity guides, maps and books on local history, art and fiction. A good selection of kids' book will keep your tots and your teenagers happy. Whet your appetite before you set out by having books delivered to your door; order online at W www.banffbooks.com or call toll-free ☎ 866-418-6613.

GIFTS

The Bear & Butterfly *(Map 2; ☎ 403-762-8911; 214 Banff Ave)* This is the place for creative gifts and souvenirs like wildflower seeds, carvings, ceramics and the essential moose slippers. They also carry some great activity guides and maps. Almost everything is locally produced, and profits go to Friends of Banff.

GROCERIES

For the best prices and selection in Banff, join the crowds at **Safeway** (*Map 2; cnr Elk St & Banff Ave, Banff Town*). In Lake Louise, the rather pricey **Village Market** (*Map 2; Samson Mall, Lake Louise Village; open 7:30am-10pm*) has a good selection of fruits and veggies in summer as well as all the essentials.

INTERNET ACCESS

Cyber Net (*Map 2;* ☎ *403-762-9226; Sundance Mall; 7/15/30/60 min CAD$1/2/4/6; 9am-midnight*) has comfortable couches and chairs to email home from. The experience is made all the more pleasant with happy music and drinks. Also try **The Underground** (*Map 2;* ☎ *403-760-8776; Sundance Mall, 211 Banff Ave; 15/30/60 min CAD$2/4/6; open 9am-1am*) for lots of new computers in a rather dark room.

LAUNDRY

After a few days in the backcountry, **Cascade Coin Laundry** (*Map 2; basement, Cascade Plaza; wash/dry CAD$2.75/0.25 for 4 min; open 9am-9pm, last wash 7:45pm*) may well be your first stop.

MEDICAL SERVICES & EMERGENCIES

For medical emergencies head to the modern **Mineral Springs Hospital** (*Map 2;* ☎ *403-762-2222; Bow Ave*). For emergencies in the backcountry, including accidents, missing persons or bear sightings, contact the emergency line at the **Banff Warden Office** (*Map 2;* ☎ *403-762-4506; 24 hrs*). For all other emergencies, dial ☎ **911**.

MONEY

At the south end of Banff Ave, you'll find a **Bank of Montreal** (*Map 2*), and there's an ATM at the entrance to **Cascade Plaza** (*Map 2; cnr Banff Ave & Wolf St*) where you can use all major cards. If you've got foreign cash to exchange, try the **Foreign Currency Exchange** (*Map 2;* ☎ *403-762-4698; Clock Tower Mall, 110 Banff Ave*) or **Custom House Currency Exchange** (*Map 2;* ☎ *403-660-6630; Park Ave Mall, 211 Banff Ave*).

POSTAL SERVICES

Send your postcards and parcels from the main **Post Office** (*Map 2;* ☎ *403-762-2586; 204 Buffalo St*), at the southern end of town.

TRASH & RECYCLING

Banff Town is as clean as you'd hope the rest of the national park is. Garbage bins are located all over town, and you'll find recycling at the corner of Banff Ave and Caribou St, as well as outside Safeway.

Whyte Museum Shop (*Map 2;* ☎ *403-762-2291; cnr Banff Ave & Buffalo St*) An outpost of the museum, this shop carries a excellent selection of prints, posters, postcards and local crafts.

Glacier Gifts (*Map 2;* ☎ *403-762-3435; Sundance Mall, Banff Ave*) An original range of beautiful prints and quality local artwork makes Glacier Gifts stand out in the crowd of souvenir shops along this block.

AROUND BANFF NATIONAL PARK

There's a lot in Banff's backyard that's worth taking the time to visit. You'll likely pass through some of these places en route to Banff; others can be visited on a day trip. Each of the surrounding parks has its own distinct character, and accommodations in these areas are often less busy and more affordable than Banff Town or Lake Louise.

Canmore
MAP 4

On Banff's eastern doorstep, Canmore is home to many outdoor enthusiasts who prefer its slower pace. Many businesses that run activities throughout the park are also based here.

Easily reached along the Trans-Canada Hwy, Canmore is just 25km/15.5 miles east of Banff Town and 6km/3.7 miles from the park's gates. To reach downtown, exit the highway and follow signs to Main St (8th Ave), where you'll find the majority of shops, restaurants and facilities.

An **Alberta Visitor Information Centre** (☎ 403-678-5277; W www.discover alberta.com; 2801 Bow Valley Trail; open 8am-8pm summer, 8pm-6pm winter) is located just off the Trans-Canada Hwy at the western edge of town. They can supply you with trail maps and information, town maps and activity brochures.

The **post office** is on the corner of Main St and 7th Ave. You can get online and sip coffee at **CyberWeb** (☎ 403-609-2678; 717 10th St; 7/15/30/60 min CAD$1/2/4/6; 9am-midnight) or log in at **Cafe Books** (☎ 403-678-0908; 826 Main St; 9:30am-9pm, 10:30am-5:30am Sun), where you can also pick up maps, guidebooks and souvenirs. For cash, head to the **Valley Credit Union** (810 Main St), where an ATM accepts all major cards.

SIGHTS & ACTIVITIES

If you have a keen interest in the history of mining, geology or the railway, visit the **Canmore Museum & Geoscience Society** (☎ 403-678-2462; 907 7th Ave; walks adult/student/child/senior CAD$25/20/15/20; open Wed-Sat 1-8pm, Sun 10am-5pm). In July and August, they hold guided walks. You can also visit Canmore's restored **North West Mounted Police Barracks** (☎ 403-678-1955; 601 Main St), which was built in 1893 and is home to a tearoom and gardens.

There are a number of short **day hikes** you can do around Canmore, both southwest of the Bow River and northeast of town off Silvertip Trail. Ask for the *Canmore Trails* brochure at the information center.

Climb through narrow passageways and descend shoots along 4km/2.5 miles of an undeveloped cave system within Grotto Mountain. Both **Canmore Cavers** (☎ 403-678-9918; W www.canadianrockies.net/wildcavetours; full/half day CAD$105/79) and **Canadian Rockies Cave Guiding** (☎ 403-678-3522; W www.caveguiding.com; intro/rappel/2-day trips CAD$65/95/300) run tours year-round.

Canmore Rafting Centre (☎ 403-678-4919; W www.canmoreraftingcentre.com; 20 Lincoln Park; from CAD$59; May–late Sep) runs white-water rafting trips along Kananaskis and Kicking Horse Rivers and through Horseshoe Canyon, with novice trips geared for families. They also run gentle float trips for those content to stay dry.

Rocky Mountain Paddling (☎ 800-656-8288; **w** www.rockymountain paddling.com; kayaking/canoeing/float trips from CAD$345/245/45) runs kayaking and canoe adventures, including historic float trips, for all levels. Group rates are much cheaper.

There is no shortage of two-wheelers in Canmore. Rent bikes with full suspension and your choice of pedals from **Altitude Sports** (☎ 403-678-0008; 801 Main St; hr/day from CAD$11/38, helmets CAD$3; open 10am-7pm). They'll also tune up your bike for reasonable rates. **Rebound** (☎ 403-678-3608; u www.reboundcycle.com; cnr Railway Ave & Bow Valley Trail; switch/front/full suspension per day CAD$45/25/35) also rents out high-performance bikes for the trail. Once you're geared up, head out along the fantastic trail system at the **Canmore Nordic Centre** (☎ 403-678-6764; u www.trail-sportsl.cab.ca; trail fees adult/teen/child/senior CAD$5/4/4/3),which also maintains cross-country ski trails in winter, rents skis and offers lessons.

For equipment rental of all sorts, including tents, camp stoves, kayaks and packs, visit Canmore Rafting Centre (previous) or **Gear Up** (☎ 403-678-1636; **w** www.gearupsport.com; 1302 Bow Valley Trail).

Tours

Alpine Helicopters (☎ 403-678-4802; **w** www.alpinehelicopters.com; heli hike/alpine walk/flight tours from CAD$375/250/145; 91 Bow Valley Trail) take you up for a bird's-eye view of the Rockies and let you escape into the alpine meadows for hiking. Helicopters are wheelchair accessible. If you're eager to reach such heights by foot, the **Alpine Club of Canada** (☎ 403-678-3200; **w** www.alpineclubof canada.ca) organizes climbing, skiing and hiking adventures in the backcountry for people of all levels.

Mahikan Trails (☎ 403 609 3489; **w** www.mahikan.com, full/half day CAD$124/69, includes lunch; 82 Grotto Way) offers hikes and snowshoe trips with First Nation guides, who share their history and culture.

PLACES TO STAY
Camping
Bow River Campground (☎ 403-673-2163; **w** www.bowvalleycampgrounds.com; off Hwy 1, east of Canmore; CAD$17, 2nd unit on same site CAD$15, seniors CAD$15) The most pleasant campground in the area has wooded sites along the river and mountain views. (Sites at the front have views of the highway.) Basic facilities include flush toilets and a shelter.

With lots of mountain views but no privacy, **Restwell Trailer Park** (☎ 403-678-5111; **w** www.restwelltrailerpark.com; 502 3rd Ave; full/electric/no hookup CAD$33/29/26, pet/extra adult CAD$2; open year-round) is best for RVs, and the basic **Canmore Municipal Campground** (☎ 403-609-0771; 100 Ray McBride St; night/week/month per person CAD$10/60/220; open mid-May–Sep) will do in a pinch.

Lodging
With over 50 B&Bs in the area, you're unlikely to be stranded without a place to stay. Prices range from CAD$60 to CAD$300; the majority are around CAD$120. Contact **Canmore Bow Valley B&B Association** (☎ 403-609-7224; **w** www.bbcanmore.com) for availability or pick up a listings brochure from the Alberta Visitor Information Centre. You'll also find a procession of motels along the Bow Valley Trail.

Canmore Clubhouse (☎ 403-678-3200; **W** www.alpineclubofcanada.ca; Indian Flats Rd; dorms members/nonmembers CAD$19/23) On the sunny, north side of the valley east of Canmore, the Alpine Club of Canada's beautifully maintained hostel is footsteps away from trailheads and is great place to meet fellow mountaineers. Facilities include laundry, a library, a kitchen and a sauna.

The Lady Macdonald Country Inn (☎ 800-567-3919; **W** www.ladymacdonald .com; 1201 Bow Valley Trail; doubles CAD$150-225 including breakfast, kids under 12 free) Twelve lovely rooms are individually decorated with sleigh or four-poster beds, warm-colored walls, lots of cushions and down duvets. All have private bath, and many have mountain views. A gourmet breakfast is included in the price. Family lofts and a wheelchair-accessible room are available.

The Georgetown Inn (☎ 403-678-3439; **W** www.georgetowninn.ab.ca; 1101 Bow Valley Trail; doubles CAD$129-189, including breakfast) Done up like an old English tudor inn, the rooms here have lovely antique furniture well mingled with modern touches like Jacuzzis and mini-kitchens. The resident Miner's Lamp Pub has oodles of character.

Rundle Mountain Lodge (☎ 403-678-5322; **W** www.rundlemountain.com; 1723 Bow Valley Trail; cabin/cabin with kitchen/standard double CAD$125/135/135) Just outside Canmore, this roadside lodge has older, cozy two-bedroom cabins with kitchens for up to four adults – a bargain at CAD$160. Standard rooms are clean but nothing special. There's also a pool and kids' playground, and staff are very friendly.

Also recommended are the following:

Rocky Mountain Ski Lodge (☎ 888-435-4222; **W** www.rockymtnskilodge.com; 1711 Bow Valley Trail; double/with kitchen CAD$100/105, 2-bedroom/with kitchen CAD$115/125)

Canadian Rockies Chalets (☎ 403-678-3799; **W** www.canadianrockieschalets.com; 1206 Bow Valley Trail; chalets sleeping 6/8 from CAD$179/239)

Bow Valley Motel (☎ 403-678-5085; **W** www.bowvalleymotel.com; 610 Main St; doubles CAD$95-110)

Canmore Motel (☎ 403-678-5158; 738 Main St; doubles CAD$40)

PLACES TO EAT

Rocky Mountain Bagel Company (☎ 403-678-9978; 102-830 Main St; mains CAD$4; open 6:30am-10pm) This is the most popular place in town for a coffee and lunch. It's worth standing in line for bagelwiches, soups and salads.

Sage Bistro (☎ 403-678-4878; 1712 Bow Valley Trail; lunch/dinner CAD$10/20; open 11am-11pm Sun-Thu, 11am-midnight Fri & Sat) The bright, spacious and contemporary atmosphere here is only outshined by the food. For brunch try smoked trout crepes or whole-wheat raspberry pancakes, and for lunch or dinner dive into maple wood–smoked duck, cranberry-stuffed quail or one of the many tasty veggie options.

Crazyweed Kitchen (☎ 403-609-2530; 626 Main St; lunch/dinner CAD$11/20; open 11:30am-3pm & 5:30pm-late) With an innovative ever-changing menu, this casual, fashionable place is a rising star in Alberta's cuisine world. Main courses like tea-smoked sable fish and homemade linguine keep customers piling in.

Mélange (☎ 403-609-3221; 107-721 Main St; lunch/dinner/tapas CAD$9/20/9; open noon-3pm & 5-10pm) For a choice of sizzling tapas and international entrées with a Gallic flair, head here .

Ziggy's (☎ 403-678-1941; cnr Main St & 7th Ave; slice/pie CAD$3.25/14; open 11am-4am) If you're looking for a quick lunch or something for the road, Ziggy's can fill you up with topping-loaded pizzas.

GETTING THERE & AWAY

Canmore is easily accessible from Banff Town and Calgary along Trans-Canada Hwy 1. All buses en route between Banff Town and Calgary stop in at the **Greyhound Bus Depot** (☎ 403-678-4465; cnr Main St & 7th Ave; open 7:30-midnight).

Kananaskis Country
MAP 7

Nestled next to each other over mountain ranges and down through deep valleys, a string of Alberta's provincial parks and reserved multiuse areas create over 4000 sq km/1578 sq miles of rural playground, known as Kananaskis Country. Bumping up against the eastern border of Banff National Park, Kananaskis Country is much quieter than its legendary neighbor yet provides excellent opportunities for heaps of outdoor pursuits. The area's look is its own, and the carved sides and fashioned peaks of the mountains may leave you feeling like you've driven into a claymation cartoon starring a moose or two, nonchalantly munching along the roadside.

ORIENTATION & INFORMATION

From Canmore in the northwest, Kananaskis Country stretches almost as far as the small town of Highwood House in the southeast. Most people visiting the area from Canmore complete a loop down the Kananaskis Trail (Hwy 40) and up along the Smith–Dorrien Rd (Hwy 742).

Near the northern end of Kananaskis Trail, **Barrier Lake Information Centre** (☎ 403-673-3985; W www.gov.ab.ca/env/parks/prov_parks/kananaskis; Kananaskis Trail, Hwy 40; open 9am-5pm summer, 9am-4pm winter) has loads of information, including maps, trail conditions and accommodations brochures. They also sell backcountry camping passes for the park.

The **Peter Lougheed Information Centre** (☎ 403-591-6322; Kananaskis Lakes Rd) provides similar information for those arriving from the south.

A third information booth and an **ATM** and **post office** are located in tiny Kananaskis Village.

SIGHTS & ACTIVITIES

In the richly forested foothills, **Jumpingpound Demonstration Forest** (☎ 403-297-8800; Hwy 68; open May-Sep) is a 10km/6.2-mile interpretive auto tour winding through spruce, aspen, fir and pine trees, with exhibits of sawmills from days of yore and of modern logging techniques. To reach the forest, follow the gravel Hwy 68 18km/11.2 miles east off the Kananaskis Trail.

For a trip around the area on horseback, stop at **Boundary Ranch** (☎ 403-591-7171; W www.boundaryranch.com; Kananaskis Trail; 1 hr CAD$30; open mid May–mid Oct). Tours can be catered to all ages and abilities.

At **Kananaskis Country Golf Course** (☎ 402-591-7154; W *www.kananaskisgolf* *.com; Kananaskis Trail, south of Kananaskis Village; greens fee CAD$70),* you can chase the little white ball around two 18-hole courses in the midst of spectacular scenery. Rent your gear at the clubhouse.

To cast a line, head for **Sibbald Meadows Pond** on Hwy 68; it's small but hopping with fish. You can also launch your boat at **Barrier Lake** on the Kananaskis Trail. **Lower Kananaskis Lake** is popular for bull trout.

Peter Lougheed Provincial Park is popular for hiking, particularly around the Kananaskis Lakes. Information centers supply trail maps and interpretive maps for short walks; **Ptarmigan Cirque** (3 hours roundtrip), **Boulton Creek Trail** (1 hour roundtrip), **Kananaskis Canyon Trail** (45 minutes roundtrip) and **Middle Lake Trail** (1 hour roundtrip) are all great places to get out and stretch your legs.

If you prefer to bike the trails, take on the challenging trail system at **Smith-Dorrien Park**. Rent mountain bikes, children's bikes and bike trailers from **Peregrine Source for Sports** (☎ 403-591-7453; *Kananaskis Village; full day CAD$6.25-12.50; open 9am-4:30pm).*

Many of the hiking trails are open to cross-country skiers in the winter. **Ribbon Creek**, **Peter Lougheed**, **Smith-Dorrien** and **Mount Shark** areas all have trails for beginners to advanced skiers. To rent cross-country skies (CAD$17), as well as toboggans, snowshoes and skates, head to **Peregrine Source for Sports** (previously mentioned).

Downhill skiers can reenact the 1988 Winter Olympics at **Nakiska** (☎ 403-591-7777; W *www.skinakiska.com; Kananaskis Trail, south of Kananaskis Village; day lift pass adult/youth/child CAD$46/36/15, under 6 yrs free),* on the slopes of Mt Allan. Snowboarders will likely prefer the more daredevil hill at **Fortress Mountain** (☎ 403-591-7108; W *www.skifortress.com; day lift pass adult/youth/child CAD$35/25/12, under 6 yrs free).*

PLACES TO STAY

Camping

Kananaskis Country has some stunning, peaceful campgrounds. Backcountry camping permits are mandatory for all hikers spending the night in the wilds; they cost CAD$3 per person per night, plus a CAD$6 administration fee per party. The backcountry sites do fill up; call the information centers to reserve ahead.

Canyon Camping (☎ 403-591-7226; W *www.kananaskiscamping.com; CAD$17; Kananaskis Lakes Rd; open mid-Jun–Sep)* has 50 sites next to Lower Kananaskis Lake and fabulous views of the mountains.

One of the most popular campgrounds in the area, **Boulton Creek Campground** (☎ 403-591-7226; W *www.kananaskiscamping.com; CAD$17; open May-Nov)* has 118 private, level sites. Loop B has big drive-through sites for RVs. Facilities include showers, flush toilets and a nearby grocery store.

Next to the lake, **Lower Lake Campground** (☎ 403-591-7226; W *www.kananaskiscamping.com; CAD$17; open May-Nov)* has 95 big drive-through wooded sites for RVs. The nine fantastic walk-in sites for tents are utterly secluded, with views of the lake and mountains.

Ask for a lakeside site at **Interlakes Camping** (☎ 403-591-7226; u *www.kananaskis camping.com; CAD$17; open May-Nov).* The grounds have 48 sites total and a boat launch.

Other campgrounds include:

Elkwood Amphitheatre Campground *(☎ 403-591-7226; u www.kananaskiscamping.com; CAD$17; open May-Nov)*

Mt Kidd RV Park *(☎ 403-591-7700; Mt Kidd Dr; full/electricity/no hookups CAD$32/26/20; open year-round)*

Sibbald Lake Camping *(☎ 403 673 2163; Hwy 68; CAD$17, CAD$15 for additional unit; open May-Sep)*

Eau Claire Campground *(☎ 403-591-7226; CAD$17, CAD$15 for 2nd unit; open mid-May–mid-Sep)*

Lodging

Rooms at **Kananaskis Resort** *(☎ 888-591-7501; W www.kananaskisresort.com; Kananaskis Village; doubles CAD$159-259)* are tastefully decorated with black and white alpine photos and beautiful furnishings, creating a modern, alpine feel. Also in the village, the **Delta** *(☎ 888-244-8666; W www.deltahotels.com; doubles CAD$190-230, family rooms & lofts CAD$260, extra adult CAD$25)* has spacious, standard rooms.

With sweeping views across an alpine meadow, you'll find lots of home comforts at **Mount Engadine Lodge** *(☎ 403-678-4080; W www.mountengadine.com; rooms & cabins per person CAD$105-150, meals included)*. Rooms and cabins are snug and prices include hearty meals that you can enjoy from the big deck or before the fireplace. Discounts for children are available.

Cozy, clean and bright, the simple **HI Kananaskis Wilderness Hostel** *(☎ 403-521-8421; W www.hihostels.ca; Kananaskis Village; dorms members/nonmembers CAD$19/23)* is close to lots of activities. The big kitchen is well equipped, and there's a comfy lounge with a fireplace. Dorm rooms have seven bunks each, and there's a private room for three.

Also check out **Sundance Lodges** *(☎ 403-591-7122; W www.sundancelodges.com; Kananaskis Trail; trapper's tent/4-person tepee/2-person tepee/tent site CAD$64/60/56/19; open mid-May–Oct)* for comfortable tepees and trapper's tents, or **William Watson Lodge** *(☎ 403-591-7227; Kananaskis Lakes Rd; cabins CAD$30-40; open year-round)*, which is designed to give people with disabilities access to the area.

PLACES TO EAT

Pick up basic groceries at **Fortress Junction**, **Mt Kidd RV Park** or **Boulton Creek Trading Post**.

There are a few places to eat in Kananaskis Village. Shoot a game of pool while you wait for your food at **Woody's Pub and Patio** *(☎ 888-591-7501; Kananaskis Mountain Lodge; mains CAD$10; open noon-2am)*. **Brady's Market** *(The Delta; mains CAD$25; open 6:30-9:30pm)* is a tiny place going for a rustic Tunisian feel and serving up seafood, tapas and pasta. The menu at **The Fireweed Grill** *(☎ 888-244-8666; The Delta; breakfast/lunch/dinner CAD$10/12/25; open 6:30-11am, noon-4pm & 5-9pm)* is more inspired than the decor, with fresh seafood and barbecued steak.

At **Rick Guinn's Steakhouse** *(☎ 403-591-7171; Boundary Ranch; mains CAD$12; open 11am-7pm mid-May–mid-Oct)*, you can feast on ranch-style steak and burgers, and at **Mount Engadine Lodge** *(breakfast buffet/lunch/dinner CAD$12/12/32, reservations mandatory)*, you'll dine on tasty set meals before a gorgeous meadow view.

GETTING THERE & AWAY

Kananaskis Country can be reached off Trans-Canada Hwy 1 along the gravel Smith-Dorrien Hwy 742 from Canmore or the Kananaskis Trail (Hwy 40), just east of Canmore. From southern Alberta, you can reach the area in summer along Hwy 40 from Highwood House.

Yoho National Park
MAP 5

A visit to Yoho National Park takes you down through the Kicking Horse Valley, alongside the surging, blue-green Kicking Horse River. Rocky, multicolored mountains tower on either side, cradling natural wonders like crashing waterfalls and brilliant lakes.

In the midst of Yoho National Park lies the quaint village of **Field**, with buildings dating all the way back to the early days of the railway. At the town's entrance is the **Field Visitor Centre** (☎ *250-343-6783; Trans-Canada Hwy; open 9am-7pm summer, 9am-4pm winter)*, which is home to a **Parks Canada** (☎ *250-343-6100;* **w** *www.parkscanada.gc.ca/yoho)* information desk. You can collect maps and information on accommodations and trails here, in addition to making reservations for backcountry camping.

Yoho lies snug against Banff's western border and the provincial boundary. About 27km/16.7 miles from Lake Louise Village and just inside British Columbia, Field is the main center for accommodations and restaurants.

SIGHTS
Lake O'Hara

While not particularly easy to reach, the gorgeous **Lake O'Hara** is the park's most popular site. You can reach the lake on a day trip, but it's worth staying overnight and setting out on one of the rigorous day hikes. The **Alpine Circuit Trail** (12km/7.4 miles) offers a smorgasbord of the surrounding scenery, with wooded hillsides, alpine meadows and glacier vistas.

The lake is accessible by foot along the 11km/6.8-mile access road or the 13.8km/8.6-mile nonmaintained forest trail. You can also reach it by public bus (June 19 to the end of September). It gets busy in summer (as does the campground), so reserve *(summer* ☎ *604-343-6418, winter* ☎ *403-762-4481; adult/child CAD$12/5)* as far in advance as possible. Reservations are allowed up to three months in advance. Catch the bus at the parking lot just off the highway, and don't leave valuables in your car while visiting the lake.

Takakkaw Falls

Named 'magnificent' in Cree, **Takakkaw** (245m/804ft) is one of the highest waterfalls in Canada. An impressive torrent of water travels from the Daly Glacier, plunges over the edge of the rock face into a small pool and jets out into a tumbling cloud of mist. To reach the falls, head north off Hwy 1 along Yoho Valley Rd (open late June to October). En route you'll pass the second **Spiral Lookout** and the **Meeting of the Rivers**, where the clear Kicking Horse runs into the milky colored Yoho. The narrow road climbs a number of tight switchbacks.

Spiral Tunnels & Kicking Horse Pass

Upon completion of the railway in 1885, trains struggled up the challenging **Kicking Horse Pass**, the steepest railway pass in North America. Wrecks and runaways were common until 1909, when the **Spiral Tunnels** were carved into Mt Cathedral and Mt Ogden. If you time it right, you can see a train exiting from the top of the tunnel while its final cars are still entering at the bottom. The main viewing platform is off the Trans-Canada, 8km/5 miles east of Field.

Emerald Lake

Gorgeously green, **Emerald Lake** gains its color from light reflecting off fine glacial rock particles that are deposited into the lake by grinding glaciers. It's a highlight of the park, so the lake sees visitors year round, either to simply admire its serenity or to fish, skate, hike or horseback ride. In summer the water warms up just enough to have a very quick dip. The lake is 10km/6.2 miles north off the Trans-Canada Hwy. En route to the lake, you'll pass an impressive **natural bridge** stretching across the Kicking Horse River.

Burgess Shale World Heritage Site

In 1909, Burgess Shale was unearthed on Mt Field – and with it, new questions and hypotheses on the evolution of life on Earth. With perfectly preserved fossils dated at over 500 million years old, the area is now a World Heritage Site and is accessible only by guided hikes, led by naturalists from the **Yoho-Burgess Shale Foundation** (☎ *800-343-3006;* **W** *www.burgessshale.bc.ca; to Burgess Shale adult/child CAD$59/27, to Mt Stephen adult/child CAD$27/16, open Jul–mid-Sep).*

ACTIVITIES

There are miles and miles of maintained **hiking trails** in Yoho; ask at Parks Canada for maps and information on backcountry camping. Favorite trails are those around Lake O'Hara, the flat walking path around Emerald Lake and the 20km/12.4-mile **Iceline** loop from Takakkaw Falls. **Historical walks** *(admission free; Tue-Sat 8pm)* are led through Field throughout the summer from Field Community Centre.

You can go **fishing** on Emerald Lake from July to November. Rent canoes from the lakeside **Emerald Sports & Gifts** (☎ *250-343-6377; 1hr CAD$20; open 9am-7pm summer, noon-4pm winter).* In winter you can rent **snowshoes** and **cross-country skis** here and set out across the frozen lake.

For guided horseback rides around Emerald Lake and the surrounding forests, visit **Emerald Lake Stables** (☎ *250-343-6082; Emerald Lake; 1hr adult/child CAD$30/25; 9am-6pm).* No shorts or sandals are permitted, and horses don't go faster than a walk.

PLACES TO STAY

Campers should head to **Kicking Horse Campground** *(Yoho Valley Rd; site/ with fire CAD$22/28; open late Jun–late Sep),* where riverside sites (loop 68–74) are forested, private and pleasant. With 92 sites, flush toilets, showers and an interpretive program, it's a popular place. The campground is also the site of an early railway construction camp; you'll see an old stone oven dating from 1884. Next door, **Monarch Camping** *(Yoho Valley Rd; CAD$14; open May 16–Sep)* is popular with RVers.

Field Information Centre keeps a list of the many private guesthouses (CAD$95-150) in town, as well as current vacancies.

Whiskey Jack International Hostel *(☎ 866-762-4122; Ⓦ www.hi hostels.ca; Yoho Valley Rd; members/nonmembers CAD$15/19; open mid-Jun– mid-Oct)* is near Takakkaw Falls and next to trailheads galore. Three basic dorm rooms each have nine bunks, a shower, toilet and heater. There's a simple kitchen but no food for sale anywhere close by.

Set in a forest below Cathedral Mountain, **Cathedral Mountain Lodge** *(☎ 250-343-6442; Ⓦ www.cathedralmountain.com; Yoho Valley Road; double/with loft CAD$274/294 including breakfast, extra person CAD$25, under 7 yrs free)* is definitely a treat. The beautiful, cozy log cabins have giant tubs, lots of pillows and a fireplace.

Between Lake Louise and Field, **West Louise Lodge** *(☎ 250-343-6311; Trans-Canada Hwy; doubles CAD$99)*, on Wapta Lake, is short of frills but is a good value. In Field, **Kicking Horse Lodge** *(☎ 250-343-6303; Kicking Horse Ave; doubles from CAD$126-172, extra adult CAD$12)* has typical, clean hotel rooms, some with kitchens and some able to accommodate up to six people.

Built in 1926, the historic and atmospheric **Lake O'Hara Lodge** *(☎ 250-343-6418; Ⓦ www.lakeohara.com; room/cabin CAD$400/500, including meals and transport; open mid-June–Oct & mid-Jan–mid Apr)* has down comforters and a stone fireplace to warm you after a day's hike. The upscale **Emerald Lake Lodge** *(☎ 403-410-7417; Ⓦ www.crmr.com; doubles CAD$470-710)* has balconies with some of the best views in the park, but rooms don't have a great deal of character, and prices seem rather steep.

PLACES TO EAT

An old-fashioned cabin full of character, **Cathedral Mountain Bistro Café** *(☎ 250-343-6442;Yoho Valley Rd; breakfast/lunch/dinner CAD$10/5/30; open 7:30-10am, 11am-4pm & 5-9:30pm)* serves tasty lunches and gourmet dinners.

In Field, **Truffles Pigs Café** *(☎ 250-343-6462; Stephen Ave; breakfast & lunch/dinner CAD$6/12; open 7am-10pm summer, 8am-7pm Mon-Thu & 8am-9pm Fri-Sat winter)* is a country shop-cum-bistro and is the most lively place in town. Try piggy-size sandwiches, huevos rancheros, burgers and panini. The eclectic dinner menu includes game and seafood off the barbecue (CAD$22), and the deli serves up sandwiches to go. Next door, **Kicking Horse Lodge** *(☎ 250-343-6303; Kicking Horse Ave; breakfast/lunch/dinner CAD$7/9/18; open 8-11am, noon-3pm & 5-9pm)* has surprisingly diverse mains, like Cajun burgers and salmon pie.

On Emerald Lake, **Cilantro** *(☎ 250-343-6321; mains CAD$20; open 11am-9pm Jun-Oct)* has big picture windows, a patio bar and a big fireplace. Gourmet dishes include grilled salmon with yam or buffalo ragout. There's also a formal dining room at **Emerald Lake Lodge** *(☎ 403 410 7417; mains CAD$32; open 6-9:30pm)* and a lounge *(CAD$13; open 11am-11pm)*, with salads, burgers and a Rocky Mountain Game Platter.

Mt Assiniboine Provincial Park
MAP 6

Nicknamed the Matterhorn of Canada, **Mt Assiniboine** reigns over 39 sq km/15 sq miles of provincial parkland. Accessible only by foot or helicopter, this small park entices backcountry campers, mountaineers and wildflower fans. For those who do make the effort, the soaring craggy peaks, the meadows and the shimmering **Lake Magog** don't disappoint. The name Assiniboine is borrowed from the Assiniboine natives who once hunted here; the game they searched for – elk, bears, moose, mountain goats and bighorn sheep – can still be seen roaming the slopes. The park's few facilities, including **park headquarters** *(☎ 250-422-4200)*, are located around Lake Magog, with rangers stationed here throughout the summer.

ACTIVITIES

The main activity in the park is **backcountry hiking**. While hikers have traditionally reached Lake Magog from Kananaskis Country, the more scenic and quieter route from Sunshine Village is deservedly gaining popularity. There are also numerous day hikes in the vicinity of the lake. For an easy walk visit **Gog Lake** (1.8km/1.1 miles) or **Wonder Pass Viewpoint** (5.6km/3.5 miles); for a demanding hike, set out for **Mt Cautley** (4.8km/3 miles).

Rock climbing in the park is very tough and should only be attempted by experienced, well-equipped climbers. These mountains are made of decaying limestone, meaning there are frequent rock falls; always check with park headquarters before setting out.

In winter, **cross-country skiing** is a popular way to experience the park; most skiers visit via Assiniboine Pass, and all should be prepared to camp en route, as conditions can vary daily. All skiers must carry an avalanche beacon. The season is generally from mid-December until the end of April.

PLACES TO STAY

The park's main **campground** *(CAD$5 per person)* is found on the west side of Lake Magog. Fires are prohibited, and water can be gathered from nearby spring-fed streams. Not far away is a **group campground** with 25 sites; reservations are mandatory.

On the eastern side of the lake, the four, rustic **Naiset Cabins** *(CAD$20 per person)* provide basic shelter. Cooking inside is prohibited, and fires in the heaters must be lit with compressed sawdust logs; bring your own or buy some from the lodge. In summer, the cabins are snatched up on a first-come, first-served basis, so be prepared to camp. From December until June, reservations are required.

The original **Mount Assiniboine Lodge** *(☎ 403 678 2883; u www.assiniboine lodge.com; double lodge rooms CAD$180, private/shared cabins CAD$230/180, all including meals, under 13 yrs CAD$110; open mid Jun Oct & mid-Feb–mid-Apr, reservations mandatory)* was the first ski lodge in the Canadian Rockies. Today's renovated and enlarged log lodge is owned by BC Parks but is family-run. Cabins command fantastic views.

GETTING THERE & AWAY

Most visitors reach the park on foot or cross-country skis. The other option is to arrive by helicopter *(☎ 403-678-2883; CAD$100 one way Fri, Sun & every other Wed)*.

Kootenay National Park & Radium Hot Springs

In 1920 the BC provincial government set out to build the first Canadian motor road across the Rockies. When funding floundered, the federal government agreed to lend a hand in return for land on either side of the road. The result was Kootenay National Park, stretching a mere 8km/5 miles to either side of Hwy 93. Incredibly, the park encompasses an extremely diverse range of scenery, from the glacier-topped peaks in the north to the drier Rocky Mountain Trench in the south. Visible from space, the trench cuts deep into the earth's surface, from the US border to the Yukon. With some excellent day hikes, intriguing natural wonders and gorgeous views, Kootenay Park makes a great day trip from Banff, or a destination in itself.

ORIENTATION & INFORMATION

Along the western ranges of the Rockies, Kootenay Park runs from Banff National Park in the north, along the Continental Divide to the town of Radium Hot Springs in the south. The 94km/58.3-mile Hwy 98 is the only road through the park.

The majority of accommodations and facilities are found in the tiny town of Radium Hot Springs, just outside the park's southern boundary. Collect maps and trail information from **Kootenay Visitor Information Centre** (☎ 250-347-9505; W www.parkscanadagc.ca/kootenay; 7556 Main St East, open 9am-7pm summer, 9am-5pm winter). There's also a desk here for **Radium Hot Springs Tourist Information** (☎ 250-347-9615). You'll find a second parks information desk at Vermillion Crossing, where you can purchase fishing licenses and park passes.

SIGHTS

If you stop once in the park, see **Marble Canyon**, which is only 6km/3.7 miles south of the Trans-Canada along Hwy 98. The easy 15-minute trail zigzags over **Tokumm Creek**, giving jaw-dropping views deeper and deeper into the canyon below. The limestone walls have been carved away by the awesome power of the water, resulting in plunging falls and bizarrely shaped cliff faces. The trail can be slippery and is not maintained in winter.

A further 3km/1.9 miles down Hwy 98, a short, flat interpretive trail leads to the intriguing red and orange **ochre ponds**. Drawing Kootenay natives for centuries – and later, European settlers – the earth was collected, mixed with oil and turned into paint. Pieces of mining equipment lay rusting where abandoned. Further along the trail are three crystal-blue springs, known as the **Paint Pots**.

The park boundary between Banff and Kootenay passes over the **Continental Divide**, where water flows either west to the Pacific or east all the way to the Atlantic. The **Fireweed Trail** is a 15-minute interpretive path that takes you along the divide.

Set in a valley just inside the southern border of the park, the outdoor **Radium Hot Springs** (☎ 250-347-9485; W www.rhs.bc.ca; Hwy 98; adult/child CAD$6.50/5.50; hot/cool pool open 9-11am/noon-9pm summer, both pools open noon-9pm Mon-Fri, noon-10pm Sat-Sun winter) has a hot pool simmering at 39°C/102°F and a second pool to cool you off at 29°C/84°F. The name stems from the small amount of radium detected in the water in 1914. Don't worry, the radiation is less than that given off by an ordinary watch dial. You can rent lockers, life jackets, towels and swimsuits here. The large tiled pools get crowded in summer.

ACTIVITIES

There are lots of options for **hiking** in Kootenay. **Stanley Glacier** (11km/6.8 miles roundtrip) is a popular trail leading to a moraine-strewn valley where the glacier hangs between the peaks of Mt Stanley. Moose and black bears often meander through here. Other popular day hikes include **Kimpton Creek Trail** (9.6km/6 miles roundtrip) and **Kindersley Pass Trail** (20km/12.4 miles roundtrip). For a worthwhile overnight hike, follow **Floe Lake Trail** (21.4km/13.3 miles roundtrip). If you've got more time, take on the full **Rockwall Trail** (55.6km/34.5 miles one way), a favorite of many seasoned hikers. Reservations for this busy route are recommended in summer. A wilderness pass is required for anyone camping in the backcountry. Visit Parks Canada for more information on trails and to buy permits.

Kootenay River Runners (☎ 250-347-9210; W www.raftingtherockies.com; Hwy 93) operates fairly tame white-water rafting trips down the Kootenay River (half-day adult/child CAD$59/45) and full-on adventures down the Kicking Horse River (CAD$78). Take a float trip (adult/child CAD$49/35) in the evening for a good chance of seeing wildlife.

Golfers will think they've found heaven in Radium Hot Springs; really it's the 18-hole, scenic **Radium Resort Spring & Resort Courses** (☎ 250-347-6266; W www.radiumresort.com; Resort Course, Hwy 93/95; Springs Course, McKay St; Resort Course Mon-Thu/Fri-Sun CAD$40/47, Springs Course Mon-Thu/Fri-Sun CAD$65/75; open late Mar-Oct).

In summer, Friends of Kootenay runs a **Junior Naturalist Program** (☎ 250-347-6525; Redstreak Campground Theatre; Mon & Wed afternoon) for children ages six to 12. Activities include fun hikes and outdoor games. Register at the Kootenay information center.

PLACES TO STAY

The majority of accommodations are found in Radium Hot Springs, where endless alpine-style hotels line the southern end of Hwy 93. The information center keeps a list of accommodations, but there is no central reservation center. If you're stuck for a bed, head east for Invermere.

Camping

Only 6km/3.7 miles from the park's northern border, **Marble Canyon Campsite** (Hwy 98; CAD$17, with fire CAD$23; open mid-Jun-Sep) has wooded sites and flush toilets. Sites on the eastern side have better views, as do sites on Loop A. Further south is **McLeod Meadows** (Hwy 98; CAD$17, with fire CAD$23; open mid-May-mid-Sep). Head to Loop J for secluded sites or Loop K for a view of the river. The campground has 98 sites, flush toilets, shelters, food-storage lockers and wheelchair-accessible sites.

At the southern end of the park, **Redstreak Campground** (Stanley St East, Radium Hot Springs; full/electricity/no hookups CAD$30/26/22, fire permit CAD$6; open May-Oct) has 242 sites in slightly wooded grounds; however, there appears to be more road than campsites. Loops F and H offer the most shelter, and you'll find full facilities here. In winter, you can camp at **Dolly Varden** (CAD$17; Hwy 98; open mid-Sep-May), with seven sites and basic facilities.

If the park is full, head 5km/3.1 miles south of **Radium Hot Springs** to Dry Gulch Provincial Park (Hwy 93/95; CAD$17, cash only) for 26 wooded and very private sites.

Lodging in Kootenay Park

If you're going to splurge on one place during your holiday, seriously consider **Storm Mountain Lodge** (☎ 403-762-4155; **W** www.stormmountainlodge.com; Hwy 98; double cabins CAD$195, including breakfast). Just inside the northern border of the park, these luxury cabins were built in 1925 and have been gorgeously restored right down to the copper piping in the bathroom. They're cozy and romantic, with a big wooden bed, fireplace and clawfoot bathtub. Meals in the equally charming lodge are gourmet.

With cabins built in the 1930s, **Kootenay Park Lodge** (☎ 403-762-9196; **W** www .kootenayparklodge.com; Vermillion Crossing, Hwy 98; double cabins CAD$90-115; open mid-May–late Sep) offers snug, rustic accommodations in the heart of the park. Set among trees and off the road, the quaint cabins have fireplaces and sheltered verandas.

The 1960s-style Radium Hot Springs Lodge (% 250-347-9341; Hwy 98; doubles CAD$130-140) has very average rooms; prices seem steep.

Lodging in Radium Hot Springs

The friendly **Black Bear's Inn** (☎ 250-347-9565; **W** www.blackbearsinn.com; 5017 Hwy 93; double CAD$70, extra adult CAD$5, under 10 yrs free) is the best deal in town, with very comfortable, renovated rooms looking out over a pine forest. Each room has a barbecue, microwave and fridge, and there's a hot tub with water from the springs.

Chalet Europe (☎ 250-347-9305; **W** www.chaleteurope.com; Madsen Rd; doubles CAD$109-149) sits on a hill above town, looking like a Swiss hotel. Newly renovated one-bedroom suites have kitchens and excellent views. Corner suites have panoramic views and a telescope.

Pinewood Motel (☎ 250-347-9529; **W** www.pinewoodmotel.ca; Stanley St; doubles CAD$65) has clean, standard rooms, each with a kitchen and sitting room. **Radium Springs Hostel** (☎ 250-347-9912; **W** www.radiumhostel.bc.ca; Hwy 98; dorms CAD$17-21, doubles CAD$54-69) offers basic dorms, a kitchen and a deck with a view. Private rooms don't seem worth the asking price.

The upmarket **Radium Resort** (☎ 800-667-6444; **W** www.radiumresort.com; off Hwy 93/95; double/suite CAD$109/179, extra adult CAD$10, youth under 15 yrs free) rests in the Columbia Valley, surrounded by forest and mountain scenery.

PLACES TO EAT

In Radium Hot Springs, **Higher Ground** (☎ 250-347-0089; Hwy 93, Radium Hot Springs; mains CAD$6; open 6am-6pm) is a relaxed place to have a coffee, indulge in cake or fill up on a bagel. At the very casual **Back Country Jack's** (☎ 250-347-0097; Hwy 93, Radium Hot Springs; lunch/dinner CAD$8/18; open Mon-Thu & Sat 11:30am-10pm, Fri 11:30am-midnight, Sun 11:30am-9pm), you can dine on hot prime-rib sandwiches, Filet a la Big Guy, chili or pasta. Kids will be kept busy with crayons and the children's menu (CAD$5). **Helna's Stube** (☎ 250-347-0047; 7547 Hwy 93, Radium Hot Springs; mains CAD$18; open 5-10pm) has Austrian fare for connoisseurs; try schnitzel cordon bleu or Vienna *rostraten*.

GETTING THERE & AWAY

From Banff, head south along Hwy 98 from Castle Junction. You can also reach the park from the south by heading north from Cranbrook on Hwy 93 to Radium Hot

Springs. In Radium Hot Springs, the Greyhound bus depot is on Hwy 93, next to the Esso station and near the junction with Hwy 98.

Golden

Once hardly given a second glance by travelers zipping through en route to Yoho and Banff, little Golden is becoming a destination in itself as the adrenaline capital of the Rockies. From white-water rafting to cat-skiing to hardcore downhill biking, you'll find something to get your heart racing. The recently developed Kicking Horse Resort is drawing skiers from across the continent, while the town itself is experiencing a boom, with some good restaurants and reasonable accommodations.

Golden is divided in two by the Kicking Horse River; the smaller, northern side, near the Trans-Canada Hwy, is where you'll find the majority of tourist facilities. For trail maps and activity brochures, visit **Golden Visitor Information Centre** (☎ 250-344-7125; W *www.goldenbritishcolumbia.com; 500 North 10th Ave; open 9am-5pm summer, Tue-Fri 10am-4pm winter).* You can get online at **180** (☎ 866-344-4609; 423 9th Ave N; 10 mins CAD$1; open 8:30am-9pm) or **Jenny's** (9th Ave N; per min CAD$0.12).

ACTIVITIES

There are lots of **hikes** directly from Golden; ask at the information center for trail conditions, descriptions and maps. If you're really eager to get out into the wilderness, hop on a flight with **Percell Heli-Hiking** (☎ 250-344-5410; W *www.purcellhelicopter-skiing.com; full/half day CAD$440/255; mid-Jun–Oct).*

With the raging Kicking Horse River running right through town, there's no shortage of **white-water rafting** companies to take you for a ride. Each offers trips for beginners, float rides for families and wild rides through the rapids for thrill seekers. The season is May to September.

Alpine Rafting (☎ 888-599-5299; W *www.alpinerafting.com; Golden View Rd; half/full day from CAD$65/105)*

Wet & Wild (☎ 800-668-9119; W *www.wetnwild.bc.ca; half/full day from CAD$60/105)*

Glacier Raft Company (☎ 250-344-6521; W *www.glacierraft.com; full/half day CAD$89/55)*

Adrenaline Descents (☎ 250-344-4679; W *www.adrenalinedscents.com; 735 Hefti Rd; full/half day from CAD$65/105)*

For a tour along the Columbia River by **kayak**, contact **Wet & Wild** *(see preceding list; CAD$60).* **Adrenaline Descents** *(see preceding; list tour CAD$65, rental CAD$25-55),* which runs kayaking tours and rents kayaks. If you prefer to **canoe**, **Kinbasket Adventures** (☎ 250-344-6012; W *www.bcrockiesadventures.com)* runs full- and half-day tours along the Columbia River, as well as **bird watching** and **wetland tours**. The Columbia River is a nesting ground for thousands of migrating birds; watch for osprey, bald eagles and herons.

For serious riders, **mountain biking** doesn't get much better than around Golden. The **Golden Cycling Club** (e *goldencyclingclub@canada.com)* produces a trail map (CAD$2), available from the information center and most cycle shops in town; try **Summit Cycle** on 11th Avenue. You'll also find 12 trails at **Kicking Horse**

Mountain Resort (☎ 250-439-5400; W www.kickinghorseresort.com; single ride/full day CAD$17/30; open noon-8pm, mid-Jun–mid-Sep), where you can take your bike up the gondola.

Very new on the scene but already snowballing into fame, the **Kicking Horse Mountain Resort** (day pass adult/youth/child CAD$50/40/20; open mid-Dec–mid-Apr) has limited grooming and lots of powder. Views are sensational, and with 78 runs, you can pack in about four days of skiing. While there are good runs for beginners, there are even better options for experts. You'll find accommodations, restaurants, ski rentals and classes.

Adrenaline Descents offers **heli-skiing**, **sled-skiing**, guided skiing (CAD$325 per day) and avalanche-awareness training for skiers and snowboarders (intro/advanced CAD$155/275). To get plowed out to the powder, try **cat-skiing** with **Chatter Creek Mountain Lodge** (☎ 250-344-7199; W www.catskiingbc.com; per day CAD$500 including meals, accommodations & guide, not including helicopter CAD$240 roundtrip).

For snowmobiling, check out **Snowpeak Rentals** (☎ 888-512-4222; W www.snowpeakrentals.com; 1025 10th Ave N; half/full day from CAD$120/175). There are 12 trails around Golden where you can zip around on the little machines. **180** (☎ 866-344-4609; 423 9th Ave N; skis, boots & poles from CAD$31 per day) rents standard and performance ski equipment.

PLACES TO STAY

You'll find lots of standard motels heading north of Golden on the Trans-Canada Hwy. **Khar** (☎ 866-344-4609) is an agency dealing with accommodations reservations in Golden.

The sites near the entrance of the **municipal campground** (☎ 250-344-5412; 9th St S; power/power & water/no hookups CAD$14/16/17; open mid-May–mid-Oct) are squished between the road and the train tracks; head further into the grounds for a wooded area near a river. There are hot showers, shelters and a total of 69 sites; reservations are accepted. South of Golden, **Sander Lake Campground** (Nicolson, off Hwy 95; CAD$14) is somewhat rough but is handy to the Moonraker Trails for mountain bikers.

The friendly **Hillside Lodge & Chalets** (☎ 250-344-7281; W www.mistaya.com/hillside; Trans-Canada Hwy; doubles CAD$128, including breakfast; cabins CAD$125-135) has lovely, cozy wood cabins with all the comforts of home and rooms in the lodge with mountain views.

Originally a 1920s rail house, **Kicking Horse Hostel** (☎ 250-344-5071; 518 Station Ave; dorms CAD$25) has a homey atmosphere, lots of videos, a deck and a spacious kitchen. Dorm rooms are far from crowded and have big sturdy bunks; the hostel sleeps a maximum of 12.

Rooms at **Mary's Motel** (☎ 250-344-7111; 603 8th Ave N; doubles CAD$56-59) are super clean and a good value. Some are more like suites with kitchenettes. Newer rooms cost a bit more but look the same as older rooms. Also check for vacancies at the **Sportsman Lodge** (☎ 250-344-2915; W www.sportsmanlodge.ca; Trans-Canada Hwy; doubles CAD$74-79, pets CAD$5).

PLACES TO EAT

With the most atmosphere in town, **Kicking Horse Grill** (☎ 250-344-2330; 1105 9th St S; mains CAD$20; open 4:30-11pm) pulls off fine dining pioneer-style. The log cabin is lit with fairy lights and candles, chairs are covered in white linen, and service is excellent. The menu is impressively eclectic – sushi, steak, pasta and curries. Reservations are recommended.

Dinner at the classy **Cedar House** (☎ 250-344-4679; 735 Hefti Rd, off Hwy 95; mains CAD$25; open 5-10:30pm) is worth the drive south of town. The views from the deck and dining room are stunning, and the food – all fresh and free range – is delicious.

Eleven 22 (☎ 250-344-2443; 1122 10th Ave S; mains CAD$15; open 4-10pm) is artsy and intimate, serving steamed mussels, pasta, steak and Asian dishes.

The mellow, colorful **Dogtooth Café** (☎ 250-344-3660; 1007 11th St N; mains CAD$7; open 8am-6pm Mon-Sat, 10am-4pm Sun) is a good place to grab a quick, healthy lunch. Fresh baked goods and tasty soups and sandwiches will keep you happy while your kids are busy in the children's corner.

GETTING THERE & AWAY

About 25km/15.5 miles west of Yoho National Park, Golden is situated next to the Trans-Canada Hwy, at the junction of Hwy 95 south. Greyhound buses pass through town twice a day, stopping on the east side of the Trans-Canada Hwy at the intersection with 14th St North.

Well known as one of the world's most scenic drives, the Icefields Parkway (Hwy 93) connects Banff and Jasper National Parks between two strings of glacier-coated peaks in the Eastern Ranges.

EXPERIENCING
ICEFIELDS PARKWAY

The road curves around mountains, climbs high passes and follows three major river systems flowing through wide hanging valleys. As the highest and most spectacular road in North America, the Icefields Parkway takes you about as close as you're going to get to the Rockies' craggy summits in your vehicle; if you get out and follow one of the many trailheads en route, you'll feel like you're on top of the world within a matter of hours. Numerous roadside stops give you the chance to take in the Parkway's brilliantly colored glacial lakes, gushing waterfalls and exquisite viewpoints. While you can cover the route in a few hours, it's worth spending a few days exploring the region; camp at one of the campgrounds along the parkway, stay in a rustic lodge, or base yourself in Lake Louise Village or Jasper Town.

Much of the route followed by the parkway was established in the 1800s by native peoples and fur traders. An early road was built during the 1930s as part of a work project for the unemployed, and the present highway was opened in the early 1960s. These days it's used almost entirely by tourists, with the exception of the occasional elk, coyote or big horned sheep meandering along its perimeter.

When You Arrive

The North Gate of the parkway is 6km/3.7 miles south of Jasper; the South Gate lies 2km/1.2 miles north of the junction with the Trans-Canada. Both gates act as tollbooths, where you'll receive *The Icefields Parkway*, a handy map and brochure detailing stops along the way. A parks pass is required to travel along this route, regardless of whether you plan to stop or not. Day passes are available for adult/senior/child CAD$6/4.50/3; year passes give you unlimited access to all of Canada's national parks for adult/group up to five people CAD$38/75. You can pay with Visa, MasterCard, American Express, travelers checks or cash. The road is officially open year-round, but heavy snows in winter frequently bring closures. Almost all services shut down from November until March.

ORIENTATION & INFORMATION

Running southeast to northwest for 230km/142.6 miles, the Icefields Parkway crosses the boundary between Banff and Jasper National Parks at 122km/75.6 miles from its southern end and 108km/67 miles from the north. The road roughly follows the Continental Divide, with the Alberta–British Columbia provincial border lying to the west.

From the south, reach the parkway from Trans-Canada Hwy 1; the turnoff is 2km/1.2 miles west of Lake Louise Village. In the north, the parkway joins Hwy 16, which heads northeast into Jasper Town and on to Edmonton or west to Mt Robson Provincial Park. About halfway along the parkway, inside Banff, is a junction with Hwy 11 at Saskatchewan River Crossing; this road heads east to Rocky Mountain House and Red Deer.

At Saskatchewan River Crossing you'll find a restaurant, hotel, telephones and a gas station. At Columbia Icefield Centre (open in summer only), just inside Jasper Park, you'll find restaurants, a hotel, telephones and a **Parks Canada Information Desk** (☎ *780-852-6288; Icefield Centre, Jasper Park; open 9am-6pm summer, 9am-5pm May-Jun & Sep-Oct, closed winter)* where you can pick up maps of maps, trail information and permits for both parks. You can also collect maps and details about activities along the parkway from Parks Canada information centers in Jasper Town, Banff Town and Lake Louise Village.

Manned from March until October, **warden stations** are located along the parkway at Saskatchewan Crossing, just north of Jonas Creek Campground and at the southern junction with Hwy 93A.

Along the parkway are a number of campgrounds, hostels and a few lodges; many have public telephones. If you are camping or cooking for yourself, you'll need to bring along your groceries and supplies.

HIGHLIGHTS

Getting soaked to the skin at **Athabasca Falls** (p138)

Pushing icebergs out into the lake beneath **Angel Glacier** (p141)

Being mesmerized by the unreal color of **Peyto Lake** (p139)

Counting the claws of **Crowfoot Glacier** (p136)

Looking between the boards of the bridge to see the water slamming past at **Mistaya Canyon** (p136)

Getting Around

Traveling by car is a fantastic way to visit the parkway, as it allows you maximum flexibility. The speed limit is 90kmh/56 mph, and the road is well maintained, although weather conditions can bring snow to the highest passes even in midsummer. Try not to drive this road in a hurry; not only will you want time to appreciate the scenery, you are also likely to be stuck behind a convoy of motorhomes and trailers that are also busy taking in the sights.

Wildlife is common along the parkway, so always be prepared for animals darting across the road, particularly if you're driving at dusk or in the dark. Also watch out for cyclists whizzing past the fleets of vehicles. The only gas station you'll find is at Saskatchewan River Crossing; head out with a full tank.

There is no public bus transportation along the parkway. **Brewster** (☎ 800-760-6934; W *www.brewster.ca)* runs regular one-way and roundtrip tours along the route. Lots of companies run tours back and forth between Banff Town and Jasper along the Icefields Parkway, stopping at major sights en route. You can either take the coach one way and spend some time in the final destination or do a marathon loop in a day. See Organized Tours in the Banff (p70) and Jasper (p165) chapters for more information.

Sights

Natural wonder after natural wonder will astound you. While major sights, like the Athabasca Glacier and Peyto Lake, pack in the tourists, many of the smaller roadside viewpoints and short walks are equally impressive, and it's worth stopping at a few of them to soak up a bit of the parkway's majesty minus the crowds. No matter how many times you drive this route, you'll find new things to see.

Sights are divided into Banff and Jasper Parks and listed from south to north. For sights along Hwy 93A, see Driving Tours (p168) in the Jasper chapter.

BANFF NATIONAL PARK
MAP 8

The stunning **Crowfoot Glacier** lies just 33km/20.5 miles north of the southern end of the parkway. Giant and impressive, its second toe of ice dangles over **Bow Lake**, just 300m/984ft from the viewpoint on the western side of the road. Named over a century ago, the glacier's third and lowest toe receded and completely disappeared by the 1940s. Its two remaining toes continue to claw the lower slopes of **Crowfoot Mountain**. At the northern end of Bow Lake lies **Bow Glacier**. This hefty mass of ice carved out the Bow Valley over 10,000 years ago and has now receded to its lair in the **Wapta Icefield**.

As you reach the crest of **Bow Pass**, the highest point of the road, you'll have spectacular views down the valley. Just past here is the turnoff for **Peyto Lake**, one of the most popular sights along the Parkway but well worth joining the throng of tourists to see it. The robin egg–blue water of the lake is runoff from **Peyto Glacier**, 5km/3.1 miles south of the lake and hidden above a rock wall. The lookout point is a short walk (0.4km/0.2 mile) up a paved hill from the parking lot (there is also wheelchair access), and from it you can see the **Mistaya River** running through the mountain-studded valley. The lake is named after Bill Peyto, one of the park's early game wardens.

At 48km/29.8 miles, **Snowbird Glacier** hugs the side of **Patterson Mountain** like a giant, motionless waterfall; the lookout on the left is unmarked. From here, the parkway follows the river to **Mistaya Canyon**, where the water surges and snakes through a narrow limestone canyon. The walls of the canyon are carved away into potholes and plunge pools by the rock dust and gravel that are carried from the glacier. The forested walk down to the canyon is 500m/1640ft.

Flowing from high up on **Cirrus Mountain**, water seeps through the cracks of the cliff face and streams out in a multitude of tiny dripping waterfalls to create the

Weeping Wall. In winter it freezes into an impressive sheet of ice. The parkway climbs round a high bend from here; stop at the lookout near the top for amazing views back across the valley and at the creviced, angular side of **Mt Saskatchewan**. Around the next bend is **Bridal Veil Falls**, named for the intricate pattern of their cascade.

Just over the high **Sunwapta Pass** you leave Banff behind and slip into Jasper National Park.

MONSTER BEAR

In the untamed land between Banff and Jasper, you may well expect to encounter a little wildlife. However, if you're anticipating elk or even a grizzly, what lurks beyond that next bend might surprise you.

In 1811, David Thompson was forging across the Rocky Mountains en route to Jasper. He was a surveyor for the Northwest Company and he recorded in his journal:

'When proceeding up the Athabasca River to cross the mountains ... we came to the track of a large animal, which measured 14 inches in length by eight inches in breadth. Report from old times had made the head branches of this River, and the Mountains in the vicinity the abode of one, or more, very large animals, of which I never appeared to give credence. But the sight of the track of that large beast staggered me, and I often thought of it, yet never could bring myself to believe such an animal existed, but thought it might be the track of some Monster Bear.'

Thompson's Monster Bear was the M-s-napeo, more commonly known as Sasquatch or Bigfoot. Such a creature has been glimpsed by Stoney natives around the Saskatchewan River throughout the past century. Big, hairy and supposedly preceeded by a foul smell, sightings of the Sasquatch have been reported by locals and visitors around Banff and Jasper National Parks up into the 1990s.

JASPER NATIONAL PARK
MAP 8

The sight that draws tour buses and crowds en masse, **Athabasca Glacier** is the only glacier accessible to the fingertips of all tourists. Head down the parking lot on the west side of the road, and walk 500m/1640ft to the toe of the glacier.

From here, with sturdy shoes, you can tread a further 1km/0.6 mile onto the icy giant, but it's essential that you stay within the ropes; one step in the wrong direction could land you at the bottom of a crevice or slide you down into the rocky moraines.

The glacier was at its grandest in 1844, when it had eked its way across the present-day parkway and covered the parking lot on the eastern side of the road. The glacier is doing its best to advance again. Its lower portion crawls forward about 20m/66ft each year, and its upper regions slide down the mountain at a rate of 127m/417ft. Nevertheless, hot summers melt the glacier back faster than it can advance; it's only with a few cool summers that the glacier manages much progress. The glacier is part of the **Columbia Icefield**, the largest icecap south of the Artic Circle.

Across the road you can catch a giant **Snocoach** (☎ 403-762-6735; w www .brewster.ca; Icefields Centre, Jasper Park; adult/child CAD$30/15, under 6 yrs free;

depart every 15-30 mins 9am-5pm Apr–Sep, 10am-4pm Oct 1-15, closed mid-Oct–Apr) for a 1.5-hour tour 5km/3.1 miles up the glacier. Reservations are only accepted for groups, so try to avoid the rush between 10:30am and 3pm. Some Snocoaches are wheelchair accessible.

Tangle Falls tumble over a series of limestone steps. Although they indeed have a tangled appearance, the falls are actually named after Tangle River, which in turn was named by early explorers for the tangle bush they encountered in the area. Watch out for bighorn sheep and for tourists wandering in the middle of the road. Up the road are **Sunwapta Falls**. Just off the parkway, the Sunwapta River takes an abrupt turn and plunges into a deep limestone canyon.

The showpiece of waterfalls on the parkway, **Athabasca Falls** lies at the junction of the parkway and Hwy 93A, 30km/18.6 miles from Jasper Town. An amazing cauldron of frothing water, the Athabasca River rushes over the brink and into a twisting gorge. Unfortunately, the bridges crisscrossing the falls are ugly cement relics of the 1960s; nevertheless, the views are spectacular. Be prepared to get wet, and wear sturdy shoes to maneuver along the slippery paths.

Up the parkway, the incredibly blue **Horseshoe Lake** often goes unnoticed by visitors but is worth a short climb. After passing the foot of the lake, take the first left along the inside of the horseshoe; the color intensifies with the depth of the water.

Day Hikes

Trailheads from the parkway take you up into the mountains for stunning views down long valleys and to sparkling glaciers. All of these hikes can be reached on day trips from either Lake Louise Village or Jasper Town. For safety and permits, see p96.

BANFF NATIONAL PARK
While sights along the southern section of the road are often busy, the following day hikes are generally quiet retreats into the backdrop of the Parkway.

BOW GLACIER FALLS
Distance: 7.2km/4.4 miles roundtrip
Duration: 2 hours roundtrip
Challenge: Easy-Moderate
Elevation Change: 95m/310ft

This well-worn trail has been followed by visitors to the area since the late 1800s. In those days, the Bow Glacier was packed into the basin at the end of the trail; today it's receded beyond sight, leaving an impressive waterfall in its wake. It's a fairly easy walk, with only one steep jaunt, passing a pretty gorge and leaving you in a moonscape of moraine.

To reach the trailhead, turn left 37km/23 miles from the southern end of the parkway. The trail begins behind the Num-Ti-Jah Lodge. The walk follows the northern shore of beautiful **Bow Lake**, the source of the long, winding Bow River. Views across the lake take in **Crowfoot Mountain** and the **Wapta Glacier**, all but concealing **Mt St Nicholas**. At 2km/1.2 miles you reach the edge of the lake and the inlet, which the path follows southwest across a rock bed. To your right are two narrow **waterfalls** streaming down the cliff face. Follow the cairns across the rocky terrain, heading for a distant staircase and the mouth of the canyon.

At 3.5km/2.2 miles the staircase leads you up a forested ridge along-side the canyon. If it has been raining or snowing, this trail grows slippery. There is a small path heading left at the top of the staircase from which you can take a perilous look into the canyon, but you're better off heading down the one at the bottom of the second staircase. From here you can take a good gander at the giant granite boulder stuck in the jaws of the canyon, as well as the water rushing past below and the distant falls to the right. Be careful along here, as the path can be slippery, there are no barriers, and it's a long drop down.

Continuing up the stairs, the steep dirt trail brings you to a giant bowl filled with boulders left behind by the glacier. At its far end, **Bow Glacier Falls** plummets 100m/328ft to the ground. If you're hankering for a closer view, pick your way carefully across the moraine to the foot of the falls.

PEYTO LAKE & BOW SUMMIT LOOKOUT
Distance: 6.2km/3.8 miles roundtrip
Duration: 2 hours roundtrip
Challenge: Moderate-Difficult
Elevation Change: 230m/760ft

From the Peyto Lake Lookout, this old fire road continues up into the hills to the lookout once used to spot fires down the Mistaya and Bow Valleys. Set on a small grassy knoll, the views from this peaceful lookout are spectacular.

From the bottom of the parking lot, follow the paved trail 15 minutes (0.4km/0.3 mile) up a steady, gradual incline to the wooden platform overlooking the incredible **Peyto Lake**. Its robin egg–blue color is most brilliant in the sunlight, and from here you have a far-reaching view of a string of small lakes that are down the valley guarded on either side by icy peaks.

Continue up the paved trail, keeping right along edge of the ridge. At the junction of three trails, follow the middle trail, which continues to climb. Where the paved trail begins to loop around to the right (1km/0.6 mile), an unmarked dirt road continues uphill; follow it as it zigzags up the hillside. You'll reach a plateau on the right from which you can look back across the lake. From here the trail continues to climb south and, as the trees thin away, you enter wildflower territory and begin to get a taste of the views you can expect at the top.

At 2.5km/1.5 miles, the road dips into a rocky bowl. Stand quietly and watch the hoary marmots bathing in the sun or practice your echo to ward off any nearby bears. A stream flows through the center of the bowl. Once on the other side, you quickly make up any lost elevation, plus some, with a steep 0.5km/0.3-mile climb over two hills to the **Bow Summit Lookout**. To the southeast is the **Bow Valley**, and to the north is **Mistaya Valley** rising up to **Bow Pass**.

HELEN LAKE
Distance: 12km/7.4 miles roundtrip
Duration: 4 hours roundtrip
Challenge: Moderate-Difficult
Elevation Change: 550m/1804ft

Leading up to a vast hidden valley dappled with wildflowers and hoary marmots, this trail is fairly tough but worth it if you're after panoramic views or solitude. Helen Lake itself is more a convenient place to turn around than a worthwhile sight; do this hike for the journey rather than the destination. Don't attempt this route if the weather looks forbidding, as the weather's almost always worse at the top. The trailhead is 33km/20.5 miles north from the southern end of the parkway.

From the parking lot, follow the dirt trail up into the forest for a steady but gradual 3km/1.9 mile-ascent heading east. As you leave the forest behind, the climb grows steeper, with brief plateaus that give you a chance to catch your breath and take in fantastic views to **Crowfoot Glacier** and **Bow Lake**. The trail heads over a giant, boulder-strewn ridge; to the left, before the top, is a great outlook.

Over the ridge, the trail heads back toward the west along a fairly level path into a giant valley carved by a receding glacier. A number of small streams cross the path, and over your shoulder is a superb view back down the valley.

At 4.5km/2.8 miles, the trail dips below a rockslide and then rises up beside **Helen Creek**. The trail appears to branch into many; cross the creek at the most convenient spot and then continue up over the ridge on the other side.

Follow the path through the open meadow where you'll be greeted by countless hoary marmots. **Helen Lake** is a further kilometer, hidden in a dip below a **Cirque Peak**. It's more of a puddle than a lake, but the setting is stunning. Return by the same route.

JASPER NATIONAL PARK

The day hikes along the northern stretch of the Icefields Parkway tend to attract more visitors, however, they also lead you through some of the area's most breathtaking scenery and to gorgeous sights.

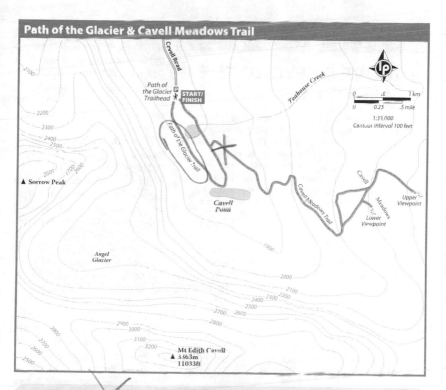

Path of the Glacier & Cavell Meadows Trail

Cavell Road

Teahouse Creek

Path of
the Glacier
Trailhead **START/
FINISH**

Path of the Glacier Trail

▲ Sorrow Peak

Cavell
Pond

Cavell Meadows Trail

Cavell

Upper
Viewpoint

Meadows

Lower
Viewpoint

1900

Angel
Glacier

2100
2000
2300 2200
2400
2500
2600
2700 2800

2900
3000
3100
3200

Mt Edith Cavell
▲ 3463m
11033ft

2100
2200
2300
2400
2500
2000
1700 1600

2800
2700
2600
2500

0   .5   1 km
0   0.25   .5 mile
1:33,000
Contour interval 100 feet

PATH OF THE GLACIER & CAVELL MEADOWS TRAIL
**Distance: to Glacier 1.6km/1 mile,
to Cavell Meadows 9.1km/5.6 miles
Duration: to Glacier 45 minutes roundtrip,
to Cavell Meadows 3 hours roundtrip
Challenge: Easy to Glacier,
Moderate Cavell Meadows to Lower Viewpoint,
Difficult Cavell Meadows to Upper Viewpoint
Elevation Change: Negligible to Angel Glacier,
400m/1300ft to Cavell Meadows**

With her wings spread mightily between the slopes of Mt Edith Cavell and Sorrow Peak, **Angel Glacier** appears to hover over a small sapphire lake afloat with icebergs. The ice blue and brilliant white is made all the more dramatic by the barren, stony surroundings created by the glacier's not-so-long-ago flight across the valley. **Angel Glacier Loop** is the most popular day trip from Jasper Town; head up to Cavell Meadows to escape the crowds and to achieve even better views. There is no shelter from sun or rain on these trails, so come prepared.

To reach the trailhead from Jasper, follow Hwy 93A south to Cavell Rd. From the parking lot at the end of the road (12km/7.4 miles), follow the stairs up to the start of the trail. Interpretive signs along the route tell

ABOVE & BEYOND THE CALL OF DUTY

Matron of a Belgian Red Cross hospital during the First World War, Edith Cavell was dedicated to assisting wounded soldiers regardless of their nationality. When two English soldiers appeared at her hospital seeking protection in 1914, Edith decided that helping them to escape was as humanitarian as tending the wounded. An underground lifeline was quickly established, and over the next year, Edith helped to smuggle over 200 Allied soldiers to neutral Holland. In 1915, she was arrested by German soldiers and sentenced to death.

The Germans, however, underestimated Edith's influence. It is claimed that members of the firing squad either refused to shoot her or fired wide, and that Edith was finally killed by an infuriated officer. Worldwide press coverage of her execution raised sympathies to such an extent as to double the number of enlisting Allied soldiers for two months and to help rally America to join the war.

The awe-inspiring 3363m/11,033ft **Mt Edith Cavell** is named in recognition of her bravery and is touched by the wing of Angel Glacier.

the story of both Edith Cavell and the glacier. The trail climbs uphill through rocky moraine. At 0.5km/0.3 mile, the trail to Cavell Meadows branches uphill to the left (see below). The Path of the Glacier continues ascending to a fantastic viewpoint of Angel Glacier, reflected in Cavell Pond at its feet.

The trail descends to the water, adrift with **icebergs**. There are a number of ice caves on the right side of the glacier, but reaching them is very dangerous business. Don't attempt to climb beneath the glacier, as chunks of ice the size of houses frequently crash down – and don't even dream about entering the caves.

From here, the path levels out and loops back to the parking lot. This area was covered by the glacier until the 1950s; small trees and plants are only just beginning to make an appearance.

A loop around **Cavell Meadows** will treat you to fantastic views and a good workout. Take a left off the Path of the Glacier trail at 0.5km/0.3 mile, and begin a steep ascent north along switchbacks. The trail levels off with clear views of the glacier to the right, beyond the moraine ridge. This area is strewn with boulders left behind by the glacier, some measuring up to 4m/13ft high. The path crosses a stream; catch your breath for the climb ahead. Switchbacks take you north into the forest; keep right at the junction (2.2km/1.4 miles), crossing two small streams and bringing you out into an open, flowery meadow. As you continue to ascend, enjoy the fantastic views back over the glacier. At 3km/1.9 miles is a short side trail right to the **Lower Viewpoint**.

Returning to the main trail, a brief climb brings you to another junction. If you've had enough, head left to meet up with the Path of the Glacier trail; if you've still got some energy and a penchant for climbs, turn right for the **Upper Viewpoint**.

The way is steep, the air grows thin and the rock-strewn trail becomes fainter and slippery. (After about 5 minutes, you're given a second chance to return down to the lower trail, with a trail branching off on the left.) Continuing uphill to the right brings you to a high subalpine meadow with an explosion of flowers. The path runs along a bank of loose shale with a steep drop on the left; then it turns right, where it becomes incredibly steep and rather treacherous.

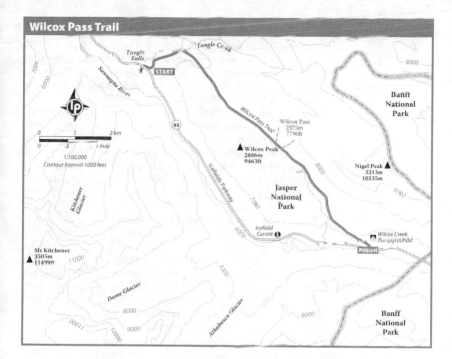

Wilcox Pass Trail

You'll know you've reached the **Upper Viewpoint** by the yellow marker; the panoramic views are also something of a giveaway. Southwest is **Mt Edith Cavell**; **Pyramid Mountain** lies to the north and **Roche Bonhomme** to the northeast. **Angel Glacier** is suspended to the west; from this height you have an impressive view of her wings and upper half.

Heading back, the descent along the loose shale is tricky. At the junction, turn right to return through lush meadows to the Path of the Glacier trail.

WILCOX PASS
Distance: 11.2km/6.9 miles one way
Duration: 3.5 hours one way
Challenge: Moderate
Elevation Change: 335m/1100ft

From this high alpine pass, you'll have exceptional views of the Columbia Icefield, some of the highest peaks in the Rockies, and perhaps even a bighorn ram or two. Wilcox Pass was forged by First Nation families avoiding the impassable Sunwapta Canyon; today it's recognized as one of the most scenic walks along the parkway but remains fairly quiet, particularly if you complete the route to Tangle Falls. If you don't have transportation from Tangle Falls back to the trailhead at Wilcox Creek Campground (3.1km/1.9 miles south of the Icefield Centre), you can go as far as the pass and return along the same route (8km/5 miles roundtrip).

143

From the trailhead parking lot, the path climbs up through the woods. The climb is steep but short, gaining 120m/394ft in about 1 km/0.6 mile. On the left watch for views to **Athabasca Glacier** as you travel through a patchwork of forest and flower-sprinkled meadows. At 2.5km/1.6 miles, you leave the forest behind, emerging into rocky, exposed terrain. To the right, **Nigel Peak** rises up 3212m/10,535ft.

At the junction head left, following the eastern ridge of a valley before turning north for a steep ascent. From the top there are fantastic, panoramic views that take in Athabasca Glacier, **Mt Athabasca** and **Mt Kitchener**. At the next junction, head right, veering away from the valley and heading between **Wilcox Peak** and **Nigel Peak**. Stepping stones lead you across a stream quickly after you reach **Wilcox Pass** (4km/2.5 miles), marked by a cairn. Have a look around for the bighorn ram that frequent these meadows.

Continuing north, go straight at the next junction, passing a pool on the right. The trail can be boggy along here, with snow into midsummer. Head left at the next fork, following the cairns across a number of streams. About half an hour from Wilcox Pass, the trail crosses a ridge, bringing the **Winston Churchill Range** into view to the northwest. You'll notice the giant **Mushroom Peak** (3200m/10,499ft) resting like a beached U-boat. Follow the cairns down to the right, away from the range and climbing into moraine; watch for cairns that mark the path across.

From here the trail becomes very faint, turning to shale as it nears the crest of a hill. From the top you'll see two hills ahead; don't mistake the rock on the furthest one as a cairn. The trail runs along the western foots of these hills, bearing left and descending steeply into a valley and then into the woods. From here the trail is more apparent, traversing the hills alongside **Tangle Creek** and with a viewpoint to **Stutfield Glacier**. The final descent brings you to **Tangle Falls**.

VALLEY OF THE FIVE LAKES
Distance: 4.2km/2.6 miles roundtrip
Duration: 1 hour 45 minute roundtrip
Challenge: Easy
Elevation Change: Negligible

This easy hike takes you past five serene lakes, each a different shade of blue and green. Popular with families, the trail winds through the woods, up and down small hills and around large boulders.

From the trailhead 9km/5.6 miles south of Jasper Town, on the eastern side of the parkway, follow the level, dirt trail through a lodgepole pine forest. At 0.8km/0.5 mile, the path dips down to cross a plank bridge over the **Wabasso Creek Wetlands**. Keep an eye open for **beavers**, who like to build dams along here. Climb up the opposite bank, heading straight at the junction. At the top of the small hill, you'll have views over your shoulder to **The Whistlers** and **Marmot Mountain**. Heading back into the woods, take a right at the Y-junction. The forest is not particularly dense, showing off its diversity of plants and trees.

After ascending and descending a few small hills, you'll see the **Fourth Lake** to your left, through the trees. While you can attempt to scramble down to its shores, you'll have much better views further along the trail. Cross a small bridge over a stream and head up the bank for views to the right of the aquamarine **Fifth Lake**. In the center of the lake is a small island, where **loons** nest and a few small boats are locked to a small dock (to rent one, visit Curries Tackle, 610 Connaught Dr, Jasper Town). This is a lovely, peaceful place to rest for a while

The trail heads north from here, along the slope of the **Fourth Lake**, which appears to change color – from aquamarine to emerald – as you travel alongside it. Up and down two more hills (the second is a little steep) brings you to a rocky point with shade to enjoy views across the lake.

Continue north to the **Third Lake**, ringed by a light green, and the multicolored **Second Lake**. Take a left between the **Second** and **First Lakes** to finish the loop; heading straight will take you on a lengthy (10km/6.2 mile) haul through the woods to **Old Fort Pointe Trail**, but the route is heavily used by bikers.

Other Activities

Backcountry hiking is popular from trailheads along the parkway. Wilderness permits are required for anyone staying overnight in the backcountry; see Banff (p96), Jasper (p179) and Planning (p34) chapters for more details. The **Alpine Club of Canada** (☎ 403-678-3200; W www.alpineclubofcanada.ca; Indian Flats Rd, Canmore) operates six backcountry huts along the these trails. Visit their website or Parks Canada for more details.

Mountain biking is allowed on several trails along the parkway; ask at the information desk at the Glacier Centre or in Lake Louise Village, Banff Town or Jasper Town for a trail map. The parkway itself is a popular bicycling route, as are **Wabasso Lake** and **Fortress Lake Trails**. For bike rentals and tours, see Activities in the Jasper or Banff chapters.

If you're eager to get up on the Athabasca Glacier on foot, join an **Ice Walk** (☎ 800-565-7547; W www.icewalks.com; Icefield Centre; adult/child from CAD$45/22.50; Jun-Sep) at Columbia Icefield. Experienced guides take groups on three- to six-hour interpretive hikes, taking in crevasses, millwells, crevasses and fantastic views.

Fishing is possible on some of the parkway's waterways, including parts of the **Athabasca** and **Sunwapta Rivers** (year-round) and **Third, Fourth** and **Fifth Lakes** in the Valley of Five Lakes (mid-May to September). A full list of regulations and restrictions is included with the required fishing permit, available from Parks Canada.

Horseback riding is also permitted on many trails; the **Athabasca Pass Trail**, **Astoria River Trail**, **Nigel Pass Trail**, **Glacier Lake** and **Howe Pass Trail** are all backcountry trails where you can trot your horse.

Come winter, **Marmot Basin** (☎ 780-852-3816; W www.skimarmot.com; Hwy 93A, Jasper Park; adult/youth 13-17/child 6-12 day pass CAD$52/42/20, under 6 yrs free; open Dec-May) ski area has 84 runs – some groomed and others deep powder. Beginners will find classes and some easy and moderate runs; experienced skiers have a huge choice of black-diamond and expert runs with chutes and open bowls. There's also a terrain park for snowboarders, equipment rental and childcare. Multiday and season packages are available.

Places to Stay

Numerous campgrounds are dotted along the parkway. Most have only basic facilities, but if you're willing to rough it a little, they are peaceful, remote and set in the midst of stunning scenery. There are also a number of basic hostels and a few private lodges, giving you easy access to hikes and a little more comfort.

CAMPING

Campsites in both Banff and Jasper National Parks are doled out on a first-come, first-served basis. See those chapters for more details, including a few hints for scoring a site and policies and regulations. For recorded information on campgrounds in Banff National Park, call ☎ 403-762-1550; in Jasper, call ☎ 780-852-3834.

Banff National Park Map 8
Mosquito Creek *(Icefields Parkway; with/without fire CAD$23/17; open Apr–mid-Sep)* Despite the name, there was nary a mosquito when we visited. Instead, you'll find 32 wooded sites next to a lovely creek. Facilities are basic – dry toilets and a water pump.

Waterfowl Lakes *(Icefields Parkway; with/without fire CAD$23/17; open mid-Jun–late Sep)* Sites are wooded, pleasant and close to the very blue lake. Those at the rear on the left back onto a stream. The grounds are fairly large, with 116 sites, wheelchair-accessible sites, shelters and flush toilets – pretty plush for this neck of the woods.

Jasper National Park Map 8
Columbia Icefield *(Icefields Parkway; with/without fire CAD$19/13, tents and vans only; open mid-May–mid-Oct)* While somewhat exposed to the elements, these sites are set back from the loop, making them some of the most secluded on the parkway. Views of the area are fantastic. Facilities are limited to dry toilets and a water pump.

Wabasso *(Hwy 93A; with/without fire CAD$23/17; open Jun–Sep)* Peaceful and remote, this campground is conveniently located, relatively near to sights and Jasper Town. Despite having 228 sites, the grounds are spread out and fairly private. Walk-in tent sites along the river are wooded and lovely. Sites A74, 76 and 78 are drive-in sites next to the water. Amenities include hot water, flush toilets and wheelchair-accessible sites.

Jonas Creek *(Icefields Parkway; with/without fire CAD$19/13; open mid-May–mid-Oct)* Sites on the south side of these grounds are sheltered by a small hill; those on the north side are wooded, pull-in sites, though they're not particularly private or far from the highway. Walk-in tent sites are small and secluded. Facilities for the 25 sites are limited to dry toilets and a water pump.

Honeymoon Lake *(Icefields Parkway; with/without fire CAD$19/13, open mid-May–mid-Oct).* With lake access, these grounds are fairly popular. Sites 26 to 28 are right next to the water, and the rest of the 35 sites are wooded and fairly large. Sites 4 to 20 are the most private. Dry toilets and a water pump are the only home comforts.

Mount Kerkeslin *(Icefields Parkway; with/without fire CAD$19/13; open late Jun–Sep)* Across from its towering namesake, this campground has 42 sheltered sites. The first half of loop 14 to 42 are larger and good for RVs, although not all are entirely level. Facilities are limited to dry toilets and a water pump.

Wilcox Creek *(Icefields Parkway; with/without fire CAD$19/13; open early Jun–late Sep)* If you score a site away from the road, you'll find trees and privacy here. Sites one to seven are exposed but have great views, and site 21 is wheelchair accessible. All 48 sites are roomy enough to pull an RV into. Facilities are minimal; there is a dry toilet, water pump and payphones.

LODGING
Banff National Park Map 8
Num-Ti-Jah Lodge *(☎ 403-522-2167; W www.num-ti-jah.com; Icefields Parkway; double lake/mountain view from CAD$210/245, including meals CAD$525/480; open Dec–mid-Oct)* Next to Bow Lake, with views to Crowfoot Mountain and the Wapta Icefield, the setting of this historic lodge couldn't get much more stunning. The library and lounge are packed with character, although rooms have a standard motel-ish feel to them.

Rampart Creek International Hostel *(☎ 403-670-7580; W www.hihostels.ca; Icefields Parkway; dorms members/nonmembers CAD$19/23; may be closed in winter)* Popular with cyclists and climbers, these 12-bed pine cabins are made all the more homey with decks, flower boxes and heaters. The kitchen is big and well equipped, and there's a sauna and a big outdoor fire pit. Up the road, the remote **Hilda Creek Hostel** *(☎ 403-670-7580; W www.hihostels.ca; Icefields Parkway; dorm member/nonmember CAD$19/23; may closed in winter)* is run on a reservation-only basis. See the manager at Rampart Creek Hostel for more information.

Mosquito Creek International Hostel *(☎ 403-670-7580; W www.hihostels.ca; Icefields Parkway; dorm member/nonmember CAD$19/23; may be closed in winter)* Next to Mosquito Creek, this cosy, basic hostel has heated dorm cabins in a forested, peaceful setting. There's also a family cabin, a sauna and a communal cabin with a kitchen lounge and fireplace. Nonguests can use the kitchen for a CAD$5 fee.

The Crossing *(☎ 403-761 7000, W www.thecrossingresort.com; cnr Hwy 11 & Icefields Parkway; doubles CAD$100; open mid-Mar–Nov)* Well located for hiking, rooms here are comfortable, with standard hotel atmosphere and fine views. It gets busy, so reserve in advance.

Jasper National Park Map 8
Athabasca Falls International Hostel *(☎ 780-852-3215; W www.hihostels.ca; Icefields Parkway; dorm member/nonmember CAD$13/18; closed Tue Oct–Apr)* This popular hostel has a big, alpine-style kitchen and sitting area, food lockers and even table tennis. Heated dorms are in wooden cabins. The forest setting is a good base for biking, hiking and cross-country skiing.

Mount Edith Cavell International Hostel *(☎ 780-852-3215; W www.hihostels.ca; Icefields Parkway; dorm member/nonmember CAD$13/18; open mid-Jun–mid-Oct)*

A great base for hiking, this rustic hostel has a comfy kitchen where you can buy mac & cheese, soft drinks and porridge. Enjoy the scenery from the deck or the outdoor firepit, and retire to basic dorms in cabins.

Beauty Creek International Hostel (☎ *780-852-3215;* W *www.hihostels.ca; Icefields Parkway; dorm member/nonmember CAD$12/17; open Apr-Oct)* With a homey kitchen, a deck with a barbecue and views, trailheads nearby and no electricity or running water, you can really get back to nature here.

Sunwapta Falls Resort (☎ *888-828-5777;* e *info@sunwapta.com; Icefields Parkway; doubles from CAD$79, suites from CAD$218; open May-Nov)* These comfortable rooms and suites are reasonably priced (relatively). Although next to the parkway, the setting is peaceful and staff is friendly. Suites sleep four adults.

Columbia Icefield Chalet (☎ *877-423-7433;* e *icefield@brewster.ca; Icefield Centre, Icefields Parkway; doubles CAD$185-195; open May-Oct)* On the 3rd floor of the Icefield Centre, rooms here are nothing exceptional, although views through the tiny windows are amazing. The atmosphere is more like a train station or shopping mall than a chalet.

Places to Eat

Banff National Park Map 8

Num-Ti-Jah Lodge (☎ *403-522-2167;* W *www.num-ti-jah.com; Icefields Parkway; lunch/dinner CAD$12/49; lunch 11am-5pm, dinner 6:30pm)* This atmospheric lodge runs an evening gourmet dinner; appetizers are served in the library, a feature entrée is dished up next to the fire in the dining room, and then it's all followed by dessert and drinks in the lounge. Reservations are required. Lunch is a little more typical, with salads, pastas and burgers.

The Crossing (☎ *403-761-7000; cnr Hwy 11 & Icefields Parkway; lunch/dinner CAD$8/20; open 11am-1:30pm & 5-9pm mid-Mar–Nov)* Trying for a bit of class, this dining room doesn't muster up much atmosphere. Nevertheless, you can fill up on wraps, fish and chips, and burgers at lunch, and lasagna, seafood and duck in the evening. If you're looking to eat and run, try the **canteen** *(mains CAD$8; open 7am-10pm mid-Mar–Nov)* for burgers and the like.

Jasper National Park Map 8

Sunwapta Falls Resort (☎ *888-828-5777; Icefields Parkway; lunch/dinner CAD$10/15; deli open 11am-6pm, dining room 6-9pm May-Nov)* With some good 'home cooking,' this is a relaxed place to stop for a meal. The deli serves burgers, salads and soups canteen-style; dinner has table service and features local seafood, lamb, beef and some interesting veggie options.

Icefield Centre Dining Room (☎ *877-423-7433; Icefield Centre, Icefields Parkway; breakfast/dinner CAD$7/17; open 8-10am & 6-9pm May-Oct)* Fantastic views of Athabasca Glacier will likely keep you from noticing the lack of atmosphere here. Fill up on pancakes, omelets or oatmeal before heading out on the trail. For dinner there's a bit of everything, including lots of Chinese cuisine. You'll also find a hectic **canteen** *(mains CAD$8; open 9am-6pm Apr-Oct)* at the Icefield Centre, good for hot dogs, noodles, soup and burgers.

MAP SECTION

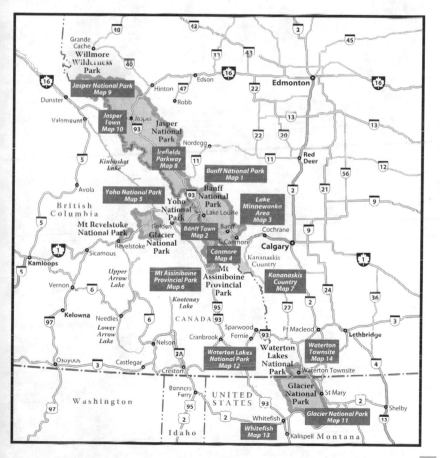

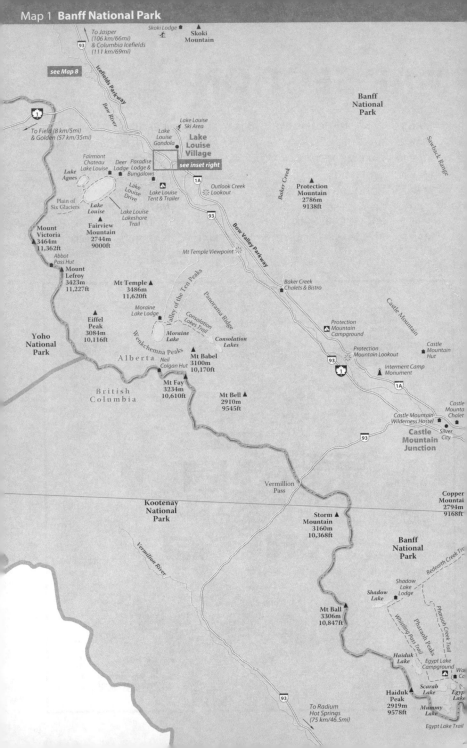

Map 1 Banff National Park

To Jasper
(106 km/66mi)
& Columbia Icefields
(111 km/69mi)

see Map 8

Icefields Parkway

Bow River

To Field (8 km/5mi)
& Golden (57 km/35mi)

Skoki Lodge

Skoki Mountain

Banff National Park

Sawback Range

Lake Louise Ski Area

Lake Louise Gondola

Lake Louise Village

see inset right

Fairmont Chateau Lake Louise

Lake Agnes

Deer Lodge

Paradise Lodge & Bungalows

Plain of Six Glaciers

Lake Louise Drive

Lake Louise

Lake Louise Tent & Trailer

Lake Louise Lakeshore Trail

Outlook Creek Lookout

Baker Creek

Protection Mountain 2786m 9138ft

Mount Victoria 3464m 11,362ft

Fairview Mountain 2744m 9000ft

Bow Valley Parkway

Mt Temple Viewpoint

Abbot Pass Hut

▲ **Mount Lefroy 3423m 11,227ft**

Baker Creek Chalets & Bistro

Mt Temple 3486m 11,620ft

Valley of the Ten Peaks

Panorama Ridge

Castle Mountain

Eiffel Peak 3084m 10,116ft

Moraine Lake Lodge

Consolation Lakes Trail

Protection Mountain Campground

Castle Mountain Hut

Yoho National Park

Wenkchemna Peaks

Moraine Lake

Consolation Lakes

Protection Mountain Lookout

Alberta

Neil Colgan Hut

Mt Babel 3100m 10,170ft

Interment Camp Monument

British Columbia

Mt Fay 3234m 10,610ft

Mt Bell 2910m 9545ft

Castle Mounta Chalet

Castle Mountain Wilderness Hostel

Silver City

Castle Mountain Junction

Vermillion Pass

Kootenay National Park

Copper Mountain 2794m 9168ft

Storm Mountain 3160m 10,368ft

Banff National Park

Vermillion River

Redearth Creek Tr

Shadow Lake Lodge

Shadow Lake

Mt Ball 3306m 10,847ft

Whistling Pass Trail

Pharaoh Peaks

Pharaoh Creek Tr

Haiduk Lake

Egypt Lake Campground

Wa Co

Scarab Lake

Egyp Lake

Haiduk Peak 2919m 9578ft

Mummy Lake

To Radium Hot Springs (75 km/46.5mi)

Egypt Lake Trail

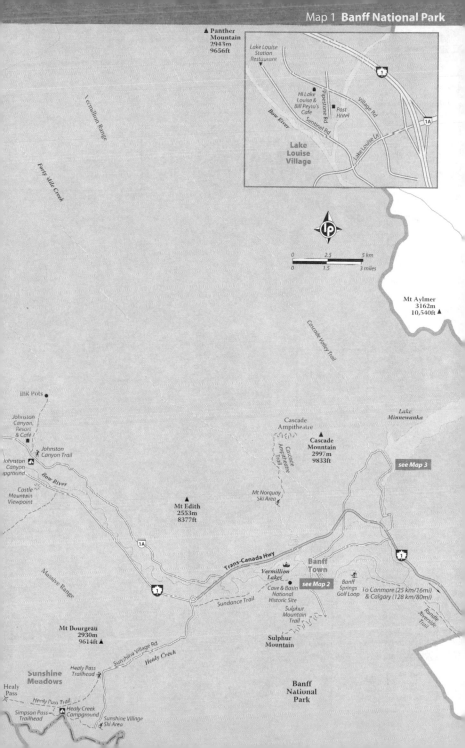

Map 1 **Banff National Park**

▲ Panther
Mountain
2943m
9656ft

Lake Louise Village

Lake Louise Station
Restaurant

Pipestone Rd

Hi Lake
Louise &
Bill Peyto's Café

Post
Hotel

Sentinel Rd

Village Rd

Bow River

Lake Louise Dr

1

1A

Lake Louise Village

Mt Aylmer
3162m
10,540ft ▲

0   2.5   5 km
0   1.5   3 miles

Vermilion Range

Forty Mile Creek

Lake Minnewanka

Cascade Valley Trail

Ink Pots ●

Johnston
Canyon
Resort
& Café

Cascade
Ampitheatre

Cascade Ampitheatre Trail

Cascade
Mountain
2997m
9833ft ▲

see Map 3

Johnston Canyon Trail

Johnston Canyon Campground

Castle Mountain Viewpoint

Bow River

Mt Edith
2553m
8377ft ▲

Mt Norquay
Ski Area

1A

Trans-Canada Hwy

Vermilion Lakes

Banff Town

1

see Map 2

Massive Range

1

Sundance Trail

Cave & Basin
National
Historic Site

Sulphur Mountain Trail

Banff Springs Golf Loop

To Canmore (25 km/16mi)
& Calgary (128 km/80mi)

Tunnel Riverside Trail

Mt Bourgeau
2930m
9614ft ▲

Sunshine Village Rd

Healy Creek

Sulphur
Mountain

Sunshine Meadows

Healy Pass Trailhead

Healy
Pass

Healy Pass Trail

**Banff
National
Park**

Simpson Pass Trailhead

Healy Creek Campground

Sunshine Village
Ski Area

Map 2 **Banff Town**

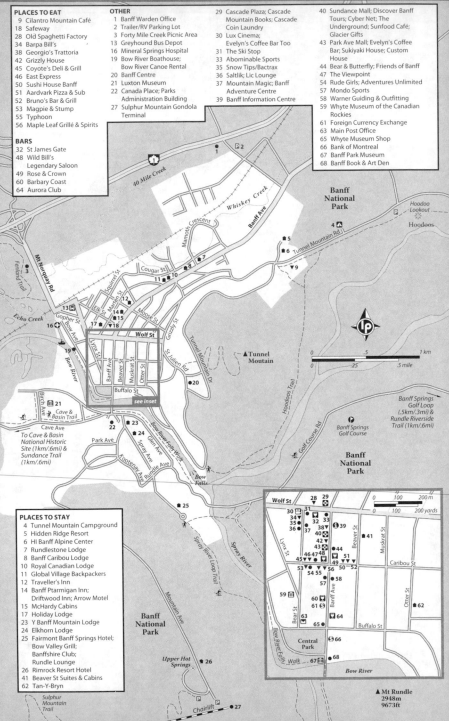

PLACES TO EAT
9 Cilantro Mountain Café
18 Safeway
28 Old Spaghetti Factory
34 Barpa Bill's
38 Georgio's Trattoria
42 Grizzly House
44 Coyote's Deli & Grill
46 East Express
50 Sushi House Banff
51 Aardvark Pizza & Sub
52 Bruno's Bar & Grill
53 Magpie & Stump
55 Typhoon
56 Maple Leaf Grillé & Spirits

BARS
32 St James Gate
48 Wild Bill's
   Legendary Saloon
49 Rose & Crown
60 Barbary Coast
64 Aurora Club

OTHER
1 Banff Warden Office
2 Trailer/RV Parking Lot
3 Forty Mile Creek Picnic Area
13 Greyhound Bus Depot
16 Mineral Springs Hospital
19 Bow River Boathouse;
   Bow River Canoe Rental
20 Banff Centre
21 Luxton Museum
22 Canada Place; Parks
   Administration Building
27 Sulphur Mountain Gondola
   Terminal

29 Cascade Plaza; Cascade
   Mountain Books; Cascade
   Coin Laundry
30 Lux Cinema;
   Evelyn's Coffee Bar Too
31 The Ski Stop
33 Abominable Sports
35 Snow Tips/Bactrax
36 Saltlik; Lic Lounge
37 Mountain Magic; Banff
   Adventure Centre
39 Banff Information Centre

40 Sundance Mall; Discover Banff
   Tours; Cyber Net; The
   Underground; Sunfood Café;
   Glacier Gifts
43 Park Ave Mall; Evelyn's Coffee
   Bar; Sukiyaki House; Custom
   House
44 Bear & Butterfly; Friends of Banff
47 The Viewpoint
54 Rude Girls; Adventures Unlimited
57 Mondo Sports
58 Warner Guiding & Outfitting
59 Whyte Museum of the Canadian
   Rockies
61 Foreign Currency Exchange
63 Main Post Office
65 Whyte Museum Shop
66 Bank of Montreal
67 Banff Park Museum
68 Banff Book & Art Den

PLACES TO STAY
4 Tunnel Mountain Campground
5 Hidden Ridge Resort
6 HI Banff Alpine Center
7 Rundlestone Lodge
8 Banff Caribou Lodge
10 Royal Canadian Lodge
11 Global Village Backpackers
12 Traveller's Inn
14 Banff Ptarmigan Inn;
   Driftwood Inn; Arrow Motel
15 McHardy Cabins
17 Holiday Lodge
23 Y Banff Mountain Lodge
24 Elkhorn Lodge
25 Fairmont Banff Springs Hotel;
   Bow Valley Grill;
   Banffshire Club;
   Rundle Lounge
26 Rimrock Resort Hotel
41 Beaver St Suites & Cabins
62 Tan-Y-Bryn

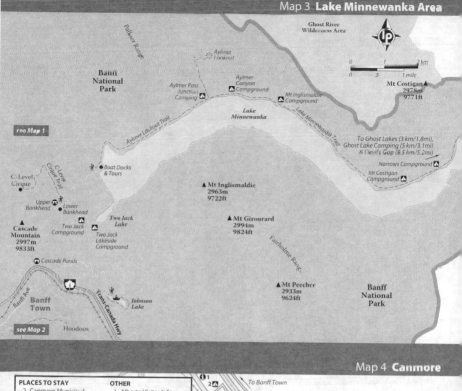

Map 3 Lake Minnewanka Area

Ghost River
Wilderness Area

Mt Costigan
2978m
9771ft

Banff
National
Park

Palliser Range

Aylmer
Lookout

Aylmer Pass
Junction Camping

Aylmer
Canyon
Campground

Mt Inglismaldie
Campground

0   1   2 km
0   .5   1 mile

Lake
Minnewanka

Aylmer Lookout Trail

see Map 1

To Ghost Lakes (3 km/1.8mi),
Ghost Lake Camping (5 km/3.1mi)
& Devil's Gap (8.5 km/5.2mi)

Narrows Campground

Mt Costigan
Campground

C-Level
Cirque

C-Level Cirque Trail

Boat Docks
& Tours

▲ Mt Inglismaldie
2963m
9722ft

Upper
Bankhead

Lower
Bankhead

Two Jack
Lake

Cascade
Mountain
2997m
9833ft

Two Jack
Campground

Two Jack
Lakeside
Campground

▲ Mt Girourard
2994m
9824ft

Fairholme Range

Cascade Ponds

Banff
Town

Banff Ave

Trans-Canada Hwy

Johnson
Lake

▲ Mt Peechee
2933m
9624ft

Banff
National
Park

see Map 2

Hoodoos

Map 4 Canmore

PLACES TO STAY
2 Canmore Municipal
Campground
3 Rundle Mountain Lodge
5 Rocky Mountain Ski Lodge
6 Canadian Rockies Chalets
8 The Lady Macdonald
Country Inn
9 The Georgetown Inn
13 Canmore Motel; Ziggy's
16 Bow Valley Motel
22 Restwell Trailer Park

PLACES TO EAT
4 Sage Bistro
11 Rocky Mountain Bagel
Company
15 Crazyweed Kitchen
19 Mélange

OTHER
1 Alberta Visitor Info
7 Gear Up
10 Rebound
12 Canmore Museum &
Geoscience Society
14 CyberWeb
17 Canmore Nordic Centre
18 Post Office;
Rusticana Grocery;
Greyhound Bus Dept
20 North West Mounted
Police Barracks
21 Altitude Sports
23 Canmore Rafting Centre
24 Alpine Helicopters

To Banff Town

McBride
St

Bow Valley Trail

Palliser Trail

Trans-Canada Hwy

1A

17 St

Fairholm Dr

Railway Ave

Sidney
St

Banchlands Trail

0   250   500 m
0   250   500 yds

Rundle Forebay

Smith-Dorrien Spray Trail

10 St
9 St
Main St (8 St)

Bridge Rd

Rundle Dr

7 Ave

5 Ave

6 St

5 St Centennial Park

4 St

3 St

2 St

1 St

7 Ave

6 Ave

4 Ave

3 Ave

Three Sisters Dr

Bow River

Spray Lakes Rd

To Bow River Campground,
Kananaskis Trail & Calgary

Bow Valley Trail

To Alpine Club
of Canada

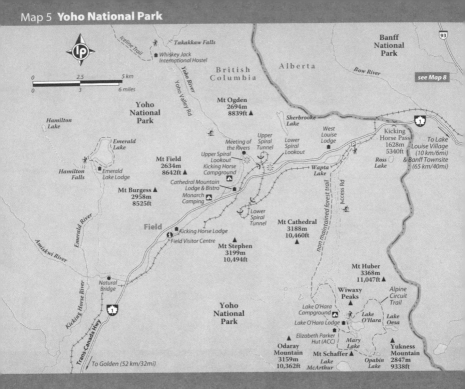

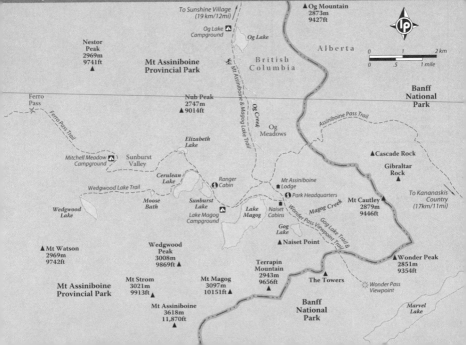

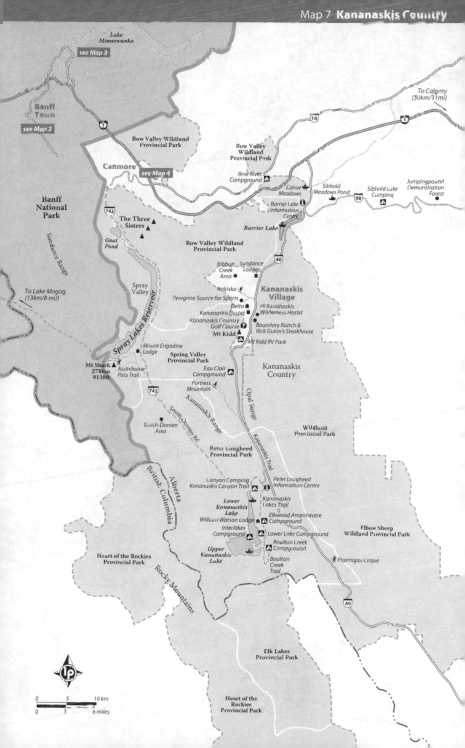

Map 7 **Kananaskis Country**

Lake
Minnewanka

see Map 3

To Calgary
(50km/31mi)

Banff
Town

see Map 3

Bow Valley Wildland
Provincial Park

Bow Valley
Wildland
Provincial Park

Canmore   see Map 4

Bow River
Campground

Canoe
Meadows

Sibbald
Meadows Pond

Sibbald Lake
Camping

Jumpingpound
Demonstration
Forest

Banff
National
Park

Barrier Lake
Information
Centre

The Three
Sisters

Goat
Pond

Bow Valley Wildland
Provincial Park

Barrier Lake

Sundance Range

Spray
Valley

Ribbon
Creek
Area

Sundance
Lodges

Kananaskis
Village

To Lake Magog
(13km/8 mi)

Nakiska

HI Kananaskis
Wilderness Hostel

Peregrine Source for Sports

Delta
Kananaskis Resort

Kananaskis Country
Golf Course

Mt Kidd

Boundary Ranch &
Rick Guinn's Steakhouse

Mt Kidd RV Park

Mount Engadine
Lodge

Spring Valley
Provincial Park

Kananaskis
Country

Mt Shark
2786m
9138ft

Assiniboine
Pass Trail

Eau Clair
Campground

Fortress
Mountain

Smith-Dorrien
Area

Smith-Dorrien Rd

Kananaskis Range

Wildland
Provincial Park

British Columbia

Alberta

Peter Lougheed
Provincial Park

Kananaskis Trail

Opal Range

Canyon Camping
Kananaskis Canyon Trail

Peter Lougheed
Information Centre

Lower
Kananaskis
Lake

William Watson Lodge

Interlakes
Campground

Upper
Kananaskis
Lake

Kananaskis
Lakes Trail

Elkwood Ampitheatre
Campground

Lower Lake Campground

Boulton Creek
Campground

Boulton
Creek
Trail

Ptarmigan Cirque

Elbow Sheep
Wildland Provincial Park

Heart of the Rockies
Provincial Park

Rocky Mountains

Elk Lakes
Provincial Park

Heart of the
Rockies
Provincial Park

0   5   10 km
0   3   6 miles

Map 8 **Icefields Parkway**

Jasper Lake

To Edmonton (98km/61mi)

To Map 9

▲ Mt Morro
1648m
5495ft

To Mount Robson Provincial Park (81km/50mi)

Jasper **see Map 10**

see inset

North Gate

Wabasso Campground

Angel Glacier

Mt Edith Cavell
3309m
11,033ft

Maligne Range

Maligne River

Maligne Lake

Honeymoon Lake Campground

Sunwapta Falls Resort
Sunwapta Falls

Continental Divide

Fortress Lake Trail

Hamber Provincial Park

Fortress Lake

British Columbia

Alberta

Endless Chain Ridge

Warden Station
Jonas Creek Campground

Beauty Creek International Hostel

▲ **Sunwapta Peak**
3262m/10,875ft

Tangle Falls & Tangle Creek

Columbia Icefield Centre

Columbia Icefield Campground
Wilcox Creek Campground
Sunwapta Pass 6635ft
Bridal Veil Falls
▲ Cirrus Mountain 3270m/10,720ft

Hilda Creek Hostel
Saskatchewan Mountain Lookout

Weeping Wall

▲ **Mushroom Peak**
3149m
10,499ft

Athabasca Glacier

Columbia Icefield

▲ **Mt Saskatchewan**
3289m
10,964ft

Rampart Creek International Hostel

▲ Mt Wilson
3210m
▲10,700ft

Jasper National Park

Brazeau River

Nordegg

11

▲ Mt Michener
2300m
7667ft

Abraham Lake

Kinbasket Lake

Banff National Park

Saskatchewan River

Saskatchewan River Crossing
● Warden Station

Mistaya Canyon

Waterfowl Lakes Campground

Mountain Time Zone
Pacific Time Zone

Continental Divide

Wapuutik Range

Mistaya River

Snowbird Glacier
Patterson Mtn ▲
Peyto Lake
Peyto Glacier
Peyto Lake & Bow Summit Lookout
Num-Ti-Jah Lodge
Bow Glacier Falls Trail
Crowfoot Glacier Lookout

Wapta Icefield

Bow Pass
▲ Cirque Peak
2945m
▲9819ft

Bow Lake

Helen Lake Trail

Mosquito Creek Campground
Mosquito Creek International Hostel

Crowfoot Mtn

Hector Lake

Bow River

Yoho National Park

Scott Duncan Hut

see Map 5

South Gate

Lake Louise Village

To Banff Town (61km/38mi)

see Map 1

Donald

Glacier National Park

Beaver River

Golden

Trans-Canada Highway

95

Columbia River

Kootenay National Park

▲ Mt Dawson
3262m
10,875ft

Grand Mtn ▲
3262m
10,875ft

95

0   15   30 km
0   10   20 miles

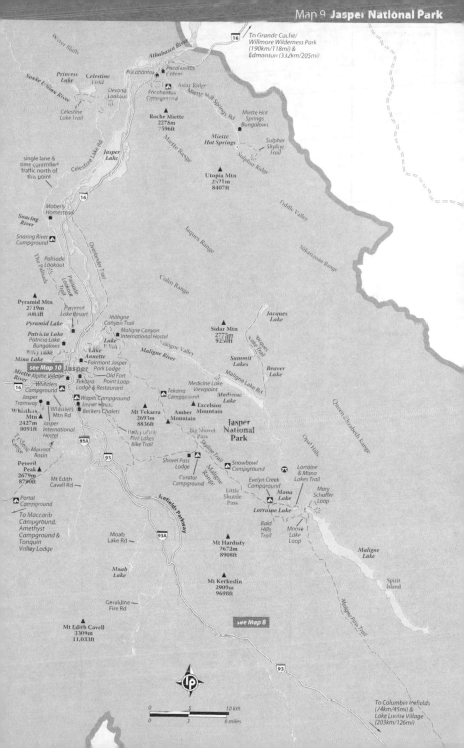

Map 9 **Jasper National Park**

To Grande Cache/
Willmore Wilderness Park
(190km/118mi) &
Edmonton (332km/205mi)

Athabasca River

Beaver Bluffs

Princess
Lake

Celestine
Lake

Pocahontas
Cabins

Pocahontas

Snake Indian River

Devona
Lookout

Pocahontas
Campground

Aster Ridge

Miette Hot Springs Rd

Celestine
Lake Trail

Miette Hot
Springs
Bungalows

Roche Miette
2278m
7596ft

Sulpher
Skyline
Trail

Miette
Hot Springs

Celestine Lake Rd

Jasper
Lake

Miette Range

Sulphur Ridge

single lane &
time controlled
traffic north of
this point

Moberly
Homestead

16

Utopia Mtn
2562m
8407ft

Fiddle Valley

Snaring
River

Snaring River
Campground

Jaques Range

Nikanassin Range

The Palisade

Palisade
Lookout

Overlander Trail

Palisade
Lookout
Trail

Colin Range

Pyramid Mtn
2719m
8083ft

Pyramid Lake

Maligne
Canyon Trail

Patricia Lake
Patricia Lake
Bungalows

Maligne Canyon
International Hostel

Jacques
Lake

Sidar Mtn
3250m

Weasel Vale Trail

Mina Lake

Miette
River

Lake
Annette

Maligne River

Maligne Valley

Summit
Lakes

Beaver
Lake

Alpine Village

Jasper

16

Whistlers
Campground

Fairmont Jasper
Park Lodge

Old Fort
Point Loop

Maligne Lake Rd

Jasper
Tramway

Tekarra
Lodge & Restaurant

Tekarra
Campground

Medicine Lake
Viewpoint

Medicine
Lake

Whistlers
Mtn
2427m
8091ft

Whistlers
Mtn Rd

Wapiti Campground

Jasper House

Beckers Chalets

Mt Tekarra
2693m
8836ft

Amber
Mountain

Excelsior
Mountain

Jasper
National
Park

Queen Elizabeth Range

Jasper
International
Hostel

93A

Big Shovel
Pass

Skyline Trail

Marmot
Basin

De Smet Range

Trails of the
Five Lakes
Bike Trail

93

Peveril
Peak
2679m
8790ft

Mt Edith
Cavell Rd

Shovel Pass
Lodge

Curator
Campground

Snowbowl
Campground

Maligne Range

Lorraine
& Mona
Lakes Trail

Opal Hills

Portal
Campground

To Maccarib
Campground,
Amethyst
Campground &
Tonquin
Valley Lodge

Icefields Parkway

Moab
Lake Rd

93A

Little
Shuttle
Pass

Evelyn Creek
Campground

Mona
Lake

Lorraine Lake

Mary
Schäffer
Loop

Bald
Hills
Trail

Moose
Lake
Loop

Maligne
Lake

Moab
Lake

Spirit
Island

Geraldine
Fire Rd

Mt Hardisty
2673m
8908ft

Mt Kerkeslin
2909m
9698ft

see Map 8

Maligne Pass Trail

Mt Edith Cavell
3309m
11,033ft

93

see Map 10

IP

0   5   10 km
0   3   6 miles

To Columbia Icefields
(74km/45mi) &
Lake Louise Village
(203km/126mi)

Map 10 **Jasper Town**

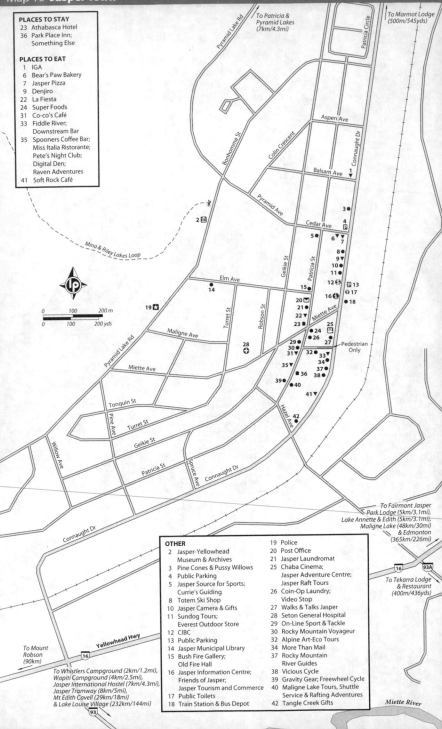

PLACES TO STAY
23 Athabasca Hotel
36 Park Place Inn;
   Something Else

PLACES TO EAT
1 IGA
6 Bear's Paw Bakery
7 Jasper Pizza
9 Denjiro
22 La Fiesta
24 Super Foods
31 Co-co's Café
33 Fiddle River;
   Downstream Bar
35 Spooners Coffee Bar;
   Miss Italia Ristorante;
   Pete's Night Club;
   Digital Den;
   Raven Adventures
41 Soft Rock Café

OTHER
2 Jasper-Yellowhead
   Museum & Archives
3 Pine Cones & Pussy Willows
4 Public Parking
5 Jasper Source for Sports;
   Currie's Guiding
6 Totem Ski Shop
10 Jasper Camera & Gifts
11 Sundog Tours;
   Everest Outdoor Store
12 CIBC
13 Public Parking
14 Jasper Municipal Library
15 Bush Fire Gallery;
   Old Fire Hall
16 Jasper Information Centre;
   Friends of Jasper;
   Jasper Tourism and Commerce
17 Public Toilets
18 Train Station & Bus Depot
19 Police
20 Post Office
21 Jasper Laundromat
25 Chaba Cinema;
   Jasper Adventure Centre;
   Jasper Raft Tours
26 Coin-Op Laundry;
   Video Stop
27 Walks & Talks Jasper
28 Seton General Hospital
29 On-Line Sport & Tackle
30 Rocky Mountain Voyageur
32 Alpine Art-Eco Tours
34 More Than Mail
37 Rocky Mountain
   River Guides
38 Vicious Cycle
39 Gravity Gear; Freewheel Cycle
40 Maligne Lake Tours, Shuttle
   Service & Rafting Adventures
42 Tangle Creek Gifts

To Patricia &
Pyramid Lakes
(7km/4.3mi)

To Marmot Lodge
(500m/545yds)

Mina & Riley Lakes Loop

To Fairmont Jasper
Park Lodge (5km/3.1mi),
Lake Annette & Edith (5km/3.1mi),
Maligne Lake (48km/30mi)
& Edmonton
(365km/226mi)

To Tekarra Lodge
& Restaurant
(400m/436yds)

Yellowhead Hwy

To Mount
Robson
(90km)

To Whistlers Campground (2km/1.2mi),
Wapiti Campground (4km/2.5mi),
Jasper International Hostel (7km/4.3mi),
Jasper Tramway (8km/5mi),
Mt Edith Cavell (29km/18mi)
& Lake Louise Village (232km/144mi)

Miette River

Pedestrian
Only

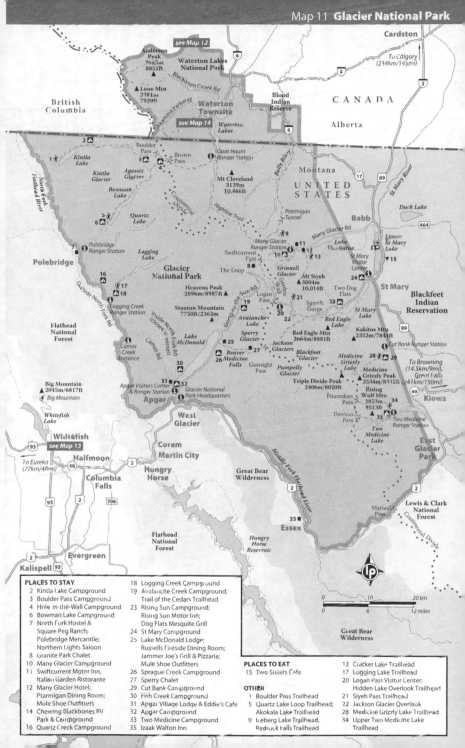

Map 11 **Glacier National Park**

PLACES TO STAY

2 Kintla Lake Campground
3 Boulder Pass Campground
4 Hole-in-the-Wall Campground
6 Bowman Lake Campground
7 North Fork Hostel &
   Square Peg Ranch;
   Polebridge Mercantile;
   Northern Lights Saloon
8 Granite Park Chalet
10 Many Glacier Campground
11 Swiftcurrent Motor Inn;
   Italian Garden Ristorante
12 Many Glacier Hotel;
   Ptarmigan Dining Room;
   Mule Shoe Outfitters
14 Chewing Blackbones RV
   Park & Campground
16 Quartz Creek Campground

18 Logging Creek Campground
19 Avalanche Creek Campground;
   Trail of the Cedars Trailhead
23 Rising Sun Campground;
   Rising Sun Motor Inn;
   Dog Flats Mesquite Grill
24 St Mary Campground
25 Lake McDonald Lodge;
   Russells Fireside Dining Room;
   Jammer Joe's Grill & Pizzaria;
   Mule Shoe Outfitters
26 Sprague Creek Campground
27 Sperry Chalet
29 Cut Bank Campground
30 Fish Creek Campground
31 Apgar Village Lodge & Eddie's Cafe
32 Apgar Campground
33 Two Medicine Campground
35 Izaak Walton Inn

PLACES TO EAT

15 Two Sisters Cafe

OTHER

1 Boulder Pass Trailhead
5 Quartz Lake Loop Trailhead;
   Akokala Lake Trailhead
9 Iceberg Lake Trailhead;
   Redrock Falls Trailhead

13 Cracker Lake Trailhead
17 Logging Lake Trailhead
20 Logan Pass Visitor Center;
   Hidden Lake Overlook Trailhead
21 Siyeh Pass Trailhead
22 Jackson Glacier Overlook
28 Medicine Grizzly Lake Trailhead
34 Upper Two Medicine Lake
   Trailhead

Map 12 **Waterton Lakes National Park**

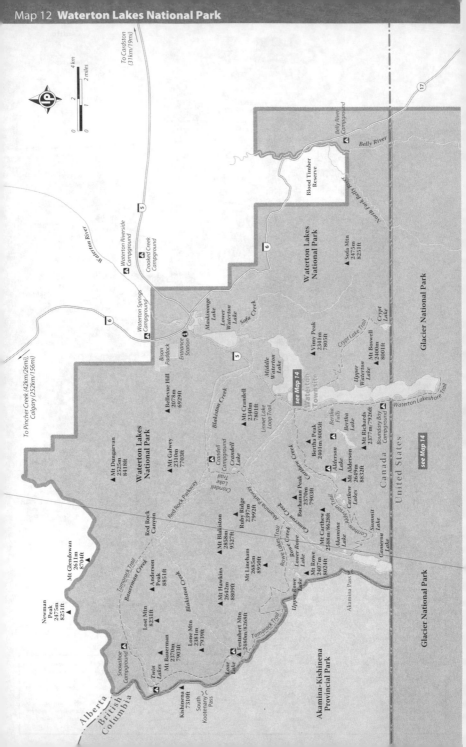

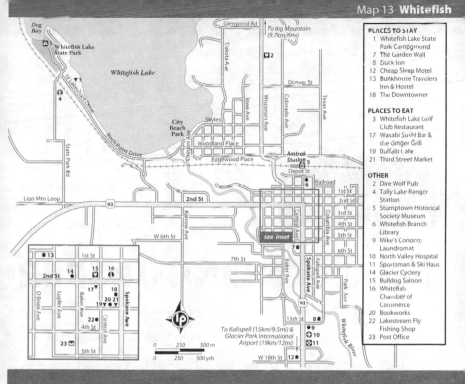

Map 13 Whitefish

PLACES TO STAY
1 Whitefish Lake State Park Campground
7 The Garden Wall
8 Duck Inn
12 Cheap Sleep Motel
13 Bunkhouse Travelers Inn & Hostel
18 The Downtowner

PLACES TO EAT
3 Whitefish Lake Golf Club Restaurant
17 Wasabi Sushi Bar & the Ginger Grill
19 Buffalo Cafe
21 Third Street Market

OTHER
2 Dire Wolf Pub
4 Tally Lake Ranger Station
5 Stumptown Historical Society Museum
6 Whitefish Branch Library
9 Mike's Conoco; Laundromat
10 North Valley Hospital
11 Sportsman & Ski Haus
14 Glacier Cyclery
15 Bulldog Saloon
16 Whitefish Chamber of Commerce
20 Bookworks
22 Lakestream Fly Fishing Shop
23 Post Office

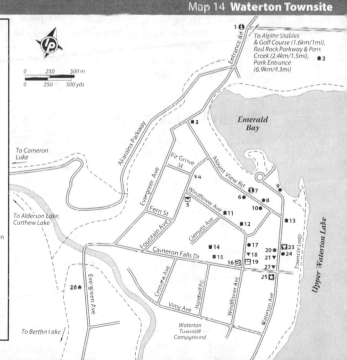

Map 14 Waterton Townsite

PLACES TO STAY
2 Prince of Wales Hotel
3 Kilmorey Lodge; The Lamp Post
11 Waterton Glacier Suites
12 Aspen Village Inn; Canadian Wilderness Tours
13 Bayshore Inn
14 Waterton Lakes Lodge
15 HI-Waterton; Waterton Health Club & Recreation Centre
26 Northland Lodge

PLACES TO EAT
4 Pizza of Waterton
18 Rocky Mountain Food Mart
21 Big Scoop Ice Cream
22 Zum's Eatery

OTHER
1 Waterton Visitor Centre
5 Post Office
6 Tamarack Village Square; Waterton Sports & Leisure; Waterton Visitor Services
7 Parks Canada Administration
8 Recycling Trailer
9 Waterton Shoreline Cruises
10 Pat's
16 Peace Park Plaza
17 Borderline Books & Coffee
19 Waterton Lakes Opera House Cinema
20 Trail of the Great Bear
23 Royal Canadian Mountain Police (RCMP)
24 Thirsty Bear Saloon
25 Waterton Heritage Centre

GLENBOW ARCHIVES ND3-384

The eastern slopes of the Rocky Mountains are rugged and remote, a vast wilderness supporting dense forests, alpine meadows and an abundance of wildlife.

EXPERIENCING JASPER

Mountain lions, wolves, caribou, beavers and bears roam freely; glaciers stretch out between mountain peaks; waterfalls thunder over slopes; and valleys are wide and lush, with rivers charging turbulently through them. This is Jasper National Park, covering a diverse 10,878 sq km/4200 sq miles.

Jasper National Park is far from built up. While activities like hiking and mountain biking are well established and deservedly popular, it's still easy to experience the solitude and remoteness that abound in this park. Some of the most popular natural wonders, like Miette Hot Springs and Maligne Canyon, are easily accessible, and many more attractions are just a short hike away. Keep a little spare time in your itinerary to take advantage of any diversions you stumble upon – a sparkling lake to laze by, a snowshoe tour to explore or a moose to watch ambling by. As the largest of Canada's Rocky Mountain parks, Jasper will quickly captivate you with its beauty and serenity.

When You Arrive

Arriving in Jasper Park, your first port of call should be the information center, where you'll receive the *Mountain Guide,* a magazine with maps, and information on local sights, and where you purchase your **parks pass** *(adult/senior/youth/family day pass CAD$7/6/3.50/14, annual pass CAD$45/38/22/89).* Passes are required for all stops within the park, including Jasper Town; if you're spending a week, an annual pass will work out cheaper and can be used in all national parks across Canada, including Banff and Yoho.

You can also purchase passes and receive information at the entrance gate at the northern end of the Icefields Parkway; other entrances are along major thoroughfares but do not have gates. The park is open year-round, though many activities and services are closed in the winter.

ORIENTATION

Jasper Park, some 200km/125 miles long and 80km/50 miles wide, lies along the Continental Divide and the border between Alberta and British Columbia. The eastern

Rockies span its length, topped with an amazing number of icefields that drain into a web of rivers and lakes. In the southeast, Maligne River flows into Medicine and Maligne Lakes. In the north, the Athabasca River rages into Jasper Lake and continues south along the Icefields Parkway, following the wide Athabasca and Sunwapta Valleys. The northern third of the park is very remote, accessible only by hiking trails and rivers.

There are two main road entrances to Jasper Park, meeting at Jasper Town, roughly in the middle of the park. Highway 16 enters from the northeast from Edmonton and from the west via Mt Robson Provincial Park. The Icefields Parkway runs south from Jasper Town, connecting the park with Banff National Park at 108km/67 miles.

Jasper Town is the main hub for the park, with lots of accommodations, places to eat, shops and activity-oriented organizations. You'll also find basic services like a post office, a bank and grocery stores.

INFORMATION

Built in 1913, the **Jasper Information Centre** (☎ 780-852-6176; **W** *www.parks canada.ca, 500 Connaught Dr; open 9am-7pm summer, 9am-4pm winter*) is a sight in itself. This is the place to pick up park and trail maps, to gather information on activities and trail conditions and to purchase permits and passes. The friendly Parks Canada staff offer lots of ideas and advice.

In the same building, **Jasper Tourism & Commerce** (☎ 780-852-3858; **W** *www .jaspercanadianrockies.com*) carries lots of brochures on accommodations and services within the park and information on commercial groups running activities in the park. **Friends of Jasper** (☎ 780-852-4767; **W** *www.friendsofjasper.com*) also has a shop here with topographical maps and specialist guides to the park.

Policies & Regulations

You must have a parks pass to stop anywhere in the park, including viewpoints and short day hikes. For wilderness permits, which are required for backcountry hiking, see p179.

It is illegal to take anything from the park, even the smallest rock or flower. Pets must be kept on a leash at all times and are not allowed in backcountry shelters.

Disturbing or harassing wildlife is also illegal; if a bedded animal gets up or a feeding animal stops chewing, you're too close. A charging elk is not an uncommon sight, particularly during spring calving and autumn mating seasons, so keep your distance. Never feed wild animals, and dispose of all litter in bear-proof bins. Hunting and firearms are not permitted within the park.

CAMPING

Camping is in designated areas only; if you set up home elsewhere you'll land a giant fine. Reservations are not accepted for frontcountry campgrounds. Checkout is at 11am, and you can stay a maximum of 14 nights. You can have one tent and up to two vehicles per site. Campfires are only permitted at designated sites, and you must purchase a fire permit (CAD$6), available at the campground entrance. The permit includes firewood, but bring your own axe for kindling.

All cooking equipment, food, toiletries and coolers must be stored in your vehicle, up a bear pole or in a bear-proof food locker. Any of these items left lying around your campsite can be confiscated by Parks Canada staff.

For information on backcountry camping, see p179.

FISHING & BOATING

Fishing is permitted in many of the park's lakes and rivers, including parts of the Athabasca, Maligne and Miette Rivers and Maligne Lake. Most of these waters are only open for short seasons, and many others are closed throughout the year. Visit the Parks Canada website or drop into one of their offices for opening dates and fishing restrictions. See p41 for information on licenses.

Rowboats and canoes are allowed on many ponds and lakes within the park; electric boats are permitted on some; and gas-powered boats are generally restricted.

BIKING, CROSS-COUNTRY SKIING & HORSEBACK RIDING

You can bike, ski and ride a horse down many park trails. Parks Canada has trail guides for all of these activities, detailing which areas are out-of-bounds and which are well suited. They also have guidelines to ensure that your impact on the environment and wildlife are minimal.

Helmets are mandatory for bicyclists in Alberta. If you're taking your horse on an overnight backcountry trip, you must purchase a grazing permit (CAD$1 per horse, per night) in addition to a wilderness pass.

Getting Around

The easiest and most flexible way to get around the park is by private vehicle. See p63 for information on car rental agencies in Jasper. Public transportation is limited in town. Tours and shuttles will get you to some of the most popular sights but not to quieter areas and trailheads.

CAR & MOTORCYCLE

Driving in Canada is on the right sight of the road, and seatbelts are mandatory. You cannot pass on a solid yellow line and cannot cross the highway to reach a pulloff on the opposite side unless there is a break in the center line. Jasper Town has lots of gas stations. Parking along the main streets is often limited to one hour; side streets and public lots are usually free game. Speed limits are clearly posted along routes; watch for temporary restrictions due to weather and wildlife. On Hwy 16 you can travel up to a speed of 90kmh/56 mph, and on smaller roads like Maligne Valley Rd and Miette Rd, the limit is 60kmh/37mph.

BUS

Hop on a **Brewster** (☎ 800-760-6934; w www.brewster.ca; adult/child to Banff CAD$57/29; daily May–late Sep, once weekly Oct-May) bus to Lake Louise Village, Banff Town or Calgary.

SHUTTLES

Maligne Lake Shuttle Service (☎ 780-852-3370; w www.malignelake.com; 627 Patricia St; to Maligne Lake/Canyon CAD$9/14; May–late Sep) runs a shuttle bus from Jasper Town to Maligne Lake, stopping at Maligne Canyon en route. The service runs three times daily from May until the end of June and six times daily for the rest of the season. They also run a shuttle service to the southern (CAD$14) and northern (CAD$9) Skyline Trailheads.

The **Mountain Hostel Connector** *(May-Oct daily)* connects hostels in Banff Town, Lake Louise Village and Jasper Town, stopping at major sights and hostels along the Icefields Parkway. Going south, the bus leaves Jasper Town at 1:30pm, reaching Lake Louise at 5pm and Banff Town at 5:45pm. Heading north, the bus departs Banff Town at 6am and Lake Louise at 8:45am (CAD$8), and reaches Jasper Town at 12:15pm (from Banff/Lake Louise CAD$51/45).

ORGANIZED TOURS

Sundog Tour Company *(☎ 888-786-3641; W www.sundogtours.com; 414 Connaught Dr; open 8am-8pm)* offers sightseeing tours of the Maligne Valley (adult/child CAD$49/35), helicopter sightseeing tours around Mt Robson (CAD$175) and trips to the Whistlers Tramway (adult/child CAD$65/54). Other tours include Columbia Icefields and half-day trips by train.

Thompson Tours *(☎ 780-852-7269; e tomtour@telusplanet.net; CAD$45)* takes small tour groups along Maligne Valley to Mt Robson and to Miette Hot Springs. Guides speak French and German and offer up lots of information about the geography and wildlife in the area. You can also head out on a longer adventure to Columbia Icefield (CAD$60) or take in the highlights around Jasper Town (CAD$35).

Jasper Adventure Centre *(☎ 800-565-7547; W www.jasperadventurecentre.com; Connaught Dr)* runs tours similar to those above, as well as a Jasper by Twilight tour (adult/child CAD$35/15).

Brewster *(☎ 780-852-3332; W www.brewster.ca)* runs one-way and roundtrip tours of the Icefields Parkway (adult/child one way CAD$95/47.50), stopping at major sites en route.

HIGHLIGHTS

You know you're in Jasper when you ...

✔ look across its peaks from the top of **Jasper Tramway** (p166)

✔ follow the route of the fur traders at the **Jasper-Yellowhead Museum** (below)

✔ see the **Old Man** sleeping on the top of Mt Roche Bonhomme (p168)

✔ row to the middle of **Maligne Lake** (p167)

✔ encounter **elk** (p270) in the middle of downtown Jasper

Sights

For sights along the Icefields Parkway, see that chapter (p134).

JASPER TOWN & AROUND
MAP 10

Jasper Town isn't brimming with sights, but the few that are here are worth the time to check out.

Jasper-Yellowhead Museum

Packed with visually compelling exhibits, the **Jasper-Yellowhead Museum** *(☎ 780-852-3013; Pyramid Lake Rd; adults/students & seniors/family CAD$4/3/10, under 6 yrs free; open 10am-9pm daily summer, 10am-5pm daily autumn, Tue-Sun 10am-5pm winter)* brings to life the nomad hunters, fur traders, travelers, explorers, artists, mountaineers, gold prospectors and pioneers who shaped both the town and park of Jasper.

Bush Fire Gallery

Housed in the Old Fire Hall, the **Bush Fire Gallery** (☎ 780-852-3554; *Old Fire Hall, cnr Elm & Patricia; open 10am-1pm & 5-9pm Thu-Mon Jul & Aug*) is a nonprofit venue for Jasper's resident artists. Run by the Jasper Artists' Guild, it displays eclectic paintings and sculptures depicting local life and landscape. You can also pick up a self-guided walking-tour map of local businesses displaying local artwork.

Jasper Tramway

Zipping 973m/3243ft in a mere seven minutes, the **Jasper Tramway** (☎ 866-850-8726; W *www.jaspertramway.com; Whistler's Mountain Rd; adult/child CAD$19/9, under 5 yrs free; open 9:30am-6:30pm late Apr–late Jun & late Aug–late Sep, 8:30am-10:30pm Jul & Aug*) carries you to a boardwalk and lookout over the eastern Rockies. You can hike a steep 1.5km/0.9 miles from here to the summit or enjoy the views from the café. Dusk sees fewer crowds and is arguably the most beautiful time for the trip. Trams depart every 10 minutes. To reach the tramway, follow Hwy 93A south.

ICY ENDEAVORS

In 1943, it was hush-hush around Patricia Lake; even if locals knew what the government was up to, they weren't likely to believe it. The idea was to build an ice ship. Invented by Englishman Nathanial Pyke and supported by Winston Churchill, Project Habakkuk would serve as an aircraft landing strip to protect Canadian convoys from German U-boats as they made their way across the Atlantic. The 280,000 blocks of ice needed to build the ship would be mixed with sawdust to create an unsinkable, indestructible streamlined iceberg that was 600m/2000ft long, with walls 15m/50ft thick. What could go wrong?

A 60m/200ft prototype was built on Patricia Lake and, cooled by an interior refrigeration plant, was kept from melting throughout a summer. Unfortunately, by this time the government realized that Habakkuk would cost CAD$70 million and require 8000 laborers and eight months to construct. The project was quite literally scuppered to the bottom of the lake, where its wooden frame remains today.

Miette Hot Springs

The hottest natural mineral springs in the Canadian Rockies, **Miette Hot Springs** (☎ 780-866-3939; *Miette Hot Springs Rd; adult/child & senior/family CAD$6.25/5.25/18.75; open 10:30am-9pm May 19–Jun 22, 8:30am-10:30pm Jun 23–Sep 4 & 11am-7:30pm Sep 5–Oct 9*) burst from the earth at a scalding 54°C/129°F. Tamed first by fur traders and later by relief workers during the Depression, the springs are cooled to 39°C/103°F with a cold pool to plunge yourself into afterward. Surrounded by mountains, the setting is peaceful; unfortunately, the small pools get rather crowded in summer. Rent a locker to store your things, and have lunch in the café.

En route to the springs, be sure to take in the giant, vertical **Ashlar Ridge** from the viewpoint at 8.9km/5.5 miles from Hwy 16.

Maligne Canyon

One of the deepest canyons in the Canadian Rockies, **Maligne Canyon** is definitely worth a gander. The Maligne River, running from the Maligne Valley, has pounded against the limestone to create this dramatic canyon in its effort to reach the lower Athabasca Valley. Plunging 23m/75ft, the deep gorge is shaped into potholes and boasts sunken gardens. To see it, follow the 20-minute trail to the first bridge (p177). You'll also find a standard café here.

Maligne Lake

In the late 1800s, Assiniboine native Sampson Beaver stood on the shores of **Maligne Lake**. Sixteen years later he sketched a map from memory, guiding Mary Schaffer and her party over the mountains to the largest and deepest lake in the park. Since their arrival in 1908, the lake has enjoyed a place of pride on most tourists' itineraries. Stretching 22km/14 miles and surrounded by rocky peaks, the lake is pretty, but the shoreline is generally crowded. The real draw is **Spirit Island**, which is a speck of an island with spiritual significance for First Nations people and is the setting of one of the most famous postcard shots in the Rockies. Unfortunately, unless you feel up to kayaking for six hours or rowing for 12, the only way to catch sight of the island is by **tour boat** (p183). These depart regularly but are busy nonetheless; reservations are recommended. Maligne Lake has some fantastic trailheads nearby and is a wonderful spot for boating (p183).

Medicine Lake

Also known as Sinking Lake, **Medicine Lake** bewildered onlookers for the better part of a century. Filled with water from Maligne River, the water level drops dramatically each year – despite the fact that there appears to be no outlet. By October, all that's left of the lake is a small stream, and in winter just a few frozen ponds remain. The secret lies on the floor of the lake, where the water flows out through small holes, creating one of the greatest underground rivers in the world. In the 1950s a ferry service across the lake was briefly attempted; efforts to plug the holes with sandbags, mattresses and bundles of magazines all proved futile.

Other Lakes

Northeast of Jasper Town, **Patricia** and **Pyramid Lakes** lie beneath the red and rust-colored **Pyramid Mountain**. Scenic and peaceful, both lakes are popular for picnicking and boating (p183). Tiny **Pyramid Island** sits in the center of Pyramid Lake; with lots of picnic tables, a shelter, a wheelchair-accessible path and beautiful views, it's a great spot for a picnic.

In summer, **Lake Annette** is just warm enough for a quick dip. Lounge on the sandy beach with half of Jasper Town and enjoy views to Mt Edith Cavell, or amble along the lakeside loop (p173). Park at the first lot on the right for clearer, deeper water and a swimming platform (but no beach). Next door, **Lake Edith** is a bit deeper, a bit colder and has a small beach, but it's also generally quieter and provides shelter. The roads around both lakes are a bit of a maze, and signs are not well posted; take the first or second parking lot on the right for Annette Lake and the first on the left for Lake Edith.

Pocahontas

The home of hundreds of miners between 1910 and 1921, all that remains of **Pocahontas** today is some overgrown ruins and the superintendent's home. A short interpretive trail (1km/0.62 mile) around the site recreates the days when the government encouraged resource extraction from the park and received handsome royalties. The coal mined from the area was used throughout WWI, as it burned hot and gave off no smoke to be spotted by German U-boats.

Driving Tours

With lots of wildlife and gorgeous rugged scenery, Jasper is a great place to explore in your vehicle.

MALIGNE MEANDER
Route: Maligne Rd from Hwy 16 to Maligne Lake
Distance: 46km/28.5 miles
Speed Limit: 60kmh/37 mph

The road to Maligne Lake is as scenic as the destination. Wildlife is rife along this route; with a little luck you'll spot a wolf, a bear and maybe a moose. Each year, animals are killed on this road by vehicles, so obey speed restrictions and watch for animals bounding across the road.

Begin the tour 2km/1.2 miles north of Jasper Town; follow Hwy 16 to the turnoff for **Maligne Rd**, crossing the **Athabasca River** and following the road left. Ahead are views of **Roche Bonhomme**, with its **Old Man** summit (below), and to the west lies the rust-colored **Pyramid Mountain**. At 3km/1.9 miles, the **Fifth Bridge** crosses the powerful **Maligne River**; if you're feeling ambitious you can head over this suspension bridge and climb the trail into **Maligne Canyon**, one of the deepest in the Rockies. An easier way to see this dramatic canyon is via the **Upper Canyon Trail** (p177); the trailhead is 7km/4.3 miles along the route.

The road continues east between the **Colin Range** to the north and the **Maligne Range** to the south. At 22km/13.6 miles there's a pulloff to Maligne River; despite the strength of the Maligne River further downstream, this rock bed only carries water if **Medicine Lake** floods. Instead, the water flows downstream in an underground waterway. Natives in the area believed that the water was whisked away by magic (or bad medicine) and feared it.

THE SLEEPING GIANT

It won't be long before you're aware of his presence. Reclining along the summit of Roche Bonhomme (Good Fellow; 2495m/8184ft), the **Old Man** was first spotted by fur traders in the 1800s. Seemingly carved into the stone, the face, headdress and upper torso of the native man are unmistakable. If you haven't seen Old Man yet, take a wander along Connaught Dr, north from the train station. There he is, up to the northeast. The carvers of Mt Rushmore could hardly have done a better job.

The next turnoff, on the northwest corner of Medicine Lake, offers superb views across the water. Along the north side of the lake, the craggy Colin Range leans flat-faced toward the road, and a delta on the far eastern side of the lake often hosts caribou in early spring and late fall.

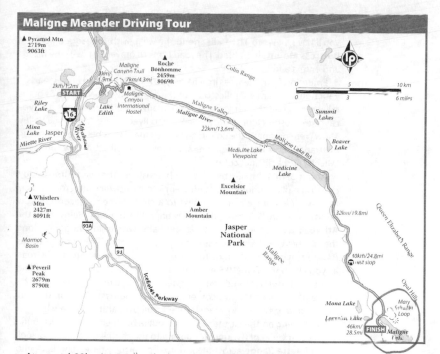

Maligne Meander Driving Tour

At around 32km/19.8 miles, look up. Above you, you'll see limestone arches cut into the summit of the **Queen Elizabeth Range**, caused by water freezing in the crevices, expanding and shattering the rock. If you've packed along a picnic and are hoping for a little peace, try the rest stop at 40km/24.8 miles, where you can relax beside the river before reaching the more hectic **Maligne Lake** (p167), 6km/3.7 miles up the road.

A SMALL ROAD WITH BIG VIEWS
Route: Celestine Lake Rd from Hwy 16
Distance: 28km/17.4 miles
Speed Limit: 40kmh/25 mph

While there is a trailhead to Celestine Lake at the end of this road, it's the drive itself and its incredible vistas that are the reason for this tour. This road is not for the faint of heart; it's a winding gravel road with lots of blind corners and a few steep climbs, and the last half is a single, dodgy track. Northbound traffic (coming from Hwy 16) can head down Celestine Lake Rd from 8am to 9am, 11am to noon, 2pm to 3pm, 5pm to 6pm, 8pm to 9pm and 11pm to midnight. Southbound traffic can return between 9:30am to 10:30am, 12:30pm to 1:30pm, 3:30pm to 4:30pm, 6:30pm to 7:30pm, 9:30pm to 10:30pm and 12:30am to 1:30am. Stick to the timetable, and honk at the blind corners in case others haven't stuck to the timetable. This road is *really* not suitable for RVs or trailers. As it's a quiet route, keep your eyes peeled for wildlife.

From Jasper Town, head north on Hwy 16, taking the exit at 10km/6.2 miles onto the paved Celestine Lake Rd. Crossing over **Snaring River**, you'll have views to **The Palisade** to the west, with the jagged peaks of **Buttress Mountain** behind. The road turns to gravel just over the bridge and enters a forest.

Emerging from the trees into fields, you'll see **Moberly Homestead** on your right at 11km/6.8 miles. Built over a century ago, before roads or the railway reached this far west, these partially restored buildings are typical of the resourceful Métis pioneers who lived in the Athabasca Valley. Métis were originally the children of mixed marriages between European fur traders and native women, and they established a new language (Michif) and a distinct culture.

About 3km/1.7 miles beyond the homestead, the road turns dodgy, crossing a plank bridge and narrowing into a one-way lane. You'll quickly pass a pleasant picnic area next to a stream, then a second narrow bridge; at 16km/9.9 miles, the views unfold to the east. Below you, the **Athabasca River** opens up into **Jasper Lake**, with trains chugging along the rails next to it, while across from you, the pointy peaks of the **Jacques Range** reach skyward. Enjoy the view and then concentrate on the road as you climb to 17km/10.5 miles, the riskiest section of the road, a blind corner with rugged terrain and no guardrail. If you're lucky enough to be in the passenger seat, this corner also offers the best views on the trip; unfortunately, there's nowhere to safely pull over and take them in.

Continuing northeast, the road levels out (a bit) then winds back around to give you views of **Pyramid Mountain** to the southwest and then a look at the **Miette Range** across the lake to the northeast. Heading back into the forest brings you to the end of the road, where you can get out and stretch your legs while waiting for the designated time to head back.

Festivals & Events

Each year Jasper hosts a number of events. Have a look at **w** www.jasper canadianrockies.com for what's happening this year.

WINTER
Jasper Welcomes Winter
To wash away the winter blues, this festival (four days, early December) brings lots of family events, such as a Festival of Trees, ice skating, fun runs and a Santa parade.

Jasper in January
For two weeks, this annual festival (the last two weeks of January) keeps tourists and locals busy with snow-sculpture contests, performances, parades, pub crawls, pie throws and hikes.

SUMMER
Canada Day
This national holiday (July 1) starts off with a patriotic pancake breakfast, progresses into a parade with marching bands and culminates with fireworks.

Take a Hike – Parks Day

Parks Canada celebrates its annual big day (third weekend in July) with free guided hikes, exhibits and kids' activities throughout the weekend.

Jasper Heritage Folk Festival

Folk performers flock to Jasper every few years to sing their hearts out for two days at the **Jasper Heritage Folk Festival** (☎ *780-852-3615*; **w** *www.jasper .ca/folkfestival; early Aug*).

Jasper Heritage Rodeo

If you're not from cowboy territory, this annual four-day event (mid-August) will be an eye opener. Check out bull riding, steer wrestling and calf roping.

Day Hikes

If you're looking to get out and stretch your legs, you've come to the right place. With more than 1200km/660 miles of trails, Jasper National Park has hikes for everyone from Grandma to GI Joe. No matter where you're staying, a trailhead is never far away. No matter how brief your stay or how full your itinerary, make time for at least one hike. For hiking along the Icefields Parkway, including at Mt Edith Cavell, see that chapter (p134).

JASPER TOWN
MAP 10

Jasper has a lovely, leisurely trail that starts right at the museum's parking lot.

MINA & RILEY LAKES LOOP
Distance: 9km/5.6 miles roundtrip
Duration: 3 hours roundtrip
Challenge: Easy-Moderate
Elevation Change: 160m/525ft

Quite literally in Jasper Town's backyard, this pleasant walk takes you deep into the woods to a group of lakes that nonetheless feel remote. Views across the lakes are tranquil and picturesque, and despite this being a popular route, you're likely to have the trail to yourself. Black bears hang out around here, so take precautions.

You'll find the trailhead in the northwest corner of the museum parking lot. Follow trail No 8 markers left behind a group of houses and then up a gentle climb into the forest. Views south along the parkway are beautiful but short-lived as you continue deeper into the woods along the now level trail. Keep to the right at the next three junctions, heading west through pine, fir and spruce trees. The path widens into a manmade meadow. Cross the gravel road and follow the trail back into the forest, which is sprinkled with stands of birch trees.

Lower Mina Lake is soon on your left; somewhat swampy, it's a popular hangout for **ptarmigan** and **dragonflies**. Just beyond is the larger **Upper Mina Lake**, where you'll spot **loons** gliding across the green surface. At the western edge of the lake, turn right along the trail sign-posted for Riley Lake.

Climbing up and down some gentle hills brings you to another junction; turn left and descend a long hill to **Riley Lake**, with **Pyramid Mountain** framed behind it. The trail skirts the moss-green edge of the lake before plunging back into the forest. Take a right at the next junction and ascend to **Cottonwood Slough**, which has open views to the **Roche Bonhomme** (only slightly obstructed by electricity wires). Continue east to the road from where Trail No 2 returns south to the original trailhead.

AROUND JASPER TOWN
MAP 10
Jasper has lots of worthwhile hikes right on its doorstep.

OLD FORT POINT LOOP
Distance: 3.5km/2.2 miles roundtrip
Duration: 1.5 hours roundtrip
Challenge: Moderate
Elevation Change: 135m/443ft

While there are a few short, steep climbs en route, this hike is a breeze, considering the panoramic views you achieve at the top. The trail itself is wooded and pleasant, leading you to the top of a *roche mountonnée* – a bedrock knob shaped by glaciers. This prominent lookout never actually supported a fort; the site was more likely named for Henry House, a fur trading post built near here in 1811. To reach the trailhead, head east on Hwy 16 and cross the Moberly Bridge to the east side of the Athabsca River.

Begin the trail from the northeast edge of the parking lot rather than up the staircase. This will give you better views and a more gradual ascent. The wooded path (indicated with yellow No 1 markers) follows a gentle sloop up through the woods, through a small meadow and on into a birch forest.

At 1.3km/0.8 mile, a steep climb takes you up past a giant chunk of **pink limestone**. Dating back 750 million years, this is the oldest rock found in Jasper National Park. You can opt out of this climb by following trail 1A for a more gradual route; take a left just before the ascent.

At the top there are many trail options; keep right, or if you're coming from trail 1A, go straight. Up a gentle slope, the trail is brightened in summer with wildflowers and butterflies. On the right, many small trails zigzag up to the **Southeast Summit**, with its peaceful meadow and great views.

From here, the trail heads west for a further 0.3km/0.2 mile to **Old Fort Summit**, unmistakable for its cairn. From the top, the red-colored **Pyramid Mountain** is one of the most distinguishable peaks, lying northwest and crowned with a microwave station. Turning clockwise from here you'll spot the gray **Colin Range** to the northeast, the jagged cliffs of **Mt Tekarra** to the east and the layered **Mts Hardisty** and **Kerkeslin** to the southeast. To the south, the snowy peaks of **Mt Edith Cavell** dominate the skyline.

Follow the trail down to the left of the outlook through a small stand of trees, and head across the small plateau for the cairn. A series of stairs leads you back down to the parking lot.

LAKE ANNETTE LOOP
Distance: 2.4km/1.5 miles roundtrip
Duration: 40 minutes roundtrip
Challenge: Easy
Elevation Change: None

Surrounded by well-known peaks, this paved stroll around Lake Annette can be finished off with a dip in the relatively warm water. The trail is wheelchair accessible, with benches and a shelter en route. From Hwy 16, turn right onto Maligne Rd and right again onto Lodge Rd. Take the left turn for Lake Annette; the trailhead is at the first parking lot on the right.

Head out right along the western side of the lake. The lake's berry bushes often draw deer and elk. You'll soon spot the rocky summit of **Roche Bonhomme** to the northeast and, after rounding the southern bend, the rust-colored **Pyramid Mountain** comes into view to the northwest. As you reach the northern shore, the trail runs between the lake and an unlikely but quite real pond of **quicksand** before bringing you to a sandy beach, from which you can take in views of the snow-capped **Mt Edith Cavell**. From here, continue along the lakeshore path to the trailhead.

MALIGNE LAKE AREA
MAP 9

Despite the rows of parked buses and gangs of tourists clambering along the shoreline, this lake's endless trails are surprisingly quiet and offer some stunning views and opportunities to really escape into the wilds.

BALD HILLS
Distance: 10.4km/6.4 miles roundtrip
Duration: 3.5 hours roundtrip
Challenge: Moderate-Difficult
Elevation Change: 480m/1574ft

This fairly hard trudge leads to a meadow offering spectacular panoramic views of Maligne Lake and the surrounding mountain ranges. Once you reach Bald Hills, the opportunities for exploring are seemingly limitless, with umpteen trails leading to various hilltops and even greater views. Venturing off these trails causes damage to the fragile alpine tundra.

The trail begins on the old fire road at the end of Maligne Rd. The road climbs west through a pine forest, following a stream. At 0.2km/0.1 mile, you'll pass a trail on the left after which the road turns right, narrows and begins to climb. The forest begins to take on an alpine look, with small buses, a few wildflowers and chirping birds. Watch for glimpses of mountain ranges through the trees.

The trail heading left at about 3km/1.9 miles is a steep, alternative route to the summit, but to best enjoy the views it affords, continue along the fire road to the top and return via this trail. At the next junction (3.2km/2 miles), stay left to climb to the top of the old fire road, checking

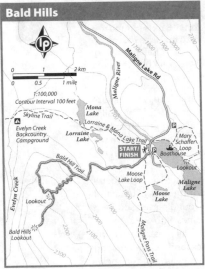

Bald Hills

over your shoulder for views of **Mona** and **Maligne Lakes**.

The old fire lookout lies just beyond the end of the fire road, at 2170m/7118ft, and is marked with a cairn. The panoramic view encompasses Maligne Lake to the southeast with **Samson Peak** behind it, **Maligne Range** to the west, the **Maligne Valley** to the north and the slate-gray **Queen Elizabeth Range** to the northwest. Continuing along the trail for 0.2km/0.1 mile brings you to an even more spectacular viewpoint, marked with a cairn and a true 360° vista.

From here, the trail climbs steeply along the crest of a hill, affording a dramatic view north of the valley and **Maligne River** and to the south of Maligne Lake. This trail ends at an isolated rocky outcrop, where you're almost guaranteed solitude to enjoy the spectacular views.

Heading back, take the alternative route down, which branches off the main trail just before the start of the fire road. The path is very steep, rocky and riddled with roots but also crosses pretty, flowery meadows and offers great views of **moose** and Maligne and Mona Lakes. Rejoining the fire road, turn right and descend to the trailhead.

MOOSE LAKE LOOP
Distance: 2.6km/1.6 miles roundtrip
Duration: 45 minutes roundtrip
Challenge: Easy
Elevation Change: Negligible

Wander through verdant forest, between mossy boulders and beneath lichen-strewn branches. A giant landslide hit this area thousands of years ago, and its effects are still evident in the pockmarked terrain followed by this easy trail. If you're after a little peace and are eager to see a moose, follow the Bald Hills Trail up the fire road.

WHERE THE WILD THINGS ARE

Keep your eyes peeled for ...

✔ **moose** taking a dip along Moose Lake Loop

✔ **big horn sheep** munching on grass on the Sulphur Skyline

✔ **deer and elk** devouring berries by Annette Lake Loop

✔ **ptarmigan and loons** hopping near the waters of the Mina & Riley Lakes Loop

✔ **caribou** along the windswept terrain of the Skyline Trail

✔ **bears** hopefully wandering away down the Jacques Lake Trail

After 0.2km/0.1 mile, head left into the woods along the Maligne Pass Trail. A further 1km/0.6 mile brings you to the junction for **Moose Lake**. Turn left and follow the trail along the water. These giant Eeyores of the forest do actually hang out here; when we last visited we were lucky enough to see one swimming across the lake. Beyond the lake you'll spot the rounded, snowy **Samson Peak**.

The trail heads north through the woods to the western shore of **Maligne Lake** and back to the trailhead parking lot.

LORRAINE & MONA LAKES
Distance: 5km/3.1 miles roundtrip
Duration: 1.5 hours roundtrip
Challenge: Easy
Elevation Change: Negligible

Along the backcountry Skyline Trail, this peaceful walk leads beneath the canopy of the forest to two small, picturesque lakes. The trailhead is on the right of the farthest parking lot on Maligne Rd, past the buildings and over the bridge.

The well-maintained dirt trail leads into a diverse forest with wildflowers sprinkled along its floor and young saplings taking root. With the sound of the **Maligne River** raging below, a gentle incline takes you over a small slope. You'll soon spot kettles, large pits left by long-ago glaciers.

At just under 2km/1.2 miles you'll cross a winding, burbling stream before ascending a short hill of red earth. Just beyond here is a small green pond on the left (perhaps a filled kettle) that's as reflective as glass. Take the next left to the jade-green **Lorraine Lake**, crossing a plank bridge over a reedy pond and following one of the many branches to the shore.

Back on the main trail, a gentle ascent gives you views down over the lake before heading back into the forest for 0.5km/0.3 mile to the next junction. Head right down this narrow path to the secluded **Mona Lake**, complete with loons and views to the **Opal Hills** beyond. Return to the trailhead by the same route.

MARY SCHAFFER LOOP
Distance: 3.2km/2.2 miles roundtrip
Duration: 45 minutes roundtrip
Challenge: Easy
Elevation Change: Negligible

Following the eastern shoreline of Maligne Lake before dipping into the forest, this trail gives you a chance to take in the view seen by the first European explorer to cross this body of water. When Mary Schaffer stepped off her raft in 1908, she wrote, 'There burst upon us ... the finest view any of us had ever beheld in the Rockies.'

To reach **Mary's viewpoint**, follow the paved trail past **Curly's historic boathouse** for about 0.8km/0.5 mile. Beyond the lookout, the trail continues inland through a spruce, pine and fir forest. After passing through a meadow, stay left at two junctions. Along the path you'll see **kettles**, giant depressions left by glacial ice trapped beneath sand and silt. At the third junction, head right to return to the boathouse.

JACQUES LAKE
Distance: 24km/14.9 miles roundtrip
Duration: 8 hours roundtrip
Challenge: Moderate
Elevation Change: 90m/295ft

Taking you to a valley surrounded by massive mountain ranges and bejeweled with the turquoise waters of Jacques Lake, this hike is packed with beautiful scenery and views, despite gaining almost no elevation. This trail is well defined and often open earlier and later than other summer trails. The hike has a distinct backcountry feel about it; while most people do this walk in one very long day, there is a backcountry campground on the northern end of the lake. This is prime bear country, and sightings are regular; be sure to take all precautions.

The trailhead is found at the southern end of Medicine Lake, at the back of Beaver Creek Picnic Area, 26km/16 miles along Maligne Rd. Following an unused, forested fire road and a babbling creek, the level trail brings you to **Beaver Lake** at 1.6km/1 mile. The lake is a destination in itself (particularly for anglers); watch for loons floating along its green surface. Beyond Beaver Lake, you begin to glimpse views of the jagged **Queen Elizabeth Range** to the east.

Continuing northwest, the trail passes **Summit Lakes**, two large ponds separated by forest and meadow. At the first of these waters, the wide, level fire road narrows into a root-riddled path, and beyond the second lake, it's often a muddy affair. The path jumps back and forth across the creek as it takes you deep within the forest.

The trail heads straight at the junction just before **Jacques Lake**. The turquoise water of the lake is reached at 11.6km/7.2 miles. To the south are the gray peaks of the Queen Elizabeth Range; to the east is **Sidar Mountain**, part of the **Colin Range**; and to the north, the **Jacques Range** crowds the skyline. On a still day, the reflections in the lake are magnificent. Follow the same route back to the trailhead.

ELSEWHERE IN THE PARK
If you're hoping to combine a day hike with a sight or a driving tour, Jasper has some excellent options in its vicinity. None of the following are easy, but all are well worth the effort involved.

SULPHUR SKYLINE
Distance: 9.6km/6 miles roundtrip
Duration: 3.5 hours roundtrip
Challenge: Difficult
Elevation Change: 700m/2296ft

For the energetic, this steep ascent is well worth the sweat entailed. Views from the summit are staggering, with deep twisting valleys and a sea of mountaintops. You're likely to see bighorn sheep along the way and will definitely find ground squirrels at the top. After descending, soak your aching muscles in the hot springs at the trailhead. Much of the trail is open, and on sunny days it can be a dry, hot haul. The area is also renowned for thunderstorms; if the weather looks ominous, don't even bother.

Park in the lot at the end of Miette Hot Springs Rd; the trailhead is on the other side of the pool, beyond the passenger drop-off loop. The initial wide, paved path becomes a narrow trail as it climbs across the open slopes for 2.2km/1.4 miles to a junction. Catch your breath and turn right; this is where the real work begins.

Switchbacks lead you up (and up and up), through flower scattered meadows and small groves. You'll pass an enormous white boulder at the treeline; during prehistoric times, this giant chunk of rock was carried by a mighty glacier from somewhere near Jasper Town. Continue climbing to the top of **Sulphur Ridge** (2050m/6724ft), where 360° views will steal away what little breath you have left. **Fiddle Valley** winds to the southeast along the eastern edge of the **Nikanassin Range**. The distinctive **Utopia Mountain** stands pyramid-shaped to the southwest among the **Miette Range**, and the jagged cliffs of **Ashlar Ridge** lie north. The return journey to the trailhead is much easier; not only is it downhill this time, but the hot springs await you at the bottom.

MALIGNE CANYON
Distance: 4.2km/2.6 miles roundtrip
Duration: 1.5 hours roundtrip
Challenge: Moderate
Elevation Change: 100m/338ft

Following one of the deepest canyons in the Rockies, this dramatic trail crosses the **Maligne River** over five bridges; if you're short on time or energy, you can turn back at any of these and still gain impressive views into this limestone gorge.

The trail starts from the parking lot 7km/4.3 miles along Maligne Rd from Hwy 16. From here, the paved **Upper Canyon Trail** takes in the canyon's highest **waterfall**, dropping 23m/75ft into a plunge pool. From the **First** and **Second** bridges you'll see potholes carved into the canyon walls and **sunken gardens** where the water's spray has brought to life small pockets of ferns deep within the gorge.

The **Lower Canyon Trail** continues down beneath the shade of the forest, crossing the **Third Bridge** for views of more waterfalls. **Springs** en route are outlets for one of the largest underground rivers on the continent, traveling from Medicine Lake 17km/10.5

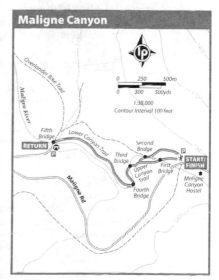

miles up the valley. The trail follows the course of the broadening water, crossing the **Fourth Bridge** and eventually the **Fifth**, a suspension bridge at 2.1km/1.3 miles downriver.

CELESTINE LAKE & DEVONA LOOKOUT
Distance: 18.4km/11.4 miles roundtrip
Duration: 5 hours roundtrip
Challenge: Moderate
Elevation Change: 325m/1066ft

A full day's hike, this route takes in two peaceful, isolated lakes before bringing you to an old fire lookout with views stretching along the Athabasca Valley. While the lakes are popular with anglers, the area remains isolated and remote, and grizzly sightings are not unheard of. Travel prepared.

The trailhead is located at the end of Celestine Lake Rd, following the final 5km/3.1 miles of Celestine Rd that is now closed to vehicles. The road loops down to cross **Snake Indian River** and then begins a steep but short uphill climb along the bank. Turning sharply to the northwest, the ascent eases up but continues to climb through the woods for the next 4km/2.5 miles or so.

Just past 5km/3.1 miles, take a right at the junction, and follow the level path northeast to **Princess Lake**. Ringed with spruce trees and probably watched over by anglers, the lake is set beneath **Beaver Bluffs** to the north. Next door, serene **Celestine Lake** is much the same.

From here the trail heads southeast, slowly climbing a narrow ridge to **Devona Lookout**. The views remain well hidden by the forest for the first 0.5km/0.3 mile; as you leave the forest behind and enter blooming meadows, the **Athabasca Valley** is spread out before you. The **lookout** is a further 2.1km/1.3 miles. Ahead of you towers **Roche Miette**, and below you can see the **Athabasca River** flowing all the way from the foothills in the northeast and disappearing behind the **Colin Range** in the south.

Backcountry Hikes

Jasper Park has an endless number of backcountry trails to help bring you face to face with the wilderness. If you're keen for an adventure but a novice at backcountry hiking, there are a number of popular trails that are well traveled and maintained. For experienced hikers, the possibilities are countless. For more information on backcountry hiking and safety, see the Activities chapter (p29).

SAFETY ISSUES
Parks Canada operates a voluntary safety registration program. If you do not have a local contact, are traveling solo or are undertaking risky activities like mountain climbing, it is recommended that you register at the Jasper Information Centre before setting out. If you do not return by your specified date, a search party will be initiated. While registration is voluntary, you must report back to the information center or call the park warden office immediately upon your return or face legal action.

PERMIT INFORMATION

Overnight stays in the backcountry require a wilderness pass (CAD$8 per night per adult over 16). Reservations are recommended, as Parks Canada limits the number of hikers on each trail; these can be made up to three months in advance and cost CAD$12. You must pick up the permit within 24 hours of heading out, at which time you'll receive updated information on trails. To refund the permit, visit Parks Canada before 10am on your departure day. You will be required to show your pass to any wardens you encounter on the trail.

BACKCOUNTRY CAMPING

If you're looking for somewhere to rough it in the wild, Jasper Park has 120 designated backcountry camping areas to fit the bill. The most lavish are found along the more popular trails (like Skyline, Brazeau Loop, Tonquin and Maligne Lake) and have pit toilets, tent pads, food-storage cables and metal fire grates. Campsites in areas designated as 'primitive' have only pit toilets, a fire grate and a bear pole. In the 'wildland areas,' random camping is permitted, but absolutely no facilities exist; pitch your tent at least 50m/164ft from the trail and 70m/230ft from any water source. You are only permitted to camp at sites you've registered for when purchasing your wilderness pass, and you can stay at one site for a maximum of three nights.

Always check with Parks Canada for current fire restrictions before you set out. Hang all food, toiletries and garbage from food-storage cables and pack out all garbage.

BACKCOUNTRY LODGING

If you'd prefer a few home comforts that are difficult to pack (like a roof), try one of these options.

Alpine Club of Canada Huts

The Alpine Club of Canada maintains a number of backcountry huts in Jasper Park. **Wates-Gibson Hut** *(Tonquin Valley; summer/winter sleeps 30/24)* is a beautiful log cabin with a wood-burning stove, sleeping mattresses and cooking utensils. **Mt Colin Centennial Hut** *(Colin Range; sleeps 6; closed winter)* has a Coleman stove, mattresses and cooking utensils. For both huts, you must bring your own bedding, food, matches, toilet paper and dishcloth and must pack out all of your garbage. For information on huts along the Icefields Parkway, see that chapter (p134).

Reservations are required for all huts and can be made through the **Alpine Clubhouse** *(☎ 403-678-3200; ꟽ www.alpineclubofcanada.ca; PO Box 8040, Indian Flats Rd, Canmore; CAD$9-24 per night, under 16 yrs half price)* and paid for with a Visa or MasterCard. You are also required to have a Parks Canada wilderness pass. Reservations for nonmembers are accepted one month in advance.

Lodges

In Tonquin Valley, **Tonquin Amethyst Lake Lodge** *(☎ 780-852-1188; ꟽ www .tonquinadventures.com; CAD$135 per person Jun-Oct, including meals, cabin for 6 CAD$210 Jan-Apr)* and *(☎ 780-852-3909; ꟽ www.tonquinvalley.com; summer/winter CAD$135/100 per person, including meals)* provides rustic accommodations in historic cabins with views of the lake and Ramparts. Both lodges run multiday horse treks to and around the lake, and in winter you can cross-country ski to the lodges.

The oldest backcountry horse camp in the park, **Shovel Pass Lodge** *(☎ 780-852-4215; ꟽ www.skylinetrail.com; CAD$140, including meals; open Jun-Sep)* has basic cabins for trekkers on the Skyline Trail. Horse-trekking trips are also available.

BACKCOUNTRY TRAILS

No matter what your fitness level, Parks Canada staff at Jasper Information Centre has lots of ideas for trips. Two of the most popular routes are detailed below, and reservations are recommended for both.

SKYLINE TRAIL
Distance: 45.8km/28.7 miles
Duration: 2 days one way
Challenge: Moderate-Difficult
Elevation Change: 1380m/4526ft

Aptly named, the Skyline is the highest trail in Jasper Park and is deservedly one of the most popular backcountry hikes in the Canadian Rockies. Taking you up above the treeline for much of the hike, the trail's infinite views across the park are stunning. Keep your eyes peeled for wildlife along the way, particularly the elusive caribou. If you have the time, it's worth stretching the trip out across three days.

The lack of trees en route means that there is little shelter, and temperatures can drop to freezing throughout the summer. If the weather turns nasty, there's nowhere to hide. The trail is only accessible from July to mid-September. Campfires are prohibited at all five campgrounds en route. For transportation to the trailheads, see Maligne Lake Shuttle Services, under Shuttles (p164).

Day One: Maligne Lake to Curator Campground *(7 hours, 20.4km/12.6 miles)* Trailheads for the hike are at Maligne Lake and at Maligne Canyon Hostel, 6km/3.7 miles east of Hwy 16, on Maligne Rd. Begin from Maligne Lake, the higher of the trailheads, and follow the Lorraine & Mona Lakes Trail (p175) through the woods for the first 5km/3.1 miles. Beyond the turnoff for Mona Lake, switchbacks leave the trees behind, passing **Evelyn Creek Campground** (keep right at the junction) and bringing you into meadows. Upon the slopes of **Maligne Range**, **Little Shovel Pass** (10.2km/6.3 miles) gives you views back over **Maligne Lake** and to the gray **Queen Elizabeth Range**, to the east. From here the trail dips down into the **Snowbowl**, a lush if somewhat boggy meadow crisscrossed with streams and stretching 7.3km/4.5 miles along the Maligne Range. **Snowbowl Campground** is at 11.8km/7.3 miles.

At the end of the Snowbowl, a short climb brings you up to **Big Shovel Pass**, which has more great views. Keep left at the junction, continuing northwest for 2.1km/1.3 miles and taking the trail left to **Curator Campground** and **Shovel Pass Lodge**.

Day Two: Curator Campground to Maligne Canyon Hostel *(8 hours, 25.2km/15.6 miles)* Begin the day with a brisk climb up to the tiny **Curator Lake**, surrounded by vast, windswept terrain. The trail becomes steep as it climbs to **The Notch**. At 2510m/8733ft, this is the high point of the trail with breathtaking views along the **Athabasca Valley** and, if you're lucky, all the way to **Mt Robson** in the northeast. Continue on to the summit of **Amber Mountain**, below which the trail switchbacks down to **Centre Lakes,** with **Centre Mountain** guarding these small ponds to the northeast. The trail heads through a small valley to **Tekarra Lake** and then fol lows around the north side of **Tekarra Mountain** amid the first trees you'll have seen all day. **Tekarra Campground** lies at 11.3km/7 miles, between the peaks of its namesake and **Excelsior Mountain**.

Coming back out of the trees, you'll have views of **Pyramid Mountain** to the northwest and the **Roche Bonhomme** to the north. It's worth taking the short detour left at 16.9km/10.5 miles to **Signal Lookout** for even better views. **Signal Campground** is just beyond this junction, and from here the old fire road descends through the forest to Maligne Canyon Hostel.

> ## TONQUIN VALLEY
> **Distance: 53.2km/33 miles roundtrip**
> **Duration: 2-3 days roundtrip**
> **Challenge: Difficult**
> **Elevation Change: 700m/2296ft**

Wildlife, lush meadows, sparkling lakes and gorgeous views make this a fantastic overnight trip. The crowning glory are the Ramparts, 10 peaks that tower like giant Gothic fortresses and house supernatural spirits of local natives. Make every attempt to do this hike in September, when the mud, bugs and horseback tours have subsided.

The trail begins from Marmot Basin Rd, off of Hwy 93A and about 16km/10 miles south of Jasper Town. While there is a shorter, less-grueling approach to Amethyst Lakes from the south, this route is far more scenic. The hike to Amethyst Campground is a full day's hike; you can break the journey by staying at one of the two campgrounds en route, or stretch it to a three- or four-day trip by continuing along one of the trails from Amethyst Lakes. Campfires are not permitted at any of the campgrounds.

From Marmot Basin Rd, the trail follows **Portal Creek** southwest and climbs into **The Portal**, a narrow canyon amid the **Trident Range**. The path crosses large rockslides beneath **Peveril Peak** and then descend into a forested valley. A gradual climb takes you past **Portal Campground** and up toward **Maccarib Pass** at 11.7km/7.3 miles. As you ascend above the treeline, you can't help but notice **Oldhorn Mountain** to the south.

Beyond the pass, you begin your descent into the meadowland of **Tonquin Valley** with ever-increasing views of **The Ramparts** to the west. **Maccarib Campground** is next to a small creek at 17.8km/11 miles. The trail heads southwest for 6km/3.7 miles to the northern shore of the glistening **Amethyst Lakes**. At the junction, head right if you've reserved a bed at **Tonquin Valley Lodge**, or continue along the shoreline to **Amethyst Campground** at 26.6km/16.5 miles. On still days, the water reflects the snow-cloaked Ramparts like glass.

Either pack up camp the following day and make the return journey along the same route or, if you have the time, spend a day exploring around Amethyst Lakes before heading back to the trailhead on the third day.

Other Activities

With so many easily accessed trails and waters, Jasper Park is popular with everyone from anglers to ice climbers. Despite being half the size of Banff

Town, Jasper Town has plenty of outfitters, and fierce competition often leads to good prices.

MOUNTAIN BIKING

With lots of trails open to cyclists, mountain biking is a favorite activity around Jasper. Great trails around Jasper Town include Old Fort Point to the Valley of the Five Lakes, Saturday Night Lake Loop and Palisades Lookout. The Overlander Trail is one of the best for beginners. Ask at the information center for trail maps and route details. Bears are prevalent in Jasper Park, so ride with caution. The season runs from May to October.

If you didn't bring your own bike, rent one from **Vicious Cycle** (☎ 780-852-1111; w *www.viciouscyclecanada.com; 630 Connaught Dr; full/front suspension/cruiser CAD$40/30/20 per day; open 9am-6pm).* Hourly and weekly rates are available. **Jasper Source for Sports** (☎ *780-852-3654; 406 Patricia St; full/front suspension/cruiser CAD$28/26/20 per day),* **On-Line Sport & Tackle** (☎ *780-852-3630; 600 Patricia St)* and **Freewheel Cycle** (☎ *780-852-3898;* w *www.freewheeljasper.com; 618 Patricia St)* also rent out bikes and gear.

WHITE-WATER RAFTING & FLOAT TRIPS

Charging rivers course their way through Jasper with rafts full of thrill-seeking adventurers. You won't run short of options for white-water rafting, whether you're after a relaxing float trip, a novice white-water trip for the family or a wild adventure. The season is from mid-May to the end of September.

Maligne Rafting Adventures (☎ *780-852-3370; u www.mra.ab.ca; 627 Patricia St; novice/intermediate from CAD$44/69)* Lots of options include paddle rafting, overnight trips and float trips.

Jasper Raft Tours (☎ *780-852-2665;* w *www.jasperrafttours.com; Jasper Adventure Centre, 604 Connaught Dr; adults/under 16 yrs/under 6 yrs CAD$47/15/free)* Float trips down the Athabasca River for some good, clean family fun.

Rocky Mountain River Guides (☎ *780-852-3777; www.rmriverguides.com; 626 Connaught Dr; novice/intermediate/float trip CAD$45/65/60)* Experienced rafters can sign up for multiday Class 4 trips.

Raven Adventures (☎ *780-852-4292;* w *www.ravenadventure.com; 610 Patricia St; novice/intermediate from CAD$45/60)*

Rocky Mountain Voyageur (☎ *780-852-3343;* w *www.jaspercanoes.com; Jasper Adventure Centre, 604 Connaught Dr; adult/child CAD$48/29)* Reminiscent of the fur-trading days, 32ft canoes float you gently down the river.

ROCK CLIMBING

Jasper is a popular destination for rock climbers. Located up the trail from Fifth Bridge off Maligne Lake Rd, **Rock Gardens** is the most popular crag and has the easiest approach. For climbers with experience (and preferably a guide), **Mt Edith Cavell** offers incredible vistas for climbers, while **Ashlar's Ridge** and **Morro Ridge** are strictly the terrain of the experts.

Paul Valiulis (☎ *780-852-1945;* w *www.climbcanada.com; CAD$60 per person)* will help you scale a cliff face, no matter what your age or ability. **Peter Amann** (☎ *780-852-3237;* w *www.incentre.net/pamann)* will introduce you to the art of rock climbing with two-day beginner courses for CAD$150 and offers personal guiding. If you already know what you're doing, **Gravity Gear** (☎ *888-852-3155;* w *www.gravitygearjasper.com; 618 Patricia St)* has all the equipment to get you to the summit.

BOATING

With all of those glittering lakes, you may well feel inclined to paddle out to the middle. Nonmotorized boating is permitted on most waters; see Fishing & Boating under Policies & Regulations (p164) for more details.

Of the easily accessible lakes with boats for hire, Maligne Lake is tops. The lake is long and indented, allowing you to escape the crowds swarming along the northern shore and appreciate the views in peace. Head to **Maligne Lake Boathouse** (☎ 780-852-3370; W www.malignelake.com; canoes & rowboats hr/day CAD$15/70, kayaks 2hr/day CAD$40/85). If you're not feeling quite so ambitious or are determined to see Spirit Island, **Maligne Lake Cruises** (☎ 780-852-3370; W www.malignelake.com; adult/child CAD$35/18; high season 10am-5pm, operates May-Oct) zips boats down the lake up to eight times daily in the height of summer. Nevertheless, they book up quickly, so reserve in advance.

For a quieter day on the water, **Pyramid Lake Boat Rentals** (☎ 780-852-4900; W www.pyramidlakeresort.com; Pyramid Lake Rd; hr/day CAD$25/75) has canoes, rowboats, kayaks and paddleboats for hire.

FISHING

Fishing is popular throughout the park, both with locals and visitors. Waters frequented by anglers include Celestine, Princess, Maligne and Pyramid Lakes. Make sure you're up-to-date on regulations before you set out.

Maligne Tours (☎ 780-852-3370; W www.malignelake.com; Maligne Lake; full/half day from CAD$170/125 per person; open May-Sep) will guide you around Maligne Lake in search of trout. **Currie's Guiding** (☎ 780-852-5650; W www.curries-guidingjasper.com; 406 Patricia St; full/half day CAD$189/149) will take you fishing in cedar canoes. **On-Line Sport & Tackle** (☎ 780-852-3630; E online@incentre.net; 600 Patricia St) rents gear, teaches flyfishing (3 hours, CAD$99) and runs lots of fishing trips, including 10-hour marathons.

HORSEBACK RIDING

You can ride your horse along a huge number of backcountry trails, some of the most popular being Tonquin Valley, Maligne Pass, Jacques Lake and Bald Hills. Permits and regulations apply.

Skyline Trail Rides (☎ 780-852 4215; W www.skylinetrail.com; 1hr rides from CAD$30) leads daily scheduled rides, as well as overnight trips (three/four days CAD$495/650, including meals & accommodations). **Tonquin Valley Adventures** (☎ 780-852-3909; W www.tonquinvalley.com; per person CAD$775, including meals & accommodations) runs popular five-day horse trips to the Tonquin Valley.

WATCHING WILDLIFE

With 69 different mammals, 277 species of bird and 16 amphibians and reptiles, your chances of spotting wildlife in Jasper Park are pretty high. A trip down Maligne Rd or Miette Hot Springs Rd may score you a bear, wolf or mountain-goat sighting, and elk tend to hang out just south of Jasper Town, at the end of Hwy 93. About 0.5km/0.3 mile north of Jasper Town, on the eastern side of the road, a salt lick is frequented by goats and sheep in the summer.

Alpine Art-Eco Tours (☎ 780-852-3709; W www.alpineart.net; Rocky Mountain Unlimited, 414 Connaught Dr; half-day winter/summer CAD$49/59 per person) runs year-round safaris in search of elk, grizzlies, moose and the like. In summer they take in the wildflowers, and in winter you can trek along on snowshoes. **Jasper Outdoor**

Adventure *(☎ 780-852-5650;* **w** *www.jasperoutdooradventure.com; half day CAD$59 per person)* also runs wildlife searches, with a chance to see animals up close through a spotting scope, and **Walks & Talks Jasper** *(☎ 780-852-4945;* **e** *walktalk@incentre .net; 614 Connaught Dr; adult/child/family CAD$40/20/90)* will take you on a morning Birding & Wildlife Watch.

If birds are more your thing, **On-Line Sport & Tackle** *(see Fishing, earlier; intro/ half day/by boat CAD$69/99/129 per person)* will help you see rosy finches, bufflehead ducks and ptarmigans. Species-specific tours are also available.

GOLF

Jasper Park Lodge Golf Club *(☎ 780-852-6090;* **w** *www.fairmont.com; adult/under 18 yrs CAD$175/33, including power cart; open mid-May–mid-Oct)* is one of the most prestigious greens on the continent. Designed in 1925 by Stanley Thompson, the 18-hole course is as stunning as it is challenging. There's also a driving range, and you can rent shoes and clubs.

RANGER ACTIVITIES

Each summer, Parks Canada sponsors live theater and free family-geared interpretive programs at **Whistlers Outdoor Theatre** *(Whistlers Campground)* and Miette Hot Springs. Friends of Jasper host interpretive walks throughout the summer, as well as lots of nature programs for kids, like butterfly-counting and bird-watching. Visit Jasper Information Centre for details.

Winter Activities

While things get pretty quiet around Jasper Town in winter, the park is a peaceful and stunning wonderland for winter activities. Along the trails, visitors are often treated to up-close encounters with wildlife that have moved down to lower elevations for the season.

Pick up a copy of *Winter Trails* from the information center for details on maintained trails and access. For details on downhill skiing at Marmot Basin, south of Jasper Town, see the Icefields Parkway chapter (p134).

CROSS-COUNTRY SKIING

Parks Canada maintains a number of trails for cross-country skiing, including the Lake Annette Loop, Moose Lake Loop and Bald Hills Lookout. Trails around Maligne Lake are a good mix of novice to expert routes. You can also cross-country ski to Tonquin Valley.

To rent gear, head to **Totem Ski Shop** *(☎ 780-852-3078; 408 Connaught Dr)*, **Jasper Source for Sports** *(☎ 780-852-3654; 406 Patricia St)* or **Everest Outdoor Store** *(☎ 780-852-5902; 414 Connaught Dr)*. All of these rent cross-country equipment for CAD$9 per day.

OTHER ACTIVITIES

Ice-skating in the wilderness is amazing, and both Lac Beauvert and Pyramid Lake are maintained, so that you can glide across the ice. Rent skates at **Jasper Source for Sports** *(see previous section)*.

Snowshoeing is popular on Mina & Riley Lakes Loop, Pyramid Outlook and the Mary Schaffer Loop. You can also tromp over Maligne, Pyramid and Patricia Lakes, but check conditions with Parks Canada first, and stay near the edge, where ice stability is a little more reliable. Snowshoes can be rented from **Everest Outdoor Store** (*see Cross-Country Skiing, previous*) or join a tour with **Jasper Adventure Centre** (☎ 780-852-5595; **W** *www.jasperadventurecentre.com; 306 Connaught Dr; adult/child CAD$45/20).*

The area around Pyramid Bench is maintained for **winter hiking**. Along these trails, you'll be sheltered by the woods and have a good chance of spotting wildlife. If you'd prefer to move a little faster, drive your own dogsledding team with **Jasper Adventure Centre** (*CAD$175 per person*).

To see frozen waterfalls and stunning ice formations, take a trip into a frozen Maligne Canyon with **Jasper Adventure Centre** (*adult/child CAD$40/20; Dec–late Mar*). For a spectacular setting, join one of the moonlight tours.

GETTING INTO SNOWSHOES

Stuck in the snow in Canada's frozen north, European explorers were impressed with how the native people navigated over the frozen terrain with relative ease, and quickly adopted the snowshoe. Other than throwing yourself down a slippery slope on a sled, snowshoeing is perhaps the easiest winter sport to learn and is a fantastic way to explore Jasper's winter wonderland. Here are a few quick tips:

Make sure that the snowshoe straps are tight enough to stop your feet from wiggling around.

Bigger shoes will best keep you on top of the snow but are heavier and more difficult to move around in. Find a happy medium.

Begin on flat ground, do your best to avoid steep hills, and consider taking along poles for balance.

Wet snow is easier to walk on top of than powder.

To avoid falling, try not to cross the tails of your shoes, and always make a U-turn rather than backing up.

Places to Stay

In addition to countless standard hotels and motels, Jasper has wonderful, atmospheric cabins, excellent B&Bs and scenic campgrounds. The majority of places to stay are based in or around Jasper Town, and campgrounds are en route to popular sights. While Jasper isn't the mecca that Banff is, good-value accommodations still fill up quickly, so it's wise to book ahead.

CAMPING

Camping in Jasper can be a relaxing getaway and an activity in itself. Nevertheless, in the height of summer, campgrounds close to Jasper Town fill up quickly, and lining up for a shower can be more tiring than a summit climb. Try campgrounds further from town and with fewer amenities for a bit more peace and quiet.

Reservations are not accepted at any of the campgrounds, and sites are given out on a first-come, first-served basis. To get a site, arrive early. Checkout is at 11am, and by that time, there can already be a line of waiting campers, particularly on weekends.

Wapiti is the only campground open during the winter. For campgrounds along the Icefields Parkway, see that chapter (p134), and for camping rules, check out Camping Rules (p105).

Pocahontas *(Map 9; Miette Hot Springs Rd; CAD$17; open mid-May–mid-Oct)* You'd never know this place has 140 sites; spacious and densely wooded, this campground is peaceful and private. Loop F is the most pleasant. Facilities are minimal, with flush toilets and wheelchair-accessible sites; however, they're very well maintained.

Wapiti *(Map 9; Hwy 98; no/full hookups/electricity only CAD$22/30/26, fire permit CAD$6; open late Jun–early Sep & mid-Oct–early May)* In summer, these grounds have full facilities and fill up quickly. All 362 sites are wooded; the ones that back onto the river are most private. In winter, only 91 sites remain open, and facilities are limited to flush toilets.

Whistlers *(Map 9; Whistlers Rd; no/full hookups/electricity only CAD$22/30/26, fire permit CAD$6; open early May–mid-Oct)* Verging on a camping city, this huge campground support 781 sites. A full list of amenities, including showers, wheelchair access and an interpretive program, keeps it packed in the summer. Sites are wooded but not particularly private. Loops 50 and 67 have good pull-through spots for RVs, and tenting is best on the northern side of the grounds. Fires are only permitted at sites without hookups.

JASPER TOWN LODGING
MAP 10
Jasper Information Centre keeps a list of vacancies for lodging around town, as well as a brochure listing accommodations throughout the park. While they won't call around for you, there are courtesy phones for you to use in your hunt for an available room.

B&Bs
Looking for an affordable private room with a bit of atmosphere? Jasper Town has over 100 B&Bs, ranging from CAD$40 to CAD$150. Many are well located and comfortable, some include breakfast, and lots have family units. Parks Canada hands out a list of inspected accommodations in private homes; to receive a copy before you arrive, contact **Jasper Home Accommodation Association** *(W www.stayinjasper .com, PO Box 758, Jasper T0E 1E0).*

Athabasca Hotel *(☎ 780-852-3386; W www.athabascahotel.com; 510 Patricia St; double with shared/private bath CAD$89/145)* Built in 1929 and one of Jasper's longest-running hotels, rooms here have an old-fashioned European feel about them, with dark wooden furniture and washbasins. Rooms in the east wing are considerably cheaper but are over the nightclub, which pumps out noise until 2am.

Marmot *(☎ 780-852-4471; W www.mtn-park-lodges.com; Connaught Dr; doubles CAD$156-189)* A standard hotel, this place looks much nicer on the inside than on the outside. Renovated rooms are comfortable and tastefully decorated, if not particularly atmospheric.

Park Place Inn *(☎ 780-852-9770; W www.parkplaceinn.com; 623 Patricia St; CAD$199-225)* Unexpectedly located above a parade of downtown shops, this is Jasper's finest hotel and is one of the best in the Rockies. Each of the 12 heritage-style rooms is luxurious and uniquely decorated, with amazing attention to detail. With king-sized beds, enormous tubs, thick fluffy robes and mountain views, you'll never want to leave. Some rooms sleep up to six, and one is wheelchair accessible. Prices are extremely reasonable and worth every penny.

LODGING AROUND JASPER
MAP 9
Everything from hostels to resorts are just outside Jasper.

Budget
Jasper International Hostel (☎ 780-852-3215; **w** www.hihostels.ca; Whistlers Rd; dorms members/nonmembers CAD$18/23) While the dorms here are big (sleeping around 40 each), there are enough activities nearby to wear you out so that you can sleep through the hubbub. Three private rooms are simple but relatively bright, and the common area is pleasant and homey. The kitchen is a tad small for the number of guests.

Maligne Canyon International Hostel (☎ 780-852-3215; **w** www.hihostels.ca; dorms members/nonmembers CAD$13/18) Well positioned for hikes and cross-country skiing, this very basic hostel is poised a little too close to the road. Dorms are six beds to a cabin; toilets are in the outhouse, and water is from a pump. Staff are friendly.

Patricia Lake Bungalows (☎ 780-852-3560; **w** www.patricialakebungalows .com; Pyramid Lake Rd; double/cottage from CAD$81/134, extra adult CAD$10, under 12 yrs free; open May–mid-Oct) Set right on the lake, these rooms are a fantastic deal. Cottages sleep four and are equipped with a kitchen, and those on the lakeside have lovely views. The atmosphere here is relaxed and family oriented.

Miette Hot Springs Bungalows (☎ 780-866-3750; fax 780-866-2214; Miette Hot Springs Rd; motel rooms with/without kitchen CAD$85/75, bungalows CAD$85-130) Motel rooms are old-fashioned and charming, with a cabin feel to them. The quaint wooden bungalows were built in 1938, sleep up to four people and fill up quickly. The restaurant here has reasonably priced, standard meals.

Mid-range
Tekarra Lodge (☎ 780-852-3058; **w** www.tekarralodge.com; Hwy 93A; double cabins CAD$164-184; open mid-May–early Sep) The most atmospheric cabins in town are set next to the Athabasca River, amid trees and tranquility. Hardwood floors, wood-paneled walls, a fireplace and kitchenette give these heritage cabins a warm, cozy feeling. You're just outside town but feel years away.

Alpine Village (☎ 780-852-3285; **w** www.alpinevillagejasper.com; Hwy 93A; double cabins CAD$110-180) Just up the road from Tekarra Lodge, this is a good alternative. The more top-end cabins are plush and beautiful, and the cheaper ones have more of a motel feel.

Pocahontas Cabins (☎ 780-866-3732; **w** www.mtn-park-lodges.com; cnr Hwy 16 & Miette Hot Springs Rd; older cabins CAD$115-155, new cabins CAD$175 190) Brand-new log cabins are extremely cozy, with wood stoves, fully equipped kitchen, microwaves and black-and-white photos of the Pocahontas area in its heyday. Older cabins have had their walls plastered in renovations and lack the character of the newer ones but are cute nonetheless.

Jasper House (☎ 780-852-4535; **w** www.jasperhouse.com; Hwy 98; standard double/suite/bungalow from CAD$140/160/195) A friendly, quiet escape just 3.5km/2.2 miles south of Jasper Town, rooms here have an alpine feel, with all-wood interiors. Standards are simple, and suites have kitchens and sleep two to six. Bungalows are a bit more flashy, with Jacuzzis, fireplaces and river-view balconies,

Beckers Chalets (☎ 780-852-3779; **w** www.beckers[...........] Hwy 98; chalet for 2/3/4 persons CAD$130/135/155) has [...] quaint cabins, but newer versions have a stuffy motel [...]

Top End

Fairmont Jasper Park Lodge (☎ 780-852-3301; W www.fairmont.com; Old Lodge Rd; double/deluxe/lakefront suite CAD$500/550/785) Once the haunt of royalty, artists and the members of the jet set, like Bing Crosby and Marilyn Monroe, this infamous lodge has a 1950s holiday-camp air about it. The lobby is a mishmash of styles but affords lovely views across Lac Beauvert. Rooms and suites have a country charm about them and lots of amenities, but prices are extremely steep, and not all rooms have views of the lake.

Pyramid Lake Resort (☎ 780-852-4900; W www.pyramidlakeresort.com; Pyramid Lake Rd; doubles CAD$269-399, extra adult CAD$15, under 17 yrs free) Tastefully renovated, these comfy rooms have pleasant views of the lake and lots of amenities but still seem a bit pricey. The top-end loft rooms with kitchenettes and can sleep four. Check here in winter; off-season rates can be as low as CAD$90.

Places to Eat

In recent years, Jasper's restaurant scene has taken on an increasingly cosmopolitan air. Whether you're looking for a basic burger or something a little more elegant, you should be able to satisfy your palate.

Budget Map 10

Bear's Paw Bakery (☎ 780-852-3233; 4 Cedar Ave; pastries CAD$3; open 7am-6pm) The fresh breads, squares, scones, tarts and muffins alone are almost worth the trip to Jasper. Spicy veggie sausage rolls and stuffed ciabatta are great trail snacks.

Soft Rock Café (☎ 780-852-5850; 622 Connaught Dr; mains CAD$8; open 7am-6:30pm) It's worth fighting for a seat in this small restaurant for the all-day breakfasts, soups, wraps, fajitas and homemade pies. There's a patio outside for sunny days and booths at the back for privacy.

Co-Co's Café (☎ 780-852-5444; Patricia St; mains CAD$6; open 7am-9pm summer, 7:30am-5pm winter) Small, relaxed and trendy, this is a great place to sip a coffee or a smoothie and read magazines. Fill up on Belgian waffles or omelets for breakfast, and burgers, croissant melts and sandwiches for lunch. Many dishes can be veganized.

Spooners Coffee Bar (☎ 780-852-4046; Patricia Plaza, Patricia St; mains CAD$8; open 8:30am-9pm) Sit on the balcony and watch the slow-paced bustle of Patricia Street. You'll find fruit and veggie smoothies galore, as well as soups, filled bagels and meal-sized salads. Daily specials are a true deal.

Mid-range Map 10

Jasper Pizza (☎ 780-852-3225; 402 Connaught Dr; 10-inch CAD$13, free delivery; open 11:30am-10pm) While you can get ribs, burgers and even some Chinese food here, the real draw is the delicious pizza, piled high with toppings and baked in a wood-burning oven. Noisy and boisterous, this isn't the place for an intimate dinner.

Miss Italia Ristorante (☎ 780-852-4004; 610 Patricia St; lunch/dinner mains CAD$10; open 8am-11pm) With twinkle lights and hanging garlic, the decor here is slightly kitsch and very atmospheric. Extremely friendly staff serve up a huge array of fresh pasta dishes and Italian sausage to a noisy crowd of patrons.

Denjiro (☎ 780-852-3780; 410 Connaught Dr; lunch/dinner mains CAD$10/15; open noon-3pm & 5-10:30pm) Noodles, tempura, sushi and grilled fish are served at low tables in traditional, private booths. The lunch menu also includes a few pan-Asian choices.

La Fiesta (☎ 780 852-0404; 504 Patricia St; lunch/dinner /tapas CAD$10/20/10; open noon 11pm) With tapas like spinach and goat-cheese frittata, you may not make it to the dinner menu for cinnamon- and chili-rubbed duck or paella. The decor is Mediterranean and casual.

Something Else (☎ 780-852-3850; 621 Patricia St; lunch/dinner CAD$12/16; open 11am-11pm) Dine on spanakopita or souvlaki in an atmospheric Greek village setting. The eclectic menu includes everything from stir-fry to chicken to pizza. It's right next to Park Place Inn.

AROUND THE WORLD IN FIVE MEALS

Jasper Town covers little ground geographically, but its culinary span stretches across the globe.

✔ Wield your chopsticks over Japanese delicacies at **Denjiro**.

✔ Follow the scent of garlic to **Miss Italia Ristorante**.

✔ Indulge in Spanish tapas at **La Fiesta**.

✔ Wash down your spanakopita with Greek ouzo at **Something Else**.

✔ Discover contemporary local cuisine at **Tekarra**.

Top End Map 10
Fiddle River (☎ 780 852-3032; 620 Connaught Dr; mains CAD$28; open 5-10pm) With the best fresh seafood in town, this place is worth the splurge. Daily specials are innovative and filling and include lots of nonfishy dishes, like game, ostrich and pastas. Staff are cheerful, the wine list is long, and views across to the train station and mountain ranges are pleasant.

Around Jasper Town Map 9
Pyramid Lake Resort (☎ 780-852-4900; Pyramid Lake Rd; lunch/dinner mains CAD$10/28; lunch noon-4pm, dinner 5-9pm) Big windows give lovely views over the lake, while high ceilings and simple décor make this a classy place to dine. For dinner try seafood ragout, maple quail, chicken masala or rock fish. The Sunday brunch (CAD$12; 11am-4pm) of eggs, crepes and trout salad will leave you pleasantly full for the day.

Tekarra Restaurant (☎ 780-852-4624; Hwy 93A; mains CAD$25; open 5:30-10pm) In a historic wood lodge, the food here is as delicious as it is gorgeous. The menu will have your mouth watering, with snapper in jungle curry sauce, macadamia nut-encrusted lamb, Black Angus beef filet, daily fresh-catch specials and tasty veggie options. Reservations are recommended, and tank tops and baseball caps are a no-go.

Entertainment

Jasper's wild side is more often centered around elk sightings than nights out on the town. Nevertheless, if you're looking for somewhere to toss back a pint and compare skiing stories, there are some options.

The **Downstream Bar** (Map 10; ☎ 780-852-3032; 620 Connaught Dr; open 4pm-late) is Jasper's most comfortable pub and has evenings filled with open-mike sessions, jazz, blues or reggae. Otherwise, choose from oodles of bottled beers, shoot a game of pool or take in the giant TV screen at **Pete's Night Club** (Map 10; Patricia St; open 5pm-3am).

For popcorn and recent releases, head to **Chaba Cinema** (Map 10; ☎ 780-852-4749; 604 Connaught Dr; adult/child CAD$7/4).

✔ ESSENTIALS

BOOKS & GIFTS

Jasper Camera & Gifts *(Map 10; ☎ 780-852-3165; 412 Connaught Dr)* has a small but great selection of books on history, ghost stories and photos of the Rockies as well as specialists guides on climbing and mountaineering.

For beautifully crafted Canadian-made gifts try **Pine Cones & Pussy Willows** *(Map 10; ☎ 780-852-5310; 308 Connaught Dr)*. **Tangle Creek Gifts** *(Map 10; ☎ 780-852-5355; 640 Connaught Dr)* has local and regional crafts as well as books on local history and wildlife.

EQUIPMENT & SUPPLIES

For ski stuff, rain gear, swimwear, camping gear, boots and lumberjack shirts, head to **Totem Ski Shop** *(Map 10; ☎ 780-852-3078; 408 Connaught Dr)*, where prices are very competitive. **Everest Outdoor Store** *(Map 10; ☎ 780-852-5902; 414 Connaught Dr)* has a good selection of hiking gear and topographical maps.

Hook, line and sinker can be bought at **On-line Sport & Tackle** *(Map 10; ☎ 780 852-3630; 600 Patricia St)*. You can also pick up camping gear and outdoor clothing. Mountaineers will find a good selection of equipment at **Gravity Gear** *(Map 10; ☎ 888-852-3155; 618 Patricia St)*.

GROCERIES

For the best prices, head to **IGA** *(Map 10; cnr Connaught Dr & Balsam Ave; open 8am-10pm)*. **Super Foods** *(Map 10; cnr Patricia St & Miette Ave; open 8am-11pm)* has a good selection of harder to find items.

INTERNET ACCESS

Getting online is easy in Jasper.

More Than Mail *(Map 10; Connaught Sq, Connaught Dr; 10 min CAD$1; open 9am-10pm)*

Soft Rock Café *(Map 10; 15/30/45/60 min CAD$2/3/4/4.50; open 7am-9pm)*

Digital Den *(Map 10; ☎ 780-852-9765; Patricia Centre, 610 Patricia St; 15 min CAD$2; open 10am-10pm)*

Video Stop *(Map 10; ☎ 780-852-5593; 607 Patricia St; 15 min CAD$2; open 10am-11:30pm Mon-Fri, 11am-11:30pm Sat & Sun)*

LAUNDRY

Wash the wilderness out of your clothes at **Coin-Op Laundry** *(Map 10; 607 Patricia St; 9am-9pm Mon-Fri, 10am-9pm Sat & Sun)* or **Jasper Laundromat** *(Map 10; Patricia St; wash/40-min dry CAD$2/2; open 9am-10pm)*.

MONEY

Take a loan from Aunt Visa, cash travelers checks or use the ATM at **CIBC** *(Map 10; Connaught Dr)*, next door to the information center.

POSTAL SERVICE

Send your postcards from the main **post office** *(Map 10; 502 Patricia St)* or **More Than Mail** *(Map 10; Connaught Sq, Connaught Dr)*.

AROUND JASPER NATIONAL PARK

If Jasper's remoteness gives you a thirst for even greater seclusion in the great outdoors, consider hiking into one of the wilderness areas along the park's border. Isolated and largely unmaintained, these areas can be reached on foot only and are the territory of resilient, experienced hikers. For drivers looking for an alternative route south from Jasper, Mt Robson Provincial Park is well worth a visit, offering excellent hikes and a chance to see the Canadian Rockies' highest summit.

Mt Robson Provincial Park

Bordering Jasper Park in the east and flanked by the Selwyn Range to the west, the drive through Mt Robson Provincial Park follows a historic pathway of fur traders. Rejected by the Canadian Pacific Railway as a route through the Rockies, it was later adopted by Grand Trunk Pacific and Canadian Northern Pacific Railways and is today a major route of the Canadian National Railway. This is one drive where you are treated to the same magnificent scenery afforded to train passengers; as you travel through winding valleys, past glacial lakes and beneath the shadow of snowy mountains, you'll hear the whistle as trains clatter past.

Highway 16 enters Mt Robson Park about 25km/15.5 miles west of Jasper Town at the **Yellowhead Pass**. Covering 224,866 hectares/555,420 acres, the park's main hub is an **information center** (☎ 250-566-4325; w www.elp.gov.bc.ca/bcparks; open 8am-5pm Jun & Sep, 8am-8pm Jul & Aug) near the western border. There you can pick up trail information, register for hikes with Parks BC staff and take in exhibits on local geography and history. You'll also find a gas station and café next door to the center.

SIGHTS & ACTIVITIES

The crowning glory and namesake of the park, **Mt Robson** towers at an impressive 3954m/12,969ft – the tallest peak in the Canadian Rockies. Approaching from the east, its sudden appearance will dazzle you. Blanketed in snow throughout much of the year, the mountain has left onlookers awestruck for centuries; Aboriginals called it 'Mountain of the Spiral Rd,' and trappers and explorers revered it as unconquerable. Viewpoints are at the information center.

It's worth stopping at **Overlander Falls**, 1.6km/1 mile east of the information center. A short, forested walk (30 minutes roundtrip) takes you down to this scenic tumble of water along the **Fraser River**. With its headwaters trickling from the southeast of the park, the river has already picked up a bit of power at the falls; by the time it reaches the west coast, it's a wide, roaring torrent.

Hiking is what draws most visitors to the park. The famous **Berg Lake Trail** (22km/13.6 miles; 2-3 days) takes you through the Valley of a Thousand Falls, next to Mt Robson. The trail is moderate until the last stretch toward the stunning, glacier-fed lake. You must register to undertake the hike; the majority of spaces are filled on a first-come, first-served basis; however, reservations are accepted for particularly busy periods (☎ 800-689-9025). Seven backcountry campgrounds are located en route (CAD$5 per person per night). Trail information, permits, maps and a video detailing the hike can all be found at the information center.

Mt Robson Park is home to oodles of animals and is a great place for **wildlife watching**. Watch for mountain goats along roadside cliffs, black bears, caribou and

WHODUNNIT

By 1909, the ambition of being the first to conquer Mt Robson was bright in many climbers' daydreams. Accessible only by packhorse through a trackless forest, Mt Robson had thwarted expedition after expedition with bad weather and next-to-impossible precipices.

None had mountaineering fever as severely as Reverend George Kinney, who had already made a number of attempts at scaling Mt Robson. When he heard that a British party had set its sights on his coveted summit, the good reverend set out for the mountain immediately. In his hurry, he left without an expedition party and so picked up Donald 'Curly' Phillips en route. Curly had never attempted mountain climbing before and had only a stick for equipment. Through a blinding storm, the two men edged their way higher and higher until they stood upon the highest summit in the Canadian Rockies, at 3954m/12,969ft. Or so they claim.

The ascent of the duo was doubted immediately, particularly by Canada's mountaineering elite. When, four years later, the climb was completed by Austrian guide Conrad Kain and a group including Arthur Wheeler (the president of the Canadian Alpine Club), it was heralded as the first ascent. In 1959, climbers from Harvard Mountaineering Club found the reverend's summit note shoved into a coffee can with a Canadian flag – 305m/1000ft short of the summit, in the Southwest Bowl. It seemed apparent that Curly and Kinney had not fulfilled their dream.

Yet Kinney's description of the top of Mt Robson is uncanny. The sheer precipice stretching all the way to Berg Lake and the natural cairns are seen from the top alone. Kinney claims to have buried his coffee can in one of these cairns, which are known to collapse and could potentially avalanche into the Southwest Bowl.

So did the reverend and his novice mountaineering companion reach the summit first? The real point was stated best by Leopold S Amery, a member of the British climbing party that Kinney was so keen to beat, 'The fact that they *apparently* did not quite reach the actual summit should not detract from the credit due to one of the most gallant performances in modern mountaineering history.'

porcupine. Moose Marsh is a good spot to see these elusive, giant beasts and head down to Rearguard Falls for salmon viewing (mid-August to early September).

Boating is popular within the park although fishing isn't particularly good. Launch your boat in the green waters of Moose or Yellowhead Lakes. On hot days, you can take a dip in the latter.

PLACES TO STAY

With large, wooded sites, the spacious **Lucerne Campground** (☎ 800-689-9025; Hwy 16, Yellowhead Lake; CAD$14) is a great place to set up home for the night. A number of the 36 sites are level and pull-through for RVs; others are built up for tents. There are two walk-in, lakeside tent sites and a water pump.

Robson River Campground (☎ 800-689-9025; Hwy 16; CAD$17) is just west of the information center. Sites 10 to 18 have river views, and all 19 sites are sheltered and wooded. Tent sites have woodchip pitches. Facilities include showers.

With level sites, **Robson Meadows Campground** (☎ 800-689-9025; Hargreaves Rd; CAD$17) is popular with RVers. Sites 40 to 70 are more private and further from the main road. Across the highway, **Emperor Ridge Camping** (☎ 250-566-8438; Kinney Lake Rd; CAD$15, campfire CAD$3) are private grounds with green, leafy sites and hot showers.

On the western border of the park, the friendly **Mount Robson Mountain River Lodge** (☎ 250-566-9899; **W** www.mtrobson.com; Hwy 16 & Swift Current Creek Rd; rooms CAD$105, including breakfast, cabins CAD$125, extra adult CAD$10) commands stunning views of the giant peak. Comfortable and relaxed, this is a good value.

Hamber Provincial Park

Tiny Hamber Provincial Park is cocooned in an alcove on the western border of Jasper Park. It is the domain of black and grizzly bears, but recent years have seen an influx of backpackers. While there is no road access into the park, an improved 22km/13.6-mile trail from Sunwapta Falls along the Icefields Parkway leads to the 11km/6.8-mile **Fortress Lake**, on the park's eastern border. **Fishing** for brook trout is popular here, and an air-accessed commercial fishing camp is located on the southern shore.

Along the lake's northeast shore are three basic campgrounds, each with a pit toilet and bear pole. You do not need a permit to camp, but you must register your vehicle with Parks Canada if you plan to leave it at Sunwapta Falls.

For more information about the park and current trail conditions, contact **BC Parks** (☎ 250-566-4325; **W** www.env.gov.bc.ca/bcparks).

Willmore Wilderness Park

Spreading across the foothills and mountain ranges north of Jasper Park, Willmore Wilderness Park has more wildlife passing through it than people. If you really want to get off the beaten track, consider the 750km/465 miles of trails crossing this park. Access is by foot only from Rock Lake, Big Berland or Grande Cache. At 95km/59 miles, **Mountain Trail** is the longest and most continuous route through the park from Rock Lake to Grande Cache. The scenic **Indian Trail** (33km/20.5 miles) is popular for hunting and wildlife watching and is in better condition than many of the other trails.

Very little trail maintenance is done here, and while there are designated camping areas, you'll find nothing at them. Water is from lakes and rivers only and must be treated before you consume it. Permits to hike or camp in the park are not required. Be sure to tell someone where you're going and when to expect you back, and be prepared to deal with any emergencies or wildlife you meet on the trail.

For more information on Willmore Park, contact **Travel Alberta** (☎ 800-661-8888; **W** www.travelalberta.com). From Jasper Town, the closest source of information is at the **Hinton Visitor Information Centre** (☎ 780-865-2777; Hwy 16, Hinton), 77km/28 miles north.

Known as the 'Crown of the Continent,' Glacier and Waterton parks together make up the world's first International Peace Park, shared by two countries boasting the longest undefended border in the world.

EXPERIENCING
GLACIER & WATERTON

In 1995, the International Peace Park was designated a UNESCO World Heritage Site for its vast cross-section of plant and animal species. Wildlife can readily migrate from one side of the USA–Canada border to the other, making the two parks part of one of the most important biosphere reserves on the continent. Under the stress of increasing development around natural preserves worldwide, international relations such as these become ever more important in protecting a fragile planet.

Glacier and Waterton have reputations for dramatic wilderness, and indeed, both places offer landscapes of glaciated valleys, lakes and peaks. Though armed with different passports, the parks are undoubtedly part of one ecosystem.

GLACIER NATIONAL PARK
Map 11

It's not uncommon to hear people say that Glacier is the most beautiful place they've ever seen. It's a biologically diverse visual feast at every turn: mountains, ancient groves, massive glaciers and surreally clear lakes and streams. The belle of its ball is **Going-to-the-Sun Rd**, which shows off phenomenal examples of glacial activity, and thus the sights and trails along that route receive the most attention from visitors.

Nearly two million people visit the park each year. Lake McDonald, St Mary and Many Glacier Valleys are highly toured areas, while Two Medicine and North Fork Valleys – both stunning – receive less traffic. It is worth exploring more than one region of the park, even on a short visit. Those who make it out of their vehicles to hike, fish, paddle or ride on horseback will unearth many possible directions to explore.

Humans share this park with a whole realm of wildlife, and you are almost certain to view more than ground squirrels on your journey through. Bears are talked about far more often than they are seen, but just knowing that you are temporarily sharing residence with the legendary animal can add intrigue (and a little adrenaline) to any trip.

Though the glaciers here, decreasing in mass, gave the park its name, it is the harmony between all of the elements of the dramatic landscape that awes most visitors. Snow-covered peaks in August, elk roaming meadows at dusk, aquamarine lakes fed by glacial masses and early morning birdsong in a sleepy forest – all of this, under a huge moody sky, keeps the enamored returning again and again.

When You Arrive

The park is open year-round. An entry pass per car or RV costs USD$20. People arriving on foot, bicycle or motorcycle pay USD$5 per person. Both types of passes are valid for seven days. An annual Glacier National Park Pass costs USD$25. Fees for Glacier entry do not include entrance to Waterton Lakes National Park.

A great value for national park fans, the annual **National Parks Pass** costs USD$50 and can be purchased at US national parks or online at **W** www.national parks.org.

The **Golden Age Passport** (USD$10) offers unlimited admission and discounted camping to US residents 62 years and older, and the **Golden Access Passport** (free) offers the same to US residents who are blind or disabled; both of these can only be purchased in person.

Free entry to the park is the custom on **Founder's Day**, August 25.

Staff at the entrance stations furnish visitors with a map of Glacier and Waterton; the quarterly newspaper *Waterton-Glacier Guide,* stocked with logistical information and opening times; and *The Glacier Explorer,* a schedule of the events and activities, including ranger-led day trips.

ORIENTATION

The delineators of Glacier's 4046 sq km/1562 sq miles are the North Fork of the Flathead River (west), US 2 (south), US 89 and the Blackfeet reservation (east) and the Canadian border (north).

Entrances

There are six entrance gates into the park. The **West Entrance**, just north of West Glacier, is the busiest one. The other entries on the west side are **Camas Creek Entrance**, on Camas Rd, east of the junction with Outside North Fork Rd, and the **Polebridge Ranger Station**, northeast of the town of Polebridge. On the east side, **Two Medicine Entrance** is on Two Medicine Rd, west of Hwy 49. The **St Mary Entrance** is at the start of Going-to-the-Sun Rd, just west of St Mary Village. The **Many Glacier Entrance**, on Many Glacier Rd, is west of US 89, near Babb.

Boards at entrances indicate which in-park campgrounds are open or full.

Main Regions

The park's main areas, clockwise roughly northeast to northwest, are the Goat Haunt region, Many Glacier, St Mary, Logan Pass, Lake McDonald and North Fork. **Goat Haunt**, at the base of Upper Waterton Lake, is the closest area to Waterton Park in the north and is frequented mainly by backpackers traveling between the two parks. On Many Glacier Rd, 21km/13 miles west of US 89 is **Many Glacier Valley**, whose mountainous terrain is popular with hikers. **St Mary**, on the eastern end of Going-to-the-Sun Rd, encompasses the area around the large St Mary Lake. On Going-to-the Sun Rd 27km/17 miles west is **Logan Pass**, on the Continental Divide. Taking in a valley and its lakes, **Two Medicine** is 19km/12 miles northwest of East Glacier and US 89. The **Lake McDonald Valley** contains Apgar Village and the hub of activity around Lake McDonald. The most remote and least visited portion of the park is the **North Fork Valley**, in the northwest corner.

Major Roads
The park's main thoroughfare is the famous Going-to-the-Sun Rd, which is also the only paved road that cuts directly across the park. The 81km/50-mile scenery-loaded road exposes many of the more photographed attractions in the park. US 2 (92km/57 miles) wraps around the southern boundary of the park, wending through national forest, Blackfeet reservation land and a little bit of national park. Camas Rd (18km/11 miles) links the Apgar area with the beginning of the 21km/13-mile stretch of Outside North Fork Rd to Polebridge.

Visitor Service Hubs
Outside the park's eastern boundaries, at the junction of US 2 and 49, **East Glacier** is on the Blackfeet Indian reservation. It offers budget to mid-range accommodations; the top-end option is Glacier Park Lodge. Amenities include restaurants, gas, a post office, an ATM, a small supply/food store and an Amtrak stop.

St Mary Village on US 89 offers gas and good restaurants, a swanky lodge and campgrounds; **Babb**, 13km/8 miles to the north, has fewer amenities.

West Glacier, outside the park's southwest boundary, is the most congested of the hubs. It offers a post office, photo processing, motels and business services. The remote **Polebridge** sits 21km/13 miles from the junctions of Outside North Fork Rd and Camas Rd. Though steeped in character, its amenities are limited: a saloon, a store and a hostel.

Within the park, **Apgar Village**, off Going-to-the-Sun Rd within the park, boasts a visitors center, restaurants, shops and a couple accommodations.

INFORMATION
Glacier National Park Headquarters (☎ *406-888-7800;* **w** *www.nps.gov/glac; West Glacier, MT 59936; open 8am-4:30pm Mon-Fri)* is just south of the west entrance station. Copious park information, including maps, is downloadable from the website. From November to April, headquarters is the locus for visitor information. From late June to early September, hours vary at visitors centers and ranger stations. See the park newspaper for operating hours.

Apgar Visitor Center (☎ *406-888-7939; open early May–late Oct, weekends in winter)* A fully stocked information center.

Logan Pass Visitor Center (*no* ☎ *; usually open early Jun–mid-Oct)* Opens when Going-to-the-Sun Rd does.

Many Glacier Ranger Station (☎ *406-732-7740; open late May–mid-Sep)* A great stop for information on area hikes.

Polebridge Ranger Station (☎ *406-888-7842; open late May–mid-Sep)* A small historic station with North Fork information.

St Mary Visitor Center (☎ *406-732-7750; open early May–mid-Oct)* Holds interesting geological exhibits and an auditorium featuring slide shows and ranger talks.

Two Medicine Ranger Station *(☎ 406-226-4484; open late May-mid-Sep)* A good source for Two Medicine area hikes.

Ranger stations, not always staffed, are also at Goat Haunt, Cut Bank, Walton, Logging Creek and Kintla Lake.

The **Alberta Information Centre** *(☎ 406-888-5743, 800-252-3782; off US 2, West Glacier; open 8am-7pm)* is an excellent resource for those bound north for Canada's Waterton, Banff and Jasper National Parks.

BOOKSTORES

The nonprofit **Glacier Natural History Association** *(☎ 406-888-5756; W www .glacierassociation.org; US 2; open 8am-4:30pm Mon-Fri)*, in West Glacier's train depot, is an excellent resource for books, maps and information. It also operates the small bookstores at visitors centers and ranger stations in the park.

Good maps include the USGS *Glacier National Park* map and National Geographic's *Glacier-Waterton Lakes National Parks* map.

Policies & Regulations

No fireworks are allowed in the park, nor are any loaded firearms permitted. It is illegal to collect even the smallest natural parts of the park (ie, rocks, flowers).

Park regulations allow visitors to collect up to a pint of berries per person per day, but think twice before making this a practice. The bears and other creatures that depend on this food for sustenance cannot just hop over to the market like most of us can (plus it isn't a good idea to get between a bear and a patch of berries).

WILDERNESS PERMITS & REGULATIONS

No permits are required for day hikes, but you must have a permit to camp in the backcountry; they go for USD$4 per adult per night and USD$2 per child aged nine to 16. A season pass is USD$50. Kids eight years old and under get free permits. Once in the park, permits can be arranged less than 24 hours ahead of time at the **Apgar Backcountry Office** *(near Apgar Visitors Center; open late May–late Oct)*, St Mary Visitor Center or the ranger stations at Many Glacier, Two Medicine or Polebridge. See Information (p196) for season openings.

Planners can reserve backcountry sites in person at the Apgar office or at St Mary Visitor Center, or by writing to **Backcountry Reservations** *(fax 406-888-5819; Glacier National Park, West Glacier, MT 59936)*. Applications postmarked before April 15 are not accepted. A map of backcountry campsites with availability information is at **W** www.nps.gov/glac/activities/bcguide1.htm.

Permits are required for backcountry camping in winter (late November to late April), though no fees are charged. You may arrange for permits in person or over the phone through the Apgar Visitor Center or park headquarters up to seven days before your intended trip.

CAMPING

Frontcountry campers should store their edibles in a hard-sided vehicle or in a bear-proof food locker. Stoves, coolers, containers and utensils (even if clean) and scented toiletries should never be left out unattended. Garbage can be disposed of in the bear-proof bins available in all frontcountry campgrounds.

Most stores within and around the park sell wood for campfires. Resist the temptation to gather fallen wood in campgrounds or at picnic areas within the park, though gathering is permitted on parts of the Inside North Fork Rd. Check with a ranger for more information.

FISHING & BOATING

A Montana state fishing license is not required within Glacier National Park. Anglers are generally limited to possession of five fish daily, with caps varying by species. Some waters, including Hidden Lake and the North and Middle Forks of the Flathead River, are purely catch-and-release zones. See the park's *Fishing Regulations* pamphlet. Portions of the North Fork and Middle Fork of the Flathead River outside the park are subject to Montana state fishing regulations. Part of Lower Two Medicine Lake is on reservation land and subject to reservation regulations.

Motorboats are permitted on Upper Waterton, Sherburne, St Mary and McDonald Lakes. For sections of Lower Two Medicine Lake, you'll need a permit from Blackfeet Nation Fish & Wildlife (p229). On Bowman and Two Medicine Lakes, motorcraft must be 10 horsepower or less. See Glacier's *Boating Regulations* pamphlet. Jet Skis are not allowed on Glacier's waters. Waterskiing is permitted only on St Mary Lake and Lake McDonald, and only during daylight hours.

Getting Around

Most visitors make their way around the park on their own wheels, though a handy hiker shuttle operates in the summer.

CAR & MOTORCYCLE

The speed limit is 72kph/45 mph on all park roads unless otherwise posted; the limit drops to 16kph/10 mph in campgrounds. Vehicle restrictions are imposed on Going-to-the-Sun Rd only. Vehicles or combinations wider than 2.4m/8ft or longer than 6.4m/21ft are prohibited between Avalanche Creek to just east of Sun Point. State law requires motorcycle operators and passengers under 18 years old to wear helmets.

SHUTTLES

Operating July through early September, the unreservable Hiker's Shuttle (run by Glacier Park, Inc; ☎ 406-892-2525) hits numerous points and trailheads in Many Glacier, St Mary, West Glacier and Logan Pass. Each of the following one-way portions is USD$8: West Glacier to Logan Pass, Logan Pass to St Mary and St Mary to Many Glacier. Schedules are posted at the shuttle stops.

Reservable services by Glacier Park, Inc include the East Side Shuttle, which runs between East Glacier and Waterton; Two Medicine Shuttle, between Glacier Park Lodge and Two Medicine; and the West Glacier Train Station Shuttle, to the Belton train station from Lake McDonald and Apgar.

ORGANIZED TOURS

Glacier Park, Inc *(☎ 406-892-2525)* runs a fleet of historic red 'jammer' buses (named for the days when the coaches did not have automatic transmission and drivers jammed the gears) that ply seven different tour routes. Tours range from a 3.5-hour trip between Lake McDonald Lodge and Logan Pass (adult/child USD$25/12.50) to an 8.5-hour journey that circles the park via US 2 (USD$65/32.50). The International Peace Park Tour departs Many Glacier (USD$40/20) and Glacier Park Lodge (USD$65/32.50) daily, trotting through the east side of the park before heading to Waterton Lakes National Park in Canada in time for an optional tea at the Prince of Wales Hotel.

Blackfeet tribal members lead interpretive tours (adult/child under 13 USD$40/15) of Going-to-the-Sun Rd run by **Sun Tours** (☎ 406-226-9220, 800-786-9220). Air-conditioned buses leave from various points in East Glacier, St Mary and Browning; tours last approximately six hours, including a one-hour lunch break.

Glacier Park Boat Co (☎ 406-257-2426; **W** www.montanaweb.com/gpboats) offers boat tours (USD$10 to $12, 45 minutes to 1.5 hours) leaving five or more times daily from the docks at Lake McDonald Lodge, Rising Sun (for St Mary Lake), Two Medicine and Many Glacier Hotel (for Swiftcurrent and Josephine Lakes). All are narrated by an interpretive guide; some include an optional short hike. Sunset cruises depart the Rising Sun (6:30pm) and Lake McDonald (7pm) docks – though don't expect to see the sun drop that early in early summer.

To get a view from on high, consider the helicopter tours run by **Kruger Helicop-Tours** (☎ 406-387-4565; **W** www.krugerhelicopters.com); hourly rates start at USD$150 per person.

Sights

The most popular sights in Glacier – like beautiful **Lake McDonald** and **St Mary Lake**, and the Continental Divide–riding **Logan Pass** – are accessed along the **Going-to-the-Sun Rd** driving tour (p200). **Jackson Glacier** is the only glacier visible from an overlook on this route; to get a glimpse of others, like **Grinnell Glacier** and **Sperry Glacier**, you must brave the trails. For its dramatic natural sights, the **Many Glacier** region (p208) is a favorite among hikers.

SHRINKING GLACIERS

You've got Lupfer and Pumpelly, Sperry and Sexton, Old Sun and Ahern and Vulture and Dixon. The sight of glaciers, the park's 50-some moving ice masses, has been treasured by visitors through the years. Blackfoot Glacier (171 hectares/423 acres) is the park's largest, but one of its indisputable present traits is testament to a condition shared by all of the park's glaciers: they are receding – and fast.

Glaciers in the park have been drastically decreasing in mass since the mid-1800s. Before then, the large bodies were actually expanding. If the warming trends in the climate continue, scientists predict that Glacier's glaciers will be gone by 2030.

While Earth through the ages has proven some resiliency to natural cycles, a predominant theory is that global warming – accelerated by the burning of fossil fuels – will put the glaciers in past tense and will tragically affect wildlife habitats, fish populations and the ecosystem at large.

Glacier's trademark peaks can be seen from just about any point in the park that isn't overshadowed by towering trees. A particularly extraordinary one is the tri-oceanic **Triple Divide Peak** – dump a bucket of water from its summit and it will end up in three different places: the Pacific Ocean, the Gulf of Mexico and the Hudson Bay, which eventually flows into the Arctic.

Driving Tours

Even a drive to a lodge parking lot can be breathtakingly beautiful. You can't go wrong in the scenery department, whatever your mode of transportation – bicycle, bus or your own feet. For people with wheels and precious little time to hit the trails, a few roads provide great overviews to the park's diverse offerings.

The impressively constructed Going-to-the-Sun Rd is almost synonymous with Glacier National Park. The section from the Loop to St Mary is generally open mid-June to mid-October but reaches its crowded height in July and August.

GOING-TO-THE-SUN RD
Route: West Entrance to St Mary Entrance (or vice versa)
Distance: 81km/50 miles one way
Speed Limit: 40kph/25 mph to 64kph/40 mph

The Going-to-the-Sun Rd is an engineering marvel, particularly considering that its construction began in 1927. Crossing the Continental Divide at Logan Pass, it rides above sheer drops, jutting through the heart of the park's wilderness. Spurning the chains of switchbacks characteristic of most alpine roads, this route was set with only two major turns.

From the park's west entrance, the route veers right at Apgar to begin its journey next to the eastern edge of 16km/10-mile **Lake McDonald**, the largest lake in the park. Stanton Mountain (2362m/7749ft) is at the lake's north end. Once the lake is out of view, the road parallels McDonald Creek, the park's longest, through a narrow valley looked upon by steep-sided mountains. At 26km/16 miles, the short **Trail of the Cedars** (p203) introduces this lush area inhabited by ancient groves.

North of Avalanche Creek, the **Garden Wall** comes into view. The 2743m/8999ft granite arête divides the west and east regions of the park, running from Logan to Swiftcurrent Passes along the Continental Divide. The **Loop**, a parking lot at the road's major hairpin turn, is a good stopover. Continuing its traverse of the Garden Wall, the road passes **Bird Woman Falls** (43km/27 miles) and **Weeping Wall** (46km/29 miles), which vary from dripping to gushing during the year.

The busy visitors center at **Logan Pass** (52km/32 miles; elevation 2036m/6680ft) is the welcome mat for a couple wonderful trails, including the **Hidden Lake Overlook** and the longer **Highline Trail** (p205). Be forewarned: The Logan Pass parking lot can resemble a shopping-mall parking lot before the holidays, particularly between 11am and 3pm.

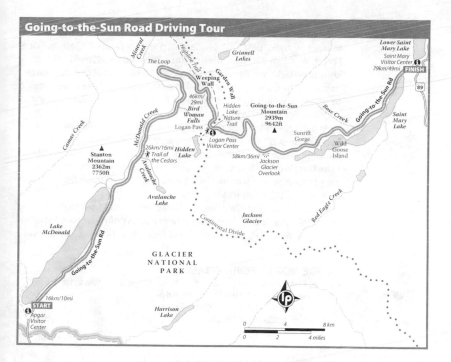

Going-to-the-Sun Road Driving Tour

At 58km/36 miles, you should visit **Jackson Glacier Overlook**. Near the west end of St Mary Lake, have a look at the vibrant Sunrift Gorge. **Going-to-the-Sun Mountain** (2939m/9642ft) is north of the road. In the lake, **Wild Goose Island** is a tiny nub of an isle with a handful of lopsided trees – proof of the extreme winds that blow through this valley.

The St Mary Visitors Center (79km/49 miles) is on the lake's east end. The plains on this side of the park stretch east from St Mary to the Dakotas.

If you go full speed ahead, the route from Apgar to St Mary can be done in an hour and a half. Plan on at least three hours, though, to savor the sights along the road. For a loop trip, drive one way on Going-to-the-Sun Rd then back along US 2 on the park's southern border.

No vehicles over 6m/21ft are allowed from east of Sun Point to Avalanche Creek.

US 2
Route: East Glacier to West Glacier
Distance: 92km/57 miles one way
Speed Limit: 88kph/55 mph to 113kph/70 mph

This segment of US 2 between East and West Glacier doesn't get the traffic found on Going-to-the-Sun Rd. Part of the Theodore Roosevelt International Hwy, the road is well used by anglers and rafters who come for the access to the Flathead River, which runs alongside much of the route.

From east to west, the highway departs the Blackfeet Indian reservation a few miles past East Glacier, then enters Lewis & Clark National Forest. At 18km/11 miles, **Marias Pass** (elevation 1590m/5216ft), once known as 'Backbone Pass' by the Blackfeet Indians, is the country's lowest pass over the Continental Divide. A memorial square here pays homage to notables, including Great Northern Railroad engineer John F Stevens and Theodore Roosevelt.

At 38km/24 miles, an access area to the Middle Fork Flathead River is a popular jump-off for rafters, floaters and anglers. A half mile later, the road enters Glacier National Park lands for just a few miles, taking in **Goat Lake Overlook**. Turn left into the parking lot, then walk down to a viewing platform, where you are likely to see salt-hungry mountain goats on rocks below. Bring binoculars.

On the left at 45km/28 miles, a 0.4km/0.2-mile road goes to the historic Izaak Walton Inn (p225). Several quiet **river access points** and overlooks dot the way to West Glacier, including Paola, Cascadilla and Moccasin Creeks.

INSIDE NORTH FORK ROAD
Route: Fish Creek Campground to Polebridge or Kintla Lake
Distance: 43.5km/27 miles to Polebridge,
**   69km/43 miles to Kintla Lake**
Speed Limit: 32kph/20 mph

OUTSIDE NORTH FORK ROAD
Route: Camas Rd junction to Polebridge
Distance: 21km/13 miles to Polebridge
Speed Limit: 56kph/35 mph

The two roads from the park's southwest into rugged and remote North Fork Valley see relatively few visitors. The Outside North Fork Rd, stretching from near the Camas Creek entrance to the Canadian border via Polebridge, is the more frequented route; it alternates between pavement, dirt and gravel. The inside road (Glacier Rte 7) – narrow, dusty, teeming with potholes – is slower but more adventurous. For variety, drive north on the Inside North Fork Rd and come down on the outer road after hanging out in the quirky village of **Polebridge** (p224).

The North Fork Valley is heavily forested but for major fire-affected areas. The **Polebridge Ranger Station** gives background on the region's fiery past. Some parts of the valley may be closed for wildlife-management reasons (ie, wolves' denning). **Spotting wildlife** is probable in this valley, particularly along the Inside North Fork Rd.

From the Fish Creek Campground entrance, driving the inside road to Polebridge (43.5km/27 miles) takes under two hours. To beautifully serene **Kintla Lake** (69km/43 miles), at the top of the road, plan on nearly three hours. **Bowman Lake**, also lovely, sits 53km/33 miles from the start of the inside road. The Outside North Fork Rd is 21km/13 miles from the junction with Camas Rd to Polebridge – a 30- to 40-minute journey.

Festivals & Events

No fireworks are present, but the weekend nearest **Fourth of July** is the year's busiest, with the smell of barbecue permeating the air. Outside the park, Polebridge celebrates with festivities, fireworks and an eclectic parade. The weekend nearest **Labor Day** (the first Monday in September) is another busy one in the park and serves as a farewell to the summer season.

Polebridge is the site of the **Root Beer Classic Sled Dog Races** for two days in January.

Day Hikes

Park roads unveil nice scenery, but to really get an eyeful, get on the trails. Even some of the shortest hikes provide a respite from the herds of Harleys and RVs. Options exist for every level, from easy nature strolls to butt-busting mountain-pass ventures. Day hikes cost neither penny nor permit, though permits (p197) are required for back-country overnights.

Park visitors centers give out basic hiking maps (divided into Lake McDonald, St Mary/Logan Pass, Many Glacier, Two Medicine, Goat Haunt and North Fork areas), which also list the length, altitude gain and trailhead locations of the hikes. Each covers six to 14 hikes.

Wildfires in the summer of 2003 affected forests near many trails. Please check in with a visitors center or ranger station for current trail information.

HIGHLIGHTS

Don't leave before you ...

- ✔ hike through the **Many Glacier Valley** (p208)
- ✔ ride horseback around **Lake McDonald** (p200)
- ✔ eat alongside a **Two Medicine** waterscape (ie, Twin Falls; p210)
- ✔ indulge in views on the **Highline Trail** (p205)
- ✔ soak your feet in the beautiful **Kintla Lake** (p202)

LAKE McDONALD VALLEY

The hikes in glacier-carved Lake McDonald Valley tread lush, forested terrain. Most of the trailheads are accessed from Going-to-the-Sun Rd.

TRAIL OF THE CEDARS
Distance: 1.3km/0.8 miles roundtrip
Duration: 30 minutes
Challenge: Easy
Elevation Change: 16m/52ft

One of the park's two wheelchair-accessible trails (the other is Running Eagle Falls Trail, in Two Medicine), this stroll can be started from the picnic parking area adjacent to Avalanche Lake Campground or directly from Going-to-the-Sun Rd. Midday in high-season, parking spaces can be in demand due to the popularity of this and the Avalanche Lake trails.

Trail of the Cedars loops through a towering old-growth forest of red cedar and western hemlock, which is more characteristic of the West Coast states than Montana. Black cottonwood and Douglas fir trees also reside here. The dim, dewy environment, with ferns and moss sprouting up from the forest floor, exudes the moist air of a rain forest, and fallen trees expose extraordinary root systems.

Benches on the loop and educational signposts encourage lingering hikes. One bench is situated to view Avalanche Gorge, now filled with swift-flowing icy-blue waters from Avalanche Lake. Birds in the area include thrushes and owls.

AVALANCHE LAKE TRAIL
Distance: 6.4km/4 miles roundtrip
Duration: 2.5 hours
Challenge: Easy
Elevation Change: 764m/475ft

This appealing trail is one of the more human-populated ones in the park. As with Trail of the Cedars (p203), you may run into parking congestion. However, even amid the foot traffic heading toward Avalanche Lake, a good chance remains for spots of quiet and maybe even a look at deer.

The hike begins on the boardwalk of the Trail of the Cedars loop trail. You will soon come to the Avalanche Lake Trail junction, from which the trail heads uphill, making its way along rushing Avalanche Creek. The mature, old-growth forests of western hemlock and cedar that are predominant on Trail of the Cedars are just as populous on this route; thus, most of the walk is shaded.

The trail is not completely level, but climbs are gentle. It is 3.2km/2 miles to the top of the alpine Avalanche Lake. Carry on another 1.3km/0.8 miles lakeside to reach the bottom end.

The destination lake is lovely, overlooked by Bearhat Mountain to the northeast and Mt Brown to the southwest. However, the hike is pleasant the whole way. Even if you do not embark on this trail, scamper up the first ascent to get a nice look at lively Avalanche Creek.

LOGAN PASS

Logan Pass boasts the Continental Divide, wildlife, refreshingly thin air and majestic views, and much of it is accessed just a short hop from the parking lot.

HIDDEN LAKE OVERLOOK TRAIL
Distance: 5km/3 miles roundtrip
Duration: 2 hours
Challenge: Moderate
Elevation Change: 150m/494ft

The grand setting, great views and wildlife easily viewed from the Logan Pass Visitors Center make this one of the park's most popular hikes.

From the rear of the visitors center, follow the paved path to the trailhead. A wooden boardwalk leads southwest. If it is covered in snow (sometimes until mid-July), follow the yellow trail markers to avoid trampling on fragile terrain – this alpine meadowland is extremely sensitive.

About 1km/0.6 miles in, the boardwalk gives way to a gravelly dirt path. If the snow has melted, the diversity of grasses and wildflowers in the meadows around you is evident. Resident trees include old Engelmann spruce, subalpine fir and whitebark pine. Hoary marmots, ground squirrels and mountain goats are not shy along this trail. The elusive ptarmigan, whose brown feathers turn white in winter, also lives nearby. Up-close mountain views include Clement Mountain north of the trail; Reynolds Mountain rises in the southeast.

The ascent is relatively gradual throughout the trail, with a couple good climbs along the way. You will cross the Continental Divide 0.3km/0.2 mile before the overlook at Hidden Lake Pass. The overlook offers stunning views of the deep-blue **Hidden Lake**, bordered by mountain peaks and rocky cliffs. **Sperry Glacier** is visible to the south.

The shores of Hidden Lake can be accessed via a 2.4km/1.5-mile trail from the overlook; a little bit more stamina is required for this leg, which steeply descends 233m/765ft.

HIGHLINE TRAIL
**Distance: 12km/7.6 miles one way to Granite Park Chalet;
18.7km/11.6 miles one way to the Loop
Duration: 5.5 hours to Granite Park; 7.5 hours to the Loop
Challenge: Easy
Elevation Change: 920m/3020ft**

This is one of the best longer hikes in the park. Superb nature can be experienced without the exertion of superpower strength. Also called the **Garden Wall** hike for its star feature, it is a popular route. Abundant scenery is revealed the whole way: dramatic peaks, wildflower-sprinkled meadows, subalpine trees, shrubby vegetation and snowfields. The trailhead sits across the road from the Logan Pass Visitors Center.

At the trail's start are immediate, mountained vistas, including jagged ridges. You will tread alongside the western boundary of the Garden Wall. Mt Clements and Mt Oberlin are west of the trail; Pollock Mountain is on the east side, ahead. Shortly after setting out, you will make your way around a rocky cliff face – a cable assists with physical (and mental) support.

After its initial ramble downwards, the trail flattens for a while, then gently ascends. After

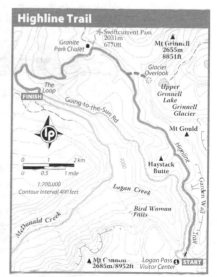

a climb, you will find yourself on a ridge connecting Haystack Butte and Mt Gould at about 5.6km/3.5 miles into the trail. Keep at it and soon you will reach the trail's apex. Breathe deep. At 10.9km/6.8miles into the trail, a junction offers a chance to climb up less than a mile for an overlook at **Grinnell Glacier**.

In order to forage onward toward the hike-in-only **Granite Park Chalet** (p212), stay left. The chalet is 12.2km/7.6 miles in, but you'll see it well beforehand.

To reach the Loop on Going-to-the-Sun Rd, head toward the southwest, hopping onto the Granite Park Trail from the chalet. Shuttles (p198) make a stop at the Loop and can return you to Logan Pass.

ST MARY VALLEY

Many of St Mary's diverse hikes launch from Going-to-the-Sun Rd. Some skirt the impressive namesake lake, and others view it from above.

RED EAGLE LAKE TRAIL
Distance: 24.5km/15.2 miles roundtrip
Duration: 8 hours
Challenge: Easy
Elevation Change: 91m/300ft

Meadows, forests and mountains alike can be appreciated on this attractive trail to Red Eagle Lake. The roundtrip from the trailhead to the lake makes for a long day trip, but the trail is largely level. To reach the trailhead from Going-to-the-Sun Rd, turn right on the road just after the St Mary entrance station.

The trail starts out from a dirt road near the northeastern edge of St Mary Lake. A little over a mile into it, a loop heads back to the historic ranger station; keep right. You will make your way through forests of

TIME OUT

- ✔ Watch the sun sink from the east shore of **Lake McDonald** (p200).
- ✔ Get a 'Flathead Hot River Rock Massage' from Remedies Day Spa at **Glacier Park Lodge** (p223) or Belton Chalet.
- ✔ Tuck into a wine-accompanied feast of locally caught whitefish at **Snowgoose Grill** (p227) in St Mary Village.
- ✔ Sit on a bench with your journal, amid the wooded tranquility of **Trail of the Cedars** (p203).
- ✔ Take an **evening boat cruise** (p199) from either Lake McDonald or Rising Sun.

fir, spruce and aspen. The grassy meadows on the route are colored with wildflowers. Red Eagle Mountain, home of mountain goats, rises ahead; Curly Bear Mountain and Kakitos Mountain look down on the trail from the southeast. At about 6.4km/4 miles, cross a suspension bridge over Red Eagle Creek. At the St Mary Lake Trail junction, keep left; you will cross another bridge over the creek and continue on to the lake.

The lovely **Red Eagle Lake** is serenely set. From the lake, view the mountains that rise southeast on the Continental Divide, including **Triple Divide Peak**.

Good bird-watching possibilities exist on the trail and at the lake; you may encounter thrushes, warblers and loons. Grizzlies are known commuters near this trail. Look for scat and other signs of their presence. To head back, retrace your steps toward the trailhead.

SIYEH PASS TRAIL
Distance: 16.6km/10.3 miles one way
Duration: 7 hours
Challenge: Moderate-Difficult
Elevation Change: 1050m/3445ft

A favorite hike among Glacier old-timers, this trail offers a vibrant range of high-alpine scenery. The trail begins from Siyeh Bend on Going-to-the-Sun Rd, jutting from Siyeh Creek through to the forested approaches toward Going-to-the-Sun Mountain.

At 4.3km/2.7 miles from the start of the trail, stay right at the junction with Piegan Pass Trail – it's another 3.2km/2 miles to **Siyeh Pass** (elevation 2512m/8240ft) via Preston Park. The path eventually traverses toward the pass via switchbacks. Once there, brave the wind that's likely blowing through for some extraordinary panoramic views. Mt Siyeh sits prominently to the northwest. Look for a pile of rocks to the right of the trail. It marks a spot where a bell once stood (it was removed for scrap metal during WWII) and was rung by passersby on horseback.

The switchbacks toward **Sunrift Gorge** head down steeply in some parts. In early summer, large snowfields over the trail can make for a tricky descent. After alternate scree and snow, open terrain gives way to sections of alpine forest.

Up on your right, **Sexton Glacier** lies in the 'V' between Going-to-the-Sun Mountain and Matahpi Peak. Continue toward St Mary Lake, part of which is seen in the distance. As you descend further, lusher plantlife includes huckleberry and thimbleberry patches. The path inches closer to the beautiful Baring Creek, with rushing streams and falls supported by red rock, before treading alongside it. Hanging valleys are visible on your right.

To catch a shuttle, you'll have to walk from Sunrift Gorge to Sun Point, 1km/0.6 mile east.

MANY GLACIER

Three trailheads lead hikers into the popular Many Glacier Valley from the end of Many Glacier Rd, which runs west from US 89. Many of the area trails go through a summer feeding ground for grizzlies – stay alert and keep singing. For more information on avoiding dangerous bear encounters, see Bear Issues (p268)

ICEBERG LAKE TRAIL
Distance: 14.5km/9 miles roundtrip
Duration: 5.5 hours
Challenge: Easy-Moderate
Elevation Change: 363m/1190ft

This hike is justifiably a common favorite. Enclosed by stunning 914m/3000ft vertical walls on three sides, Iceberg Lake is one of the most impressive glacial lakes anywhere in the Rockies. The 366m/1200ft ascent is gentle, and the approach is mostly at or above the tree line, affording awesome views. Wildflowers fans will go ga-ga in the meadows near the lake. The Iceberg/Ptarmigan Trailhead is just past the Swiftcurrent Motor Inn. The trail should be mostly free of snow by the end of June; if you crave icebergs go early in the season.

The trail climbs steeply at first, passing a couple junctions before emerging onto scrubby slopes. You'll get great views across the valley to **Grinnell Point**. While climbing, open meadows and patches of stunted pine allow views of rock walls encircling Iceberg Lake. After 3.2km/2 miles in, the path enters mature forest and arrives at

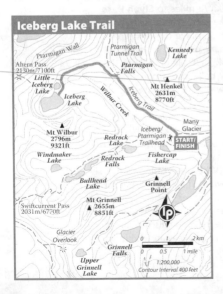

Ptarmigan Creek, crossed by footbridge, just upstream from Ptarmigan Falls. The trail climbs gently through pine to the Ptarmigan Tunnel Trail junction (p216), which heads right. Continuing toward Iceberg Lake, the trail reaches the first of several beautiful meadows under Ptarmigan Wall. Descend for a short distance to cross Iceberg Creek via a footbridge, and then climb up past **Little Iceberg Lake** before dropping down to the shores of the destination, the icy-blue cirque lake.

Iceberg Lake is 45.7m/150ft deep and about 1.2km/0.75 mile across; the granite walls average 914m/3000ft in height, easily on a par with the big walls of Yosemite. The glacier is now inactive, but surface ice and avalanche debris still provide sizeable flotillas of bergs as the lake melts out in early summer.

When ready, head back the way you came.

CRACKER LAKE TRAIL
Distance: 19.6km/12.2 miles roundtrip
Duration: 7 hours
Challenge: Moderate
Elevation Change: 378m/1228ft

The trail to gorgeous Cracker Lake begins from the south part of Many Glacier Hotel's parking lot. Those looking for solitude will find more of it on this trail than on many of the other popular walks in Many Glacier. The first 2km/1.3 miles of the Cracker Lake Trail is popular for short horseback trips, so the chopped-up path (sometimes muddy) sees its share of horse manure. Don't fret! This hike is worth persevering for, and the spectacular scenery will prove to be a reward.

The hike treads near Allen Creek, before crossing over it and climbing a ridge. It soon begins to follow Cracker Creek through its canyon, where 1250m/4100ft cliffs rise up on both sides. The heavy forest eventually encountered is made up willows, mountain alder, mountain maple (in shrub form) and isolated lodgepole pines. The forest thins out a bit as the approach to Cracker Lake begins. About 1.2km/0.7 mile before reaching the lake, some great scenery comes into view.

Turquoise **Cracker Lake** is in a cirque capped by 3052m/10,014ft Mt Siyeh, and the views of **Siyeh Glacier** are dramatic. A backcountry campsite sits at the south end of the lake. If camping here, stake your tent down sturdily, as winds have been known to sweep unsuspecting tents into the water. Behind the campground are, curiously enough, some leftover relics from the privately owned **Cracker Mine**. Follow the trail back the way you came.

REDROCK FALLS
Distance: 5.8km/3.6 miles roundtrip
Duration: 2 hours
Challenge: Easy
Elevation Change: 64m/212ft

This hike on the Swiftcurrent Pass Trail departs from the west side of the Swiftcurrent Motor Inn parking lot. Stay to the left and cross a bridge over Wilbur Creek. The trail heads northwest, north of the path cut by Swiftcurrent Creek. The low lodgepole forest sprinkled with aspen is regrowth following the 1936 Heaven's Peak fire that burned out much of the upper Swiftcurrent Valley.

From the trail, the highest visible summit is Mt Wilbur to the northwest. The jagged Grinnell Mountain is south, on the left. Swiftcurrent Mountain, which this path eventually ascends, is southwest. North Swiftcurrent Glacier is visible from the trail.

Hiking through the potentially hot open terrain, you will soon find relief amid the foliage, including Englemann spruce, subalpine fir, fireweed, maple and the shade-giving quaking aspen. Wildflower spotters will enjoy colorful landscapes dotted with forget-me-nots, paintbrush, harebell, yellow columbine and Siberian chive. Watch for stinging nettle along the way.

Less than 2.4km/1.5 miles into the trail, the trail touches a northern tip of Red Rock Lake, and the waterfalls become visible in the distance. No fish are native to the lake, but eastern brook trout now reside within. Beavers are active along streams in this valley; look out for beaver lodges on the other side of the lake. At pretty Redrock Falls, the inlet cascades in several stages over red mudstone. Relax here, before heading back or onward to **Swiftcurrent Pass** (2064m/6770ft).

TWO MEDICINE VALLEY

The majority of the trails in this area begin at the north end of Two Medicine Campground, or they begin 0.8km/0.5 mile south, at the east end of Two Medicine Lake, just past the boat dock. A boat ride across the lake shaves almost 4.8km/3 miles off trails that pass the west end of the lake.

UPPER TWO MEDICINE LAKE
Distance: 15.1km/9.4 miles roundtrip
Duration: 5 hours
Challenge: Easy
Elevation Change: 101m/330ft

Beginning on the North Shore Trailhead, the trail is accessed from the Two Medicine Lake Campground. The hike starts as a pleasantly green and relatively flat ramble beside the north shore of Two Medicine Lake. Avalanches are responsible for the many clumps of felled trees along the way.

At 5.1km/3.2 miles, the trail splits, offering a moderate-to-difficult 2.4km/1.5-mile ascent northwest to No Name Lake. To continue to Upper Two Medicine Lake, continue southwest at this junction. Less than 0.5km/0.3 mile further, a short spur trail shoots over to **Twin Falls**, which should be visited on the way to or from the lake. True to its moniker, two falls crash into a rocky pool.

On the main trail, it's a little over a thinly forested mile to **Upper Two Medicine Lake**, which rests majestically in a cirque below Lone Walker Mountain. Pumpelly Pillar rises in the northeast, while Mt Helen peaks at the northwest.

Be aware that the lake attracts a swarming mosquito population, so come armed with a coat of repellent.

A quicker means to Upper Two Medicine Lake involves taking a boat tour to the upper boat dock on Two Medicine Lake and hiking northwest on the South Shore Trail until it reaches a junction; turn left toward Twin Falls and Upper Two Medicine Lake. From the boat dock to Upper Two Medicine Lake, the trail is 6.4km/4 miles roundtrip, though you can cut that distance in half by settling for Twin Falls as your destination. For diversity, take the boat one way and walk the other.

MEDICINE GRIZZLY LAKE TRAIL
Distance: 19.8km/12.4 miles roundtrip
Duration: 6.5 hours
Challenge: Easy-moderate
Elevation Change: 165m/540ft

The Medicine Grizzly Lake Trail has been closed for whole seasons at a time in recent years because of run-ins with bears. People leaving picnic remnants behind taught bears that humans come with food, and the bears began to charge or follow visitors on the trail.

Offering this hike as a ranger-led activity has improved the situation, both by educating visitors and letting resident bears know that humans are here to stay. Enjoy the access to this beautiful country, but remember that you are sharing it.

Access this hike from the trailhead immediately preceding the Cut Bank Campground, 8km/5 miles off US 89 via dirt road. Forests of fir, spruce, quaking aspen and lodgepole pine shade part of the way, and patches of open meadow are aglow with wildflowers.

In the first part of the trail, **Bad Marriage Mountain** looms up on the left; if you look straight ahead, you will see the prominent **Medicine Grizzly Mountain**.

Even if you do not see wildlife on this hike, you may see signs of their presence. Look for bear hair on bark or bark worn down on tree trunks used as moose rubs. Much of the trail is level; none of the climbs are too difficult.

Atlantic Creek Campground is 6.9km/4.3 miles from the start of the trail. At 7.4km/4.6 miles, the path forks The option to the right leads to **Triple Divide Pass**. Stay left for Medicine Grizzly Lake. When you arrive at the lake, home to brook and rainbow trout, continue alongside it until you reach its head – a perfect spot for a picnic. Razor's Edge Mountain looks down as its waterfalls bellow. To head back, retrace your steps on the same trail.

NORTH FORK VALLEY

Most trails in Glacier's northwest corner follow a creek through dense pine forest to a southwest–northeast trending lake.

The **Quartz Lake Loop** is favorite trail in the North Fork Valley for its wonderful scenery and vistas. The trip is a moderate 7.5 hours over 20.5km/12.8 miles roundtrip. It goes in and out of forest, though you will see that much of the area was affected by the Red Bench Fire of 1988. **Cerulean Ridge** (elevation 5500ft/1676m) affords fantastic views of Quartz, tiny Middle Quartz and Lower Quartz Lakes below.

The generally well-maintained **Logging Lake Trail** can be muddy in the spring. The hike takes in thick greenery in lieu of dramatic vistas. It's an easy excursion covering 14.5km/9 miles roundtrip.

The 28.7km/11.6 miles roundtrip **Akokala Lake Trail** contains thickly forested areas and ascents rewarded with good views. It traverses portions of the Numa Ridge.

Other hikes in the North Fork Valley include Bowman Lake, Dutch Lake, Hidden Meadow, Numa Lookout, Quartz Creek and several trails to the Kishnehn Ranger Station.

Backcountry Hikes

If a day hike introduces more wilderness than a drive ever could, a backcountry trip is really cracking open the experience.

Pick up the park's *Backcountry Guide* for the ins and outs of heading into the wilderness; it's downloadable in PDF form from **W** www.nps.gov/glac/activities/bcguide1.htm.

PERMIT INFORMATION

See Wilderness Permits & Regulations (p197) for fees and reservation details. If you don't have a reservation, getting sites on your preferred route can be difficult at times, but it's worth a try. Head to a permit-issuing ranger station or visitors center early in the morning the day before your intended departure. Have a backup route in case your first choice is booked.

BACKCOUNTRY CAMPING

From early May to late November, backpackers must camp in designated backcountry campgrounds, a rule set in place to minimize impact on a highly used environment.

The most popular backcountry sites are the ones at higher elevations, particularly along the Continental Divide. Other backcountry sites that you'll want to reserve early on include those along Dawson-Pitamakan Trail, Gunsight Pass Trail and the North Circle. **Hole-in-the-Wall Campground**, on Boulder Pass Trail, is a spectacular pick.

BACKCOUNTRY LODGING

Built by the Great Northern Railroad, two gorgeously set lodges in Glacier's backcountry can be accessed only by hiking or horseback. Reservations are a must. Both are open July to mid-September.

The 17-room historic **Sperry Chalet** (☎ *406-387-5654*, *888-345-2649*; **W** *www.sperrychalet.com*; *USD$155 1st person, USD$100 each additional, USD$40 deposit*) opened in 1914. There's still no road to it: The 10.5km/6.5-mile trail there, with a 1006m/3300ft elevation gain, begins at Lake McDonald Lodge. Rates include three meals. Bring a flashlight for midnight trips to the outhouse, and warm sleeping clothes.

Run by Glacier Wilderness Guides, the circa 1914 **Granite Park Chalet** (☎ *406-387-5555*, *800-521-7238*; **W** *www.glacierguides.com*; *USD$72 per person*) is used as a hikers' shelter. It has a kitchen and dining room for use, and linen (USD$10) and packaged meals are available. The easiest approach is the 12km/7.6-mile Highline Trail from the Loop on Going-to-the-Sun Rd.

BACKCOUNTRY TRAILS

Following are some favorite backcountry trips in the park. Justifiably popular, the campgrounds along them often get snatched up early. Rangers can suggest alternate approaches on the following routes, or altogether differ ent itineraries.

Justifiably popular, Gunsight Pass is one of the park's most scenic hike-able passes, taking in snowfields, glaciers and lakes along its journey over the Continental Divide. Though you can start the hike from Lake McDonald Lodge and end it at Jackson Glacier Overlook, doing it vice versa (east to west) is easier. You are almost guaranteed to see wildlife, particularly mountain goats, near this trail. Usually the pass is not safely free of ice until mid-July.

If starting on the east end, the trailhead is at Jackson Glacier Overlook (Piegan Pass Trailhead), roughly 6.4km/4 miles east of Logan Pass on Going-to-the-Sun Rd. You will end at Lake McDonald Lodge, 10.9km/6.8 miles from West Glacier on Going-to-the-Sun Rd.

Day 1: Jackson Glacier Overlook to Sperry Chalet (6-9 hours, 21.6km/13.4 miles) Follow the trail southeast through fir and spruce forest until it stumbles upon Reynolds Creek. The trail follows the creek past Deadwood Falls; there is a junction at about 2km/1.3 miles with the Gunsight Pass Trail. Choose the trail on the right. It crosses a footbridge past Reynolds Creek campground, and then heads alongside the St Mary River. At 6.4km/4 miles, a junction offers a 1km/0.6-mile trail to Florence Falls.

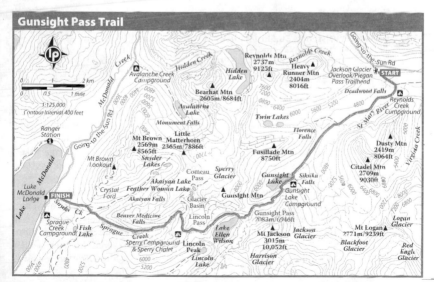

Gunsight Pass Trail

Carry on up the valley below **Citadel** (east) and **Fusillade** (west) Mountains. Take in views of glaciers clinging to the high ridge between Blackfoot Mountain and Mt Jackson as you pass **Gunsight Lake Campground** (a little over 9.6km/6 miles in), a short stretch before Gunsight Lake. A suspension bridge gets you over St Mary River. You soon tackle switchbacks up, foraging through cow parsnip and alder shrub.

It's a two- or three-hour hike from the campground to **Gunsight Pass** (2117m/6946ft). Reaching the pass involves walking over cliff ledges high above the lake, but the trail is broad. A basic emergency shelter (day-use only) stands on this narrow saddle.

Steeply descending switchbacks lead almost to the north shore of **Lake Ellen Wilson**, a spectacular alpine lake lying in a deep trough ringed by sheer, glaciated rock walls. The trail continues around the lake's western shore, passing above Lake Ellen Wilson Campground.

Go up the slope to a high shelf overlooking Lincoln Lake. The trail turns gradually to cross the apex of the hike, **Lincoln Pass** (2149m/7050ft), just north of Lincoln Peak, then winds its way down past Sperry Campground. Four scenic sites here overlook Lake McDonald far below. Mountain goats regularly visit the camp, so always use the pit toilet.

The trail leads to the historic **Sperry Chalet** (p212).

Day 2: Sperry Chalet to Lake McDonald Lodge *(2.2-3 hours, 10.3km/6.4 miles)* Drop quickly past the Sperry Glacier Trail and across small Sprague Creek. The trail leads down into fir-spruce forest, past **Beaver Medicine Falls**. It continues 4km/2.5 miles down the valley to cross Snyder Creek on a footbridge. Pass in quick successive turnoffs to Fish Lake, Snyder Lakes and Mt Brown Lookout. The trail descends through a mossy forest of cedar, hemlock, grand fir, larch and yew to reach Going-to-the-Sun Rd.

BOULDER PASS
Distance: 50.5km/31.4 miles
Duration: 4 days
Challenge: Moderate-Difficult
Elevation Change: 1273m/4175ft

This challenging hike through Glacier's isolated northwest corner features beautiful glacial lakes, an alpine pass and stunning mountain scenery. Beginning at the Boulder Pass Trailhead at Kintla Lake, the route travels northeast, skirting the north shores of Kintla and Upper Kintla Lakes, climbing steeply over Boulder Pass – snow can persist here until late July. It descends via the superb Hole-in-the-Wall cirque to Brown Pass.

Those with time for the main route culminate at Goat Haunt Ranger Station and the southern shore of Upper Waterton Lake – a gateway into Waterton Lakes National Park. At the lake, you can hop on one of the daily boat services to **Waterton Townsite** (p235). Bring your passport. For those who want to finish on foot, an easy 9.7km/6 mile trail runs from Goat Haunt along the western shores of Upper Waterton Lake to Waterton Townsite.

Backcountry campgrounds are along the way. Those who want to loop back down to North Fork, rather than head to Waterton, can head southwest from Brown Pass, which leads to the southern end of Bowman Lake.

The trailhead is near the Kintla Lake Campground, at the top of Glacier Rte 7 in North Fork Valley.

Day 1: Kintla Lake to Upper Kintla Lake *(5-6 hours, 18.7km/11.6 miles)*
The trail quickly reaches the forested shore of Kintla Lake. After a few miles along the shore, you'll climb away from the water before dropping back down to it about 3.2km/2 miles from the lake's head.

Passing the head of **Kintla Lake Campground**, plunge through some dense vegetation and pass a patrol cabin before starting the ascent to Upper Kintla Lake. Climb steadily along a winding trail that provides occasional glimpses of Kintla Creek. The trail climbs into a meadow with great views of the Kintla Glacier (south) and the ring of peaks surrounding it. Dead trees on that side of the valley are testament to a wildfire. After you've reached Upper Kintla Lake, the trail follows its north shore to arrive at **Upper Kintla Campground**, with stunning looks at Kinnerly Peak and Gardner Point as you progress

Day 2: Upper Kintla Lake to Boulder Pass Campground *(3.5-4.5 hours, 9km/5.6 miles)* The trail leaves Upper Kintla Lake and crosses Kintla Creek on a bridge. For the next 3.2km/2 miles the forested trail climbs steadily, with views opening up across the cascades on Agassiz Creek to **Agassiz Glacier**. The east faces of Kinnerly and Kintla Peaks loom over the valley. The trail begins to climb more steeply, switchbacking through lush vegetation. Past this section the gradient eases as the trail soon enters a series of long, drawn out switchbacks. Eventually the trail goes south, through wildflower meadows before reaching tree line and **Boulder Pass Campground**. The strenuous ascent to this campground only takes a few hours but will constitute a full day's effort for most hikers.

(You *could* continue for an extra two hours, crossing Boulder Pass to reach the even more dramatically sited **Hole-in-the-Wall Campground**.)

Day 3: Boulder Pass Campground to Lake Francis *(4-5 hours, 12.2km/7.6 miles)* It's a gentle climb from Boulder Pass Campground to the top of **Boulder Pass**. The view from the pass itself is restricted by the steep slopes and cliffs of Boulder Peak and Mt Custer. Descend into the beautiful cirque on the east side of the pass, where several small tarns have formed since Boulder Glacier's retreat. Here, you get your first glimpse (south) of the spectacular **Thunderbird Mountain**.

Continue, soon descending steeply over ice-scoured rock slabs (potentially dangerous if still under snow) into another basin colored by meadows. Traverse across and pass a junction, where a path leads right, to **Hole-in-the-Wall Campground**, one of the most spectacular backcountry sites in the park. Continue your traverse around increasingly steep slopes, with views across the 914m/3000ft cliffs that drop into Bowman Valley. Next is a short section of very exposed rock ledge only a few feet wide. The

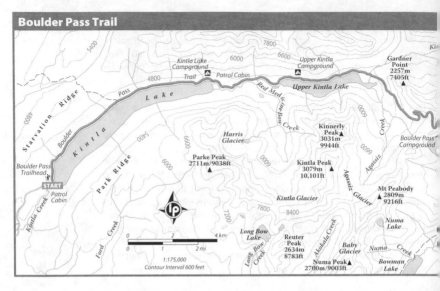

Boulder Pass Trail

trail then descends across meadows to **Brown Pass** (1906m/6253ft) on the Continental Divide. The **Brown Pass Campground** is nearby. Hikers returning to the west side of the park via Bowman Lake should turn right here. Goat Haunt is 13.8km/8.6 miles east of Brown Pass (all downhill), and up-to-it hikers who have reached the pass early could continue to the finish.

Descend steeply on switchbacks to a small, unnamed lake beneath Thunderbird Glacier, and then descend more gently through forest to **Lake Francis Campground**.

Day 4: Lake Francis to Goat Haunt Lake *(3 hours, 10.6km/6.6 miles)*
Continue your descent from Lake Francis, traversing forest all the way, past **Lake Janet Campground** to Goat Haunt. The trail descends more steeply 3.2km/2 miles before Goat Haunt Lake, reaching a junction 1.4km/0.9 mile from Goat Haunt. Hikers wishing to walk to Waterton Townsite can continue straight ahead for 9.7km/6 miles; **Boundary Bay and Bertha Bay Campgrounds** are en route. Turn right for Goat Haunt, crossing a bridge over the Waterton River before arriving at the ranger station and **campground**. The boat launch is a few hundred yards further along the lakeshore.

HIGHLINE TRAIL/PTARMIGAN TUNNEL LOOP
Distance: 80.8km/50.2 miles
Duration: 6 days
Challenge: Moderate-Difficult
Elevation Change: 853m/2800ft

In Many Glacier, the six-day **Highline Trail/Ptarmigan Tunnel Loop**, also called the 'North Circle,' arguably offers the most varied scenery of any longer hike in the park. The route combines several popular trails –

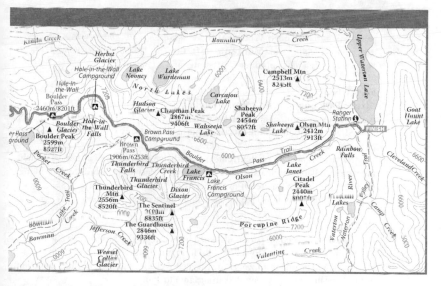

Highline (p265), Stoney Indian Pass and Ptarmigan Tunnel – to give up to a week of spectacular hiking. The loop stretches around the northern Lewis Range; it includes numerous long, slow ascents and descents, as well as several strenuous ones.

Check at Many Glacier Ranger Station for help in planning your route and for the state of the trails. A tricky section of the Highline Trail near Ahern Pass sometimes requires an ice axe and crampons. Stoney Indian Pass and the western approach to Ptarmigan Tunnel may remain closed well into July. From June through September thunderstorms with heavy lightning often occur in the early afternoon.

The trailhead is 110m/120 yards past the Swiftcurrent Motor Inn, on the northwestern side of the large parking lot. An alternative route gets its start on the Highline Trail, beginning from the parking lot atop Logan Pass.

Backcountry campgrounds on the route include Granite Park, Fifty Mountain, Stoney Indian, Mokowanis Junction, Glenns Lake Head, Glenns Lake Foot, Cosley Lake and Elizabeth Lake Foot.

Other Activities

Had enough hiking? There are loads of other things to keep you occupied in Glacier, and a lot of people to help you do it.

WHITE-WATER RAFTING & FLOAT TRIPS

The North and Middle Forks of the Flathead River are very popular with rafters, though all rafting tours take place on or outside the park's boundaries. **Glacier Raft Co** (☎ 406-888-5454, 800-235-6781; w www.glacierraft co.com) is arguably the most reputable raft company in the area. Prices for trips down the North Fork and Middle Fork of the Flathead River start at adult/child USD$40/30 for a half-day and from USD$65/48 for a full day. Similarly priced, **Great Northern Whitewater** (☎ *406-387-5340, 800-735-7897;* **w** *www .gnwhitewater.com)* and **Montana Raft Co** (☎ *406-387-5555, 800-521-7238;* **w** *www.glacierguides.com)* offer white-water and scenic tours.

BOATING

Glacier Park Boat Co (☎ *406-257-2426)* rents out small boats (kayaks, canoes and rowboats) in the summer at Apgar, Lake McDonald, Two Medicine and Many Glacier for USD$10 per hour. Motorboats, available at all but Many Glacier, go for USD$15 per hour.

McDonald, Bowman, Swiftcurrent, Two Medicine and St Mary Lakes have launching ramps available for boats. Sailors might find St Mary Lake's winds to their liking. If bringing your own watercraft to Glacier, see Policies & Regulations (p187).

See Organized Tours (p198) for boat-tour information.

CYCLING

Bicycles are prohibited on park trails. Road bikes can ply the park's pavement, though restrictions exist on Going-to-the-Sun Rd from mid-June to Labor Day, when cyclists are not allowed to ride from Apgar to Sprague Creek Campground in either direction or from Logan Creek to Logan Pass from 11am to 4pm.

The closest thing to a mountain biking venture in the park is Inside North Fork Rd (Glacier Rte 7) to Kintla Lake. Bikers craving trails should consider Waterton.

Good road biking near the park is along its eastern boundary on Hwys 49 and 89, which parallel the Continental Divide for 50km/31 miles between East Glacier and St Mary.

Hiker-biker campsites go for USD$3 per person at Apgar, Avalanche, Fish Creek, Many Glacier, Rising Sun, Sprague Creek, St Mary and Two Medicine Campgrounds. Spaces are first-come, first-served until 9pm; sites at Fish Creek and St Mary can be

TREAD LIGHTLY

Late-19th century conservationist Gifford Pinchot may have said it best: 'Conservation is the foresighted utilization, preservation and/or renewal of forests, waters, lands and minerals, for the greatest good of the greatest number for the longest time.' National parks were designated for both the protection of the wilds and the enjoyment of people, but it is crucial for incoming parties (people, in this case) to delight in nature conscientiously, respectfully and mindfully.

Urging the traveler to leave nothing behind, the national Leave No Trace program inspires and encourages sensitive wilderness travel. Its basic tenets include maintaining respect for wildlife and others (including humans), packing out what you pack in, and steering clear of fragile terrain.

Leave No Trace (☎ *800-332-4100;* **w** *www.lnt.org)* is run by a nonprofit in conjunction with the National Park Service and other federal agencies. See its website for extensive advice, as well as details on educational and volunteer opportunities.

FAMILY FUN

It may not have a jungle gym, monkey bars or a zillion-megahertz processor with the capacity to read minds, but the playground of Glacier National Park boasts hundreds of miles of skippable terrain. And seeing as how it's bear country, being loud and (somewhat) rowdy is not such a bad thing.

Kids shouldn't even need a sugar lure to keep them going on the trails. The gentle **Avalanche Lake Trail** is a half-day dose of scenery. Once everybody's ready for a challenge, a full day out on the marvelous **Siyeh Pass Trail** (p207) will get everybody sleeping well at night. Take a day out from hiking to paddle on one of the lakes.

After a day's work, campfire programs around the park provide education and entertainment. Blackfeet tribal members often lead programs, from storytelling to traditional drumming and dance; see the *Glacier Explorer* for information.

Need a time-out from nature? You may or may not want to alert the kids to **Big Sky Water Park** (☎ 406-892-5025; Hwys 2 & 206; adult/child 3-10 from USD$18/14; open Memorial Day–Labor Day) in Columbia Falls, halfway between Glacier and Whitefish. It's one big party, with waterslides, miniature golf, a carousel and arcade games.

reserved (☎ 800-365-2267). Rentals are available at **Glacier Cyclery** (☎ 406-862-6446; 326 2nd St) in Whitefish.

FISHING

The park's season for streams and rivers is late May to late November, though lakes are open for fishing year-round. While anglers explore easily accessible waters like Lake McDonald and St Mary Lake, it is some of the hike-in destinations that can prove the most tranquil, such as Hidden Lake, Oldman Lake and Red Eagle Lake. Glacier's store of fish includes cutthroat trout, northern pike, whitefish, burbot, kokanee salmon, brook trout, rainbow trout, mackinaw and grayling.

Great Northern Fishing Guides (p218) runs various fishing trips on the Flathead River.

HORSEBACK RIDING

Riders can bring their own horses into the park, but no stable rentals are available. A pamphlet offered at visitors centers explains the park's dos and don'ts.

Mule Shoe Outfitters (open early May–early Sep) runs guided horseback trips within the park, lasting one hour (USD$27) to all day (USD$110 to $120) from its **Lake McDonald Corral** (☎ 406-888-5121) and **Many Glacier Corral** (☎ 406-732-4203). Anything longer than a one-hour ride must be reserved.

ROCK CLIMBING

Rock climbing and bouldering are not popular undertakings in Glacier, as the rock is sedimentary, much of it metamorphosed mudstone and limestone. Because of the crumbly nature of the rocks, technical climbing is not the sport of choice. The best relevant resource is *A Climber's Guide to Glacier National Park*, by J Gordon Edwards, available at visitors center bookstores. Climbers should sign the register at visitors centers and ranger stations before heading out.

Other Activities

Hit the golfing greens in the summer months at the **Glacier Park Lodge Golf Course** (☎ *406-226-5642*) in East Glacier or **Glacier View Golf Club** (☎ *406-888-5471*) in West Glacier.

In winter, when Going-to-the-Sun Rd and most services are closed, the park is left to wildlife and those cross-country skiing and snowshoeing. Lessons, cross-country tours and a network of groomed trails are available from the **Izaak Walton Inn** (p225). The year-round **North Fork Hostel** (p224) in Polebridge has cross-country ski and snowshoe rentals (free for guests).

Places to Stay

Glacier's noncamping accommodations can get booked solid in July and August. Thankfully, plentiful lodging in gateway towns should leave even the most last-minute travelers sweetly dreaming by nightfall.

CAMPING

Even on the busiest days, there is usually space in at least one of the campgrounds run by the National Park Service. Camping options (with showers) are also available in gateway towns.

Glacier National Park

The NPS (☎ *406-888-7800*) maintains 13 campgrounds in the park. Sites at **Fish Creek and St Mary Campgrounds** (☎ *800-365-2267*; W *http://reservations.nps.gov*) can be reserved up to five months in advance. All other sites are first-come, first-served.

SPOTTING ANIMALS

Patient waits at the following places may result in eruptions of 'Look! Over there!' Bring binoculars or a spotting scope.

✔ **Mt Henkel**: From the Swiftcurrent Motor Inn parking lot, scope these slopes for mountain goats, bighorn sheep and bears.

✔ **Two Dog Flats**: Elk roam these grasslands along Going-to-the-Sun Rd at dusk.

✔ **Goat Lick Overlook**: See mountain goats contented by rock salt at this viewpoint off US 2.

✔ **Rising Wolf Mountain**: Scan its looming sides and surrounding greenery trail in Two Medicine.

Campgrounds generally open mid-May to the end of September. Only Apgar Picnic Area and St Mary Campground offer primitive winter camping (USD$7.50).

If you haven't reserved a site, stake your claim as early as possible. In July and August, sites fill quickly. Sprague Creek on the west side and Many Glacier on the east tend to fill first, often before 11am. In summer, weekdays are as busy as weekends.

RVs are allowed at all sites except Sprague Creek, though footage regulations vary. Large units are not recommended at those accessed via dirt road, Bowman Lake, Cut Bank, Kintla Lake, Logging Creek and Quartz Creek.

Apgar is popular for activities and amenities, and Sprague Creek is a quieter lakeside beauty. Visitors coming in from the east head to windy Rising Sun. Many Glacier is a hit with hikers.

Apgar Campground (*next to Apgar Village; USD$15; open early May–early Sep*) This large wooded campground is a good choice for its proximity to Apgar Village. Loop A can be bustling, but the other loops feel more relaxed.

Avalanche Creek Campground (*off Going-to-the-Sun Rd btwn Lake McDonald & Logan Pass; USD$15; open mid-Jun–early Sep*) This lush campground gets more rainfall than others in the park. Some sites are overshadowed by old stands of hemlock, cedar and Douglas fir.

Bowman Lake Campground (*North Fork, 9.7km/6 miles up Inside North Fork Rd from Polebridge; USD$12; open mid-May–mid-Sep*) Usually only about a third full, this campground offers spacious sites in forested grounds. There is a visitors information tent here with reference books and local hiking information.

Cut Bank Campground (*8km/5 miles off US 89 via dirt road; USD$12; open late May–late Sep*) This small, remote campground is deserted during the day, meaning only that people come here to hike the less-populated trails that the area offers.

Fish Creek Campground (*5.6km/3.5 miles northwest of the main park entrance; USD$17; open early Jun–mid-Oct*) In dense cedar-hemlock forest, this campground offers sites that are tucked among the trees. Book early for one in Loops C and D, which are nearest the lake.

Kintla Lake Campground (*North Fork, top of Inside North Fork Rd; USD$12; open mid-May–mid-Sep*) If you've come to Glacier to catch up on novels, this primitive campground is ideal. No motorboats are allowed on the gorgeous lake, so it stays wonderfully quiet.

Logging Creek Campground (*North Fork, on Inside North Fork Rd 27.4km/17 miles north of Fish Creek Campground; USD$12; open early Jul–early Sep*) It takes some determination to reach this primitive campground, but it is worth it if you're looking for tranquility amid the trees. It's very still here but for the sound of a flowing creek.

Many Glacier Campground (*Many Glacier, next to Swiftcurrent Motor Inn; USD$15; open late May–late Sep*) Its access to phenomenal trails makes this campground one of the park's most popular with the hiking set. You can't go wrong with any site you choose, though the even numbers among site Nos 90 to 104 feel quite tucked away.

Quartz Creek Campground (*North Fork, on Inside North Fork Rd 31.2km/19.4 mi from Fish Creek Campground; USD$12; open early Jul–early Sep*) The campground here is similar to the one at Logging Creek, though its thicker vegetation lends a more private air. It is ultraquiet, and as at Logging, a creek babbles romantically nearby.

Rising Sun Campground (*8km/5 miles west of St Mary entrance station; USD$15; open late May–mid-Sep*) Drive around to see what suits you here, as the sites in this somewhat unprotected campground do vary. The lush and diverse vegetation provides lots of shade.

Sprague Creek Campground *(off Going-to-the-Sun Rd on upper shores of Lake McDonald; USD$15; open mid-May–mid-Sep)* Because this small campground draws mostly tents (no vehicles over 6.4m/21ft allowed), it feels more intimate than many of the park's others. Get there early to claim a site overlooking the lake.

St Mary Campground *(just west of St Mary entrance station; USD$17; open late May–late Sep)* Cottonwood and aspen trees predominate in the most shaded sites here: Nos 5 to 19 and 33 to 44 in the A Loop. Sites in the B Loop, which are bedecked with shorter and shrubbier plantlife, are more open and unprotected. There is almost always space here.

Two Medicine Campground *(4.8km/3 miles southwest of Two Medicine entrance station; USD$15; open mid-May–late-Sep)* This campground below Rising Wolf Mountain is great for families – amenities, trailheads and the lake are all close by. Good sites near the lake include Nos 34 to 38 and 83 to 95; Nos 23 to 33 and 44 to 55 are nice wooded spots.

East Glacier

The campgrounds at East Glacier are generally open June to late September; call for specific season information.

Firebrand Pass Campground *(☎ 406-226-5573; off US 2; sites USD$18)* This small campground, 4.8km/3 miles west of East Glacier, has 26 sites for both tent and full RV hookup. The grassy, shady grounds have an air of seclusion; the bathroom and laundry facilities are clean.

Sears Motel & Campground *(☎ 406-226-4432; e eglacier@aol.com; 1023 Hwy 49 N; camp/RV site USD$10/15)* Very convenient to East Glacier amenities, this pleasant campground offers tucked-away tent sites. Bathrooms and one shower are available.

St Mary

Campgrounds at St Mary are usually open mid-May to early October; call for specific season information.

Johnson's of St Mary *(☎ 406-732-4207; off US 89; hike/bike site USD$12, camp/ RV site USD$19/20-28)* The RVs get sublime views of St Mary Lake and surrounding mountains, but tents here get peaceful shade from alder trees. Kids will appreciate the plethora of grassy space. Sites have fire pits.

Chewing Blackbones RV Park & Campground *(☎ 406-732-9263; US 89; camp/ RV site USD$16/21-27)* North of St Mary by 9.7km/6 miles, this large campground is owned by the Blackfeet Nation. Request one of the partly shaded tent sites along the lake. There's a playground and recreation on the lake.

West Glacier

Campgrounds in West Glacier are generally open from May 1 to September 30.

San-Suz-Ed RV Park & Campground *(☎ 406-387-5280, 800-305-4616, fax 406-387-5924; US 2; camp/RV site USD$19/22-25)* On US 2, 4km/2.5 miles west of the park, this pine-scented campground is quiet but for the distant whoosh of the highway. The showers are spotless, and the owner's homemade pies are delicious. Self-contained sites are available in winter.

Glacier Campground (☎ 406 387 5689; off US 2; camp/RV site USD$18/19-24, cabin USD$30-40) West of West Glacier 1.6km/1 mile, this campground offers sites spanning 16 hectares/40 acres of lovely wooded grounds, as well as a cute cluster of basic wooden cabins.

Lake Five Resort (☎ 406-387-5601; W www.lakefiveresort.com; 540 Belton Stage Rd; camp/RV site USD$25/25-30, cabins USD$60-115) West of the park entrance 5km/3 miles and 0.8km/0.5 mile north of US 2, this recreation area is thronging with water-skiers, speedboats and sunburned people all summer. It's popular with families.

LODGING IN GLACIER NATIONAL PARK

In the early 1910s James Hill's Great Northern Railroad built a series of grand hotels to lure rich tourists to Glacier National Park. Guests arrived by train and were transported by 'jammer' bus or horse-drawn carriage to their lodge of choice. The historic lodges are now operated by **Glacier Park, Inc** (☎ 406-892-2525 for reservations; W www.glacierparkinc.com). All are nonsmoking, and rooms do not have air-conditioning or TV. All offer at least one wheelchair-accessible room, but none have elevators. Contact Glacier Park, Inc to book a room at the Village Inn, Lake McDonald Complex, Rising Sun Motor Inn, Swiftcurrent Motor Inn, Many Glacier Hotel or Glacier Park Lodge.

Most of the lodges within the park open mid- to late May and close some time in September.

Mid-range

Swiftcurrent Motor Inn (☎ 406-732-5531; W www.swiftcurrentmotorinn.com; Many Glacier Valley; cabin USD$43-73, room USD$92-100; open mid-Jun–early Sep) The least expensive lodging in the park, Swiftcurrent has no-frills, comfortable-enough rooms and cabins that are a pebble's toss from fantastic trailheads. Cabins come with or without bath – if you want one with, book way ahead.

Rising Sun Motor Inn (☎ 406-732-5523; W www.risingsunmotorinn.com; USD$92-100; open mid-Jun–early Sep) On the upper north shore of St Mary Lake, Rising Sun is quieter than the big lodges in the park and is less busy. Its motel-style rooms are pleasant, and its cute duplex cottages are also a good option.

Apgar Village Lodge (☎ 406-888-5484, fax 406-888-5273; room USD$75-100, cabin from USD$90; open May–mid-Oct) The only privately owned accommodations within the park, this lodge offers well-maintained motel-style rooms and cabins. The cabins are spacious, and most come with kitchenette, while the smaller rooms are more rustic.

Top End

Glacier Park Lodge (☎ 406-226-5600; W www.bigtreehotel.com; East Glacier; USD$135-400; open mid-May–late Sep) Sixty old Douglas fir timbers support interior balconies surrounding the lobby in this grand flagship hotel. Rooms are modern and elegant, and the lobby is always abuzz with activity. An onsite spa service offers massages and other you-deserve-it treatments (USD$25 to $170).

Many Glacier Hotel (☎ 406-732-4411; W www.manyglacierhotel.com; Many Glacier Valley; USD$110-220; open mid-Jun–early Sep) On the north shore of Swiftcurrent Lake, this large chalet-like lodge is surreally immersed in a dramatic peak-laden scape. The rooms are comfortable rather than luxurious, and you can choose lake views, mountain views or no views at all ('value' rooms).

Lake McDonald Lodge *(☎ 406-888-5431; www.lakemcdonaldlodge.com; cottage USD$94-142, room USD$100-142; open late May–mid-Sep)* The rooms in this cozy lodge are comfortably simple, and many of them face the lake. A lot of visitors prefer the quiet of the cottages, which come in large or small.

Village Inn *(☎ 406-888-5632; w www.villageinnatapgar.com; USD$105-170; open late May–late Sep)* At the southern end of Lake McDonald in Apgar Village, this well-placed hotel is a first-rate choice for travelers with children. It's near restaurants, ranger activities and plenty of lakeside. Stay in one of the 1st-floor rooms for your own spot of beach.

LODGING IN POLEBRIDGE

The wonderfully unique little Polebridge has no electricity, which makes a stay in the **North Fork Hostel & Square Peg Ranch** *(☎ 406-888-5241; w www.nfhostel.com; 80 Beaver Dr; tent/tepee USD$10, dorm USD$15, cabins USD$30-65)* all the more rustic and homey. It is 0.4km/0.25 mile southeast of the village shop. Guests can use the hostel's bikes, skis, snowshoes and kayaks for free. A ride from the Amtrak station in West Glacier is USD$30.

LODGING IN ST MARY

St Mary Lodge & Resort *(☎ 406-732-4431, 800-368-3689; w www.glcpark.com; USD$110 and up; open mid-May–early Oct)* The spacious, comfortable rooms in this privately owned resort's Great Bear Lodge are pricier than those in its main lodge, but they present delicious mountain views. Wheelchair-friendly rooms are available in both lodges, and cabins are also on offer.

Red Eagle Motel *(☎ 406-732-4453; US 89; USD$65-85; open late May–late Sep).* Perched up above St Mary Village, this basic motel has good views from its grounds. Rooms are on the small side, but rates are determined by the bed as opposed to by the person, which means it's a good value for bigger groups.

LODGING IN EAST GLACIER

All rooms and cottages in East Glacier are within a half-mile of the junction of US 2 and Hwy 49. Most places are open from May to October.

Brownie's *(☎ 406-226-4426; w www.brownieshostel.com; 1020 Hwy 49; dorm USD$16, s/d USD$21/29)* Above Brownie's Grocery & Deli, this casual HI-AYH hostel is packed with travelers staying in eight-person single-sex dorms or private doubles. It has a common room and kitchen, and lockout is roughly 10am to 4pm. Sheets, blankets and pillows are provided free of charge.

Backpacker's Inn *(☎ 406-226-9392; Dawson Ave; dorm USD$10, s/d cabins USD$20/30)* This quieter alternative sits behind Serrano's Mexican Restaurant and offers two four-bed single-sex dorm rooms plus two private cabins. A yard acts as the hostel's only common area, and there is no kitchen.

East Glacier Motel & Cabins *(☎ 406-226-5593; w www.eastglacier.com; cabin/room from USD$45/65)* On the west side of Hwy 49, this place offers motel rooms and a row of attractive cottages with flowerpots and perchable front stoops.

Bison Creek Ranch *(☎ 406-226-4482, 888-226-4482; e bison@bigsky.net; cabin USD$45-50, A-frame USD$65-70)* With unobstructed views of nearby peaks, this property is a pleasure, owned and managed by the same family for over 50 years. The basic cabins are comfy, and the two-level A-frames are big (great for families), with kitchenettes and lounge spaces.

Izaak Walton Inn (☎ *406-888-5700;* **w** *www.izaakwaltoninn.com; 290 Izaak Walton Inn Rd; rates from USD$108; open year-round)* In Essex, a quarter mile off US 2 between East and West Glacier, this hotel is popular with cross-country skiers in winter. The small rooms are cozy, and caboose cottages, part of the hotel's railroad memorabilia, come with kitchenette.

LODGING IN WEST GLACIER

Rooms in West Glacier are more expensive than comparable rooms in East Glacier. Most are open from mid-May through late September.

Glacier Highland Resort Motel (☎ *406-888-5427, 800-766-0811; US 2; s/d from USD$65/75)* This attractive place offers 33 units and an indoor hot tub; there's one wheelchair-friendly room. It sits across from the Amtrak station in West Glacier.

Belton Chalet (☎ *406-888-5000, 888-235-8665;* **w** *www.beltonchalet.com; from USD$120/95 high/low season)* This lovely Swiss-style chalet is a fully histored historic building. The rooms exude a simple elegance (no TVs), and the gardened grounds are well maintained. Its restaurant serves dinner (mains USD$15 to $20) nightly.

West Glacier Motel (☎ *406 888-5662, 888-838-2363;* **w** *www.westglacier.com/motel.html; room/cabin from USD$75/125)*, is the closest motel to the park entrance. It's located on the north side of the railroad tracks and US2.

Vista Motel (☎ *406-888-5311; US 2; s/d/t $65/75/80)* is located 3.2km/2 miles west of the park entrance. It has 26 rooms and an outdoor pool.

Places to Eat

In and around the park, standard American fare – generally meat-oriented – can be expected. Vegetarians will usually find *something* to order but may have to settle for less than exciting choices.

GLACIER NATIONAL PARK

Food within Glacier won't win any culinary awards, but it is usually decent. Almost all of the in-park restaurants (note the similar menus) are run by Glacier Park, Inc, the corporation that operates the park's lodges.

Filler-up breakfast buffets are served daily at Russels Fireside Dining Room, Ptarmigan Dining Room and Great Northern Steak & Rib House. They cost USD$9 for adults, USD$4.50 for kids. Restaurants' seasons correlate with lodge openings.

Jammer Joe's Grill & Pizzaria (*Lake McDonald Lodge; breakfast USD$5-8, lunch & dinner USD$7-15; open 6:30am-9:30pm)* This casual, vibrant eatery across from Lake McDonald Lodge has tummy-filling menu offerings, like pizza and lasagna. Portions are generous.

Russells Fireside Dining Room (*Lake McDonald Lodge; lunch USD$6-8, dinner mains USD$10-20; open 6am-9:30am, 11:30am-2pm, 5-9:30pm)* This handsome restaurant affords a tranquil dining experience. Ribs, fish and more are on at dinner.

Ptarmigan Dining Room (*Many Glacier Hotel; lunch USD$6-8, dinner mains USD$12-20, open 6:30-9:30am, 11:30am-2pm, 5-9:30pm)* The elegant feel of Many Glacier Hotel's restaurant encourages slow dining while soaking up views of the lake. Steak, seafood, pasta and usually one vegetarian main are among the many supper offerings.

HUCKLEBERRIES: JUST ANOTHER BLUEBERRY?

Consume them in chocolate, jam, syrup, taffy, brownies and even beer. Their purple-blackish coat and cute round figure are found on everything from hiking trails to postcards. What is this berry, why the fuss, and is it really what it says it is?

Different varieties of huckleberries are found from Alaska and California to Idaho and Montana. Their bushes begin to bloom in May; ripening starts around August. In northwest Montana, huckleberries are loved above just about anything smaller than a breadbox.

You may find that the huckleberry you sample in northwest Montana tastes very similar to a blueberry, just a tad more tart. Indeed, some horticulture experts claim that the 'Montana huckleberry' would be more accurately called a blueberry, an assertion that irks proud locals. Huckleberries and blueberries do indeed belong to different genera.

No matter the scientific evidence, many locals will stand by their berry, and bears continue to feast regardless of what the damn thing should be called. Next time you're given a juicy slab of huckleberry pie, you'd do well to stay quiet, nod and enjoy.

Italian Garden Ristorante (*Swiftcurrent Motor Inn; breakfast USD$5-7, lunch & dinner USD$7-11; open 6:30am-10am, 11am-3pm, 5-9:30pm*) Sporting checkered tablecloths, this restaurant has a limited menu that includes breakfast of the eggs-and-pancakes variety (and good biscuits). Later in the day, chow on pizza and burgers.

Great Northern Steak & Rib House (*Glacier Park Lodge; open 7-9:30am, 11am-2pm, 5:30-9:30pm; lunch USD$7-9, dinner mains USD$12-20*) This big restaurant is a smooth operation, serving steak, seafood, chicken and more to refortify you after a day on the trail.

Two Dog Flats Mesquite Grill (*Rising Sun Motor Inn; dishes USD$7-12; open 6:30-10:30am, 11am-9:30pm*) This small, airy eatery doesn't go out on any limbs with its menu. American standards, mostly meaty, pervade all three meals. It has limited breakfast offerings.

Eddie's Cafe (☎ *406-888-5361; Apgar Village; meals USD$6-13; open 7am-9:30pm*) The at-ease, privately owned Eddie's serves hearty portions of pancakes, sandwiches, burgers and baked potatoes. A picnic lunch to go is USD$7, and a kiosk out front sells espresso and ice cream.

Groceries

Small grocery stores (with limited camping supplies) are in Apgar, Lake McDonald, Rising Sun and at the Swiftcurrent Motor Inn.

Just outside the park you can load up with food, including some fresh produce, in St Mary, Babb and West Glacier. For better prices and selection, head to Whitefish or Kalispell; both have natural-foods markets.

POLEBRIDGE

The **Northern Lights Saloon** (☎ 406-888-5669; *Polebridge Loop Rd; dishes USD$6-12; open 4pm-midnight, May-Sep*) is worth the dusty drive to Polebridge. In a casual setting, dig into healthy choices (finally) like tempeh and veggie burgers (meat offered, too). It will go down especially smooth with an organic beer.

Dubbed 'the Merc' by those in the know, **Polebridge Mercantile** (☎ 406-888-5105; *Polebridge Loop Rd*), next door to the saloon, creates sweet and savory pastries (USD$2.50) that are talked about the park over. The small shop also stocks some foods.

ST MARY VILLAGE

Snowgoose Grill (☎ 406-732-4431; *US 89; breakfast & lunch USD$6-9, dinner mains USD$15-25; open 7-10:30am, 11:30am-4pm, 5:30-10pm*) Its homemade scones with honey butter are the steaming hot stuff of dreams. The staff here is welcoming, the atmosphere soothing and the wild huckleberry pie (USD$5) delicious. The restaurant is wheelchair-accessible.

Park Cafe (☎ 406-732-4482; *US 89; open 7am-10pm*) Ever bustling, the attractive Park Cafe boasts an outdoor deck, cozy interior and a menu full of satisfying, never boring American fare. A few interesting choices exist for the vegetarian. No alcohol is served.

Two Sisters Cafe (☎ 406-732-5535; *US 89; breakfast USD$6-9, lunch & dinner USD$8-15; open 8am-9pm*) This place, halfway between Babb and St Mary, lives up to the eclectic expectations set by its colorful exterior, with heaps of random decor, like inflatable aliens, nuns and flamingos. Its food, too, boasts flair and flavor.

EAST GLACIER

Serrano's Mexican Restaurant (☎ 406-226-9392; *29 Dawson Ave; mains USD$7-12; open 5-10pm*) Serrano's serves up very good Mexican food at dinner in casual environs both inside and outside on its deck. It's usually packed with hungry, hungry hikers, and is known for its excellent margaritas.

Whistle Stop Restaurant (☎ 406-226-9292; *Hwy 49; dishes USD$6-12; open 7am-9pm*) This homemade-goods haven is a nice choice breakfast, lunch or dinner. Start the day with French toast, and end it with a savory portobello sandwich or something else that's just been sizzled on the grill.

Brownie's Grocery & Deli (☎ 406-226-4426; *1020 Hwy 49; open 7am-10pm*) Head here for strong coffee, sandwiches and baked goods.

Two Medicine Grill (☎ 406-226-5572; *314 US 2; breakfast & lunch USD$4-7, dinner USD$7-10; open 6:30am-9pm*) This no-glamour-needed grill is open year-round.

Entertainment

Nothing is flashy about the nightlife around Glacier National Park, but 'strong' defines the drink here.

Kip's Beer Garden (*no ☎; US 89*) in St Mary Village is neither pretty nor predictable. Whether mingling with the permanent residents of its barstools or off-duty seasonal workers, you won't leave sober. It has pool tables, and the garden is open sometimes.

East Glacier's drinking hole is the **Trailhead Saloon** (*US 2*). Come prepared to down shots.

✔ ESSENTIALS

EQUIPMENT & SUPPLIES

Glacier Outdoor Center (☎ 406-888-5454, 800-235-6781; 11957 US 2 E, West Glacier) rents and sells gear for rafting, fishing, mountain biking, camping and backpacking. Minimal camping supplies can be found at stores in the park, as well as in East Glacier, West Glacier and St Mary.

For photo processing, the closest option is **Glacier Photo** (☎ 406-888-5233) in West Glacier.

INTERNET ACCESS

East Glacier's only Internet stop is **Brownie's** (☎ 406-226-4426; 1020 Hwy 49), where a surf is USD$7 per hour. In St Mary, log on at **Mountain Chief Trading Post** (☎ 406-732-9242; US 89), just north of the village, which charges USD$2 per 15 minutes. In West Glacier, the **Nomad Technologies trailer** (☎ 406-755-1721), near the post office, charges USD$15 per hour for high-speed access.

MEDICAL SERVICE & EMERGENCIES

Basic first-aid is available at visitors centers and ranger stations in the park. The closest hospitals to the west side are **Kalispell Regional Medical Center** (☎ 406-752-5111; 310 Sunnyview Lane) and **North Valley Hospital** (☎ 406-863-3500; 6575 Hwy 93 S).

If you're in the northeast, you may find that **Cardston Municipal Hospital** (☎ 403-653-4411; 144 2nd St W, Cardston), in Alberta, Canada, is the closest bet, though customs could consume time en route.

MONEY

Canadian currency is not widely accepted in Glacier. The nearest banks are in Columbia Falls and Browning. The lodges at Lake McDonald, Glacier Park and Many Glacier have 24-hour ATMs. Other ATM sites include Eddie's Camp Store in Apgar and the St Mary Supermarket.

POSTAL SERVICE

Post offices are located in West Glacier (zip code 59936) and East Glacier (zip code 59434), and substations where you can post mail and buy stamps are in Lake McDonald, Polebridge and in the St Mary Supermarket.

SHOWERS & LAUNDRY

The campstores at **Rising Sun** and **Swiftcurrent Motor Inns** have showers (USD$1.25 per 8.5 minutes); the latter also has laundry facilities. Showers are open 6:30am to 10pm; expect a wait.

In North Fork, the **North Fork Hostel** offers showers (USD$4) or baths (USD$5). **Johnson's** of St Mary has showers (USD$3) and laundry. In West Glacier, **SanSuzEd Campground** has the cleanest showers (USD$5) around. In West Glacier, a laundry is behind Glacier Raft Co, near the Alberta Visitor Centre.

TELEPHONES

All park lodges have public phones, as do the nonprimitive campgrounds. Local calls are USD$0.50. Cell-phone reception in the park is spotty and depends largely on your service. Certainly don't count on it on the trail.

TRASH & RECYCLING

Brown bear-proof bins for trash are all over the park. Sadly, Glacier's recycling efforts are not as polished as those of Waterton. Aluminum cans can be tossed in designated bins in certain areas around the park, including visitors centers. The entrance to St Mary Campground holds designated containers for plastic, aluminum and newspaper.

AROUND GLACIER

Blackfeet Indian Reservation

The shortgrass prairie east of Glacier is home to the Blackfeet Nation, which includes the Northern Piegan (Blackfeet), Southern Piegan and Blood tribes that came south from the Alberta area in the 1700s. Originally an agrarian people, the Blackfeet took quickly to horses and guns, eventually developing a reputation as the fiercest warriors in the West. Today, approximately 7000 tribal members reside on or around the reservation (W www.blackfeetnation.com); major industries are ranching, farming and pencil manufacturing. Browning, 29km/18 miles east of Glacier Park, is where most of the reservation's amenities lie.

The **Museum of the Plains Indians** (☎ 406-338-2230; Hwys 2 & 89, Browning; adult/child 6-12 USD$4/1; open 9am-5pm daily Jun-Sep, 10am-4:30pm Mon-Fri Oct-May) is one of Montana's better Native American museums. Extensive descriptions accompany fascinating exhibits of costumes, art, craftwork and more

Rising Wolf Wilderness Adventures (☎ 406-338-3016; W www.risewolf.com) runs guided hikes and fishing trips in and around the Blackfeet Indian reservation. The activities, run by Blackfeet women, are geared toward women.

Sleep in a traditional tepee looking onto the plains at the **Lodgepole Gallery & Tipi Village** (☎ 406-338-2787; tipicamp@3rivers.net; US 89; USD$40 per person, USD$10 each additional).

Whitefish

MAP 13

A fine gateway to Glacier National Park, Old West Whitefish wears a New West coat of good restaurants, shops and bars. It sits next to large Whitefish Lake, in the shadow of Big Mountain, one of Montana's premiere year-round resorts. Summer is the most all-around vibrant season, though when the snowfall is good in winter, the nightlife can rollick.

ORIENTATION & INFORMATION

US 93 goes through town as Spokane Ave (north–south) and 2nd St (east–west), connecting to Kalispell 20.9km/13 miles south, and US 2; Glacier is 38.6km/24 miles west via US 2. Wisconsin Ave goes north from downtown to Big Mountain.

Whitefish Chamber of Commerce (☎ 406-862-3501, 877-862-3548; W www.whitefishchamber.org; 520 E 2nd St; open 9am-5:30pm Mon-Sat summer, 9am-5pm Mon-Fri winter) has ample area information. The **Tally Lake Ranger Station** (☎ 406-862-2508; 1335 Hwy 93 N; open 8am-4:30pm Mon-Fri) is 1.6km/1 mile west of Whitefish.

Wash your clothes while you get gas at **Mike's Conoco** (☎ 406-862-6453; 13th St & Spokane), which has a 24-hour laundry. Use the Internet for free at the **Whitefish Branch Library** (☎ 406-862-6657; 9 Spokane Ave).

Bookworks (☎ 406-862-4980; 244 Spokane Ave) has a good selection of books and maps. For gear and rentals, head to **Sportsman & Ski Haus** (☎ 406-862-3111; 6475 US 93 S).

SIGHTS

Whitefish's star attraction is the **Big Mountain Resort** (☎ 406-862-2900, 800-858-4157; **W** www.bigmtn.com), 11.2km/7 miles from downtown. It has a whopping 1214 hectares/3000 acres of skiable terrain and a snowboarder-hopping Terrain Park. The winter season runs late November to mid-April. From June to September, 32.2km/20 miles of trails host aficionados of **hiking** and **mountain biking**. The **gondola** to the mountaintop offers great views of Flathead Valley; ride or hike down.

The **Stumptown Historical Society Museum** (☎ 406-862-0067; 500 Depot St; admission free; open 10am-4pm Mon-Sat summer, 11am-3pm Mon-Sat winter), in the old Great Northern Railroad Depot, displays train memorabilia and fascinating photos of early Whitefish.

The **City Beach Park** (admission & parking free), on the southern shore of Whitefish Lake, is full of the county's children (and their adults) when the sun is out. The swimming area is roped off.

PLACES TO STAY

Prices are usually 20% lower Labor Day to mid-December and mid-March to Memorial Day.

Whitefish Lake State Park Campground (☎ 406-862-3991; State Park Rd; day use USD$5, campsites USD$15; open late May–early Oct) On the southwest edge of the lake, shady forested grounds hold 25 first-come, first-served sites, including one that is wheelchair-friendly.

Bunkhouse Travelers Inn & Hostel (☎ 406-862-3377; 217 Railway St; dorm/room USD$15/34) In a quiet residential area convenient to town, this tidy operation boasts a laundry room, communal kitchen, friendly owners and no curfew (though lockout is 11am to 4pm). Linen costs USD$3.

The Downtowner (☎ 406-862-2535, 224 Spokane Ave; dorm USD$20, s/d from $61/72) Centrally situated, this hotel with spacious, comfortable rooms also has a well-kept hostel. All guests get free use of its outdoor Jacuzzi, sauna and adjacent gym.

Duck Inn (☎ 406-862-3825, 800-344-2377; room USD$80) A lovely choice, the lodge has 10 quiet doubles, stocked with TV, phone, fireplace and balcony. Off the highway, it overlooks the Whitefish River.

The welcoming **Cheap Sleep Motel** (☎ 406-862-5515; 6400 Hwy 93 S; **W** www.cheapsleepmotel.com; s/d from USD$40/50) is a good value, and **The Garden Wall** (☎ 406-862-3440, 888-530-1700; **W** www.gardenwallinn.com; 504 Spokane Ave; s/d USD$125/145) is an elegant B&B.

PLACES TO EAT & DRINK

Third Street Market (☎ 406-862-5054; 3rd St & Spokane Ave; open 9am-6pm Mon-Sat) A great little grocery, this place sells a range of natural foods, bulk-bin items, vitamins, organic produce and even healthful grub for your pet.

Buffalo Cafe (☎ 406-862-2833; 514 3rd St; mains USD$4-6; open 6am-2pm Mon-Fri, 7am-2pm Sat, 9am-2pm Sun) Eat till you're overfull at this great spot. Always buzzing with local crowds, it serves huge plates of hot food, from tofu scrambles to burritos and infinite coffee.

Wasabi Sushi Bar & the Ginger Grill (☎ 406-863-9283; 419 2nd St E; meal USD$14-20; open 5pm Tue-Sat) Locals have the sushi addiction, and it's all because of this hip eatery, which serves very good traditional and fusion sushi. For those who don't crave raw, it offers a cooked array of pan-Asian entrées.

Whitefish Lake Golf Club Restaurant (☎ 406-862-5285; Hwy 93; mains USD$16-22; open 5:30pm) At the golf club, this locally praised restaurant is a hole-in-one for classy dining. Racks, roasts and ribs galore, as well as appetizing seafood, are served. Reservations are advised.

Dire Wolf Pub (☎ 406-862-4500; 845 Wisconsin Ave; open 11am-10:30pm Mon-Sat, noon-10:30pm Sun) North of town, the nonsmoking Dire Wolf has tables big enough to sleep on. It's warm and comfy, and the pub fare is good and filling. Bands perform weekly.

Bulldog Saloon (☎ 406-862-5601; 144 Central Ave, open 11am-2am) In this popular place, walls are aflutter with sports flags and bulldogs, hard drinkers are playing poker, and the bathrooms boast X-rated decor.

GETTING AROUND

Intermountain Transport (☎ 406-755-4011) connects the train depot in Whitefish to Kalispell; its buses also mosey to Missoula, Helena, Bozeman and Seattle.

The free **Shuttle Network of Whitefish** (SNOW) connects Whitefish to Big Mountain during ski season. **Eagle Transit** (☎ 406-758-5728; open 8am-5pm Mon-Fri) provides bus service around Whitefish (USD$1), and to and from Kalispell (USD$3).

Kalispell

Kalispell, 20.9km/13 miles south of Whitefish, is Flathead Valley's commercial hub. Though not as charming as Whitefish, it's a pleasant enough place to refuel on supplies. Its concentration of budget lodging makes it a frequented gateway to Glacier, less than an hour's drive northeast. It's also used by visitors to the popular Flathead Lake, 15 to 20 minutes south by way of US 93.

Kalispell Chamber of Commerce (☎ 406-758-2800; 15 Depot Park, open 8am-5pm Mon-Fri) has maps and information. Check out **Books West** (☎ 406-752-6900; 101 Main St) for its great stock of titles, including area guides.

The completely restored 1895 Norman-style **Conrad Mansion** (☎ 406-755-2166; Woodland Ave & 3rd St E; adult/child USD$7/2; open 10am-6pm, mid-May–mid-Oct), built in 1895, is worth touring. Contemporary work by Montana artists is displayed at **Hockaday Museum of Art** (☎ 406-755-5268; 302 2nd Ave E; adult/child 6-18 USD$5/1; open 10am-6pm Mon-Sat, to 8pm Thu noon-4pm Sun).

Kalispell has a good range of lodging and eateries. **Rocky Mountain 'Hi' Campground** (☎ 406-755 9573, 800-968-5637; W www.kalispell.bigsky.net/rmhc; 825 Helena Flats Rd; camp/RV site USD$16/19-21, cabin USD$40-50), off US 2 east of Kalispell, is great for families, but kids will also appreciate the pool at **Vacationer Motel** (☎ 406-755-7144, 888-755-7144; 285 7th Ave; s/d USD$55/60). The best downtown pick is **Kalispell Grand Hotel** (☎ 406-755-8100, 800-858-7422; W www.kalispellgrand.com; 100 Main St; s/d from USD$75/80 summer, USD$60/70 winter).

For myriad coffee choices and healthy baked goods, stop by **Montana Coffee Traders Cafe** (☎ 406-756-2326; 326 W Center St; dishes USD$4-7; open 7am-5pm Mon-Sat). The vibrant **Knead Cafe** (☎ 406-755-7510; 25 2nd Ave; lunch USD$7-9, dinner mains USD$9-14; open 8am-3pm Sun-Mon, 8am-9pm Tue-Sat) has delicious Mediterranean-style fare. The menu at elegant **Café Max** (☎ 406-755-7687; 121 Main St; mains USD$17-25; open 5:30pm Tue-Sat) stands out, with choices like ginger-and-sesame seared tofu and 'cowboy steak.'

WATERTON LAKES NATIONAL PARK
Map 12

The 525-sq-km/203-sq-mile Waterton, though small compared to its southern neighbor, is full of dramatic diversity. Here the land rises from the prairie into rugged, beautiful alpine terrain with plentiful valleys, lakes and waterfalls. Upper Waterton Lake, the deepest lake in the Rockies (146m/479ft), and Cameron Falls, which cascade across rock 600 million years old, are two easily accessed draws. Spotting wildlife amid the wilds here is common.

According to Blackfeet tradition, the god of wind watches over Waterton. It is, in fact, one of the gustiest places in Alberta. In the spring and fall, storm-watching is a fascinating activity. And in the summer, the sunny park is blanketed in color, with 800 wildflower species and the photogenic beargrass, brought over from Glacier by pollinators.

Waterton makes for a convenient national-park experience once you've reached it. From your hotel or campground within the townsite, which is well inside the park, you can walk to several trailheads. Everything you might need for your trip – from equipment to a packed lunch – is located in the few blocks of the townsite.

When You Arrive

The park is always open: You can enter any day of the year at any hour, though many amenities and a couple park roads close in winter. Entry costs CAD$5 per adult per day and CAD$2.50 per child six and up. Passes, to be displayed on your vehicle's windshield, are valid until 4pm on the date of expiration. If you enter the park when the booth is shut, get a pass early the next morning at the Waterton Visitor Centre or park administration office. An annual Waterton pass costs CAD$30. Available at Waterton or any fee-charging national park, the National Parks of Canada Pass (adult/child six to 16 CAD$45/22) is good for unlimited admission to Canadian national parks for one year.

Free park admission is de rigueur on Canada Day (July 1) and Parks Day (third Saturday in July).

Upon entering, you'll receive a map of Waterton and Glacier Parks and the quarterly information-packed newspaper, *Waterton-Glacier Guide*.

ORIENTATION
Waterton lies in Alberta's southwestern corner, 130km/81 miles from Lethbridge. From the British Columbia border to Chief Mountain Hwy, it is 525 sq km/203 sq miles. That border is traced by the Continental Divide, which separates the provinces of Alberta and British Columbia.

Entrances
The one road entrance into the park is in its northeast corner along Hwy 5. Most visitors coming from Glacier and the USA reach the junction with Hwy 5 via Hwy 6 (Chief Mountain International Hwy) from the southeast. From Calgary and Pincher Creek to the north, Hwy 6 shoots south toward Hwy 5 into the park. From the east, Hwy 5 through Cardston heads west and then south into the park.

Major Regions & Roads

Unlike the vast Glacier, Waterton is not divided into distinct regions, but rather its main roadways delineate the accessible attractions for most visitors. Highway 5 south leads past the park entrance to Waterton Townsite, the services hub within the park. Chief Mountain Hwy (Hwy 17 on the US side) wends its way northwest over Belly River, through the Blood Timber Reserve and into the park. Red Rock Parkway (open mid-May to mid-October) jets off from Hwy 5 and is a popular scenic stretch, particularly for Red Rock Canyon, its destination point. In early May, this road is often under repair. Akamina Parkway, used mainly by cross-country skiers in winter, begins closer to the townsite, following Cameron Creek to Cameron Lake.

Visitor Service Hubs

Waterton Townsite sits prettily on the west side of sparkling Upper Waterton Lake, which crosses the border into the USA. Upper Waterton Lake is a major centerpiece of the park, with boat tours, shuttles and limited motorboats. Waterton Ave (Main St) and its surroundings are full of lodging, restaurants and other services, such as bicycle rentals, a post office, ATMs, Internet and phones.

The closest town with full services is Pincher Creek (population 3665), 55km/34 miles north via Hwy 6. To the east, Cardston (population 3475) is 56km/36miles from the park on Hwy 5. En route to Cardston, the small hamlet of Mountain View, 20km\12.6 miles from the park, has limited amenities.

INFORMATION

Waterton Visitor Centre *(Map 14; ☎ 403-859-5133; W www.parkscanada.gc.ca/ waterton; open 8am-7pm, early May–early Oct)*, across the road from hilltop Prince of Wales Hotel, is the central stop for information (front- and backcountry). Call for an information package to be sent to you before your trip. The park has no separate ranger stations, though staff at Waterton Townsite and Crandell Mountain Campgrounds can provide area information. From early October to early May, **Parks Canada Administration** *(Map 14; ☎ 403-859-2224; Waterton Lakes National Park, Box 50, Mount View Rd, Alberta T0K 2M0; open 8am-4pm Mon-Fri)* serves as the visitors center.

Parks Canada maps of the park and townsite are available at the visitors center, as well as at hotels and restaurants around town. **Borderline Books & Coffee** *(Map 14; ☎ 403-859-2284; 305 Windflower Ave)* has a great range of books on the park and region. **Waterton Heritage Centre** *(Map 14; ☎ 403-859-2624; Main St)* also sells books and maps.

Policies & Regulations

Enjoy Waterton's diverse wildlife, but from a distance. Resist the temptation to remove anything (even the minutest pebble) from its natural environment

CAMPING

Rules for food storage at campgrounds are similar to those in Glacier. Waterton's informative *Bare Campsite Program* brochure is handed out in park campgrounds. Campgrounds hold central steel bear-proof lockers and have designated areas for wastewater.

Campfires are OK in designated areas, but be particularly cautious when it is windy, which is often.

WILDERNESS PERMITS & REGULATIONS

Permits are not required for day hikes, but overnight trips require them. Up to 24 hours before the start of your journey, make arrangements at the visitors center. The nightly fee is CAD$8 per adult. Kids 16 and under get free permits. All of the back-country sites are reservable, and advance reservations can be made up to 90 days ahead by calling ☎ 406-859-5133; an extra fee of CAD$12 is charged. You can also put in your request by mail to Parks Canada Administration (see Information).

FISHING & BOATING

A Parks Canada permit is required to fish in Waterton. Permits cost CAD$6 for seven days or CAD$13 for the season and can be purchased at the visitors center, park headquarters or at campground entry booths.

Waters that open for fishing in mid-May include Upper and Middle Waterton Lakes, Akamina Lakes, Crandell Lake, and Cameron Lake and Creek; these are generally open through late August. All other lakes are open from early July to late October, except for those that are completely closed to anglers. Off-limits waters include Sofa and Dungarvan Creeks, Maskinonge Lake, Blakiston and Bauerman Creeks and North Fork Belly River. Cutthroat trout caught on Middle and Lower Waterton Lakes and Belly River must be released. Inquire about the park's seasonal regulations.

Motorboats are permissible only on Upper and Middle Waterton Lakes. **Waterton Shoreline Cruises** (☎ *403-859-2362; wscruise@cadvision.com*) manages the docking facilities at the townsite's Marina. Stalls rent for CAD$13 per night or CAD$150 for the season.

Getting Around

Since public transportation is nonexistent in Waterton, a car or bicycle is the most convenient way to get outside of the townsite.

CAR & MOTORCYCLE

The speed limit in the townsite is 30kph/19 mph unless otherwise posted; campgrounds post 20kph/12 mph. Akamina Parkway has a limit of 50kph/31 mph, unless otherwise posted.

The town's two gas stations are at Pat's and Tamarack Village Square, both on Mount View Rd and open May to October only; to fuel up in winter, head to Mountain View. Parking is a piece of cake around town. There are no meters or any unusual restrictions curbside, and the townsite has a few free lots (no parking between 11pm and 6am).

TRANSPORTATION

Waterton Townsite is easy enough to walk around. The following services run in the summer season.

Waterton Sports & Leisure (☎ *403-859-2378*) runs hiker shuttles departing from Tamarack Village Square. The Cameron Express (CAD$9 per seat or CAD$30 for whole shuttle), handy for Carthew-Alderson trailbound hikers, leaves daily at 8:30am and 9:30am. Its run is contingent upon the opening of the trail, which sometimes isn't clear until early July. Reserve your seat at least a day in advance; reservations can be made in person or by phone. The reservation-only Tamarack Shuttle (CAD$15 per person) is for Tamarack Trail backpackers. The shuttle bus follows you and your car to whichever end of the trail is your final destination. After you park your vehicle, the shuttle transports you to the trailhead. Another shuttle heads to Goat Haunt/Chief Mountain Customs in the USA. This service must be reserved; call for current rates.

Glacier Park, Inc (☎ 406-892-2525) runs a daily shuttle from Prince of Wales Hotel to the following points in Glacier Park: Chief Mountain (USD$8), Many Glacier (USD$16), St Mary (USD$24) and Glacier Park Lodge (USD$34.50).

Sights

You don't need to hike uphill for days to get a taste of Waterton wilderness. Even the strollable town boasts impressive sites

WATERTON TOWNSITE MAP 14

The attractive village within the park is both functional and charming. It is a relatively peaceful place, thanks to the lack of tour-bus traffic that can overtake Banff and Jasper. A 3.2km/2-mile **loop trail** along Upper Waterton Lake and around the townsite provides a good introduction to the area.

The **Waterton Heritage Centre** (☎ 403-859-2624; Main St; admission free; open 10am-6pm mid-May–late-Sep), a small museum run by nonprofit Waterton Natural History Association, is a worthwhile stop for exhibits of park flora, fauna and history.

At the west end of Cameron Falls Drive, **Cameron Falls** is a much-photographed body of water rushing into a turquoise pool. Supporting the falls are some of the oldest observable rocks (1.2 to 1.5 billion years old) in the Rockies. The lookout here is paved for wheelchair access.

UPPER WATERTON LAKE

The deepest lake in the Canadian Rockies, Upper Waterton Lake sinks its heels down 120m/394ft. Many visitors take in a boat ride across its beautiful waters, which have their far shore in Montana, USA. **Waterton Shoreline Cruises** (☎ 403-859-2362; wscruise@cadvision.com) operates boats holding up to 200 passengers. A limited operation (with no stops in the USA) begins in May; the full schedule operates in July and August. Boat guides tend to be knowledgeable and amusing. Most cruises (45 minutes one way) stop at Goat Haunt, Montana for a half-hour. The roundtrip costs adult/child 13 to 17 CAD$25/13; only cash or travelers checks are accepted. Roundtrip boat passengers to Goat Haunt do not have to go through customs before heading toward the Canadian sector again, though if you take the boat one way, hiking to or from Goat Haunt, you'll need to flash your passport.

CAMERON LAKE

Glacier-born Cameron Lake (elevation 1660m/5445ft), now fed by snow and ice, sits beautifully before snow-dressed Mt Custer. The sparkling blue lake has an area spanning 172 hectares/426 acres and drops to 39m/128ft at its deepest. The surrounding area is popular with families. When the sun is out, sunbathers and picnickers speckle the grassy patches lakeside. From foamflowers to fireweed, copious **wildflower species** thrive. Permitted anglers visit for the lake's brook- and rainbow-trout **fishing**.

An unstaffed **educational exhibit** near the lake is tailored toward children. It offers interested tidbits on Cameron Lake flora, climate and geology. A number of **trails** start from around the lake.

Driving Tours

It's not unusual to see traffic backed up along any of these scenic roads when any wildlife is spottable nearby.

AKAMINA PARKWAY
Route: Waterton Townsite to Cameron Lake
Distance: 16km/10 miles one way
Speed Limit: 50kph/31 mph unless otherwise posted

The road begins 0.5km/0.3 mile from the townsite center. After you've climbed your first 0.5km/0.3 mile on the road, you'll get a sideways glance at the town and lake below. Rocky faces on your right and many-treed slopes on your left predominate the first few kilometers, and soon you'll glimpse **Cameron Creek**.

The curious structure 7.6km/4.7 miles from the start of your journey is the **Lineham Discovery Well National Historic Site**, the first oil well in Western Canada. It was struck in 1902, along with premature optimism

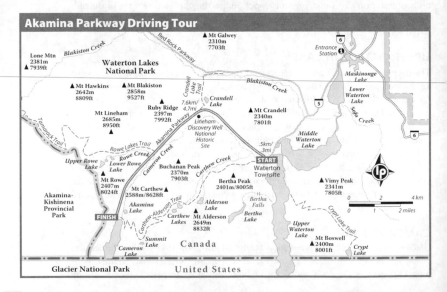

Akamina Parkway Driving Tour

that led to dubbing the area 'Oil City.' After two years the flow was poor, and the well dripped her last in 1936.

The parkway ends at the stellar **Cameron Lake** (p235).

RED ROCK PARKWAY
Route: Red Rock Parkway (at Hwy 5) to Red Rock Canyon
Distance: 15km/9 miles one way
Speed Limit: 50kph/31 mph unless otherwise posted

Red Rock Parkway gets its start at a junction with Hwy 5, about 8km/5 miles south of the park entrance. This road, running alongside Blakiston Creek for much of its route, is full of wildflower-speckled prairie spilling onto incredible mountains. South of the parkway, the awe-inspiring **Mt Blakiston** (2910m/9580ft) is Waterton's tallest peak.

A few picnic spots are along the way, and 4.8km/3 miles in, a small **native history exhibit** is worthwhile.

Most visitors persevere to the end of the road, 15km/9miles in, where **Red Rock Canyon** sits colorfully aglow. A 0.7km/0.4-mile self-guided loop trail circuits the edge of a canyon. Consisting of ancient Grinnel argillite, the canyon is a fantastic introduction to one of the geologically wondrous aspects of Waterton.

CHIEF MOUNTAIN HIGHWAY
Route: US/Canada border to junction with Hwy 5 south,
on Chief Mountain Hwy (Hwy 6)
Distance: 21.6km/13.4 miles one way
Speed Limit: 80kph/50 mph unless otherwise posted

This is the roadway vein between the two parts of the International Peace Park, Glacier and Waterton. It is most dramatic for those entering from the USA for the first time. A little over a kilometer after the border, a turnoff on the left gives a good first view of the region's divine mountainous terrain. Belly River Campground's entrance is 3.9km/2.4 miles north of the border.

The **Blood Indian Timber Reserve** is 1639 hectares/4050 acres that has been owned and used by Blood Indians since a treaty drawn in 1883. About 6.4km/4 miles before you reach the route's end, a turnoff to the left showcases much of Waterton from above – it's an introduction to this land where, as they say, 'the mountains meet the prairie.'

Festivals & Events

The **Waterton International French Film Festival** (W *www.waterton internationalfrenchfilmfest.com*) is a two-day affair at the Waterton Opera House in early June. Check the website for program information.

Canada Day (July 1) takes in a pancake breakfast, flag-raising ceremony and kids programs, and **Parks Day** (3rd Saturday in July) is celebrated with games and other festivities. Contact the visitors center for details.

In mid-September, the **Heritage Ball** (☎ 403-859-2624), organized by the Waterton Natural History Association, sashays into the Prince of Wales Hotel.

Day Hikes

North of the Canadian border, the approaches to sensational hikes are shorter than in Glacier National Park, since roads penetrate quite far into the 'backcountry.' Lacing the park are 255km/159 miles of hiking trails, some of which are good for cycling and horseback riding. In winter many become cross-country skiing and snowshoeing trails.

Waterton is a day hiker's destination. Backpackers will find plenty to keep them occupied as well but will have less-limited opportunities at the larger Banff, Jasper and Glacier parks.

To stretch a bit after you arrive to Waterton, you can try out a short stroll near the townsite, like the tree-shaded **Linnet Lake Loop Trail** (1km/0.6 mile). It's a paved and wheelchair-accessible circuit of the small, green Linnet Lake.

CARTHEW-ALDERSON TRAIL
Distance: 19km/11.8 miles one way
Duration: 6.5 hours
Challenge: Moderate
Elevation Change: 600m/1968ft gain

Many seasoned visitors rate this hike the best in the park. It can get well trafficked, but fans love it for its multifarious beauty and incredible sweeping views. You can embark westward on the trail from the townsite and end at Cameron Lake (at Akamina Parkway's end). However, starting at Cameron Lake and hiking east (to Cameron Falls in the townsite) is the usual choice because of a gentler elevation gain. Find somebody to drop you at Cameron Lake to start, or reserve a seat on the hiker shuttle (p234). The trail is sometimes not hikeable until mid-June or later due to snow.

The trail heads southeast from the Cameron Lake boat ramp and enters the pines along the eastern shore, climbing through a series of switchbacks to **Summit Lake**. This pool, surrounded by meadow and pine, marks the top of the steepest climb. The Carthew Lakes Trail is signed left (northeast) at a junction shortly after Summit Lake. The ascent lets up slightly as the trees give way to scrub and then grass, before all vegetation disappears. Views over Lake Wurdeman and Carcajou Lake soon become more and more striking. A narrow path switchbacks up scree to the ridgeline, where you'll get an expansive panorama: northern Glacier summits to the south, Carthew Lakes to the north.

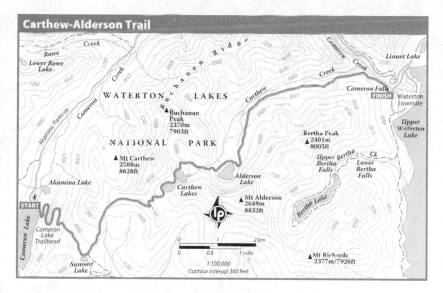

Carthew-Alderson Trail

After the climbing is done, the trail descends from the ridge and weaves between the two starkly located **Carthew Lakes**. A steep cliff is negotiated at the exit of the Carthew basin before **Alderson Lake** becomes visible below. The trail reenters the trees shortly before the lake; a detour of 0.5km/0.3 mile leads to the water itself.

From here the trail follows the Carthew Creek valley, descending gradually through the forest to Waterton Townsite. A fitting end to the day is the impressive **Cameron Falls**.

CRYPT LAKE TRAIL
Distance: 17.2km/10.3 miles roundtrip
Duration: 6.5 hours
Challenge: Moderate-Difficult
Elevation Change: 700m/2296ft gain

A couple decades ago, a leading magazine rated this hike Canada's best, and the modifier has stuck. 'Best' is a strong word; however, there's no doubt that this is one of the more interesting hikes out there and does make for a very fun day out.

It was once possible to make an overnight of it at two different backcountry camps along this trail, but the park service discovered that removal of the sites greatly decreased problems with bears. Now you must complete the trail in one day, planning it to coincide with the boat that will take you to and from the trailhead. The Waterton Shoreline Cruises boat (CAD$13 roundtrip) leaves the townsite marina at 10am daily (also 9am July to August) and picks up the weary and exhilarated at the Crypt Lake trailhead at 4pm and 5pm. Most hikers will find these timings allow time for a relaxed lunch break at Crypt Lake.

Once off the boat and at the Crypt Lake trailhead, the ascent quickly begins. The way up is, well, *up* most of the way as it climbs through thick green vegetative areas, though there are a few level stretches. Don't forget to stop and smell the wildflowers along the way. Particularly in the first couple of miles of lush terrain, make plenty of noise for the bears residing nearby. Once in more open terrain, you'll take in up-close views of waterfalls, mountains and an unnamed lake below.

This hike comes with its thrills. Just when you're hoping to throw off your sweaty socks and soak your aching feet in the Crypt Lake of your dreams, you encounter delightful diversions. First, go through a glacial cirque by crouching (or crawling) through a tunnel, reached via a narrow ladder up. (The tunnel, though natural, was enlarged in the 1960s.) Soon after your body is vertical again, you reach a sheer rock face that must be negotiated with the assistance of a cable. It is not as terrifying as it sounds, but take extra care when it's raining. You've made it? Your reward then, quite soon, is the gorgeous **Crypt Lake**, nestled in an amphitheater-like setting. You won't likely be the only human there, but plenty of spots exist in which to eat your lunch and drink in the surrounding beauty.

Ensure that you allow enough time for your return trip down, as the boats to the townsite are the only easy way back!

ROWE LAKES
Distance: 12.6km/7.8 miles roundtrip
Duration: 5 hours
Challenge: Moderate
Elevation Change: 548.6m/1800ft

Another favorite of Waterton visitors, the Rowe Lakes hike takes in beautiful alpine meadowland and lakes en route a creekside trail. Those who don't feel up to tackling the steep ascent to Upper Rowe Lake can still have a satisfying day visiting Rowe Meadow and Lower Rowe Lake.

If you're coming from the townsite, the Rowe-Tamarack trailhead is accessed from a pullout 10.1km/6.3 miles down the Akamina Parkway. The trail calmly moves alongside Rowe Creek before ascending into forested bunches of lodgepole pine.

At an avalanche slope covered in lodgepole pine you'll take in wondrous mountainous vistas. After hiking through more forested area, you'll pass a waterfall and then, 3.9km/2.4 miles from the initial trailhead, begin a short trail that juts over to **Lower Rowe Lake**.

The main trail makes its way through forested terrain until, at 4.9km/3 miles, you reach **Rowe Meadow**. It's a vibrant expanse, cut through by a stream and colored with wildflowers; it provides a dramatic look up at Lineham and Rowe Mountains. Those who have retained energy can carry on for a climb to the alpine **Upper Rowe Lake**. At 5.1km/3.2 miles, the trail junctions with the Tamarack Trail (p242), which leads to Lineham ridge. When ready, head back the way you came.

CRANDELL LAKE TRAIL
**Distance: 4km/2.4 miles roundtrip from Red Rock Pkwy,
2.4km/1.4 miles from Akamina Pkwy
Duration: 1.5 hours from Red Rock Pkwy, 1 hour from Akamina Pkwy
Challenge: Easy-Moderate
Elevation Change: 100m/328ft gain**

To reach the Crandell Lake, choose from one of two access points. Those staying at Crandell Mountain Campground can begin the trail directly from the campground. Day-trippers arriving from Red Rock Parkway should park in the lot on Canyon Church Camp Rd and walk over the pedestrian bridge to the trailhead. On Akamina Parkway, the trailhead is visible 6.4km/4 miles from the road's junction with Hwy 5.

Both approaches to the lake are great for families and anybody wanting a relatively easy scenic walk: the ascents are gentle. The clear lake, with Mt Crandell visible to its southeast, is a serene setting with sandy areas and rocks perfect for a picnic perch. Retrace your steps to get back to the trailhead from where you began.

AVION RIDGE LOOP
**Distance: 22.5km/14 miles
Duration: 8.5 hours
Challenge: Moderate-Difficult
Elevation Change: 981m/3218ft gain**

For spectacular views of the peaks of Waterton and southern British Columbia, try this unusual route traversing Avion Ridge. This is one of the best, and most remote, high-elevation hikes in the park. The signposted trail is generally easy to follow, but it is only partly maintained and is not fully marked on most maps. The ridge may be partly covered by snow until late June. It is also very exposed, so avoid windy conditions and plan to be off the ridge early if afternoon thunderstorms may occur. The hike begins and ends at Red Rock Canyon parking area, 14.5km/9 miles from Waterton Townsite, at the end of Red Rock Parkway.

From the trailhead, cross the bridge over Red Rock Creek and head along forested Bauerman Creek. Pass the Goat Lake Trail junction after 3.9km/2.4 miles and continue west to **Snowshoe Campground**. The Avion Ridge Trail makes an abrupt right turn here onto a smaller path. Climb through forest, and stay right at a signed junction where the trail to Lost Lake veers to the left. The ascent gradually steepens until a point just before the saddle of Castle River divide. The Avion Ridge is signed to the right from the main trail; continue the climb up the shoulder. As the trees begin to shrink, you'll view Lost Lake and the peaks of northwest Waterton.

The trail levels out a while, crosses a saddle in a clearing and then passes the first marker indicating Waterton's north boundary. The trail more or less follows this boundary for the next 3.2km/2 miles. Ascend through pine forest before the trail reemerges from the trees for the last time. The climb is more gradual now, and the trail picks its way along the southern

INTERNATIONAL PEACE PARK HIKE

The International Peace Park hike, led by interpretive rangers from Glacier and Waterton, departs from the Bertha Lake trailhead, just south of Cameron Falls, at 10am every Saturday from the end of June to the end of August. On the 13.7km/8.5-mile trip to Goat Haunt, attendees will be asked to consider the cross-border cooperation between two countries that makes preservation of Glacier and Waterton parks possible. It's an easy stroll and one potentially packed with education. Beware, crowd-o-phobes, the number of attendees is rarely ever less than 30 – it has been known to bring in 100 hikers in one go! Consider it an opportunity to make new friends.

The hike is relatively easy, with gradual ascents. Though most of it (along the Waterton Lakeshore Trail) is through shady forest, you will get fine views of Upper Waterton Lake and mountains beyond. The guided hike ends at Goat Haunt, USA, where you'll check in with the customs ranger before boarding a boat (CAD$15) back to Waterton's marina.

side of scree slopes, heading toward the main summit. This peak is bypassed to the south, with the trail passing around scree slopes to avoid the steep cliffs to the north. The path returns to the airy ridge just east of the peak and – voila – more magnificent views. A sheer drop falls away to the Castle River valley to the north.

Make a short, steep descent along the ridge to a saddle. Don't drop into the cirque below, as there is no safe descent. Instead, cross the saddle and begin to contour around the western slopes of the scree-covered mountain ahead. Follow the sometimes narrow trail to the next saddle and, from this point, Goat Lake is clearly visible in the cirque to the southeast.

Backcountry Hikes

Waterton does not offer a vast number of backcountry camping options. Still, an overnighter is possible and will really add to your park experience. Permits (p234) are mandatory to stay in one of the park's nine backcountry campgrounds. The nicest, and more popular, options include **Alderson Lake**, **Lone Lake** and **Bertha Lake**. All backcountry campgrounds have bear poles and pit toilets.

A spectacular backcountry trip traverses the 31.6km/19.6-mile, moderately difficult **Tamarack Trail**, which visitors generally take two days to do, camping at Lone Lake, Upper Twin Lake or Snowshoe. Choose between two starting points: the Rowe Lakes Trail off Cameron Lake Rd for a clockwise loop or the Lone Lake Trail from Red Rock Canyon to head counterclockwise. From the Rowe Lakes Trail, the trail junctions with the main Tamarack Trail at 5.1km/3.2 miles before ascending Lineham ridge. This ridge, offering breathtaking panoramic views, is a true highlight of this trip. Tricky descents over scree, extreme winds at high altitude and long stretches without treatable water sources are potential difficulties that must be considered before heading out. The recompense is immersion among the scenic beauty of northwestern Waterton, with views sweeping over the mountainous grandeur of Waterton and Akamina-Kishinena Provincial Park. Glacial moraines and wildflowered meadows, lakes and larch, and perhaps even an animal or two are viewed along the way.

Because of snow at higher elevations, the whole of this trail is often not open until early July. Check with the visitors center for trail status. Early autumn is a nice time to make the journey, particularly to see the namesake tamarack tree, an alpine larch, at its most colorful. A reservation-only shuttle (p234) is available.

Other Activities

Waterton offers those who are about to undergo a 'hazardous activity' the opportunity to preregister at the visitors center.

Four trails in the park are open for **cycling**: the **Akamina Pass Trail** (1.3km/0.8 mile one way), the **Snowshoe Trail** (16.4km/26.4 miles roundtrip), **Crandell Loop Trail** (20.6km/12.8 miles roundtrip) and **Wishbone Trail** (21km/33.8 miles roundtrip).

Cyclists on park trails should adhere to a few basics. Ride single file when in groups to prevent trail damage or erosion; alert hikers ahead of you if you want to pass, and then pass slowly; and when encountering a horse, get off your bike and stand aside until it passes. Always stay on the trail, and be careful not to surprise wildlife.

Mountain bikes can be rented at **Pat's** (☎ 403-859-2266; 224 Mount View Rd) for hour/day CAD$4-6/30. Helmets are included.

Visitors interested in **horseback riding** can giddyup down the trail with the help of **Alpine Stables** (☎ 403-859-2462, off Hwy 5), across the road from the golf course. It has handsome horses suited for all levels, from never-ridden-before to advanced. Reserve at least a day ahead, and ride for an hour up to all day.

Fishing is popular in Waterton National Park. Waterton's waters are swimming with 24 species of fish, including Northern pike; whitefish; and cutthroat, rainbow, bull and lake trout. See the Fishing & Boating (p234) for regulations. A favorite hike-in destination for anglers is **Bertha Lake**, for setting, serenity and rainbow trout.

Rent boats for **kayaking**, **canoeing** or **rowing** (from CAD$20 for first hour; open 7:30am to 7pm) at the exquisite Cameron Lake.

Because its sedimentary rock is soft and crumbly, Waterton is not hugely popular for **rock climbing**, but the upper and lower bands of **Bear's Hump** offer ten approaches ranging from grades 5.4 to 5.8.

Scuba diving is possible in the frigid waters of Waterton. The most popular spot to get down under is Upper Waterton Lake's Emerald Bay, where a paddle wheeler named *Gertrude* sits 20m/66ft below. The closest place to rent equipment or get air fills is **Awesome Adventures** (☎ 403-328-5040; www.awesomeadventure.com; 314 11th St S), in Lethbridge.

Sterling scenery is part of the game at **Waterton Lakes Golf Course** (☎ 403-859-2074); call for prices and hours.

In the winter, Akamina Parkway is the most popular access point for **cross-country skiing**, and the Cameron Lake area is a favorite for **snowshoeing**. Waterton is also known for its range of **ice climbing**.

Places to Stay

If you want to stay in the park between late June and August, booking early is key. Accommodations at this time usually get booked completely, both on weekdays and weekends.

CAMPING

The park holds three vehicle-accessible campgrounds. At the time of writing, none accepted reservations, though plans to eventually establish a system were in the works. Since sites are first-come, first-served, strive to seek out a site as early as possible in the day.

Open fires are permitted at Crandell and Belly River Campgrounds but not at the townsite campground. Crandell has a cluster of sites without fire pits available, for visitors who prefer a smoke-free environment.

Inside the Park

In high season, Waterton Townsite Campground can fill by late morning. If staying at Crandell Mountain or Belly River Campgrounds, you can use the showers at Waterton Townsite Campground free of charge.

Waterton Townsite Campground (*Map 14; on Hwy 5 at the southern end of town; site CAD$19-30; open mid-May–mid-Oct*) The park's largest campground has full facilities on grassy grounds. Though largely unshaded, it is near the waterfront and the townsite center. Due to gusty winds, RVs are usually placed near the lake, and tents get more shelter near the creek.

Crandell Mountain Campground (*Red Rock Pkwy; site CAD$17; open mid-May–Sep*) Much of this tranquil campground is wooded with lodgepole pines, but many people prefer loops K and L, which are filled with aspen and low-lying vegetation. Fortunately mosquitoes are not too rampant here.

Belly River Campground (*Chief Mountain Hwy; site CAD$13; open mid-May–early Sep*) Outside of the pay area of the park, this primitive campground sits in placid parkland terrain with aspen trees and far-off views of the mountains.

Outside the Park

A few campgrounds not far from the park entrance are good values.

Waterton Springs Campground (☎ *403-859-2247, fax 403-859-2249; Hwy 6; camp/RV site CAD$17/19-24*) Little ones have lots of room to roam in this campground 3km/1.9 miles north of the park. While RVs are out in the open, tent sites are much more secluded in a shady treed area. It has a few fishing ponds.

Waterton River Campground (☎ *403-653-2888; Hwy 5; camp/RV site CAD$16/20*) Pleasant sites dot this relaxed campground with 60-plus sites. There is no running water or dump station, nor are reservations accepted. Its rocky entry road is 4km/2.5 miles away from the junction with Hwy 6.

Crooked Creek Campground (☎ *403-653-1100; Hwy 5; camp/RV site CAD$11/15-18*) Waterton Natural History Association owns this open, unshaded campground with 46 sites; it's 5.6km/3.5 miles from the park. Tenters should request a site next to the creek as opposed to the highway side. There are no showers.

LODGING

MAP 14

All of the lodging in the townsite is no further than an easy stroll to amenities. The last (and priciest) three offer wheelchair-friendly rooms.

HI-Waterton (☎ *403-859-2151, 888 985-6343,* **c** *info@watertonlakeslodge.com; Cameron Falls Dr at Windflower Ave; member/nonmember dorm CAD$31/35, room CAD$93/105; open mid-May–Nov)* This spotless hostel is just about the only budget accommodations in Waterton and thus is busy with travelers staying in small but comfy co-ed dorms and private rooms (based on triple occupancy). It has a well-equipped kitchen, lounge and laundry. Hostelers get a discount at the attached recreation center.

Aspen Village Inn (☎ *403-859-2255;* **w** *www.aspenvillageinn.com; Windflower Ave; room from CAD$98, cottage from CAD$102; open May-Oct)* This is a great pick for families, with good-value rooms, barbecue grills, a small playground and a hot tub. A couple of rooms on the ground floor are wheelchair-accessible.

Northland Lodge (☎ *403-859-2353;* **w** *www.northlandlodgecanada.com; 408 Evergreen Ave; room CAD$100-170; open mid-May mid-Oct)* Just a half mile from Main St and within hearing distance of Cameron Falls, this lodge has nine pretty rooms, a kitchen and outdoor grill. Continental breakfast is included.

Kilmorey Lodge (☎ *403-859-2334;* **w** *www.kilmoreylodge.com; 117 Evergreen Ave; room CAD$108-213, off-season CAD$93-185; open year-round)* The historic lakefront Kilmorey, dating from the late 1920s, has an upscale-rustic ambience and 23 snug, charming rooms with neither TV nor phone. Two suites are wheelchair-friendly.

Bayshore Inn (☎ *403-859-2211, 888-527-9555;* **w** *www.bayshoreinn.com; 111 Main St; high/low season from CAD$140/100; open Apr–mid-Oct)* The Bayshore's nicest asset is its prime lakefront location. All rooms are spacious and comfortable, with balcony. Some ground-floor rooms offer immediate lake access.

Waterton Glacier Suites (☎ *403-859-2004, 866-621-3330;* **w** *www.watertonsuites .com; Windflower Ave; high/low season CAD$170-260/125-175; open year-round)* This polished place knows how to make its guests happy. It offers spacious, sparkling rooms, all with porch or balcony, air-conditioning, microwave, fridge and at least one fireplace.

Waterton Lakes Lodge (☎ *403-859-2150, 888 985 6343;* **w** *www.watertonlakes lodge.com; 101 Clematis Ave; summer/winter from CAD$195/100; open mid-May–late Oct)* This serene place offers a variety of tastefully decorated, well-equipped rooms. Guests get free entry to the pool/health club/recreation center.

Prince of Wales Hotel (*in season* ☎ *403-859-2231, other times* ☎ *406-756-2444;* **w** *www.princeofwaleswaterton.com; Prince of Wales Rd; from CAD$260; open mid-May–Sep)* This national historic site perches on a rise overlooking the lake. Though photogenic from afar (we're talking cover-model material), up close, the hotel looks less grand. But the views alone are worth raving about. The 5th- and 6th-floor rooms are considered the most haunted.

Places to Eat

MAP 14

Waterton offers a diversity of good restaurant options; most are open May to early October.

Rocky Mountain Food Mart (☎ *403-859-2526; 307 Windflower Ave; hours vary*) For food to rattle in your camping tins, stop by this small year-round grocery store next to the cinema. It stocks a good range of packaged goods, frozen foods, teas, fresh deli meats and more.

Zum's Eatery (☎ *403-859-2388; 116B Main St; breakfast & lunch CAD$6-10, dinner mains CAD$13-17; open 8am-9pm*) The people like Zum's for its good homestyle food and cheerful atmosphere. The selection of grub includes lots of meat, some fish and a few veggie items from the US and Canadian Plains.

The Lamp Post (☎ *403-859-2334; 117 Evergreen Ave; breakfast & lunch CAD$6-12, dinner mains CAD$18-30; open 7:30am-10pm year-round*) Exuding rustic elegance and charm, this restaurant has a menu that leads one to indecisiveness. Alberta beef or something lighter? Fresh seafood or rich pasta? The desserts are scrumptious, the service excellent.

Pizza of Waterton (☎ *403-859-2660; 103 Fountain Ave; dishes CAD$7-12, pizza CAD$12-20; open noon-10pm*) This inviting eatery has a cozy interior and relaxing outdoor patio. The handcrafted pizza is, unsurprisingly, the star, but salads, sandwiches and wraps are on offer, too.

Big Scoop Ice Cream (☎ *403-859-2346; Main St; items CAD$3-5; open 10am-10pm*) Children with chocolate mustaches may be sighted as you near this very popular stop. The smell of waffle cones will pull you in to this tempter offering sundaes, milkshakes and 32 hand-dipped ice cream flavors.

Entertainment

MAP 14

Waterton Townsite doesn't exactly bustle with nightlife. Seasonal workers and visitors down a few at **Thirsty Bear Saloon** (☎ *403-859-2211; Main St; open 7pm-2am*). Its large space is busy after 10pm, with people playing pool or even wiggling to DJ-driven music.

See recent mainstream movies at the small, historic **Waterton Lakes Opera House Cinema** (☎ *403-859-2466; cnr Cameron Falls Dr & Windflower Ave*).

EQUIPMENT & SUPPLIES

Pat's (☎ 403-859-2266; 224 Mount View Rd) sells camping and fishing gear, outdoors clothing and other equipment. It also rents out bikes, scooters, tennis racquets, binoculars and more. Waterton Outdoor Adventures in Tamarack Village Square (☎ 403-859-2378; Mount View Rd; open 8am 8pm) is a one-stop shop for a range of camping supplies.

MEDICAL SERVICE & EMERGENCIES

The summer-only number for ambulance service and other medical emergencies in Waterton is ☎ 403-859-2636. Full medical help is available at **Cardston Municipal Hospital** (☎ 403-653-4411; 144 2nd St W) and **Pincher Creek Municipal Hospital** (☎ 403-627-1234).

For fire emergencies, call ☎ 403-859-2113. Waterton's **Royal Canadian Mounted Police office** (☎ 403-859-2244) is open May to October. Otherwise, contact the **park warden** (☎ 403-859-2224; Cameron Falls Dr & Main St).

MONEY

Change US and Canadian cash and travelers checks at **Waterton Visitor Services** (☎ 403-859-2378; Tamarack Village Square, Mount View Rd; open 8am-8pm). ATMs are in the Prince of Wales Hotel, Rocky Mountain Food Mart and a few other locations in the townsite.

Most places accept travelers checks and credit cards, though you'll receive change in Canadian currency (loonies and toonies are more fun, anyway). The closest banks are in Cardston and Pincher Creek.

POST & COMMUNICATIONS

The **post office** (☎ 403-859-2294; 102A Windflower Ave) is open weekdays.

Check in with the web at **Borderline Books & Coffee** (☎ 403-859-2284; 305 Windflower Ave), which charges CAD$0.25 per minute; the same rate goes at **Peace Park Pita** (☎ 403-859-2259; Windflower Ave & Cameron Falls Dr).

Pay phones are along Main St and in all hotel lobbies. Local calls are CAD$0.35.

SHOWERS & LAUNDRY

The Waterton Health Club & Recreation Centre has public showers (CAD$3) and laundry; you can use the whole facility (pool, spa, sauna and gym) for CAD$6 per day.

TRASH & RECYCLING

Waterton gets an A+ for its recycling efforts. Park brochures can be deposited in boxes in the townsite and visitors center for reuse. Brown bear-proof trash bins are all over the townsite and campgrounds, as are blue recycling bins for glass, plastic and aluminum containers. Green bins for cardboard can be found in the townsite.

A green trailer in the Marina parking lot accepts all of the aforementioned recyclables, as well as office paper, tin cans, newspapers and magazines.

People first set foot upon the wilderness of the Rockies over 12,000 years ago.

HISTORY

Believed to have ventured over a frozen land bridge across the Bering Strait during the last ice age, these people roamed throughout the Americas. Those that eventually settled around the Rockies became known as the Blackfeet, Kootenay, Cree, Peigan and Stoney tribes. As nomadic tribes, they followed wildlife like bison, bighorn sheep and elk through the lush valleys of the region, and by the 1700s, the area was firmly established as their home and hunting grounds.

European traders and explorers began arriving in the mid-18th century. They depended upon the natives for survival skills and as guides; unfortunately, the relationship was not often mutually beneficial. Europeans also brought new diseases, alcohol, guns and cultural ideas that clashed with indigenous ways of life – such as the desire to conquer and claim the land. Eventually pushed off what became federally owned land, the region's first inhabitants' stories are largely left untold, lost in the fame of hot springs, the challenge of railways and the endeavors of mountaineers. Nevertheless, from today's roadways – which continue to follow indigenous hunting and trading routes – to inventions like the snowshoe, the impact of the First Nations in the Rockies continues to resound.

Banff National Park

Explorers began eyeing and then tramping through present-day Banff National Park in the early 1800s. As governor of the Hudson Bay Company, George Simpson traveled through the area in 1841 and sparked exploration throughout the Canadian Rockies. In 1857, the Palliser Expedition was sent out by the British government to determine resource and settlement potential for the West; James Hector led the party through the Banff area, naming many of the mountains he passed en route. While the expedition initially reported back that the land was unfavorable to settlement and utterly unsuitable for a railway, the government's later promise of a train link to British Columbia in exchange for the province joining the Confederation meant that the meticulous work of the Palliser Expedition would take on national importance.

In 1871, railway surveyors followed Stoney natives through the land in search of a pass to the West Coast. Kicking Horse Pass, just west of Banff in Yoho National Park, was eventually chosen. While it was by no means the easiest route for a train (in fact, it was the highest rail pass on the continent), it gave the Canadian Pacific Railway the opportunity to compete with American lines to the south. During their explorations, railway surveyors also took in some of Banff's spectacular sights, including Lake Louise, spotted by Tom Wilson in 1882.

News of the area's potential for exploration soon found its way into the thoughts of mountaineers and adventurers in Europe and throughout the USA; the allure of Banff had begun.

BANFF TIMELINE

10,000 BC– AD 1700	Natives settled and hunted throughout the Rockies.
1750	European explorers and traders arrive in the area.
1800s	Europeans begin exploring the area in search of a railway pass to the West Coast.
1885	The Trans-Canada Railway is completed, and a federal reserve is established around Cave & Basin Hot Springs.
1892	The reserve is enlarged to include Lake Louise as mountaineers begin scaling the area's peaks.
1911	A road from the east is opened to Banff, increasing the number of visitors.
1914–18	Prisoners of war are detained in camps within the park; their labor is used to improve park's infrastructure.
1930	National Parks Act is passed, establishing Banff's present-day boundaries.
1990	Banff town becomes self-governing, and Canadian Pacific Railway service is discontinued.
1996	Banff National Park Management Plan is implemented.

THE BIRTH OF A PARK

While Stoney natives had been soaking in the healing bubbly stuff for as long as anyone could remember, it wasn't until three railway workers stumbled upon the Cave & Basin Hot Springs at the foot of Sulphur Mountain that the establishment of Banff National Park was set in motion. The three hopeful entrepreneurs came up with a plan to develop the springs and attract wealthy patrons, but their application for a homestead lease was unsuccessful. Instead, the disgruntled men were bought out by the government, which, it soon became apparent, had similar plans for the area.

In 1885, as the last spike was driven into the transcontinental railway, a 26-sq-km/10-sq-mile federal reserve was established around Cave & Basin Hot Springs.

The next year, the head of the Canadian Pacific Railway (CPR) announced, 'If we can't bring the mountains to the people, then we'll bring the people to the mountains.' His name was William Van Horne, and his idea to build a luxurious, massive and astronomically expensive hotel at what was then little more than a railway camp seemed ludicrous to many. Van Horne named the would-be townsite Banff, after the Scottish county of Banffshire – the birthplace of two of the original CPR investors.

Van Horne saw the hotel, the hot springs and the reserve – which had expanded to 673 sq km/260 sq miles by 1887 – as a carrot for wealthy Victorians who would arrive in Banff as paying passengers on CPR trains. Little did he know how successful his plan would be. By 1888, over 5000 tourists had visited to be rejuvenated in the spring-water. Banff Town boasted 300 permanent residents, as well as churches, hotels, saloons and shops. The reserve was named Rocky Mountains Park and was the beginning of both Canada's national park system and its tourism industry.

The next year brought extreme forest fires; in an effort to build access routes to fight the blazes, bridle paths were cleared into remote areas of the park. The paths were also promoted to tourists, who would head off down these initial backcountry trails to camp for weeks at a time. In 1892, Rocky Mountains Park was expanded to include the area surrounding Lake Louise.

Over the next decade, the number of visitors to Banff continuously increased. Having run out of unclimbed peaks in Europe, mountaineers were crossing the Atlantic and hopping on a train for Banff, where they had their pick of virgin peaks to scale. Banff's first mountaineering death occurred in 1896, on Mt Lefroy near Lake Louise. In an effort to ensure this didn't affect tourism, CPR hired Swiss guides to lead novice climbers up the slopes (see Peak Experience, p93). They needn't have worried; the sense of danger simply heightened interest in the sport, and climbers continued pouring in.

At the turn of the century, the CPR expanded its attempts to bring in funds for the railway by opening coal mines near Lake Minnewanka, resulting in a mining community called Bankhead, home to 1000 people. The mined coal was not suitable for locomotives and had to compete with other mines in Alberta for domestic and industrial sales. This, coupled with employee strikes, caused the mine to close in 1922, and Bankhead quickly disappeared.

WELCOMING THE MASSES

A coach road was opened to Banff in 1911, and the following year, public traffic was allowed into the park. The park was suddenly accessible to visitors other than wealthy Victorians. Campsites were set up on Tunnel Mountain and at Two Jacks Lake. Affordable lodging began to appear, and the north side of the Bow River took on the look of a prairie town, while the ritzier folks continued to hold turf on the south side. Pursuits diversified; skiing, the arts and short-lived sports like ice boating all drew participants and spectators. A road was built to Norquay ski slopes, and Lake Louise soon began to welcome skiers as well. The year 1917 saw the initiation of the Banff Winter Carnival, a week of everything from dances to dogsled races that continues to be celebrated each year.

Throughout WWI, immigrants from enemy countries were detained in camps below Castle Mountain and near Cave & Basin Hot Springs. Forced to labor, they established much of the infrastructure throughout the park, including making horse trails car-friendly (see Silent Legacy, p76). Similar work was taken up in the 1930s by relief workers during the Depression, when the Icefields Parkway was first initiated. Relief workers also built gardens in Banff Town and an airfield for private planes.

The National Parks Act passed in 1930, establishing the boundaries of the park much as they are today, along with many of the conservation laws that are still in place. Rocky Mountains Park was renamed Banff National Park. While the number of tourists to the park diminished throughout WWII, Banff became a popular honeymoon destination throughout the 1940s and 1950s for returning veterans and their brides. By 1962, when the Trans-Canada Hwy officially opened, Banff was well established as an international holiday destination.

BALANCING ACT

Banff gained further global recognition as a summer and winter destination with the 1988 Winter Olympics, in nearby Calgary. Although events were actually held at Nakiska ski resort in Kananaskis Country and the Nordic Centre in neighboring Canmore, the Olympics drew tourists and publicity to the park. Banff Town's economy boomed, further strengthening the tourism infrastructure. In 1990, after over a century of being governed federally, Banff Town was granted the right to become a self-governing community. That year, the CPR train service that was at the root of the town's beginnings was discontinued, as trains carried on through Banff Town to the West Coast.

These days, more than eight million people pass through Banff annually. Many feel the wilderness is being compromised by the expansion of tourism, and that Banff Town's capacity has been stretched to its limits (see Under New Management, p71). Throughout history, native peoples, explorers, mountaineers and tourists have voyaged through much of Banff, yet today over 95% of the park still remains wild and undeveloped. With a balance between conservation and human access, it is hoped that the park's unique character can be preserved for future generations.

TINSEL TOWN

With the completion of the railway and the opening of the West, the CPR wasn't alone in hoping to make a penny or two off visitors and entrepreneurs drawn through the Rockies.

In 1883, a few (unnamed) enterprising individuals claimed that silver was struck in the shadow of Castle Mountain. While minute amounts were eventually found in the area, many believe that the purveyors of the claim went so far as to plant decoy deposits of silver ore in hopes of luring prospectors. The promoters' aim was to get rich – not off the silver that wasn't there but off the miners themselves. Almost overnight, a town of 3000 was established and christened Silver City, as miners with silver fever flooded in. The nearby town of Cache even changed its name to Golden in order to compete for prospectors and settlers.

The prospectors soon came to realize that they'd been swindled, and by 1885, only two years after the town's birth, there was but one resident left in Silver City. With the exception of a hotel that was floated down the Bow River to Banff Town, Silver City was completely dismantled. All that remains today is a small monument to the prospectors' grand, if thwarted, ambition.

Jasper National Park

Natives traditionally used the land that is now Jasper National Park as seasonal hunting and gathering grounds. It wasn't until the 1800s, when fur traders began to push west across the continent and further dislocated indigenous groups, that some First Nations tribes began exploring the Athabasca Valley as new territory in which to reside more permanently.

Soon after, Howe Pass, in present-day Banff, was abandoned due to deteriorating relations with native peoples there. David Thompson set out to find a new route across the Rockies to the resource-rich West Coast. In 1806, Thompson was the first European to cross the Athabasca Pass, following the native people's pitching trails through the valley and establishing a transportation route favored for nearly 70 years by traders and trappers wanting to reach the Columbia Valley. Thompson established posts near present-day Jasper Town, and traders that ensued named many of the mountains and natural wonders that they passed en route.

In an effort to built good trade relations, the traders were encouraged to take native wives. In doing so, a distinct culture was formed, and the unique language of *Michif* arose. Many of the descendents of this mixed ancestry, called Métis, continued to farm in the Athabasca Valley for nearly a century, greatly influencing the area's development. In 1910, the Métis were given compensation payments and forced to leave their land, which by then had become federal reserve.

ADVENTURERS AND MOUNTAINEERS

In the mid-18th century, around 200 pioneers set out from Ontario with their sights on the gold rush in British Columbia. The Overlanders, as they would come to be known, passed through Jasper and struggled over Yellowhead Pass, the park's present-day boundary with Mt Robson Provincial Park. The two-month journey turned into six months of near starvation. Poorly equipped and inexperienced, a number of men died en route, either swept away by turbulent rivers or from hypothermia. The only

JASPER TIMELINE

10,000 BC–AD 1700	Natives settled and hunted throughout the Rockies.
1750	European explorers and traders arrive in the area.
1800s	Dislocated native tribes begin to settle in their hunting grounds along the Athabasca Valley
1806	David Thompson is the first European to cross the Athabasca Pass and establishes a post near present-day Jasper Town.
1850s	Adventurers and mountaineers explore region.
1907	Jasper Forest Park is established.
1911	Grand Trunk Pacific's railway reaches Jasper Town.
1928	Road to Edmonton opens.
1930	National Parks Act passed, establishing Jasper's present-day boundaries.
1940	Icefields Parkway opens.
1950s	Jasper is well established as a tourist destination.

JASPER GOES TO HOLLYWOOD

With its fantastic alpine backdrop, Jasper first made it onto the big screen in *Under Suspicion*, an early talkie filmed in 1931. Bing Crosby brought the park into the limelight again in 1948 with *Emperor Waltz*, and in 1953, James Stewart costarred with Mt Edith Cavell in *The Far Country* and Howard Keel lounged by Lac Beauvert in *Rose Marie*. More recently, Christopher Reeve passed Athabasca Glacier faster than a speeding bullet in *Superman II* (1980).

By far the film best loved by residents of Jasper Town, *River of No Return*, brought Marilyn Monroe and Robert Mitchum to the small community in 1953. The script is based around a treacherous journey down a raging river, and much of the footage was filmed at Maligne Canyon. The stars were required to perform their own stunts, meaning some dodgy trips over rapids on a makeshift raft. On more than one occasion, Monroe and Mitchum had to be rescued from the icy waters. Monroe also took a tumble over the Bow Falls in Banff Town, making her one of few to survive going over the falls.

woman to accompany the group managed to survive, giving birth upon reaching Kamloops.

Around this time, as the fur trade fell steadily into decline, explorers, mountaineers and adventurers began heading into Jasper's rugged wilderness in search of unnamed peaks and fabled glacial lakes. In 1927, botanist David Douglas made his way through the area and, upon reaching Athabasca Pass, named Mt Brown and Mt Hooker. He mistakenly attributed the mountains' heights at nearly 5200m/17,000ft; while this would make them the highest peaks between Alaska and Mexico, his calculations were overestimated by around 2500m/7216ft. The error was perpetuated by atlases, igniting a flame of interest in mountaineers. For around 70 years, climbers sought out these mythical peaks and instead found Columbia Icefield, Miette Hot Springs and Maligne Canyon. Mary Schaffer, a widow from Philadelphia, was perhaps the most famous mountaineer to explore the area. In 1908, Mary was the first nonnative to reach Maligne Lake, guided only by a map sketched from memory by a Stoney native.

THE EMERGENCE OF A PARK

The dawning of the new century also brought a proposal by the Grand Trunk Pacific Company for a railway line from the West Coast through Yellowhead Pass. The pass had originally been considered for the main CPR route but abandoned for Kicking Horse Pass in Banff. The Grand Trunk's proposal was granted, prompting the government to establish Jasper Forest Park in 1907. Construction of the railway reached the site of Jasper Town in 1911, bringing an immediate influx of adventurers, mountaineers and railway workers. The tiny town of Jasper jumped from a population of 125 to around 800. Seeing the potential for business, a number of outfitters from the Banff area also began packing their bags for Jasper. Plans for an enlarged town were laid out, a school was built, and clearing began for roads and climbing trails. The first grocery store opened in 1914, meaning that residents no longer had to wait for a month's supply by train from Edmonton. The following year, 10 crudely constructed tents were set up for visitors on the shores of Lac Beauvert; eventually this would become Jasper Park Lodge.

In 1910, a coal mine was established at Pocahontas, near the eastern boundary of the park. A small mining town grew around it but was short-lived. The coal that was mined from the area burned at a high heat and was virtually smokeless, useful for warships during WWI. Following a major employee strike in 1919 and competition with larger operations east, the mine was shut down and the town dismantled by 1921.

SHARING THE LIMELIGHT

The road from Jasper to Edmonton was opened in 1928, and by the end of the next decade, the Icefields Parkway linked Jasper to Banff. In 1930, the National Parks Act was passed, fully protecting Jasper as the largest park in the nation. Tourists began visiting Jasper as an alternative to Banff, and famous guests, such as King George VI, put the park on the international map. By 1948, Athabasca Glacier had become a major sight, with ski-equipped Model A Ford trucks carting tourists out over the ice.

Since the 1950s, Jasper's tourism infrastructure has been gradually strengthened. Major highways into the park have been paved, and roads to sights like Maligne Lake and Miette Hot Springs were cleared or upgraded. In recent years, Jasper Town has grown by leaps and bounds – not so much in size as in services and facilities. Tourism has steadily increased in the park, with more than two million visitors now arriving annually. Nevertheless, the park continues to remain a rugged and remote alternative destination to its southerly neighbor.

Glacier National Park

At the time of European contact, many different Native American groups occupied the Rocky Mountains region. In the mid-18th century, when trappers and explorers began to arrive, the Blackfeet controlled the northern plains and the western

GLACIER TIMELINE

10,000 BC–AD 1700	Natives settled and hunted throughout the Rockies.
1750	European explorers and traders arrive in the area.
1896	The Blackfeet reluctantly accept the US government's offer to purchase what is now known as Glacier National Park, for USD$1.5 million.
1910	US President Taft signs a bill creating Glacier National Park.
1912	Great Northern Railroad begins building grand hotels and chalets within Glacier National Park (and later, Waterton Lakes) to promote its railway line.
1932	Canada and the USA declare Glacier and Waterton Lakes an International Peace Park – the world's first.
1932	The scenic Going-to-the-Sun Rd in Glacier National Park is completed, connecting the east and west sides of the park.
1995	Glacier and Waterton Lakes National Parks are designated a UNESCO World Heritage Site.
1997	Going-to-the-Sun Rd is designated a national historic landmark.
2003	Larger-than-normal fires tear through Glacier National Park, resulting in over 40,469 hectares/100,000 acres of burned forests, many closures and a drop in tourism.

mountain passes along the Front Range. The Blackfeet resisted the European invaders to their territory in the upper Missouri, Milk and Marias Rivers and the Judith Basin. Their population peaked at about 30,000 before the smallpox epidemic of 1837. The Blackfeet knew Glacier as the 'Backbone of the World.' Within the area of the park, many sites were considered sacred to the people.

James Willard Shultz lived for months at a time among the Blackfeet people, whom he considered his relatives and closest friends, and was among the nonnative men who first laid eyes on much of Glacier's interior. He introduced the area to Dr George Bird Grinnell, editor of the popular *Forest & Stream* magazine, and together with their Blackfeet friends, they explored the area and named many of its mountains, rivers and lakes. Grinnell dubbed the area the 'Crown of the Continent' and lobbied Congress for 10 years until, in 1910, President Taft signed the bill creating Glacier National Park.

Bird-rattler, Blackfeet Nation, at dedication of Going-to-the-Sun Rd, 1933

But the historical handover of the parklands from the Blackfeet to the US government was preceded by a series of injustices. Not long after a treaty was drawn in 1855 between the Blackfeet and the USA, the government showed a lack of follow-through regarding promised payments and other services, such as protection, aid and education. Furthermore, the government found ways to decrease the reservation extents. When supplies of bison – so central to the survival of the Blackfeet people – disappeared in the winters of 1883 and 1884 from overhunting for hide and food, starvation hit, as well as a need for federal funds. Not much had improved for the reservation by 1896, when the Blackfeet relented to the government's push to purchase Glacier for USD$1.5 million.

After Glacier National Park was dedicated and (soon after) Waterton Lakes Dominion Park was created, Canada and the USA, along with Rotary International, declared the two parks an International Peace Park. Its purpose was to signify harmonious relations between the two countries. Preserving the parks' unique biological corridor was a backseat issue at that point.

When Major William R Logan, the park's first superintendent took office in 1910, he was thrown into the hot seat, so to speak: Over 20,234 hectares/50,000 acres of park forest were burning in a summer of raging fires. Glacier's history with fire goes back thousands of years. Native people were thought to have set blazes purposely, having recognized the significance of fire in managing forest and wildlife habitat.

Visitors began coming regularly to the park around 1912, when the Great Northern Railroad's James J Hill instigated an intense building phase to promote his Empire Builder line. Railway employees built grand hotels and a network of tent camps and mountain chalets, each a day's horseback ride from the next. Visitors would come for several weeks at a time, touring by horse or foot, and stay in these elegant but rustic and rather isolated accommodations.

The popularity of motorized transportation increased quickly, and in 1921 federal funds were appropriated to connect the east and west sides of Glacier National Park by building Going-to-the-Sun Rd. It took until 1932 to complete the project.

WWII forced the closure of almost all hotel services in the park, and many buildings fell into disrepair and were eventually demolished. The grand old lodges still standing – Glacier Park Lodge, Lake McDonald Lodge, Sperry Chalet, Granite Park Chalet and, in Canada, the Prince of Wales Hotel – were updated and are used for accommodations today.

Over the years, the 80km/50-mile scenic Going-to-the-Sun Rd has been the primary travel artery in the park, and, for many, the park's highlight. It has been continually repaired, improved and expanded. In 1997, it was designated a national historic landmark. Park access via roads like Going-to-the-Sun has provided education to millions of visitors throughout the years, fostering an appreciation and awareness of the natural world. However, retaining and supporting the stunning wilderness has become an increasingly larger challenge with the encroaching influences of a surrounding civilization that has become evermore modern. Encouraging the public to ditch their cars for the services of a touring bus like the 'jammers' (which are partially run on biofuel) is a move in the right direction.

Fire management has always be a source of concern, and sometimes disagreement, among park officials. On average, about 2023 hectares/5,000 acres burn within the park each year. In the summer of 2003, lightning-started fires blazed over large areas – 55,240 hectares/136,500 acres – in the park, burning a large hole in the area's tourist-dependent economy. At time of writing, tourism officials were running a full-force effort to let the public know that Glacier National Park was, in fact, still gloriously standing.

Waterton Lakes National Park

The Kootenay and Blackfeet people have roots in this part of Southern Alberta, and their ancestors are thought to have shifted location by season. Bison, which native people followed to the eastern prairies, were central to the tribes' survival for thousands of years. Hunters used animals' meat, hide, bone, horns and nearly everything else for their supplies and materials. South Kootenay Pass was crossed by Kootenay people headed to the area around Chief Mountain to hunt bison. Blackfeet people stampeded bison over cliffs like the famous Head-Smashed-In Buffalo Jump, about 18km/11 miles northwest of Fort Macleod, which is now a UNESCO World Heritage Site. The site was last used for hunting bison in the early 19th century.

Horses brought to the region in the early 1700s provided efficiency in hunting, but also warring between tribes. The Blackfeet were introduced to rifles, which they used to expand their territory, eventually edging out the Kootenay. Over the next century and a half, European-born diseases inflicted many deaths among the tribes. The bison were also decreasing in number, and would soon dwindle to zero.

Englishman Peter Fidler of the Hudson Bay Company is thought to be the first European to have explored this southern portion of the Canadian Rockies; he set out in 1792. Explorer Thomas Blakiston came upon Waterton Lakes in 1858, naming them after famous British naturalist Charles Waterton.

WATERTON LAKES TIMELINE

10,000 BC– AD 1700	Natives settled and hunted throughout the Rockies.
1750	European explorers and traders arrive in the area.
1895	The Canadian government grants protective status to the land around Waterton Lakes, paving the way to national park status.
1902	Oil is struck, but only briefly, in Waterton's Cameron Valley.
1911	George 'Kootenai' Brown is appointed the first superintendent of Waterton Lakes National Park.
1979	Waterton Lakes National Park is designated a biosphere reserve.

The seed to designate the area a reserve was largely sown by Fredrick William Godsal, a rancher and conservationist in southern Alberta who had the prescience to see that if the beautiful lakes region was not soon set aside as protected land, private interests would soon take hold. In 1893, Godsal wrote a letter to William Pearce, the superintendent of mines, who had himself once advocated for preserving the region. Pearce urged government officials in Ottawa to consider the issue, and in 1895, what is now known as Waterton was given protective status by the Canadian federal government as a forest park.

Cameron Valley had a stint as 'Oil City' that began in 1902, when barrels of the liquid money poured out from Western Canada's first oil well there. After two years the flow was poor, and the well dripped her last drops in 1936. The Lineham Discovery Well was declared a national historic site in 1968; it can be visited along what is now called Akamina Parkway.

After Glacier National Park was officially dedicated, Canada expanded Kootenay Lake Park – what it was called in that incarnation – and boosted its status to create Waterton Lakes Dominion Park. Waterton's most famous figure is George 'Kootenai' Brown, who was appointed the first superintendent of Waterton in 1911. A jack of many trades throughout his colorful life, he became an early settler of the Waterton area and is now remembered at a gravesite off of Hwy 5, within the park.

Great Northern Railroad's James J Hill did not neglect Waterton when it came to fulfilling his plan of railway-linked recreation. After handpicking the spot where it would stand, overlooking Upper Waterton Lake, he ordered construction of the Prince of Wales Hotel. In 1927, while it was being built, 144kph/89 mph winds blew through, and the building was jolted off its base by 20cm/8 inches. Still, it survived, and opened on July 25, 1927.

Southern Alberta is cattle-ranching country, with a strong wheat presence, but, Waterton, with its small townsite, is completely driven by tourism. In 1979, the park received the designation of a biosphere reserve, and it, along with Glacier, became a UNESCO World Heritage Site in 1995. Now, with decreasing native fish populations and the increasing fragility of the ecosystem, the goal is to find a way to keep a park like Waterton enjoyable as well as sustainable.

Geologically speaking the Canadian Rockies are a fascinating place – a simple landscape of monotonously layered sediments nearly 32.2km/20 miles thick that have been fractured and crumpled in many complex ways.

GEOLOGY

It's a region of multiple mountain chains and rocks in all colors of the rainbow; and it's a region with countless fossils, including a site that is considered one of the most important fossil localities in the world. Everywhere you look there is evidence of 1.5 billion years of Earth history, including fossilized ripple marks from ancient beaches, and shadows of the earliest known forms of life. Most dramatically of all, the landscape displays in full view the awesome power of Ice Age glaciers and icefields.

With generations of geologists poring over every minute detail of this landscape, it comes as no surprise that there are several excellent books on the region's geology. *Geology Along Going-to-the-Sun Road, Glacier National Park, Montana,* by Omer Raup and other authors, is a self-guided tour for motorists. This book excels in giving visitors a stop-by-stop pictorial explanation of roadside geology. A broader explanation can be found in *How Old Is That Mountain? A Visitor's Guide to the Geology of Banff and Yoho National Parks,* by CJ Yorath, and a detailed examination of every rock formation in the region is included in Ben Gadd's *Handbook of the Canadian Rockies.*

Laying It All Down

In a sense the story of the rocks in the Canadian Rockies is a very simple and orderly sequence of events. Over many millions of years ancient seas gently laid down layers of sediment, followed by a long quiet spell, then a steady pushing that uplifted some mountains. But a full reading of this story is complex beyond the scope of this book, because the layers have been cracked and buckled in a dizzying variety of patterns. Every site in the Canadian Rockies has to be read with a fresh eye, because layers have been tilted sideways, vertically, horizontally and even reorganized so that older layers lay on top of younger layers. Depending on your point of view it's either a mess or a geologist's dream come true.

THE FIRST SUPERCONTINENT

Just about 1.5 billion years ago sediments began to be laid down in an inland sea within the supercontinent called Rodinia (a combination of landmasses that later broke apart into the continents we recognize today). Consisting of sands, silts and cobbles, these ancient sedimentary layers are now so deeply buried that they appear on the earth's surface in only a few places, one of which is Waterton and Glacier National Parks. On the west side of the parks, the oldest layer, the **Pritchard Formation**, preserves evidence of a deep sea that can be seen in thin layers of fine green rock along MacDonald Creek. On the east side of the parks, layers laid down in shallow margins of the same sea are called the **Altyn Formation**. Pale whitish Altyn rocks are visible around Geology Stops 2 and 3 (there are 21 signed Geology Stops along the Going-to-the-Sun Rd), where you can find crossbedding and ripple marks characteristic of shorelines. Altyn rocks also preserve fossil algae (actually cyanobacteria) that grew in cabbagelike colonies called stromatolites within shallow waters.

Next in this sequence of ancient layers is the **Appekunny Formation**, which appears as dark gray-green and purple rocks on the lower slopes of Waterton and Glacier These rocks are conspicuous along the north shore of St Mary Lake around Geology Stop 4. Appekunny rocks document a time when the weight of accumulated sediments pushed the earth's crust downward and deepened the water at the margins of the ancient sea. Over time new sediments filled this basin to recreate shallow tidal flats now preserved in the next layer, called the **Grinnell Formation**. Bright brick red, the Grinnell Formation is the easiest layer to recognize in the Waterton-Glacier region, and it is spectacularly exposed in Red Rock Canyon, in Waterton National Park.

Hard, erosion-resistant rocks of the **Empire and Helena Formations** form the bulk of the parks' peaks and cliffs. These rocks represent very shallow waters where algae precipitated out minerals to form limestone and dolomite. In the upper portions of the Helena Formation, super dense stromatolites occur in a 100ft-thick band that can be seen miles away.

WHOSE ROCKIES ARE THEY?

Most visitors will be readily familiar with the term 'Rocky Mountains' but may be confused by the separate label 'Canadian Rockies.' However, there's quite a bit of difference between the Rockies in Canada and those in the United States, and it has nothing to do with a border crossing. In fact, as a distinct geologic unit, the Canadian Rockies extend south of the international border to include peaks in Glacier National Park, and the American Rockies continue from Montana south to New Mexico. The difference lies in how the ranges were formed. In the Canadian Rockies, the forces of compression can be visualized as acting like a bulldozer scraping materials across a hard-packed road. By contrast, in the American Rockies, these forces buckled and fractured the underlying 'roadbed.' The Canadian Rockies show tilted and folded sedimentary layers (the surface materials), but the American Rockies are formed mostly of ancient continental rock (the 'basement' materials).

Other differences between the two ranges include the substantial amount of volcanism in the American Rockies (consider Yellowstone National Park), something that's quite rare in the Canadian Rockies. Conversely, extensive glaciers and icefields were largely absent in the American Rockies, while playing a significant role in shaping the Canadian Rockies.

Above the grayish-tan Helena Formation is an abrupt switch to the red and green **Snowslip Formation**, which is readily visible on the higher slopes both north and south of the Logan Pass Visitors Center. These easily eroded rocks were laid down on shoreline mudflats, and the few stromatolites present are a unique reddish color, as seen at Geology Stop 13.

THE BIG BREAKUP

About 750 million years ago, the supercontinent Rodinia began to break up along a giant rift, creating a new shoreline where North America split off from the future continents of Australia and Antarctica. As with the older inland sea, this coastal area on the west side of North America accumulated sediments being washed out into the water. Over several million years, layers of the **Miette Group** formed and became the oldest rocks visible in Banff and Jasper National Parks. But this was not necessarily an orderly laying down of sediments, because the new continental edge was raw, with bits of the continental plate fracturing off as the rift pulled apart. Earthquakes and underwater landslides were probably the norm, and consequently, many rocks in the Miette Group are very coarse gritstones and conglomerates of rough debris.

A significant transition occurred 570 million years ago, when the period of geologic history known as the Precambrian came to an end, about the time that the rift had widened into a wide ocean. The transition to the Cambrian period sparked an incredible proliferation of life known as the 'Cambrian explosion.' Many fossils of multicellular organisms remain from this period, including elegant trilobites. At this time, the Canadian Rockies region hovered near the equator, and the land was an arid desert (terrestrial plants and animals had not yet evolved). Fossils from the Cambrian explosion are remarkably well preserved at the world-famous Burgess Shale site in Yoho National Park.

Until 200 million years ago, there was a long period of relative stability as desert landmasses eroded and sedimentary layers accumulated along the continental coastline. Meanwhile, marine organisms developed remarkably complex forms, including early fishlike animals, and primitive plants had moved onto land. The long period from 570 to 200 million years ago is documented in dozens of sedimentary layers that comprise the bulk of the peaks in the Canadian Rockies, a record that shows seas advanced and retreated numerous times across the region.

Building It Back Up

This period of stability came to a close around 200 million years ago when the continental plate began a steady march westward, pushing against the part of the earth's crust that lies under the Pacific Ocean. Like a slow-motion collision, the leading edge of the continental plate buckled against the impact. At first, the buckled edge may have simply created folds in the earth's crust, but over time these folds became steeper and started to fracture under the stress. In addition, the crumpling extended eastward, reaching the region of the Canadian Rockies about 100 million years ago.

Geologists estimate that the westward edge of the North American continent was eventually compressed about 322km/200 miles. Since rocks can't absorb this much pressure, it all had to go somewhere – so the land fractured and layered up from west to east much like shingles on a roof. This process is called **thrust faulting**, and Mt Rundle, near the town of Banff, is a classic example of a mountain formed this way.

The main period of compression reached its peak 60 to 80 million years ago, then subsided slowly, by which time the basic form of the Canadian Rockies had been established. The wreckage that lay behind this massive compression included layers of deep old rock wedged up over the top of younger layers, layers folded up so tightly that they bent back on top of themselves and layers that shattered in long series of parallel cracks. The eastward edge of this zone of crumpling and fracturing can be clearly seen in the prominent McConnell Thrust, which rears up as one final cliff at the edge of the great prairies. Mt Yamnuska, just east of Canmore, is a dramatic portion of this feature.

Tearing It Down Again

For the past 60 million years, the forces in the Canadian Rockies have been those of erosion, not of deposition. Erosive forces have included chemical weathering, mineral dissolving, mechanical weathering, freezing, biological breakdown, running water and at least a dozen other impacts. Over time these will combine to break high peaks down into flat prairies, although the change is extremely gradual.

In the last two million years, however, one force has dramatically sculpted the Canadian Rockies like no other – the great glaciers and icefields of the Ice Age. No one knows exactly what caused the onset of the Ice Age, but when summers weren't warm enough to melt the previous winter's snow and ice, they accumulated into sheets of ice that, over several million years, grew to cover large portions of several continents. At a northern latitude, the Canadian Rockies were buried under so much ice that only the tips of major peaks poked out into the open sky. These giant sheets of ice produced unbelievable amounts of weight and pressure, and as tongues of ice crept across the landscape they tore apart rocks, carved mountains like soft butter and transformed narrow V-shaped ravines into broad open valleys. Trillions of tons of debris were left behind when the ice finally retreated 10,000 years ago, much of it forming distinctive ridges called **moraines** such as the one that The Chateau at Lake Louise is perched on.

Nearly every feature seen in the Canadian Rockies today is a legacy of the Ice Age. Peaks that were carved on multiple sides at once left behind sharp spires called **horns**, as can be seen at Mt Assiniboine. A few peaks, like Tunnel Mountain, were completely overrun by ice and are now rounded on the upstream side and abruptly steepened on the downhill side. Mountains that had glaciers cutting along two sides could end up as sharp ridges known as **arêtes**. Side streams flowing into valleys that were deepened by glaciers were often left hanging in midair, creating **hanging valleys** with the streams pouring out as waterfalls down sheer cliffs.

Glaciers Today

Even though the Ice Age ended 10,000 years ago and the great icefields retreated, the story of ice and glacier is not over in the Canadian Rockies. Along the spine of the Continental Divide, 16 smaller icefields remain as evidence of this great era. From these icefields, tongues of ice called **glaciers** still run down side valleys in multiple directions.

The largest icefield is the Columbia Icefield, and thanks to the Icefields Parkway, it is also the most accessible, but because this icefield sits higher up on the mountain slopes, most visitors are content with a quick stop at the toe of the great Athabasca Glacier that streams down from the high country. Here one can quickly get a sense of the scale and nature of glaciers.

Icefields and glaciers are created when winter snows remain through the summer and snowflakes become compacted into granular **firn**. Accumulating layers of firn squeeze

Before (inset) and after a glacier's retreat

out microscopic air pockets, compressing the snow into ice like that which builds up in your freezer. Due to its incredible weight, ice begins to flow down-hill and is then called a glacier. Generally, these tongues of ice try to conform to the shape of the underlying landscape, but many cracks, called **crevasses**, form on the glacier's surface. On the Athabasca Glacier, crevasses are known to reach 90ft deep and pose a great danger to unwary visitors; in fact anyone traveling more than a few feet onto a glacier is advised to use experienced guides.

While glaciers continue to flow downhill (as evidenced by the sounds of ice breaking over cliff edges), the warming of the climate over the past century has dramatically reduced the scale and length of glaciers in the Canadian Rockies. This is particular-ly evident in comparing old photographs with the view we see today. The tip of Athabasca Glacier has retreated upslope nearly a mile in the past 100 years, and continued warming could result in its disappearance.

Shape of the Land

The Canadian Rockies today are a composite of parallel ranges and valleys that reflect their long and varied history. At their highest elevations they form the Continental Divide, the spine of North America, from which waters flow west into the Pacific Ocean and east into the Atlantic. In fact the hydro-graphic apex of North America sits on a little peak called Snow Dome, locat-ed at the top of the Athabasca Glacier. From Snow Dome, waters divide and run into three oceans, the Pacific, Atlantic and Arctic. In terms of water, this is the epicenter of North America.

These parallel mountains can be divided into four groups: eastern foothills, front ranges, main ranges, and western ranges, all of which are like-ly to be encountered by visitors. The **foothills** lie on the east side of the parks and represent the eastern edge of the compression that formed the Rockies 60 million years ago. Most of this area consists of flat areas of deep rich soil that has been washed down from peaks to the west. Protruding from this are smaller ridges that are actually the tips of tilted layers lying underground.

Approaching from the east, visitors can't help but notice the towering wall of the **front ranges** rising 3000ft over the foothills. Uplifted along the McConnell Thrust, these higher rocks are 400 million years older than the younger foothills below. Formed of highly resistant limestones, these upthrust rocks haven't eroded as easily as the soft shales and sandstones of the foothills, further accentuating the height difference. Upended like shingles, the front ranges create a series of nearly identical parallel ridges stacked between the foothills and the main ranges. Mt Rundle and the peaks around Banff are included in the front ranges.

This symmetry has been lost in the **main ranges** due to the intense sculpting of Ice Age glaciers and icefields. Here giant peaks of the hardest rocks in the Rockies stand over broad, glacially carved valleys. Many of these peaks still have active glaciers or lakes tucked into bowls left behind by glaciers. Rock layers are mostly horizontal, which has helped these peaks resist erosion (layers tilted to one side are more easily eroded).

Western ranges consist of old rocks that are highly compressed and tilted at complex and crazy angles. These ranges are distinct because there is a switch from limestones of the main ranges to shales in the western ranges. Because this region largely escaped glaciation, valleys are not broad and open like in the main ranges but have maintained their ancient V-shaped profiles.

These four groups of ranges are just one aspect of what makes the Canadian Rockies such a diverse and interesting place. The region's complexly tilted layers of sediments and majestically sculpted landscape make even nongeologically inclined visitors wonder how to read the history of rocks, and there's no better classroom than the Rockies for learning this story.

MOUNTAIN TYPES

It may seem at first glance that there are an infinite variety of mountain shapes and types in the Canadian Rockies, but geologists divide them into a handful of easily recognized categories to help understand underlying forces in the landscape.

Thrust fault mountains are layers of sedimentary rock tilted about 45 degrees, with an inclined southeast-facing slope and a steep northeast-facing cliff. Typical of the front ranges, they show how layers of rock can be fractured and stacked like a dominoes; Mt Rundle is a classic example.

Dogtooth mountains, found in the front and main ranges, show layers of sedimentary rock that have been tilted vertically. The mountains then stand upright as weather-resistant spires after softer rocks have eroded away. Mt Edith and Mt Louis are good examples.

Sawtooth mountains are similar to thrust fault mountains but tilt nearly vertically, so they erode into rows of angular sawlike teeth. This is a common feature in the front ranges, but Sawtooth Range is perhaps the best example.

Castellated mountains arise from alternating layers of resistant rock (like limestone) and softer rock (like shale) that lie in horizontal bands. The harder rocks break off in blocks and form vertical steps as softer layers erode out from under them, forming towering castlelike shapes. Peaks like Castle Mountain and Mt Blakiston are trademark shapes of the Canadian Rockies.

Horn mountains form where glaciers grind mountains on multiple sides at once, leaving a single isolated tower in the center. Outstanding examples include Mt Assiniboine and Mt Chephren.

As the earth's crust buckles, it creates two distinct structures, upward-bending U-shaped folds called **anticline mountains** and downward-bending folds called **syncline mountains**. Anticline mountains are rare, but valleys commonly erode into the crests of these upward folds. In fact, most major valleys in the Canadian Rockies originate along the crests of anticlines. Conversely, synclines form the bases of many ranges, because the rocks become so compressed that surrounding rocks erode and leave the synclinal structure standing as a mountain range; Cirrus Mountain and Mt Kerkeslin are good examples.

Complex mountains combine anticlinal and synclinal features or attributes of other mountain types in such a manner that they defy categorization; Cascade Mountain, near Banff, is one of many examples.

The Rocky Mountains are one of the most important landscape features of North America; in fact, they form the backbone of the continent.

ECOSYSTEM

This region has unsurpassed scenic beauty, vast unspoiled wilderness and remarkable opportunities to observe large mammals. From massive glaciers and snowcapped peaks to turquoise-blue lakes and lush meadows, there's no better place to find wild places and wild animals.

Stretching south to Glacier National Park, the Canadian Rockies are geologically distinct from the American Rockies that continue south from Montana to New Mexico. This relatively cold, wet northern stretch consists mainly of montane forest, rock, ice and water. Glacier National Park, for instance, is about one-third water and one-third alpine (ie treeless) country. Luxuriant vegetation can be found in the broad, glacier-scoured valleys that also characterize the region. Because Jasper, Banff and Glacier National Parks are all in the Canadian Rockies and lie in close proximity to each other, their floras and faunas are nearly identical and are treated as a single ecological unit here.

These elevated slopes and peaks rise far above the surrounding plains and prairies, creating a wild corridor that stretches across the continent from northern Canada to Mexico. With adjacent lowlands taken over by roads, farms and cities, these mountains have become a final refuge for wolves, mountain lions, bears, elk, deer and many other charismatic mammals. While populations of these animals are only a fraction of their former numbers, they are still impressive enough to be one of the main reasons for visiting these national parks.

To learn more about this rich realm of plants, animals and habitats, there's no better guide than the astonishing *Handbook of the Canadian Rockies,* by Ben Gadd. A smaller and simpler handbook is the *Rocky Mountain Nature Guide,* by Andy Bezener and Linda Kershaw. For more extensive natural-history reading try the informative *Exploring Glacier National Park,* by David Rockwell, which is generally applicable to the whole region.

Life Zones

CH Merriam developed the concept of life zones in 1889 while exploring the Grand Canyon region and trying to describe the distinct bands of vegetation that differed between high mountain peaks and adjacent desert valleys. Although his life-zone system has been replaced by more sophisticated models as ecological knowledge has grown, the very concept profoundly shaped ecological thought for over 100 years and is used here in a modified form. Three distinct zones of life can be found in the Canadian Rockies, each with its own local environment and species. An understanding of these zones will help visitors locate and appreciate the region's plants and animals.

At the lowest elevations, a great variety of plants and animals find their homes in the **montane zone**, a band of cool, damp, mostly continuous forest. This zone occupies major valley bottoms and the sunny lower slopes of mountains. Despite its ecological significance, this zone covers only about 5% of the parks' total area, and much of that area has been significantly impacted by the construction of roads, buildings and towns, as well as the passage of millions of visitors each year.

The montane zone occurs below 1524m/5000ft and is characterized by forests of Douglas fir, white spruce, lodgepole pine and quaking aspen. Streams along river bottoms are lined with two types of cottonwoods. These valley bottoms are critical winter habitat for elk, deer, bighorn sheep and their predators – wolves, coyotes and mountain lions – as well as other mammals that are pushed downslope by deep winter snows.

By one definition, the **subalpine zone** extends from the highest-growing aspen to treeline, about 1524m/5000ft to 2286m/7500ft. This is also the zone where the greatest accumulations of snow occur, and accordingly, these 'snow forests' are damp, cold and mossy. At the upper limits, where summer temperatures are barely adequate for trees to replace winter-killed needles, trees of the subalpine zone become stunted and barely grow knee high. At lower elevations, trees such as subalpine fir and Engelmann spruce grow in tall, dense stands.

Subalpine habitats cover roughly 50% of the Canadian Rockies, making them a dominant feature of these parks. This is the zone of mountain goats, grizzly bears, golden eagles, broad-tailed hummingbirds and Clark's nutcrackers. During the summer, deer, elk, and moose are frequently in this zone, though they leave for lower elevations with the onset of winter.

The highest and most austere zone is the land above the trees, the **alpine zone**, where few plants and very few animals are hardy enough to survive the extreme cold and wind. Surprisingly, in many areas it's even too cold and windy for snow to accumulate. In this region of rock and ice, the main animals are pikas and marmots, although grizzly bears, elk, deer and bighorn sheep can be common in alpine meadows during the late-summer growing season. Numerous alpine plants have bright, dramatic flowers, making this a favorite destination for wildflower enthusiasts.

Douglas fir cone

Mountain lion

Life Through the Seasons

Conditions in January are about as difficult for animals as they could possibly get. Piercing cold along with rain creates thick sheets of ice that take a heavy toll on many of the parks' animals. With food already hard to come by, elk, deer, bighorn sheep and other hoofed animals congregate in valleys hoping to paw through thinner layers of snow in search of the previous year's withered grass stems. This is a month when many animals die either of starvation or predation by the wolves, coyotes and mountain lions that gather to feed on weakened prey.

Late winter provides something of a respite, when the famous warm Chinook winds arrive to take the edge off the chill and melt enough snow and ice that animals can more easily dig down for food. This is a good time for viewing woodland caribou in Jasper National Park. Throughout the region, ravens, jays and magpies begin courtship and nesting. Well fed from a steady supply of meat, coyotes and wolves make this their mating season as well.

Mule deer

Chinooks alternate with passing storms until April, when the first spell of springlike weather settles in, melting large areas of snow and bringing out the first green buds. Even a few hardy wildflowers, like pasqueflower and silverweed, make an appearance. Overwintering insects such as mourning-cloak butterflies start flying around, and frogs return to melting ponds and start singing.

Although cold weather may return briefly in May, this is perhaps the best wildlife month out of the whole year. It's the peak time for breeding amphibians; small mammals are coming out of hibernation in great numbers; songbirds are singing like crazy; and bears show up along roadsides in search of green plants. This is also the calving time for elk, caribou, mountain goats and bighorn sheep. With days mostly sunny and warm, plants do much of their growing in these weeks, many already putting out flowers.

Summer is characterized by rapid melting of snow at progressively higher and higher elevations. Dramatic wildflower displays quickly claim each newly exposed site, with peak diversity and color occurring in alpine meadows in late July. Large mammals also move into these mountain meadows.

By September there is an evident cooling trend, with temperatures starting to nudge below freezing. Seeds and berries reach their peak numbers and are quickly harvested by eager birds and mammals. Migratory birds head south, and southbound golden eagles appear in large numbers. This is the time when male elk fill the woods with their haunting bugling and the clashing of antlers between rivals.

Weather conditions take a serious turn for the worse at the end of October, prompting waterfowl to leave and bears to dig their hibernation dens. When elk, deer, moose and caribou finish mating, males drop their antlers and try to rebuild their energy. The depths of winter are a very hard time, and all the animals need to conserve their strength for the days ahead.

Animals Great & Small

Whether you come for a glimpse of grizzly bears, wolves or woodland caribou, the Canadian Rockies offer stupendous wildlife-viewing opportunities. This is one of the few regions in North America where you can be sure you'll see *something*

BEST WILDLIFE VIEWING

- ✔ **Going-to-the-Sun Rd** (Glacier National Park): The stupendous ascent over 2012m/6600ft Logan Pass provides easy access to the upper edges of the subalpine zone, offering views of mountain goats, ptarmigans and pikas.
- ✔ **Bow Valley Parkway** (Banff National Park): Many consider this the best wildlife viewing road in Canada. The parkway is the epicenter of wildlife viewing in the park and is the best place for any of the charismatic megafauna.
- ✔ **Cave and Basin Marsh** (Banff National Park): One of many excellent wildlife sites around the town of Banff; perhaps the premier bird-watching site in the Canadian Rockies.
- ✔ **Maligne Rd** (Jasper National Park): Hot spots for viewing bighorn sheep, harlequin ducks and trout are located along this road; this is one of the only sites to reliably find woodland caribou in winter.
- ✔ **Red Rock Parkway** (Waterton Lakes National Park): Visitors have opportunities to see moose, coyotes, bears and bighorn sheep along this winding, scenic road.

---

impressive every day, and many days you can see upwards of a half-dozen species of large mammals. So exciting are these wildlife-viewing opportunities that visitors frequently overlook the many fascinating birds, small mammals, fish and insects that also make their homes in the parks. Be sure to include these smaller animals in your itinerary as well.

Several excellent books, in addition to those mentioned above, are available. At the top of the list of must-have books for wildlife enthusiasts is *The Canadian Rockies Guide to Wildlife Watching,* by Michael Kerr, which includes lots of details on the best places to view wildlife in the Canadian parks. Two other books, *Birds of the Rocky Mountains,* by Chris Fisher, and *Mammals of the Rocky Mountains,* by Chris Fisher, Don Pattie and Tamara Hartson, can also be helpful.

LARGE MAMMALS

While the prospect of seeing 'charismatic megafauna' is one the region's biggest draws, the Canadian Rockies supports nearly 70 species of mammals, including eight species of ungulate (hoofed mammal). In the fall and winter, many large mammals move down into valleys for protection against the weather; high concentrations can be seen along the Icefields Parkway during these seasons.

Bears

Black bear

The **black bear** roams montane and subalpine forests throughout the Canadian Rockies in search of its favorite food: grasses, roots, berries and the occasional meal of carrion. Frequently, they can be seen along roadsides feeding on dandelions. While most black bears are black in color, they can also be light reddish brown (cinnamon). Black bears are somewhat smaller than grizzlies and have more tapered muzzles, larger ears and smaller claws. Small claws help them climb trees and avoid their main predator, grizzly bears, which are known to drag black bears out of their dens to kill them.

ECOSYSTEM

Although they are generally more tolerant of humans and less aggressive than grizzlies, black bears should always be treated as dangerous.

Grizzly bear

The endangered **grizzly bear** once roamed widely in North America, but most were killed by European settlers, who feared this mighty carnivore. Today a hundred or so may inhabit the parks covered in this book, but with males roaming 3885 sq km/1500 sq miles in their lifetimes, they aren't particularly easy to see or count. Male grizzlies reach up to 2.4m/8ft in length (from nose to tail) and 1.05m/3.5ft high at the shoulder (when on all fours) and can weigh more than 315kg/700lb at maturity. Although some grizzlies are almost black, their coats are typically pale brown to cinnamon, with 'grizzled,'

BEAR ISSUES

Although people have an inordinate fear of being hurt by bears, the Canadian Rockies are a far more dangerous place for the bears themselves. In Banff National Park alone, 90% of known grizzly bear deaths have occurred within 0.4km/0.03 mile of roads and buildings, with most bears either being killed by cars or by wardens when bears and people got mixed up.

Bears are intelligent opportunists who quickly learn that humans come with food and tasty garbage. Unfortunately, once this association is learned, a bear nearly always has to be shot. Remember: 'A fed bear is a dead bear,' so never feed a bear, never improperly store food or garbage, and always clean up after yourself.

Bears are also dangerous creatures that can sprint the length of a football field in six seconds. Although such encounters are rare, bears will readily attack if their cubs are around, if they're defending food or if they feel surprised and threatened. Your best defenses against surprising a bear are to remain alert, avoid hiking at night (when bears feed) and be careful when traveling upwind near streams or where visibility is obscured.

If you do encounter a bear, there are several defensive strategies to employ, but no guarantees. Assuming the bear doesn't see you, move a safe distance downwind and make noise to alert it to your presence. If the bear sees you, slowly back out of its path, avoid eye contact, speak softly and wave your hands above your head slowly. Never turn your back to the bear and never kneel down.

Sows with cubs are particularly dangerous, and you should make every effort to avoid coming between a sow and her cubs. A sow may clack her jaws, lower her head and shake it as a warning before she charges.

If a bear does charge, do not run and do not scream (which may frighten the bear and make it more aggressive), because the bear may only be charging as a bluff. Drop to the ground, crouch face down in a ball and play dead, covering the back of your neck with your hands and your chest and stomach with your knees. Do not resist the bear's inquisitive pawing – it may get bored and go away. Climbing a tree is one option, but only if you have time to climb at least 4.5m/15ft.

If a bear attacks you in your tent at night, you're likely dealing with a predatory bear that perceives you as a food source. In this extremely rare scenario, you should fight back aggressively with anything you can find; don't play dead.

While it has not been proven that bears show an affinity for menstruating women, more than one woman has been attacked by a bear during her period. If you have your period while hiking in bear country, be sure to carry plenty of tampons (pads are not recommended) and sealable plastic bags in which to dispose of them. If you accidentally bleed on clothing or gear, wash it out immediately. Women who have a heavy menstrual flow may want to schedule their trip for before or after their period.

white-tipped guard hairs (the long, coarse hairs that protect the shorter, fine underfur). They can be distinguished from black bears by their concave (dish-shaped) facial profile, smaller ears and more rounded ears, prominent shoulder hump and long, nonretractable claws.

Both bears are omnivorous opportunists and notorious berry eaters with an amazing sense of smell – acute enough to detect food miles away. Their choice of food varies seasonally, ranging from roots and winter-killed carrion in early spring to berries and salmon in the fall. Before hibernation, bears become voracious. Black bears will eat for 20 hours straight and gain an incredible 1.8kg/4lb each day before retiring to their dens, and grizzly bears are known to eat 200,000 buffalo berries a day.

Some time in October, bears wander upslope to where snows will be deep and provide a thick insulating layer over their winter dens. There bears scrape out a simple shelter among shrubs, against a bank or under a log and sink into deep sleep (not true hibernation, since their body temperatures remain high and they are easily roused). Winters are particularly hard, since bears live entirely off of their fat and lose up to 40% of their body weight. Females who have been able to gain enough weight give birth to several cubs during the depths of winter, rearing the cubs on milk while she sleeps.

Dogs

The cagey **coyote** is actually a small opportunistic wolf that devours anything from carrion to berries and insects. Its slender, reddish-gray form is frequently seen in open meadows, along roads and around towns and campgrounds. Coyotes form small packs to hunt larger prey such as elk calves or adults mired in deep snow. Frequently mistaken for a wolf, the coyote is much smaller (11.3kg to 15.8kg/25lb to 35lb, versus 20.3kg to 65.3kg/45 to 145lb for a wolf) and runs with its tail carried down (a wolf carries its tail straight out).

Coyote

The **gray wolf**, once the Rocky Mountains' main predator, was nearly exterminated in the 1930s, then again in the 1950s. It took until the mid-1980s for them to reestablish themselves in Banff, and today they are common only from Jasper National Park north; in Glacier National Park, wolves can be found in North Fork Valley. Wolves look rather like large, blackish German shepherds. Colors range from white to black, with gray-brown being the most common color. They roam in close-knit packs of five to eight animals ruled by a dominant (alpha) pair. The alpha pair are the only members of a pack to breed, though the entire pack cares for the pups. Four to six pups are born in April or May, and they remain around the den until August. Packs of wolves are a formidable presence, and they aren't afraid of using their group strength to harass grizzly bears or kill coyotes, but more often they keep themselves busy chasing down deer, elk or moose for supper.

Gray wolf

Hoofed Animals

No other group of animals brings as many visitors to the Canadian Rockies as the large hoofed mammals; in fact this region is one of the best places in North America to see the following species.

Living on high slopes near rocky ridges and cliffs, **bighorn sheep** are generally shy creatures of remote areas. Unlike other parts of their range, however, bighorn sheep in the Canadian Rockies come down to roadsides in search of salts – invariably causing traffic jams of excited visitors. Males, with their flamboyant curled horns, spend summer in bachelor flocks waiting for the fall rut, when they face off and duel by ramming into each other at 96.6kph/60 mph. Their horns and foreheads are specially modified for this brutal but necessary task. When not hanging around roadsides looking for salt and handouts (strictly forbidden), bighorn sheep use their extraordinary vision and smell to detect humans up to 300m/1000ft away and keep their distance, making them extremely difficult to approach.

Occupying even steeper cliffs and hillsides, pure white **mountain goats** are a favorite with visitors. Finding one is another matter altogether, because goats live high on remote cliffs and are seldom observed close up. These cliffs provide excellent protection from predators, and both adults and kids are amazingly nimble on impossibly sheer faces. Occasionally they descend to salt licks near roads. In Jasper they occur in high densities on Mt Kerkeslin; around Banff try scanning the slopes of Cascade Mountain, and in Glacier National Park you might see goats at Logan Pass.

Mountain goat

Two species of deer are common in valleys and around human dwellings throughout the region. More common by far are the **mule deer** of dry, open areas. Smaller, and with a large prominent white tail, are the **white-tailed deer** of heavily forested valley bottoms. Both species graze extensively on grasses in summer and on twigs in winter. Delicate, white-spotted fawns are born in June and are soon observed following their mothers. Adult males develop magnificent racks of antlers in time for their mating season in early December.

Elk

Weighing up to 450kg/1000lb and bearing gigantic racks of antlers, male **elk** are the largest mammals that most visitors will encounter in these parks. Come September, valleys resound with the hoarse bugling of battle-ready elk, a sound that is both exciting for its wildness and terrifying, because hormone-crazed elk are one of the area's most dangerous animals. Battles between males, harem gathering and mating are best observed from a safe distance or from your car. While numbers increase dramatically in winter, quite a few elk now spend their entire year around towns like Banff and Jasper, where they can be dependably observed grazing on yards and golf courses.

Moose

At 495kg/1100lb, the ungainly **moose** is the largest North American deer. Visitors eagerly seek this odd-looking animal with lanky legs and periscope ears, but they are uncommon and not easily found. Moose spend their summers foraging on aquatic vegetation in marshy meadows and shallow lakes, where they readily swim and dive up to 6m/20ft. Visitors can look for moose in the Miette Valley of Jasper, around Upper Waterfowl Lake of Banff, in the McDonald Valley of Glacier, and in similar areas. The male's broadly tined antlers and flappy throat dewlap are unique, but like their close relative the elk, moose can be extremely dangerous when provoked. Moose are no longer as common as they were in the days when they freely wandered the streets of Banff; numbers have been reduced due to vehicle traffic (roadkills), a liver parasite and the suppression of the wildfires that rejuvenate their favorite foods.

SMALL MAMMALS

Hardly noticed among their giant brethren are dozens of smaller mammals roaming mountain forests and meadows. Common around picnic areas and roadside view-points are **golden-mantled ground squirrels**. Striped on their bodies like a chipmunk, these bulging beggars are fearless in their pursuit of handouts, climbing onto visitor's shoes and legs, doing everything possible to look cute and hungry. Because they hibernate and need to put on a lot of fat, ground squirrels become extremely focused on gaining weight in late summer and start looking like butterballs by September.

Hikers into the realm of rock and open meadow will quickly become familiar with two abundant mammals. When you encounter a **pika**, you are likely to hear its loud bleating call long before you spot the tiny, guinea pig–like creature staring back at you with dark beady eyes. Pikas live among jumbles of rocks and boulders, where they are safe from predators, but they still have to dart out into nearby meadows to harvest grasses that they dry in the sun to make 'hay' for their winter food supply.

Pika

Another rock dweller is even more of a tempting morsel for predators; **hoary marmots** are plump and tasty, but they have a system for protecting themselves. First they stay near their burrows and dart in quickly when alarmed. Second, all the marmots on a hillside cooperate in watching out for predators and giving shrill cries whenever danger approaches. Marmots may shriek fiercely when humans come near, warning everyone in the neighborhood about the approach of two-legged primates. The Whistlers, a mountain outside Jasper, is named after these common rodents.

Nearby forests are home to **red squirrels**, whose unmistakable scolding and restless movements are hard to miss. Running from tree to tree along elevated pathways, making death-defying leaps and scrambling up and down trees so fast that the bark flies off in pieces, these squirrels stop only to chatter loudly at intruders who dare enter 'their' forest. Signs of squirrel activity can be found everywhere, especially the piles of fragments they leave behind as they dismantle pinecones in search of seeds.

Sometimes the boundless energy of red squirrels takes on a desperate tone, which is when you might be lucky to see the Canadian Rockies' most common carnivore, the fearless little **pine marten**. Whether racing headlong after squirrels in the treetops or popping in and out of boulder fields in search of pikas, this reddish-brown weasel relative strikes terror in the hearts of small animals everywhere. Though rarely observed, martens are curious and may show up to steal food inside houses or left on picnic tables.

There's hardly a more sedentary animal in the forests than the slowly plodding **porcupine**. Protected by 30,000 deadly barbed quills, porcupines have few predators to run from, and their diet of tree bark provides scant calories for extraneous activity. These solitary animals are fairly common wherever conifer forests grow, and they spend most of their time in treetops. Missing from their diet, however, are sources of salt, so porcupines descend to nibble on salty things wherever they can find them – even roadside signs, car tires, brake linings, leather shoes, outhouse toilet seats and plywood.

The aquatic **beaver** has had a long history of relations with humans. Reviled for its relentless efforts to block creeks and praised for its valuable fur, the Canadian Rockies' largest rodent is now widely recognized as a 'keystone species,' an animal whose activities have a tremendous influence on the lives of many other species. Dozens of animals, like ducks, frogs, fish, moose and mink, depend on beavers for their livelihood. Although their numbers have declined as much as 90% in recent decades, beavers are still fairly common around marshes and ponds in valley bottoms. Here each beaver cuts down as many as 200 aspens and willows per year, feeding on the sweet inner bark and using the trunks and branches to construct dams.

Beaver

BIRDS

Although more than 300 species have been found in the Canadian Rockies, birds are readily overshadowed by the presence of so many charismatic large mammals. It takes a real bird nut to turn their attention to a diminutive mountain chickadee when they could be watching male elk battle over harems of females or bighorn sheep scale rocky cliffs. However, casual observers will notice some of the more conspicuous species without even trying.

Crows & Jays

Noisy and fearless around humans, members of the crow family are prominent in the Canadian Rockies. All are intelligent (ranking right up there with chimpanzees and dolphins), witty and social. In addition to being conspicuously large black birds, **common ravens** are highly visible because they've learned to hang out along roads looking for roadkilled mammals and birds. Ravens mate for life and are most frequently observed in pairs, though family groups are a common sight during the summer months. If there are any birds with the capacity for play, it would be ravens, for they engage in countless antics, including chasing each other in mock aerial battles, spinning somersaults, playing with dogs and tossing things at humans.

Clark's nutcracker

You'd be hard pressed to find a campsite or picnic table where you aren't quickly approached by **gray jays** hoping for a handout. These grayish little tricksters glide in silently and sidle up confidently next to your food. After a few moments they may help themselves to as much as they can carry – there's good reasons why they've been nicknamed 'camp robbers.' Most of their food they stash away in small caches for winter.

The stash master, however, is the larger **Clark's nutcracker**. Each nutcracker buries up to 98,000 seeds in thousands of small caches across miles of landscape then returns to dig them up over the course of several years – an unbelievable test of memory. Seeds that are left behind, either accidentally or intentionally, sprout Into future forests. Scientists estimate that most of the subalpine forests in the Northern Hemisphere have been planted by nutcrackers, making these birds the architects of mountain forests. With dependable supplies of food for themselves and their chicks, both nutcrackers and gray jays nest as early as February.

Included in this group of crow relatives are the showy and rather flamboyant **black-billed magpies**. With long streaming tails, iridescent black and white plumage and wonderful antics, these birds of valleys and towns draw curious stares from many visitors. Magpies are gregarious and spend the year living in complex social groups that nest colonially and cooperate in scavenging food.

Birds of Prey

Two large raptors (birds of prey) are worth mentioning because they are so frequently encountered. Working their way along rivers and lakes are white and brown fish hawks, better known as **ospreys**. Fairly common from May to September, when the ice is melted, ospreys specialize in diving into water to catch fish. Ospreys are most often seen soaring over lakes, scanning the water for fish. Plunging feet first into the water, ospreys grab fish up to 0.9m/3ft deep then fly off to eat their scaly meal on a high perch. Osprey nests are enormous mounds of sticks piled on top of dead trees or towers.

Osprey

In recent years the Canadian Rockies has gained some fame for its spectacular **golden eagle** migration. Each year 6000 to 8000 golden eagles migrate both north and south along a narrow corridor on the east side of the main mountain divide (the official count site is near Mt Lorette, in Kananaskis Country, just east of Banff). Spring migration peaks at the end of March, and fall migration peaks in October. Over a thousand golden eagles have been counted in a single day, so bring your binoculars. While migrating, golden eagles do little feeding, but some pairs stay for the summer and nest on high, remote cliffs. These massive birds are impressive predators, feeding mainly on rabbits and ground squirrels but also taking down adult deer, swans and cranes on occasion.

Of the region's eight species of owl, only the **great horned owl** is familiar to most visitors. Fearless around humans, highly vocal and sometimes active in the daytime, these large birds are a perennial sight around towns and campgrounds at lower elevations. These owls have been called the 'wolves of the bird world' because they are such ferocious predators. Even other owls and hawks move out of the neighborhood when a pair of great horned owls moves in. Great horneds will eat almost anything they can catch, including skunks, cats, snakes, fish and scorpions. Also active in the daytime is the sparrow-sized **northern pygmy owl**, an alert and curious little bird that will readily sit out in the open and call in broad daylight. Whether it's the region's largest or smallest owl, songbirds relentlessly mob and scold any owl they find during daylight hours – if you hear a group of birds causing a ruckus in the woods it's nearly always because they've found an owl to harass.

AMPHIBIANS

Very few amphibians and even fewer reptiles do well in the relative cold of these northern latitudes. Only the couple of frogs covered here could be considered fairly common, though on occasion other frogs, toads, salamanders and snakes may be encountered.

The definitive Canadian frog (found as far north as the Arctic Circle) is the **wood frog**, which occurs from low elevations up into the alpine zone. At the highest elevations, their season of activity is shortened to mere months – not much time to wake from hibernation, breed, fatten up and prepare for the next winter. Easily recognized by its dark mask, the wood frog wanders far and wide and is often found far from the nearest water. During winter they take refuge under leaves or logs, where amazingly they survive being frozen solid in the frigid cold.

More attached to water are the tiny **boreal chorus frogs**, who fill the night with their trilling songs in late April. Active at night around marshes and ponds, chorus frogs are identified by long dark stripes running down their brownish bodies. They are unlikely to be observed unless you go out at night with a flashlight (which is not a good idea, since this is grizzly feeding time).

FISH

According to some people, parks and mountains are a place where you go to camp and fish. Since high mountain lakes have no native fishes; wildlife agencies, parks and concerned citizens have for decades added countless millions of fish to lakes in order to 'improve' the visitors' experience. For instance, at least 119 lakes in Banff have been stocked with nonnative fish, even though a mere 26 lakes contained fish historically. As a consequence native fish populations and aquatic ecosystems have suffered, and several species of nonnative fish are now doing quite well. As an official policy, fish stocking in these parks was phased out only recently, in 1971 in Glacier and 1988 in Banff and Jasper.

Native fish include the threatened **bull trout**, whose dwindling populations are protected by law. Once the most widespread native fish in the Canadian Rockies, bull trout are now seen reliably at only a few sites. Your best bet is Peter Lougheed Provincial Park south of Canmore, where they migrate up creeks out of Lower Kananaskis Lake from late August to mid-October. They are distinguished from other trout by their lack of black lines or spots, so fishermen use the motto 'no black, put it back' as a reminder to return bull trout to the water if one is accidentally caught.

Representative of the nine nonnative fishes that have become common, **brook trout** are now found in most low elevation streams and lakes. Prized for fishing, brook trout can be recognized by their olive-green color, reddish belly and yellow squiggly lines along their back.

Aquatic habitats in the Canadian Rockies support many more kinds of fish than just trout – 40 species in all. Healthy populations of **mountain whitefish** make this one of the more readily seen native species. These bottom-feeders prey on small invertebrates in the major watercourses and lakes. Uniformly gray and growing to 25.4cm/10 inches, whitefish are best seen while spawning in mid-October at Banff's Fenland Picnic Site.

Verging on the bizarre, however, are the various aquarium fish that locals have introduced into the warm waters of Banff's Cave and Basin Marsh. Here, sailfin mollies, jewelfish and mosquito fish have replaced the now extinct Banff longnose dace. This is a classic example of where tinkering with nature's ecosystems can have dire consequences.

INSECTS

Except for mosquitoes and a handful of conspicuous butterflies, most of the Canadian Rockies' 20,000 or so insect species go unnoticed. Very little is known about the distribution and life history of most species, even though these organisms are extremely sensitive to environmental change and serve as key indicators of ecosystem health.

Come in the right season, however, and you'd be hard pressed to avoid buzzing hordes of **mosquitoes**. Fortunately, the mosquito season in most areas peaks for only a few weeks, in late June to early July. This season is shifted into July and August at higher elevations, but around marshy areas it can persist all summer. Mosquitoes are specialized flies that use long, piercing mouthparts to feed on plant juices. After mating, males die, while females seek a meal of blood to get enough proteins to produce her eggs. Adult mosquitoes are an extremely important food for many birds and bats (who eat hundreds per hour), and countless aquatic animals live on mosquito larvae in ponds and marshes. Mosquitoes transmit a variety of diseases, so it's best to avoid being bitten whenever possible.

Although butterflies are a showy and widespread feature of nearly every habitat, nothing compares to the spectacle of **hilltopping**. Many flying insects, including butterflies, congregate on sunny peaks to court and mate, and on a good day you may witness thousands of fervent insects. As a group, the various **checkerspots** and **fritillarys** are easy to recognize as they flit around hilltops and open meadows. All have an overall orange appearance marked with dark checkerboard patterns that may be bold bars or reduced to mere dots.

TICK FEVER

Recent concern over Lyme disease, Rocky Mountain spotted fever and other infections carried by **ticks** makes it important to check for these diminutive insects every day you are in the mountains, especially if you've been picnicking in meadows or wandering through bushes. Looking like tiny flat spiders, ticks roam among grasses and low vegetation, waiting to grab onto passing mammals with their long clawed legs. Once aboard, a tick moves slowly in search of tender skin (back of your neck, armpits, groin, etc) where it can pierce the skin and draw a meal of blood. Bites are usually subtle and go unnoticed until it's too late, making it imperative to check yourself completely at the end of each day. Use a mirror or friend to search hard-to-see places, and be alert for young ticks that are no bigger than a pinprick. If attached, ticks are best removed with a gentle steady pull, but hopefully the tick is not attached and is simply wandering in search of a good dining spot. Dispose of them in the toilet or with a match, squishing them between your fingernails may simply transfer diseases onto your fingertips. If bitten, pay careful attention to the wound and to your health; problem bites may develop red 'bull's-eye' marks, and you may experience nausea and flu-like symptoms. Unfortunately, not all problem bites result in symptoms, and diseases like Lyme may progress into serious life-threatening conditions without prompt medical attention. Your best bet is constant vigilance and frequent checking of your clothing and skin – don't take a chance on this one.

Plants

The Canadian Rockies are home to over 1000 species of plants, comprising a fairly diverse mix for such a relatively cold, northern climate. One of the main reasons for this mix is that the Continental Divide not only creates a strong elevational gradient but also splits the region into westside and eastside habitats. With a wet, ocean-influenced climate on the westside and a dry, interior climate on the eastside, this geographic split is a very significant division. Adding to the region's botanical diversity are alpine plants from the arctic, grassland plants of the eastern prairies and forest plants from the Pacific Northwest.

Because the parks cover such a span of habitats and elevations, it's possible to find flowers from March until the end of August, and taking time out to smell the flowers will definitely enrich your park visit. One comprehensive and accessible introduction to the subject is *Plants of the Rocky Mountains,* by Linda Kershaw, Andy MacKinnon and Jim Pojar. A simple picture book that could be useful is *Plants of Waterton-Glacier National Park,* by Richard Shaw and Danny On.

TREES

Except for areas of rock, ice or water, landscapes of the Canadian Rockies are mostly covered with coniferous forest. Only a handful of species are present, and these are easy to identify – learning to recognize these species is a lot of fun, plus it makes it easier to understand the layout of life zones and to predict where you might find specific animals.

Montane and subalpine forests are dominated by two spruces, **white spruce** and **Engelmann spruce**. Both have sharp-tipped needles that prick your hand if you grasp a branch. White spruce occurs mainly on valley bottoms, and Engelmann spruce takes over on higher slopes, but the two frequently overlap and hybridize. Cones on white spruces have smooth, rounded tips on their scales, but Engelmann spruces have narrow, jagged tips on theirs. Many animals feed on spruce seeds or rely on spruce forests for their livelihood in some way.

Sharing the higher slopes with the Engelmann spruce is the abundant **subalpine fir**, the namesake tree of the subalpine zone in the Canadian Rockies. Recognized by their flattened, blunt-tipped needles, subalpine firs have characteristically narrow, conical profiles. This shape allows the trees to shed heavy winter snows so their branches don't break off under the weight.

At the uppermost edges of the subalpine forest, mainly growing by themselves on high windswept slopes, are **whitebark pines**. Intense wind and cold at these extreme elevations can cause these trees to grow in low, stunted mats. Their squat, egg-shaped cones produce highly nutritious seeds favored by Clark's nutcrackers and grizzly bears, but an introduced disease is threatening this important tree and the animals that depend on it.

Engelmann spruce

One of the oddest trees of the Canadian Rockies is the **subalpine larch**, a rare tree found most easily in Larch Valley (imagine that!) just south of Lake Louise. Although it's a conifer, this remarkable tree has needles that turn golden in September then drop off for the winter in October. This makes places like Larch Valley a photographer's paradise during the peak display.

After fires or other disturbances, **lodgepole pines** quickly spring up and form dense 'doghair' thickets. In some areas, lodgepoles cover many square miles so thickly that the forests are nearly impossible to walk through. These conditions eventually promote hot fires that create seedbeds for more lodgepoles; in fact, lodgepole cones are sealed in resin that only melts and releases seeds after a fire.

A beautiful tree of dry open areas, the **quaking aspen** has radiant, silver-white bark and rounded leaves that quiver in mountain breezes. Aspen foliage turns a striking

ECOSYSTEM

276

orange-gold for just a few weeks in fall (call parks before visiting, because each year the display peaks on different dates). Aspens consist of genetically identical trunks arising from a single root system that may grow to be more than a 40.5 hectares/100 acres in size and include up to 47,000 stems. By sprouting repeatedly from this root system, aspens have what has been called 'theoretical immortality', and some aspens are thought to be over a million years old.

Two other aspen relatives, **black cottonwood** and **balsam poplar**, occupy habitats along rivers and in moist areas. Because they hybridize so readily, the two species are very difficult to distinguish and can be considered as one. Leaves are 7.6cm to 12.7cm/3 to 5 inches long and egg-shaped, with long tapering tips. New buds exude a sweet-smelling resin sometimes called 'balm of Gilead'. In the fall these trees produce million of seeds with cottony tufts that accumulate ankle-deep in places and give people with allergies a real headache.

SHRUBS

The term 'shrub' is a somewhat arbitrary label for small woody plants with multiple stems, but it can be hard to decide whether a plant is a shrub, since some trees can have many stems as well. These small woody plants may grow as low alpine mats, dense thickets or single plants on slopes or meadows.

Lodgepole pine

One common example of plants that sometimes grow as treelike shrubs are the two dozen species of **willow** that grow abundantly around water and marshy meadows. Willows range from 9m/30ft **Scouler's willows** to inches-high **arctic willows**, though most species have the form of low bushes. These ecologically important plants provide browse for mammals and ptarmigan, dense branches for countless nesting birds and homes for many insects. All willows have catkins that produce tiny clustered flowers, then fuzzy seeds later in the spring.

Shrubby relatives of their tree cousins are **common juniper** and **creeping juniper**. Very common in montane and subalpine zones, both have the same bluish berrylike cones found on all junipers (originally used to flavor gin). Common junipers grow up to 0.9m/3ft high and have stout, prickly needles, and creeping juniper forms a prostrate trailing mat with scaly leaves. Squirrels and grouse snack on the bitter berries.

With blue berries that are delicious and sweet instead of bitter, **blueberries** provide an immensely popular treat for humans and bears alike. Half a dozen species occur in the Canadian Rockies, with common names like huckleberry, grouseberry, bilberry and cranberry. Often these plants grow in patches large enough that berries for a batch of pancakes or muffins can be harvested within minutes.

Blueberry

Closely related and similar in appearance to blueberry plants is the **kinnikinnik**, also known as bearberry. This ground-hugging shrub has thick glossy leaves and reddish woody stems. Its leaves were once mixed with tobacco to make a smoking mixture, and the berries have been a staple food for many native peoples.

Buffalo berry occurs widely in mountain forests, where it is the most common shrub over large areas. Although the berries possess a bitter component, bears may eat 200,000 a day in preparation for winter. This plant is readily recognized by its dark green leaves, which underneath are silvery fuzzy with brown dots.

Shrubby potentilla ranks among the most conspicuous flowering shrubs because it is found nearly everywhere, and its brilliant yellow flowers bloom throughout the summer. Growing up to 1.2m/4ft, this potentilla has shredding reddish-brown bark and needlelike leaves in groups of five. Both livestock and native animals, such as deer and bighorn sheep, browse the foliage only when no other food is available, so nibbled potentilla is a useful indicator of overgrazing.

It's something of a surprise to encounter **wild roses** growing deep in these woods, but at least five types grow here. All look like slender, somewhat scraggly versions of what you'd see in a garden, but otherwise, there's no mistaking them. Their fruits are pear-shaped and turn red-orange during fall; popularly known as rose hips, these fruits are rich in vitamins A, B, C and E and are used to make tasty jams or teas.

WILDFLOWERS

The flowering season in the Canadian Rockies begins as soon as the snows start to melt. Though delicate in structure, the early rising **glacier lily** pushes up so eagerly that the stems often unfurl right through the snow crust. Abundant in montane and subalpine forests or meadows, each lily produces several yellow flowers, with six upward-curled petals. Wherever lilies occur in great numbers, grizzlies paw eagerly through the soil in search of the edible bulbs.

Within days of snowmelt, pretty purple **pasqueflowers** (or prairie crocuses) cover montane slopes. Growing close to the ground on short, very fuzzy stems, these brilliant flowers stand out because of their yellow centers. Later in the summer, 'shaggy mane' seed heads replace the flowers. All parts of this plant are poisonous and may raise blisters on sensitive skin if handled.

One of the most photographed flowers of Glacier National Park is the striking **beargrass**. From tufts of grasslike leaves, the plant sends up 1.5m/5ft stalks of white, star-shaped flowers that may fill entire subalpine meadows. Grizzlies favor the tender spring leaves, hence the plant's common name.

Hike almost anywhere in these mountains and you're bound to encounter the easy-to-recognize **bluebell**, with its large, bell-like flowers held up on a long, skinny stem. This plant's other common name, harebell, comes from Scotland, but its meaning is not certain. After flowering, seeds are produced in capsules that close in wet weather then open in dry winds to scatter the seeds far and wide.

Many visitors know the familiar **indian paintbrush** for its tightly packed red flowers, but fewer know that the plant is a semiparasite that taps into neighbors' roots for nourishment. By stealing some energy from other plants, paintbrushes are able to grow luxuriantly in desolate places like roadsides or dry meadows, where they are often the most conspicuous wildflower. Of the dozen species in the Canadian Rockies, a great number attract hummingbirds, making paintbrush patches one of the best sites for finding the beautiful birds.

Bluebell

Another very common roadside flower, **gaillardia**, or brown-eyed Susan, looks like it belongs in a garden somewhere and is in fact a source of some favorite garden varieties. Like small, brown-centered sunflowers, these plants present a bright sunny face that makes them a welcome addition to the landscape in July and August. A closer look reveals a characteristic feature; each petal ends in three deep lobes that give the flower a frilly-edged look.

Tucked away in damp conifer woods you will find the **dwarf dogwood**, or bunchberry, which seems like a little, ground-hugging version of the well-known flowering tree. Four large white bracts (structures that look like petals but are not) surround each cluster of tiny greenish flowers, giving the superficial impression of one big flower clusters mature into tight clumps of red berries in August, hence their other common name. The berries are a favorite food of birds and mammals and are edible for humans, though not particularly flavorful.

The big, showy **cow parsnip**, with its huge, celery-like stalks and umbrella-shaped flower clusters, is a familiar sight along streams and in moist aspen groves throughout the region. This plant can grow over 1.8m/6ft, and walking among them can make you feel small. The stems are eaten by many animals and favored by grizzlies, so caution is urged when approaching a large cow parsnip patch. Humans are advised against eating these plants because of their similarity to several deadly species.

More localized in its distribution, but sometimes confused with cow parsnip because it has the same large leaves, is the aptly named **devil's club**. This stout, 2.7m/9ft plant practically bristles with armor. Completely covered in long, poisonous spikes (even the leaves are ribbed with rows of spines) that break off in the skin when contacted and cause infections, this plant further announces itself with its strong odor and large clusters of brilliant red berries. Despite these features, devil's club has a rich and important history of medicinal use among native tribes of the area.

LICHENS, FUNGI AND MOSSES
Out of several groups of lesser-known and mostly unappreciated species (mosses, fungi, liverworts etc), lichens are worthy of pause. Arising from an odd symbiotic relationship between algae and fungi, lichens have become so successful at growing in all parts of the landscape that hundreds of species occur in the Canadian Rockies, and many more have yet to be discovered.

Obvious in subalpine conifer forests are the neon-yellow strands of **wolf lichen** growing on tree trunks everywhere. Look closely and notice how the lichens stop abruptly at a line that's several feet off the ground. This is the height of the winter snowpack. This is the only species of lichen that's known to be poisonous, and it was formerly mixed into bait set out to poison wolves, hence its name. Its scientific name, Letharia, means 'deadly' (similar to the word *lethal).

Of the many species that grow on rocks, none are as common or easy to identify as the **map lichens**. This familiar group of species covers rocks with yellow-green crusts that have black mottling, creating a maplike look in older specimens. These lichens live a very long time, at least 10,000 years, and grow at a rate that's measured in fractions of a millimeter per century. Scientists have been able to measure lichen colonies and use this data to calculate the advance and retreat of Ice Age glaciers, a technique that's described on the Path of the Glacier interpretive trail at Mt Edith Cavell.

Stresses on the System

By a stroke of good fortune, much of the Canadian Rockies has always been protected by the very nature of its remote, rocky terrain and relatively late discovery. Although the region has been logged, grazed and mined, scars from these activities are scarcely noticeable within the parks, except to the trained eye.

Even more subtle, and far more overwhelming, is the ongoing impact of millions of visitors crowding areas favored by wildlife. Large mammals in particular need a high degree of solitude and space in order to carry out their normal activities of finding food, shelter and a place to raise their young. Constant intrusions by well-meaning humans disrupt these cycles over and over again, making it difficult if not impossible for some species to maintain healthy populations. Posted signs and temporary area closures help to reduce this impact so long as the rules are followed.

The opposite problem arises when animals learn to rely on handouts of human food around popular viewpoints. Such animals become a nuisance at best, and a life-threatening problem at worst. Every year, people are hurt or killed from approaching animals too closely, and 'problem' animals, especially bears, have to be killed even when the problem stems from human behavior. Animals that hang around viewpoints are animals whose natural life cycles have been disrupted by the human presence, and visitors are reminded to avoid behavior that encourages these animals (no feeding!).

Each visitor contributes to the overall experience of being in the park, for both good and ill. We all bring with us car exhaust, congestion on roads, campfire smoke and heavy foot traffic on trails – and in parks where thousands of acres are dedicated to visitor use, the cumulative effect can be quite large. From backpacking to tour-bus sightseeing, each type of tourism has its own consequences, but together they reshape a region that's being punished by too much love. Meanwhile, park personnel do all they can to preserve the feeling of wilderness and nature for all visitors. Do your part to minimize your impact as much as possible – stay on trails, avoid trampling fragile areas, and respect park regulations – and this experience can be preserved for generations to come.

THE INFLUENCE OF FIRE

Frequent wildfires have long been the norm in the Canadian Rockies, especially over the past 7000 years, when native people took up the practice of setting fires in order to open up forests and ensure abundant berry crops in future years. Even without human intervention, naturally occurring fires sweep through an area every four to five years in dry grasslands, or every couple hundred years in wetter forests. During the 1900s, however, an aggressive policy of fire suppression meant that all wildfires were stamped out as quickly as possible, and the result has been a tremendous buildup of shrubs, trees, and dead wood. Eventually realizing that these conditions created extremely hot, destructive fires, park managers have in the last couple of decades started allowing natural fires to burn on their own wherever possible. Under carefully monitored conditions, firefighters will now start controlled fires designed to burn 'cooler' and clean out smaller shrubs and accumulated dead wood without escalating into fiery infernos. Ecologically, this new policy has been highly beneficial, because it opens up new habitats, prompts the growth of new seedlings and sprouts, and replenishes soil nutrients. Not everyone enjoys the sight of burned stumps and blackened hillsides, but take a moment to appreciate the power of fire to reset the ecological clock. If you're visiting in the spring, you'll see the most dramatic wildflower displays in burned areas.

APPENDIX

Banff National Park

GENERAL PARK INFORMATION
Banff National Park Information Centre ☎ 403-762-1550;
W www.parkscanada.gc.ca/pn-np/ab/Banff
Lake Louise Visitor Centre ☎ 403-522-3833
Banff Tourism Bureau ☎ 403-762-8421; W www.banfflakelouise.com
Lake Louise Tourism Bureau ☎ 403-762-8421
Trail Conditions ☎ 403-760-1305
Road Conditions ☎ 403-762-1450
Avalanche Hazard ☎ 403-762-1460
Park Warden Office ☎ 403-762-1470
Mineral Springs Hospital ☎ 403-762-2222

ACCOMMODATIONS
Alpine Club of Canada ☎ 403-678-3200; W www.alpineclubofcanada.ca
National Park Hotel Guide 24-hour toll-free ☎ 866-656-7124;
W www.nationalparkhotelguide.com

TRANSPORTATION
Banff Transit Service ☎ 403-760-8294
Greyhound ☎ 800-661-8747; W www.greyhound.ca

TOUR OPERATORS
Brewster ☎ 403-762-6750, 877-791-5500; W www.brewster.ca
Discover Banff Tours ☎ 403-760-5007; W www.banfftours.com
Gray Line Sightseeing ☎ 800-661-4919; W www.grayline.ca
Lake Minnewanka Boat Tours ☎ 403-762-3473;
W www.minnewankaboattours.com
Rocky Mountaineer Rail Tours ☎ 800-665-7245;
W www.rockymountaineer.com

USEFUL ORGANIZATIONS
Alpine Club of Canada ☎ 403-678-3200; W www.alpineclubofcanada.ca
Friends of Banff ☎ 403-762-8918; W www.friendsofbanff.com

MAPS
Atlas W www.atlas.gc.ca
Gem Trek Publishing ☎ 403-932-4208; W www.gemtrek.com
Map Art Publishing ☎ 403-278-6674; W www.mapart.com

BOOKS

Lonely Planet's *Canada,* by Mark Lightbody et al
Lonely Planet's *British Columbia,* by Ryan ver Berkmoes and Graham Neale

Canadian Rockies, by Douglas Leighton. Canmore, AB: Altitude Publishing Ltd, 2000
Handbook of the Canadian Rockies, by Ben Gadd. Jasper, AB: Corax Press, 1986
How to Be a Canadian, by Will Ferguson and Ian Ferguson. Vancouver, BC:
    Douglas & McIntyre, 2003
Switchbacks: True Stories from the Canadian Rockies, by Sid Marty. Toronto, ON:
    McClelland & Stewart, 1999
Raven's End, by Ben Gadd. San Francisco, CA: Sierra Club Books, 2003
The Group of Seven in Western Canada, edited by Catherine Mastin. Toronto, ON:
    Key Porter Books, 2002

History

A Short History of Canada, by Desmond Morton. Toronto, ON: McClelland &
    Stewart, 2001
Castle of the North: Canada's Grand Hotels, edited by Barbara Chisholm. Toronto,
    ON: Lynx Images Inc, 2001
Rocky Mountain Madness: An Historical Miscellany, by Edward Cavell and Jon
    Whyte. Canmore, AB: Altitude Publishing Ltd, 2001

Ecology

A Guide to Rocky Mountain Plants, by Roger Williams. Lanham, MD: Roberts
    Rinehart Pub, 2002
Bears, by Kevin Van Tighem. Canmore, AB: Altitude Publishing Ltd, 1997
Leave No Trace, A Guide to the New Wilderness Ettiquette, by Annette McGivney.
    Seattle, WA: Mountaineers Books, 2003
Plants of the Rocky Mountains, by Kershaw, MacKinnon and Pojar. Edmonton, AB:
    Lone Pine Publishing, 1997
The Bear's Embrace, by Patricia Van Tighem. Toronto, ON: Anchor Canada, 2003
Wild Flowers of the Yukon, Alaska & Northwestern Canada, by John Trelawny.
    Madeira Park, BC: Harbour Publishing Company, 2003

Activities

Lonely Planet's *Hiking in the Rocky Mountains,* by Lindenmayer, Fairbairn and
    McCormack

Backpacker's Field Manual, by Rick Curtis. New York, NY: Three Rivers Press, 1998
Canadian Mountaineering Anthology: Stories from 100 Years on the Edge, by
    Bruce Fairley. Edmonton, AB: Lone Pine Publishing, 1994
The Canadian Rockies Trail Guide, by Patton and Robinson. Banff, AB:
    Summerthought Ltd, 2000

Photography

Lonely Planet's *Travel Photography,* by Richard I'Anson

National Geographic Photography Field Guide, by Peter Burian and Robert
    Caputo. Washington, DC: National Geographic, 2003
National Geographic Photography Field Guide: Landscapes, by Robert Caputo.
    Washington, DC: National Geographic, 2002

Jasper National Park

GENERAL PARK INFORMATION
Jasper National Park Information Centre ☎ 780-852-6176;
  W www.parkscanada.ca
Icefields Centre Parks Information ☎ 780-852-6288
Jasper Tourism & Commerce ☎ 780-852-3858;
  W www.jaspercanadianrockies.com

ACCOMMODATIONS
(also see Banff)
Jasper Home Accommodation Association **W** www.stayinjasper.com

TRANSPORTATION
Brewster ☎ 800-760-6934; **W** www.brewster.ca
Greyhound ☎ 780-852-3926, 800-661-8747; **W** www.greyhound.ca
Jasper Express ☎ 800-661-4946
Maligne Lake Shuttle Service ☎ 780-852-3370; **W** www.malignelake.com
VIA Rail ☎ 888-842-7245; **W** www.viarail.com

TOUR OPERATORS
(also see Banff)
Brewster ☎ 780-852-3332; **W** www.brewster.ca
Ice Walk ☎ 800-565-7547; **W** www.icewalks.com
Jasper Adventure Centre ☎ 800-565-7547; **W** www.jasperadventurecentre.com
Maligne Lake Cruises ☎ 780-852-3370; **W** www.malignelake.com
Snocoach ☎ 403-762-6735; **W** www.brewster.ca;
Sundog Tour Company ☎ 888-786-3641; **W** www.sundogtours.com
Thompson Tours ☎ 780-852-7269; **C** tomtour@telusplanet.net

USEFUL ORGANIZATIONS
(also see Banff)
Friends of Jasper ☎ 780-852-4767; **W** wwwfriendsofjasper.com

BOOKS AND MAPS
(also see Banff)
A Hunter of Peace: Old Indian Trails of the Canadian Rockies, by Mary Schaffer.
  Banff, AB: Whyte Museum of the Canadian Rockies, 1980
No Ordinary Woman: The Story of Mary Schaffer, by Janice Sanford Beck. Surrey,
  BC: Rocky Mountain Books, 2001

Glacier National Park

GENERAL PARK INFORMATION
Glacier National Park ☎ 406-888-7800, TDD 406-888-7806; **W** www.nps.gov/glac/
Apgar Visitor Center ☎ 406-888-7939
St Mary Visitor Center ☎ 406-732-7750
Kalispell Regional Medical Center ☎ 406-752-5111
North Valley Hospital ☎ 406-863-3500 (in Whitefish)

ACCOMMODATIONS
Glacier Park, Inc ☎ 406-892-2525; **W** www.glacierparkinc.com
Camping Reservations ☎ 800-365-2267; **W** reservations.nps.gov
Apgar Village Lodge ☎ 406-888-5484; **W** www.westglacier.com/lodge.html

TRANSPORTATION
Glacier Park, Inc ☎ 406-892-2525; **W** www.glacierparkinc.com
Amtrak ☎ 800-872-7245; **W** www.amtrak.com
Airport Shuttle Service ☎ 406-752-2842 (in Whitefish)
Eagle Transit ☎ 406-758-5728 (in Whitefish)
Intermountain Transport ☎ 406-755-4011 (in Kalispell)

TOUR OPERATORS
Adventure Cycling Association ☎ 406-721-1776; www.adv-cycling.org
Backroads ☎ 800-462-2848; **W** www.backroads.com
Glacier Park, Inc ☎ 406-892-2525; **W** www.glacierparkinc.com
Glacier Park Boat Co ☎ 406-257-2426; **W** www.montanaweb.com/gpboats
Glacier Wilderness Guides ☎ 406-387-5555, 800-521-7238;
  W www.glacierguides.com
Montana Rockies Rail Tours ☎ 208-265-8618, 800-519-7245;
  W www.montanarailtours.com
Off the Beaten Path ☎ 800-445-2995; **W** www.offthebeatenpath.com
Rising Wolf Wilderness Adventures ☎ 406-338-3016; **W** www.risewolf.com
Sun Tours ☎ 406-226-9220, 800-786-9220

USEFUL ORGANIZATIONS
Glacier Institute ☎ 406-756-1211; **W** www.glacierinstitute.org
Glacier Natural History Association ☎ 406-888-5756;
  W www.glacierassociation.org
Blackfeet Nation Fish & Wildlife ☎ 406-338-7207; **W** www.blackfeetnation.com
Montana Wilderness Association ☎ 406-443-7350; **W** www.wildmontana.org
Montana Fish, Wildlife & Parks ☎ 406-994-4042, 406-994-5700;
  W www.fwp.state.mt.us/
Montana Outfitters & Guides Association ☎ 406-449-3578;
  W www.moga-montana.org
Montana Tourist Board ☎ 800-847-4868; **W** www.visitmt.com
US Forest Service ☎ 202-205-8333; **W** www.fs.fed.us

MAPS
Glacier/Waterton Lakes National Parks, National Geographic/Trails Illustrated
USGS Map Index ☎ 888-275-8747; **W** mapping.usgs.gov

BOOKS
Lonely Planet's *Rocky Mountains,* by Mason Florence, Marisa Gierlich and Andrew
  Dean Nystrom
Lonely Planet's *Hiking in the Rocky Mountains,* by Clem Lindenmayer, Helen
  Fairbairn and Gareth McCormack

A Climber's Guide to Glacier National Park, by J Gordon Edwards. Guilford, CN:
  Falcon Publishing Company, 1991
Blackfeet Tales of Glacier National Park, by James W Schultz. Beaufort Books, Inc,
  1987

Hiking Glacier & Waterton Lakes National Parks, by Erik Molvar. Guilford, CN: Falcon Publishing Company, 1999

Hiker's Guide to Glacier National Park, West Glacier, MT: Glacier Natural History Association

The Old North Trail: Life, Legends and Religion of the Blackfeet Indians, by Walter McClintock. Lincoln, NE: University of Nebraska Press, 1999

Waterton Lakes National Park

GENERAL PARK INFORMATION

Waterton Lakes National Park ☎ 403-859-2224;
  W www.parkscanada.gc.ca/waterton
Waterton Visitor Centre ☎ 403-859-5133
Ambulance service ☎ 403-859-2636 (summer)
Fire emergencies ☎ 403-859-2113
Royal Canadian Mounted Police ☎ 403-859-2244

ACCOMMODATIONS

Glacier Park, Inc ☎ 406-892-2525; W www.glacierparkinc.com
Aspen Village Inn ☎ 403-859-2255; W www.aspenvillageinn.com
Bayshore Inn ☎ 403-859-2211, 888-527-9555; W www.bayshoreinn.com
HI-Waterton ☎ 403-859-2151, 888-985-6343;
  W www.watertonlakeslodge.com/hostel.html
Kilmorey Lodge ☎ 403-859-2334; W www.kilmoreylodge.com
Northland Lodge ☎ 403-859-2353; W www.northlandlodgecanada.com
Waterton Glacier Suites ☎ 403 859 2004, 866 621 3330;
  W www.watertonsuites.com
Waterton Lakes Lodge ☎ 403-859-2150, 888-985-6343;
  W www.watertonlakeslodge.com

TRANSPORTATION

Greyhound Canada ☎ 403-627-2716, 800-661-8747; Pincher Creek;
  W www.greyhound.ca

TOUR OPERATORS

Canadian Wilderness Tours ☎ 403-859-2058
Routes to Learning ☎ 613-530-2222, 866-745-1690
True North Tours ☎ 403-934-5972; W www.backpacker-tour.com

USEFUL ORGANIZATIONS

Waterton Natural History Association ☎ 403-859-2624

MAPS

(also see Glacier)
Centre for Topographic Information ☎ 800-465-6277; W maps.nrcan.gc.ca

BOOKS

When the Mountains Meet the Prairies: A History of Waterton Country, by Graham A MacDonald. Calgary, AB: University of Calgary Press, 2000
Waterton & Northern Glacier Trails for Hikers & Riders, published by Waterton Natural History Association

INDEX

MAP LEGEND

ROUTES
.... Freeway
.... Primary Road
.... Secondary Road
.... Tertiary Road
.... Dirt Road
) -- -- (........... Tunnel
.... Trail

AREAS
.... National Park
.... Wilderness Area
.... National Forest

Place to Stay

🏕 .... Airfield
✈ .... Airport
⚒ .... Archeological Site; Ruin
💲 .... Bank
⚾ .... Baseball Diamond
⚔ .... Battlefield
🚲 .... Bike Trail
🚌 .... Bus Station; Terminal
🚠 .... Cable Car; Chairlift
⛺ .... Campground
⚓ .... Canoe Area

ROUTE SHIELDS
🛡 Trans-Canada Highway
🛡 Canadian Highway
🛡 Canadian Local Highway
🛡 US Interstate Freeway
🛡 US Highway
🛡 US State Highway
🛡 US County Road

POPULATION SYMBOLS
◉ **STATE CAPITAL** .... State Capital
◐ **Large City** .... Large City
◑ **Medium City** .... Medium City
○ **Small City** .... Small City
○ Town; Village .... Town; Village

MAP SYMBOLS
▼ .... Place to Eat

⚱ .... Cave
⛪ .... Church
🎬 .... Cinema
)—(........... Footbridge
⛽ .... Gas Station
⛽ .... Gas Station
✚ .... Hospital
ℹ .... Information
@ .... Internet Access
☀ .... Lookout
⚒ .... Mine

HYDROGRAPHY
.... River; Creek
.... Canal
.... Lake
.... Spring; Rapids
.... Waterfalls
.... Dry; Salt Lake
.... Swamp; Mangrove
.... Glacier

BOUNDARIES
.... State/Provincial Boundary
.... Country Boundary

● .... Point of Interest

🏔 .... Monument
▲ .... Mountain
🏛 .... Museum
🌳 .... Park
🅿 .... Parking Area
)(........... Pass
⛱ .... Picnic Area
🚓 .... Police Station
🏊 .... Pool
✉ .... Post Office
🍺 .... Pub; Bar

🚐 .... RV Park
🛍 .... Shopping Mall
⛷ .... Skiing - Cross Country
⛷ .... Skiing - Downhill
☎ .... Telephone
🚻 .... Toilet - Public
🚶 .... Trailhead
🚋 .... Tram Stop
🚍 .... Transportation
▲ .... Volcano

Note: Not all symbols displayed above appear in this book.

CLIMATE CHARTS

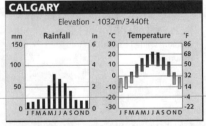

CALGARY
Elevation - 1032m/3440ft

VANCOUVER
Elevation - 3m/9ft

LONELY PLANET OFFICES

Australia
Locked Bag 1, Footscray, Victoria 3011
☎ 03 8379 8000 fax 03 8379 8111
talk2us@lonelyplanet.com.au

USA
150 Linden Street, Oakland, California 94607
☎ 510 893 8555, TOLL FREE 800 275 8555
fax 510 893 8572
info@lonelyplanet.com

UK
72–82 Rosebery Ave, Clerkenwell, London, EC1R 4RW
☎ 020 7841 9000 fax 020 7841 9001
go@lonelyplanet.co.uk

France
1 rue du Dahomey, 75011 Paris
☎ 01 55 25 33 00 fax 01 55 25 33 01
bip@lonelyplanet.fr
www.lonelyplanet.fr

www.lonelyplanet.com
Lonely Planet Images: lpi@lonelyplanet.com.au